Rice and Beans

Rice and Beans
A Unique Dish in a Hundred Places

Edited by
Richard Wilk and Livia Barbosa

London • New York

English edition

First published in 2012 by
Berg
Editorial offices:
50 Bedford Square, London WC1B 3DP, UK
175 Fifth Avenue, New York, NY 10010, USA

Berg is an imprint of Bloomsbury Publishing Plc.

Library of Congress Cataloging-in-Publication Data

Rice and beans : a unique dish in a hundred places / edited by Richard Wilk
and Livia Barbosa.
pages cm
ISBN 978-1-84788-904-1 (pbk.) — ISBN 978-1-84788-905-8 — ISBN 978-1-
84788-903-4 1. Food habits—Cross-cultural studies. 2. Cooking—Social
aspects. 3. Cooking (Rice)—History. 4. Cooking (Beans)—History.
I. Wilk, Richard R. II. Barbosa, Livia
GT2850.R54 2012
394.1'2—dc23   2012004412

British Library Cataloguing-in-Publication Data
A catalogue record for this book is available from the British Library.

ISBN 978 1 84788 903 4 (Cloth)
978 1 84788 904 1 (Paper)
e-ISBN 978 1 84788 905 8 (individual)

Typeset by Apex CoVantage, LLC, Madison, WI, USA.
Printed in the UK by the MPG Books Group

www.bergpublishers.com

Contents

List of Illustrations

Notes on Contributors

Mari-Jose Amerlinck was born in Mexico City, where she was trained as a social anthropologist. She has an MA and PhD in Social Anthropology from the State University of New York at Stony Brook (1980). She has done research on Pentecostalism and religious conversion; on the historical and socioeconomic aspects of Mexican haciendas and peasant society, before becoming interested in their architectural and spatial aspects. While this is her first incursion into culinary anthropology, though not in cooking, she is interested in the history of anthropology, anthropological theory, ethnic identity, and Mexican indigenous architecture, particularly of Michoacán Purépechas. She is coauthor with Juan Fernando Bontempo of *Antropología y entorno construido* (1994), and editor of *Hacia una antropología arquitectónica* (1995) and *Architectural Anthropology* (2001), among other articles. She lives in Guadalajara, Mexico, with her husband and recently retired as Professor and Researcher from the Universidad de Guadalajara.

Livia Barbosa is Professor of Anthropology, and Research Director, Center of Advanced Studies of Escola Superior de Propaganda e Marketing at the Universidade Federal Fluminense, in the state of Rio de Janeiro, Brazil. She holds a doctoral degree in Anthropology from the Museu Nacional of Rio de Janeiro. She has published three books on culture and consumption during the last four years, and has written extensively on food trends and habits in Brazil.

David Beriss is Associate Professor and Chair of the Department of Anthropology at the University of New Orleans. He is the coeditor (with David Sutton) of *The Restaurants Book: Ethnographies of Where We Eat* (2007, Berg) and author of *Black Skins, French Voices: Caribbean Ethnicity and Activism in Urban France* (2004, Westview Press). He is currently pursuing a research project focusing on the relationship between foodways and ideas about cultural distinctiveness in postdiluvian New Orleans, although more broadly his work focuses on Southern U.S. culture, ethnicity, and applied anthropology, as well as on France, Europe, and the French Caribbean.

Riva Berleant is Professor of Anthropology (Emerita) at the University of Connecticut, where she taught at the Torrington campus. Her Caribbean research has been published in such journals as *New West Indian Guide*, *American Ethnologist*, *Geographical Review*, and *William and Mary Quarterly*. She is author of the critical bibliography *Montserrat*, and joint author of *Antigua and Barbuda*. In 2005 she gave to the National Anthropological Archives of the Smithsonian Institution a body of her professional papers and field notes, where they may now be consulted by other Caribbeanist researchers.

Carlos Alberto Dória is the author of *A formação da culinária brasileira*. He has a PhD in Sociology from Campinas University (São Paulo/Brazil) and is a researcher and collaborator of IFCH-Unicamp. He is the author of numerous books on topics of Brazilian food, literature, and history, and publishes a blog at http://ebocalivre. blogspot.com/.

Carla Guerrón Montero is a cultural and applied anthropologist trained in Latin America and the United States. Dr. Guerrón Montero received her doctorate in Cultural Anthropology at the University of Oregon. She is Associate Professor of Anthropology in the Department of Anthropology at the University of Delaware. Dr. Guerrón Montero's areas of expertise include gender, ethnicity, and identity; processes of globalization/nationalism, and particularly tourism; and social justice and human rights. Her research on food studies has been published in *Food, Gender, and Society*, *Ecology of Food and Nutrition*, *Food and Nutrition Bulletin*, and the *Food Cultures of the World Encyclopedia*. Her geographical and historical area of interest is the African diaspora. She has conducted ethnographic research with Afro-Latin American populations in Panama, Ecuador, Grenada, and more recently, Brazil.

B. W. Higman is Emeritus Professor of the Australian National University and Emeritus Professor of the University of the West Indies. He is the author of several works on the history of the Caribbean, including *Jamaican Food: History, Biology, Culture* (2008, University of the West Indies Press) and *A Concise History of the Caribbean* (2011, Cambridge University Press). His most recent work is *How Food Made History* (2012, Wiley-Blackwell).

Sidney Mintz is Research Professor of Anthropology at Johns Hopkins University, has authored, coauthored, and edited fifteen books and three hundred articles during nearly sixty years of teaching and research. Mintz studies Caribbean social history and the anthropology of food. His recent work focuses on the importance of food in material and symbolic life. Mintz's *Sweetness and Power* (1985) looks at the history of sugar as a tool for studying the rise of consumer economies, and sugar's role in linking tropical colonies to Europe. In *Tasting Food, Tasting Freedom* (1996), Mintz studied food behavior anthropologically, to ask what cuisine really means when applied to societies such as the United States.

Anna Cristina Pertierra is an ARC Postdoctoral Research Fellow at the Centre for Critical and Cultural Studies, University of Queensland. She has a PhD in Anthropology from University College London and her research interests include consumption, media anthropology, and material culture studies. In addition to her book *Cuba: The Struggle of Consumption* (2011, Caribbean Studies Press), her work has appeared in various edited collections and journals, including the *Journal of Latin*

American Studies and the *International Journal of Cultural Studies*. More recently, Anna has been doing ethnographic research on television consumption in Mexico and the Philippines.

Theresa Preston-Werner is an advanced graduate student in the Department of Anthropology at Northwestern University. Her research interests include the anthropology of work and consumption, with particular emphasis on class and gender. She has conducted fieldwork in Costa Rica's southern zone and the Central Valley since 1998. Currently she is completing her dissertation, entitled "The World in a Bottle: Gender, Age, and Direct-Sales in Costa Rica." Her foodways publications can also be found in the *Journal of American Folklore* (2009) and the *Journal of Folklore Research* (2008).

Gillian Richards-Greaves is a dual PhD candidate in Ethnomusicology and Social-Cultural Anthropology at Indiana University, Bloomington. Her area of focus is the African diaspora of the Caribbean, with specific theoretical emphases on issues and concepts pertaining to ritual performance, ethnicity/identity, linguistics, and rediasporization. She has conducted dissertation research on the role of kweh-kweh (an Afro-Guyanese prewedding ritual) in Afro-Guyanese communities in New York and Guyana, and is currently writing her dissertation. She plans to complete all doctoral degree requirements by spring 2012 and to pursue a career in higher education.

Michael W. Twitty is a recognized culinary historian, community scholar, and living history interpreter focusing on historic African American food and folk culture. He is webmaster of www.afroculinaria.com, the first website/blog devoted to the preservation of historic African American foods and foodways. He has conducted classes and workshops, written curricula and educational programs, given lectures, and performed cooking demonstrations for more than one hundred groups including the Smithsonian Institution, Colonial Williamsburg, Thomas Jefferson's Monticello, Library of Congress, and the Oxford University Symposium on Food and Cookery. He is well known for his expertise in the history and heritage of enslaved African Americans and their foodways and his expertise in growing African American heirloom crops, open hearth cooking, heritage breed livestock, and wild flora and fauna used by enslaved Africans and their descendants. He is author of *Fighting Old Nep: The Foodways of Enslaved Afro-Marylanders, 1634–1864*, and has contributed to several encyclopedias and edited volumes including *World of a Slave: The Material Life of Slaves in the United States*, *Icons of American Cooking*, and the *Oxford Encyclopedia of American Food and Drink*.

Richard Wilk is Provost's Professor of Anthropology at Indiana University where he directs the Food Studies Program. He has also worked as an applied anthropologist with UNICEF, USAID, USDA, Cultural Survival, and a variety of other development organizations. Much of his recent work has turned toward the history of food, the linkages between tourism and sustainable development, and the origin of modern masculinity. His publications include more than 125 papers and book chapters, a textbook in Economic Anthropology, and several edited volumes. His most recent books are *Home Cooking in the Global Village* (2006, Berg), *Off the Edge: Experiments in Cultural Analysis* (2006 with Orvar Lofgren, Museum Tusculanum Press), *Fast Food/Slow Food* (2006, Altamira Press), and *Time, Consumption, and Everyday Life* (2009 with Elizabeth Shove and Frank Trentmann, Berg).

A Unique Dish in a Hundred Places

Richard Wilk and Livia Barbosa

This book provides a portrait of the way different cultures combine two foods into a single dish. This particular combination is common in a broad region from West Africa, through the Caribbean and then in parts of North, Central, and South America, an area that shares a common history of commerce and slavery, coexistence and conflict, darkness and light. Our comparison of the production, consumption, and preparation of rice and beans in these different regions shows us how history is materialized into culture—in the sense of symbols and values—and how that culture also turns back into history.

The Brazilian case is a good example of this. The historical and economic trajectories of these two staples converged when a Portuguese prince, fleeing from his country with Napoleon on his tail, came to Brazil and had to face the challenge of feeding an army. Today rice and beans in Brazil are the embodiment of different values, ranging from the Brazilian myth of origin of being a racial democracy, to the expression of "Brazilianness" when away from home, the essence of family food, and the values of a mestizo nation.

There are many ways to write about the history and culture of food, but two approaches seem to be the most popular. The first keeps the focus on a particular place and tracks the way foods come and go as a unique local cuisine develops and changes. The second follows a particular foodstuff, like codfish, curry, or hamburgers as it spreads around the world, moving from place to place. The place-centered account usually tells a story about new foods being absorbed and adapted, how a unique culture and geography influences the growth of a distinctive cuisine. It often finishes up telling us how globalization, fast food, and supermarkets are now in danger of destroying local distinction, washing away age-old traditions. Food is the vehicle for stories about the changing position of local cultures in a globalizing world, part of a struggle for distinction and variety on a planet threatened by uniformity, where every cuisine is reduced to the bland mediocrity of franchised fast food.

Even though it has a different dramatic structure, the "follow that food" genre often tells the same story. As we track the codfish or curry on a global odyssey, we also follow migrations and global commerce. The potato from Peru eventually feeds, and then starves millions of Irish, many of whom then migrate and carry the potato further on its journey. The story of chop suey includes migration, oppression, and syncretism, as Chinese food finds its home in America (Coe 2009), while the travels of the soybean testify to the spreading influence of agribusiness and the industrialization of the food supply (Du Bois, Tan, and Mintz 2008). Whether we are stuck in one place, or chasing after one food as it races around the globe, we are really hearing variations on a theme, which depends on a dramatic opposition between the local and the global, tradition and mobility.

Given the right circumstances, a food can gradually set down roots and become embedded in culture, to the point where it joins with *terroir*, that blending of the geography, climate, and culture that makes a food synonymous with place; Parmesan cheese and the region of Parma become reflections of each other. Just as often foods suddenly defy their roots and head off into the global economy as commodities; sushi conquers the New World, a Starbucks pops open like a weed on top of the Great Wall. Even Parmesan cheese gets into the act and develops a global following of sophisticated consumers who want to taste its terroir, and poorer masses that are willing to accept a cheap industrial powdered substitute in a green plastic canister.

The many dramas that play out in the battle between local and global—ruthless agribusiness against the wily peasant, forced migration and the building of new homes, tradition against modernity—lend an allure to modern food history that has led to an explosion in the number of books and studies. The genre of studies of the cuisines of particular localities and regions is well represented, for example, by the Food Cultures around the World series published by Greenwood Press, and edited by Ken Albala, which now runs to twenty volumes. Popular cuisines like Chinese have been covered by literally hundreds of books, while other places are blanks on the culinary map, with only a few local cookbooks in an indigenous language. A study of the geography of food scholarship might be very revealing of where the hot spots and blanks are, and why some regions seem to attract so much attention, while others lie fallow. Popular writing in the "food of a particular place" genre has an even more complex geography, with hundreds or even thousands of cookbooks and travel guides devoted to defining the cuisines, methods, flavors, and festivals of some places, while other whole regions might be covered by only one or two (McCann 2009). Andrew Zimmer and Anthony Bourdain lead weekly video safaris out to explore the "hot" cuisines and to put new places on the culinary map.

Since the success of Sidney Mintz's *Sweetness and Power*, and then Mark Kurlansky's "Cod," books on single foods have become so popular as to become uncountable. In 2006 one of us (Wilk) started putting together a bibliography of single food books for a class reading assignment, but gave up after 140 titles, everything from 5 books on apples to 3 books on vanilla. It was not a new genre either, with books on spices, tea, and coffee appearing in the eighteenth century. Currently there are at least two entire book series specializing in single foods, the Routledge Series for Creative Teaching and Learning in Anthropology (which started off with milk, coffee, and alcohol, among other nonedible substances), and Reaktion Books Edible Series, listing

24 titles from lobster to cheese. These are just the relatively scholarly books and series, though the dividing line between popular and scholarly is often difficult to find in food writing. Moving even slightly across that line reveals more than 12 books published in 2010 on coffee alone.

The growth in publishing of all kinds on the origins of food reflects people's growing awareness of how interdependent we have all become in a global food economy where even a basic and flavorless consumable like bottled water can travel from Fiji to thirsty folk halfway around the world. But in fact most foodstuffs do not move on their own, in isolation. The raft of new books on spices, bananas, rice, and potatoes is missing an important point—we don't consume any of these products by themselves—they are *ingredients* in dishes that form parts of *cuisines*, ensembles of ingredients, cooking methods, and styles of serving and eating. What does it mean to compare the steamed glutinous rice eaten as a main course by temple monks in Thailand with the instant parboiled rice appearing as a side dish in Texas next to a sixteen-ounce grilled sirloin steak? About the only thing the two substances have in common is their origin as seeds of the same species of plant, which hardly seems significant for understanding the similarities and differences between Thai and Texas dinners.

The fact is that individual foodstuffs are rarely consumed by themselves, in isolation. The great anthropologist Mary Douglas laid the foundation for our understanding of the relationship between food and culture when she pointed out that food has a grammar, a set of underlying organizing principles that put a series of separate foods into relationships, much the way language takes meaningless sounds and puts them together into words and sentences (Douglas 1971). The individual foodstuffs themselves carry very little meaning—it is the relationship between them that makes raw *food* into a significant *meal*. First people group individual foods together into cultural categories like "sweet," "savory," and "vegetables."[1] Then they assemble them into a meal following rules, for example, the principle that savory is for main courses and sweet is for dessert, or that a balanced dinner requires meat, starch, and vegetable.

The Rice and Beans Complex

By the same token, this kind of food grammar may be characteristic of a particular "culture," but what does that really mean? Over the last forty years social scientists have become increasingly skeptical of the idea that the world is composed of individual islands of unique cultures, with little lines marking the boundaries that separate them. This is not just because today globalization is blurring those lines by moving people and ideas around so freely. There is very good evidence that cultures have been like this for a long time, maybe back as far as we can trace the very idea of culture into our evolutionary past. Ideas, practices, ingredients, and people themselves have always moved from place to place, and almost as soon as people began to domesticate plants and animals, those new foods and products began to move by land and sea across huge distances.[2] Traditional people even traded and exchanged religious ceremonies, dances, and costumes; learned new languages; and suddenly changed food preferences and staple diets (Harrison 1993). Cultures often overlap, when people of several cultures live together in the same communities, and some cultural groups seem to have a particular penchant for the role of long-distance traders, cultural intermediaries, and epic voyaging in search of new and unsettled land.

The best we can say now is that cultural groups have "fuzzy" boundaries, and they are subject to all kinds of change, but there are also "core" elements that seem to go very deep, which connect people to their historical roots, and provide a deep sense of identity, and food is often one of those elements. This basic cultural identity is rarely grounded in an individual ingredient but instead in what Douglas calls the grammar, which includes a group of fundamental ingredients, recipes, flavors, and textures, which can be combined into the kinds of meals that people find filling and satisfying. It is this persistence that can make food such an important tool in tracing cultural histories, helping us understand how a group of cultures may be related to one another through common origins and shared experiences.

This book is therefore essentially different from the "follow that food" genre, or the "cuisine = terroir = culture" cookbook or ethnography. Instead this is an experiment in looking at how foodstuffs combine into meaningful dishes over long periods of time and large geographic spaces. We want to show how sometimes foods move, and other times they stay in place, and become embedded in locality, ethnicity, nationalism, and other kinds of human groups.

We start from the simple observation that the two foods, rice and beans, taken together are more than simply the sum of the parts. Thousands of cultures and hundreds of nations consume beans, defined loosely as a leguminous seed, as a regular part of their diets (see Albala 2007). In many countries they are the major source of protein in the diet of poor and rural people. Even more places include rice in their cuisines, often as a staple starch. On a global basis, rice is the most popular basic grain, if we exclude grains eaten by animals—more than half the world's population depend on it for daily subsistence (Nguyen and Ferrero 2006).[3] More than twenty percent of the calories consumed by the human species come from rice (Smith 1998). It is also one of the few crops where the majority of the crop raised in every country is consumed in that country; though there is a vast global trade, it is only a small proportion of global production (Sharma 2010).

Whatever their importance as separate foodstuffs, something almost magical happens when the two are combined and eaten together. This is not just a matter of nutrition—most of the people who eat rice and beans together do not know anything about complementary proteins (e.g., Chavez and Pellett 1976). It is also not just having the two foods in the diet, or even having them on the same plate at dinner time. Many cultures eat rice, and also eat beans. But it is something very different to eat *rice and beans*, a recognized dish in which the two ingredients are combined with other ingredients according to a culturally defined formula. In the chapters in this book we define something akin to what anthropologists used to call a "culture complex," a group of traits that tend to occur together, which can be used to define a culture area, cultures that are related to each other through common historical connections (e.g., Kroeber and Holt 1920). To a surprising extent the distribution of rice and beans maps out the Atlantic world, the Caribbean basin with extension and expansion into the mainlands to the north, west, and south.

The way the dish is prepared and eaten also marks, within this region, the division between the historical spheres of Spanish, Portuguese, and English colonialism.[4] As the reader will see in the chapters of this book, tracing the ancestry, distribution, and variation in rice and beans is a broad, straight avenue right into the heart of the history of the Atlantic world, from the trauma of conquest, to the tragedy of African slavery, and onward into the more recent saga of nation-building and neocolonialism. It is not that the rice and beans combination cannot be found elsewhere in the world—the Japanese, for example, eat a dish made from white glutinous rice and red adzuki beans (*Osekihan*) to celebrate holidays—but this dish is historically unconnected with the phenomenon we are concerned with in this book. We will not try to cover all the different ways the two foods can and have been combined all around the world, and it is hard to imagine what you could learn from such a project.

Rice and beans defines an Atlantic region and a shared history, but that alone does not justify the kind of energy and passion that the authors of this book bring to their topics. Why not pick some other dish or condiment that can be found everywhere in the region, like fish fried in coconut oil, or a condiment like hot peppers in vinegar?

The Meaning of Rice and Beans

The striking thing about the dish of rice and beans is that it has such strong local meaning in so many places. In many countries and regions where people eat rice and beans, the dish is a tangible symbol of identity, a basic part of what identifies people as members of larger groups. The identification of a people or culture with this particular dish is so close that they speak of it as a "national flag," "coat of arms," or a "national dish." The sight, smell, and taste of the dish stand for a whole set of deep meanings and memories that have a powerful affect; they evoke loyalty, sentimentality, and even passion. Because of this, people show an extraordinary connection to the particular savor of the version of rice and beans they define as their own. Through the vehicle of rice and beans, we can better understand what it means to have a "staple food" and a "national dish" rooted both in the taken-for-granted habitus of daily meals, and the passionate assertion of pride in place.

To an outside observer it may be hard to tell the difference between a plate of rice and beans cooked and served by a Jamaican, and the same dish prepared in Cuba, but to someone born and raised in those two nations, the differences are obvious and glaring. One looks and tastes right, and the other is a sorry excuse for a meal. Better perhaps than no rice and beans at all, but no substitute for what they were born and raised with. And like a lot of cultural differences, the contrasts between different versions are organized in a way that anthropologists call *segmentary*, after a common kind of political organization in East Africa (Sahlins 1961; Evans-Pritchard 1940). This means that at the highest level of generality, all the people of the rice-and-beans Atlantic world have a common identity, setting them apart from, say, the average Anglo- or French Canadian, or the potato-eaters of Andean South America.

But outside of that context, a Cuban and a Jamaican together in a room will be divided as representatives of the Spanish versus English Caribbean. Similarly, a roomful of Jamaicans may well find that they differ a great deal on what is the best style of "rice and peas," and it may turn out that some parts of the island favor a "wetter" style or a different proportion of beans to rice. At an even lower level, each cook has her own large or small variation that may provoke loyalty and passion, when the taste of her rice and beans is compared with neighbors or relatives. David Sutton's studies of Greek food are a convincing demonstration that very particular and subtle smells and tastes provide a kind of sensory key to deep and powerful memories, which play a very basic role in establishing and reminding people of who they are, where and how and by whom they were raised (2001).

It should therefore not seem odd that Costa Rica and Nicaragua are ready to fight over who really owns rice and beans, just the way Israelis and Palestinians fight over falafel. This pattern of arguing over what seem like minor differences is widespread as anthropologists have observed in many parts of the world. Simon Harrison argues that the most vicious and energetic fights over cultural meaning can *only* occur between groups of people who already share a lot of common culture (2003). We could add a corollary, that the very same thing that unites people can also divide them. Rice and beans does more than divide people; if people did not share so much, they would not have so much to fight over, because their differences appear so magnified. Many of the chapters in this volume explore this level of what might otherwise be considered minor variations in the way rice and beans are prepared, showing often-subtle variation that follow regional, class, ethnic, and national differences.

These variations in turn tell us a lot about the long history of globalization and cultural mixture in the Atlantic world, which has given its people so much in common, and at the same time divides them into so many different factions and divisions. The political economy of this turbulent Atlantic world made them in many ways the world's first *modern* people, in the sense that they were uprooted from their land of origins and immersed in the first great flood of capitalist development, through the slave trade, migrations and displacements, and the formation of plantation economies devoted to producing goods like sugar for export into a market economy.[5] The region demonstrates the inveterate cultural creativity of human beings, and their ability to craft and establish new cultures out of oppression and resistance. Rice and beans can stand as a symbol of this spirit and strength, a dish assembled cheaply from simple ingredients, themselves displaced from many parts of the world, combined anew into something that sustains both the body and soul. The dish shows us that even amid the most dramatic forms of globalization, despite dislocation, migration, poverty, and natural catastrophes, people continue to create culture and maintain locality. Like the people themselves, rice and beans dishes are both persistent and rapidly changeable, descended from original ancestors and constantly reinvented.

Creolization and Geography

One of the oldest arguments among historians is about how to explain the existence of cultural complexes like the sharing of rice and beans over a large territory. On one extreme, diffusionists want to trace all of the individual cases back to a specific origin or point of invention, through migrations, trade, or some other means of communication. At the other extreme are adaptationists who explain a shared trait or practice as a common adaptation to similar circumstances or environments (Eltis, Morgan, and Richardson 2007). The Caribbean variations on this theme alternatively trace the common shared characteristics of the region back to separate African, indigenous, and European models, or as common cultural adaptations to the same kinds of colonial economies and neotropical ecologies. The rediscovery of the African roots of Afro-Caribbean cultures has been an important movement in bringing respect and legitimacy to the history of the region, and the important contribution that African cultures played in making the New World (Fields-Black 2008; Carney 2001). But the task of writing the history of the region does not end with tracing the origins of contemporary culture. Rather than the survival of ancestral traits, what really distinguishes the greater Caribbean is the way the many African cultures of slaves were mixed and transformed in the process that has long gone under the regional name of "creolization."

It is accepted in greater Caribbean research that the experiences of slavery and colonial oppression and the creation of new societies out of transplanted peoples from around the globe have fundamentally shaped the Creole cultures that emerged across the region. In his book *Afro-Creole*, Richard Burton traces many modern West Indian rituals historically back through the days of slavery to the African diaspora (1997). Like Twitty's chapter in this volume on rice and beans, he finds strong African antecedents for many of the social and cultural practices of historical Caribbean people. Yet Burton tells us it is very wrong to interpret Creole Caribbean rituals as simple survivals from the past, tokens of black resistance against white domination. Nor are they just creolized and mixed blends of African and European, or signs of the emergence of an entirely new cultural synthesis. He suggests instead that public ritual was part of a process whereby slaves, free Creoles, and masters, rich and poor, male and female, all publicly negotiated and transacted their many and multiple differences from each other. He heroically resists a simple division between diffusionists and adaptationists by portraying Caribbean culture as the very means by which people understood themselves and created their society. Caribbean dance, dress, language, and food are about difference and boundaries, about power and resistance, about the local and the foreign, so they can't be reduced or explained through any of those polarities. We have to look at the connections and processes, not the points at the extremes.

For this reason, the editors of this volume take a position that should be familiar to those who have read Sidney Mintz's interpretation of the history of the Caribbean, and his opinion of the controversy between what we are calling diffusionists and adaptationists (e.g., Mintz 1974). Neither position has any particular power to explain the specific history of rice and beans in the Atlantic world. If in some places it may be a "survival" from Africa, we still have to explain why and how this particular dish survived and changed identity, why cuisine from some parts of Africa were maintained while others were lost. Similarly, if rice and beans represents some sort of adaptation to environment or the economic system of this area, why is its history so varied, and why of all foods did rice and beans become a symbol of local identity? The chapters in this volume give ample evidence that there can be no single explanation for the ubiquity and significance of rice and beans in the countries and regions of the Americas.

Each case study reveals a different historical path along which rice and beans were constituted as a pair and acquired a place within the many national cuisines and in everyday meals. In most countries rice and beans were firmly established as a dish around the end of the nineteenth century, and since then they have followed very diverse paths. We learn the role they play in constructing sociability, which opens up an entirely new historical geography among these countries, where their actual physical proximity can be redeployed and new continents of practices and meaning formed inside the geography of the Americas.

Most of the chapters present rice and beans as a unit prepared together in one pot, or cooked separately and brought together in one meal. We can also consider them in the light of their degree of independence from each other—the importance they assume as dishes in their own right. In this respect, the truly continental countries, including Brazil, Mexico, and the United States are very distinct from the countries clustered around the Caribbean basin.

As discussed in Amerlinck's chapter, in Mexico beans have the highest degree of independence from rice. They are the basis of many different dishes that are eaten without the company of rice. They can be eaten as a filling for tortillas or as a spread for nachos. They can be roasted or cooked and served warm and simply, as in *frijoles de la olla*, as a soup, as a side dish, or even as a sweet, which links Mexico to Japan and China, two countries where beans are often eaten as dessert and in confections. Unlike the Caribbean and South America, Mexico preserves and builds upon many indigenous pre-Hispanic cuisines that combined beans with corn in complex ways, and this is also probably the source of the much-loved refried beans (*refritos*) that accompany so many meals in Mexico and highland Central America. In Mexico rice is eaten most often without beans, as cooked white rice, as a side dish that complements other dishes, mainly meats, and its importance in the diet as a whole is still overshadowed by corn and wheat.

Brazil is another country where beans and rice have a certain independence from each other, a product of a unique history and the specific character of Portuguese colonialism. Beans were an essential part of the diet of early colonists and the indigenous cultures of the area, and they were combined with cassava flour, corn, and dried/salted meats in various combinations. Initially African rice, a distinct species, was more popular, and Asian rice came much later. Today rice very seldom constitutes a central dish in itself, though it is the universal side dish for Brazilian main meals. Alongside meat or covered with sauce it performs the same role as bread and potatoes in Europe. Unlike in Mexico, however, beans are not as independent and capable of standing on their own as rice. While rice is often served without beans, beans are almost always served with rice, even when they are the center of a meal, as in the example of *tutu de feijão*, a kind of creamy black bean puree. In all the other places discussed in this book, rice and beans are predominantly eaten as a pair as in "*moros y cristianos*," "cookup rice," and "congri," among others.

Nevertheless, for most Brazilians rice and beans is a basic combination, and the majority of the population eats it at every meal. In most of the country it is prepared without the coconut milk that is so ubiquitous and basic in the British-descended Caribbean, nor are the beans and rice cooked together, which is the common mode in the Hispanic Caribbean and Central America. As in Central America, it is not clearly identified with African-descended people, and is not as clearly associated with poor or rural people. Instead, as Dória's chapter shows, in Brazil the mode of preparation and the choice of beans are the key markers in distinguishing rich from poor, and region from region.

This geographic distribution helps us define a kind of core and periphery to the rice and beans complex, where the Afro-Caribbean islands like Jamaica and Cuba are in the core. Adjacent areas on the mainland that have a substantial Afro-Caribbean population, like Guyana, Belize, the Atlantic coasts of Panama and Costa Rica, and New Orleans, share the same general pattern. The continental nations of Mexico, the United States, and Brazil form a periphery, where rice and beans have taken an important place in much more diverse cuisines that show individual complexities founded in their unique histories. Each of these large and populous countries incorporated the cultures and cuisines of large numbers of African slaves, each in distinct ways, which have tended to be underappreciated. Beriss's chapter on rice and beans in New Orleans is particularly important in showing how a dish that was once identified with black slaves has become much more broadly emblematic of a regional identity that partially transcends, and sometimes conflicts, with its ethnic roots. A similar kind of process of broader identification is clear in Dória and Barbosa's chapters on Brazilian foodways.

How rice and beans are prepared can present us with another kind of geography. In this context, the Anglo-Caribbean countries form a unit on their own. They use coconut milk for cooking the rice and beans in a single pot as a dry dish, and for this reason it is usually complemented with a meat stew (chicken, goat, beef, or fried fish). In the Hispanic Caribbean, in New Orleans, and in most of Mexico and Brazil, rice and beans are cooked together in water or in a broth, and the dish can appear more often as a side dish than a main course.

Seasoning forms another geographic configuration. Most countries begin with salt, garlic, and onions, and then add seasonings like peppers of different kinds, chili, and tomatoes as in Mexico, celery in Panama, or bay leaves in Brazil. The Hispanic Caribbean countries base most rice and bean dishes on the *sofrito*, a sauce of sautéed tomatoes and vegetables that forms the foundation of many different dishes. The direct addition of other foods to the beans themselves is also geographically varied. At one end is the plain beans in a heavy broth formed by the beans as they soften, through dishes like that in Belize, which often have salted pigtail as a flavoring, to the Brazilian *feijão gordo*, in which the beans are crowded together with three or more kinds of meat.

The centrality of rice and beans to the overall diet varies a great deal through these case studies as well, creating yet another grouping of countries. While in some countries rice and beans are so central to both the diet and the national consciousness that they are called the "staple food" and "national dish," in places like New Orleans they are more symbolically central than they are essential as a source of calories. People may actually eat it less than once a week, while Costa Ricans may eat it twice or even three times a day. While many Brazilians see *feijoada* as their national dish, it only includes rice and beans as part of a larger ensemble including cassava flour, oranges, greens, meat, and other ingredients. Clearly there is no close connection between how important rice and beans may be in people's minds, and how often they put it in their stomachs. We do not have complete statistics that would allow us to judge how important rice and beans may be in the diet of each country, class, and region in this book. Figure 1.1 shows that there is considerable variation in rice consumption throughout the region, from the extremes of providing one-quarter of all calories in Panama, to only two percent of calories in Mexico and the United States. Statistics on bean consumption are harder to come by, and are generally distorted by the non-dietary consumption of soybeans, but the pattern of high-consuming countries in the region shown in Figure 1.2 seems equally random.

The popularity and significance of rice and beans has developed along different historical paths in each of the countries covered in this book. Rice and beans started as a festive meal, a Sunday dish, in Belize and Panama, only gradually becoming an everyday food. While red beans and rice remains a Monday (washing day) meal in New Orleans homes, it has become symbolically representative of a whole week of meals as the city has become more self-conscious following Hurricane Katrina (Beriss this volume). In most countries, however, they can be eaten at any time at

Brazil	Costa Rica	Cuba	Dominican Rep	Guyana	Haiti	Honduras	Jamaica
12	20	22	20	18	24	6	10

Mexico	Nicaragua	Panama	Trinidad and Tobago	United States
2	16	25	12	2

Figure 1.1 Rice consumption, per capita as percentage of total calories consumed, 2005.

Source: International Rice Research Institute, Table 16. Available at: http://beta.irri.org/solutions/index. php?option=com_content&task=view&id=250. Accessed July 4, 2011.

Belize	Cuba	Guatemala	Haiti	Nicaragua	Trinidad and Tobago
10	16	11	18	16	12

Figure 1.2 List of developing countries where pulses contribute more than 10 percent of per capita total protein intake.

Sources: Global and Regional Trends in Production, Trade and Consumption of Food Legume Crops, Sitou Akibode and Mywish Maredia. Available at: http://impact.cgiar.org/sites/default/files/images/ Legumetrendsv2.pdf. Accessed September 14, 2011.

home and in restaurants, markets, and street stands. In many places, eating dinner is synonymous with eating rice and beans, it is the default option, that which goes without saying. This "ordinariness" does not prevent rice and beans from also appearing in ritual moments as in the Old Year Eve of the Guyanese (Richards-Greaves this volume), a wedding in Belize (Wilk this volume), or on November 6 among the people of Bocas del Toro, Panama (Guerrón Montero this volume). Nor does it prevent them also from being a dish for social occasions, as in *feijoada* in Brazil, which is served to family gatherings in restaurants on Saturday or Wednesday, or in a reunion with friends on Sunday, or whenever people are invited home for a meal.

Materiality

We should not forget that rice and beans are *commodities*, and in many places their significance and status as staples depends on the fact that they are cheap sources of calories and protein, whose prices are at least partially subject to a global marketplace. Before the late eighteenth century, if any country depended on rice and beans for subsistence, it had to grow both crops itself. Rice entered the world of commerce when it became a plantation crop in the Carolinas in the United States and in northeastern Brazil in the early 1700s. It was an effective competitor with wheat flour as a carbohydrate only in some times and places, and it was usually more expensive than flour. Rice's main advantage was that it was easier to prepare, requiring no more than boiling, and in this sense it was the first global convenience food. Beans entered the world of global commerce a bit later than rice, though good statistics are lacking. Pulses like dried peas and garbanzos were being used as ship's rations in European navies and merchant ships as early as Elizabethan times, but they did not become cheap bulk trade goods in any quantity until the middle of the nineteenth century, when they were exported in bulk from ports on the northeast coast of the United States (Simmonds [1859] 2001).

As special and significant as rice and beans may be in the abstract, the specific manifestations are no more or less than a filling, cheap, and relatively simple meal. The chapters in this book are very much concerned with the mundane details of everyday life, and they all show how big abstractions like *nationalism* or *creolization* appear on the plate, in the cookpot, and in the belly. The taken-for-granted presence of rice and beans on the table of many American nations, their "blinding obviousness" as Miller and Woodward (2007) would call it, lead us to forget them, ignoring their immense variety and diversity. Most people eat the stuff instead of talking, or even thinking, about it very much.

This journey from national food to ordinary commodities reaches its final stop on each individual plate, when "the way I particularly like to eat my rice and beans" turns impersonal goods into that most individual, intimate, and specific item, my dinner. This is never the same substance for another person. Nor is the food eaten or mixed in the same way, so each person adds salt or hot sauce in his own way, and makes an individual combination of rice and beans with other side dishes, sauces, and other dishes in each bite. Like snowflakes, no two bites are ever exactly the same. Some catch in the conscious mind, and others are shoveled down without a thought.

The ordinariness of rice and beans responds to some of the paradoxes of modernity, including the burden of having too many choices. When other things are unstable, subject to question, requiring us to make up our minds and figure our way through complex choices, things taken for granted and unquestionable can be a haven, a form of escape. Habit and regularity can be a huge relief and provide a deep sense of security in what has been described as a "risk society" where so many things are being questioned (Wilk 2009; Shove, Trentmann, and Wilk 2009). Every day, rice and beans dishes relieve millions of people from having to think about "what's for dinner?"

In comparison to a plethora of new foods that separate people by class, gender, age, and income, rice and beans tends to bring people together, as the food of everyone. We can point to a whole range of forces of globalization that fragment society into segments, not the least of which is the increasing gulf between rich and poor in countries where neoliberalist reforms have destroyed the social safety net, lowering standards of living for many while creating new classes of super-rich. A tour through the countries of the greater Caribbean region reveals a growing social division between those who migrate and those who stay at home. Some are shopping in supermarkets jammed with thousands of highly processed foodstuffs, while others are supporting themselves on corn and beans raised on tiny farms hacked from the rainforest. Smartphones connected to the wireless Internet are coexisting with oxcarts and woodstoves. Hardly any communities have escaped the twin scourges of drug trafficking and violence. Rice and beans stands out as one of the few things that all these different people have in common, even if they disagree over what nation the dish comes from and the correct color of the beans, and even while some people can afford a lot more meat in the sauce than others.

Conclusions

Most of the authors who wrote the chapters in this volume have never met. We editors contacted them individually and asked them to write papers that discussed the specifics of how rice and beans are cooked and consumed in the areas they know best. We sought out scholars with specific geographical areas in mind, but we also wanted a broad topical coverage. Our goal was to find people with prior experience studying food, so each chapter would be rooted in broader cultural knowledge of the wider region. The charge to each author was to cover some common ground on the history of the dish and the sources of supply, but beyond that we did not constrain the direction the authors wanted to take their essays. The result is that there is some duplication, particularly in tracing the early history of the introduction of rice into the New World and the selection and popularity of the many different genera of beans in different places. Here we are using the term *beans* very loosely to refer to the dried seeds of all legumes, including ones often called peas, lentils, and chickpeas.

As editors we have encouraged the authors to use the nomenclature common in the area where they work, so some say "rice with beans," while others say "beans and rice" or "rice and beans." In some chapters this reflects an actual variation in the way the dish is served; in Brazil rice and beans are prepared separately, and may either be consumed separately on the same plate, or mixed together. In Belize "rice and beans" is used when the two are cooked together, and "beans and rice" when they are cooked apart, though most people mix them on the plate. Given all this variation, we have left it up to each author to explain how the two foodstuffs are prepared and consumed in each specific area, region, and group, and to use the names and labels that are most appropriate.

There is really no inherent order to the chapters because, as we explain above, none of the conventional divisions of the area into regions (e.g., Anglo/Hispanic, Island/Mainland) really works in explaining the distribution of rice and beans and its many variations. Instead we have used a geographic movement that begins in Africa with possible antecedents and precursors, then goes across the Atlantic to the Antilles, covering Cuba, Jamaica, and the Eastern Caribbean, before jumping to Brazil for two chapters and heading north through Guyana, Panama, Costa Rica (including a short border violation into Nicaragua), Belize, Mexico, and finally New Orleans in the southern United States.

Because every journey is better on a full stomach, we have asked the authors to provide a local recipe, and most have complied. Because these come from so many sources, they follow different formats, and most lack the kinds of precise directions and quantities one would expect in a cookbook. This reflects something very important about the vernacular nature of such a popular staple food—it is rarely prepared from written recipes, but is instead a dish that each cook prepares so often that it becomes ingrained in her kitchen habits. The dish is often so familiar that it hardly takes a cook's full attention; we have seen cooks prepare rice and beans while talking on the phone, watching TV, yelling out the window to neighbors, and telling a long, involved story.

At the same time, the same mundane dish signifies so much, it lives in folklore and proverbs, and has been richly treated in literature, poetry, and song. In some settings, a diet of rice and beans comes to signify poverty, the state where the eater has no other choice but the same monotonous food every day, as in Jamila Strong's poem "Rice and Beans."

Rice and Beans

I do not want to eat rice and beans any more
I want a new meal
I'm ready to throw this pot out the door
I'm sure I've had my fill
Rice and beans is my poor folks food
You know when you barely have money
After four days it taste like it's already been chewed
But you smile and eat it like it's sweet honey
I wish I had a grilled burger smothered in cheese with fries on the side
Or a roasted turkey with cornbread stuffing and a side of apple pie
But instead I dread I have rice and beans to keep me fed.[6]

Perhaps a better balance is provided by the vegan rapper/poet/singer Michael Franti and his band Spearhead, whose song "Red Beans and Rice" makes a more complex point:

Most people on the planet / eat beans and rice
some can't afford beef or they think cows are nice.

And their chorus is clearly something all the authors, and we hope, readers can agree on:

Red beans and rice, red beans and rice, red beans and rice,
make everything nice
red beans and rice, red beans and rice, red beans and rice
I could eat a plate twice. So nice. So nice. So nice.[7]

Notes

1. This is not a scientific classification, but a cultural one, since some of the things considered vegetables, like canned corn, are actually starchy, and other things considered starches, like potatoes, are actually vegetables. Other cultures classify foods in dramatically different ways, for example, in Ghana where the main classifications are "starchy staples" and "sauce ingredients."
2. We do not know if people were trading foods before the development of agriculture and pastoralism, because we lack evidence. We do know that they traded tools and the raw materials for tools over very long distances.
3. It is interesting to note that rice is the only major grain crop that is not fed to animals in any quantity. Of the beans, only the soybean has the distinction of being food fit for animals.
4. Despite a number of attempts, we were unable to obtain chapters for this book on the place and significance of rice and beans in the cuisines of the French, Dutch, and North American–influenced portions of the greater Caribbean and Atlantic worlds. Colleagues have told us that rice and beans is indeed a favorite food in Haiti, where it is called *diri ak pwa*, but it is much less common in the still-French Eastern Caribbean islands of Guadeloupe and Martinique. Dutch Curacao is also rice and beans territory.
5. The idea that the Caribbean basin and its hinterlands were the first really modern part of the world has a considerable lineage—even contemporary observers recognized that there was something quite unique about the region. Kurlansky, author of "Cod," provides one of the best general historical introductions to the region (1992).
6. This poem does not seem to have appeared in print, and can be accessed at the Poetry Soup website at http://www.poetrysoup.com/poems_poets/poem_detail.aspx?ID=255783.
7. This song appears on the Franti/Spearhead album "Home." Lyrics were viewed at http://www.lyricsdepot.com/spearhead/red-beans-rice.html.

References

Albala, Ken. 2007. *Beans: A history.* London: Berg.
Burton, Richard D. 1997. *Afro-Creole: Power, opposition, and play in the Caribbean.* Ithaca, N.Y.: Cornell University Press.

Carney, Judith. 2001. *Black rice: The African origins of rice cultivation in the Americas.* Cambridge, Mass.: Harvard University Press.

Chavez, Joe, and Peter Pellett. 1976. "Protein quality of some representative Latin American diets by rat bioassa." *Journal of Nutrition* 106: 792–801.

Coe, Andrew. 2009. *Chop suey: A cultural history of Chinese food in the United States.* New York: Oxford University Press.

Douglas, Mary. 1971. "Deciphering a meal." In *Myth, symbol and culture*, ed. Clifford Geertz, 61–82. New York: Norton.

Du Bois, Christine M., Chee-Beng Tan, and Sidney Mintz. 2008. *The world of soy.* Urbana: University of Illinois Press.

Eltis, David, Philip Morgan, and David Richardson. 2007. "Agency and diaspora in Atlantic history: Reassessing the African contribution to rice cultivation in the Americas." *American Historical Review* 112 (5): 1329–58.

Evans-Pritchard, E. E. 1940. *The Nuer.* New York: Oxford University Press.

Fields-Black, Edda L. 2008. *Deep roots: Rice farmers in West Africa and the African diaspora.* Bloomington: Indiana University Press.

Harrison, Simon. 1993. "The commerce of cultures in Melanesia." *MAN* 28 (1): 139–58.

Harrison, Simon. 2003. "Cultural difference as denied resemblance: Reconsidering nationalism and ethnicity." *Comparative Studies in Society and History* 45 (2): 343–61.

Kroeber, A. L., and Catharine Holt. 1920. "Masks and moieties as a culture complex." *Journal of the Royal Anthropological Institute of Great Britain and Ireland* 50: 452–60.

Kurlansky, Mark. 1992. *A continent of islands: Searching for the Caribbean destiny.* Cambridge, Mass.: Addison-Wesley.

McCann, James C. 2009. *Stirring the pot: A history of African cuisine.* Athens: Ohio University Press.

Miller, Daniel, and Sophie Woodward. 2007. "Manifesto for a study of denim." *Social Anthropology* 15 (3): 335–51.

Mintz, Sidney W. 1974. *Caribbean transformations.* Chicago: Aldine.

Nguyen, Nguu, and Aldo Ferrero. 2006. "Meeting the challenges of global rice production." *Paddy and Water Environment* 4 (1): 1–9.

Sahlins, Marshall D. 1961. "The segmentary lineage: An organization of predatory expansion." *American Anthropology* 63: 322–45.

Sharma, S. D. 2010. *Rice: Origin, antiquity and history.* Enfield, N.H.: Science Publishers.

Shove, Elizabeth, Frank Trentmann, and Richard Wilk. 2009. "Introduction." In *Time, consumption and everyday life: Practice, materiality and culture*, ed. Elizabeth Shove, Frank Trentmann, and Richard Wilk, 1–16. Oxford: Berg.

Simmonds, Peter. [1859] 2001. *The curiosities of food.* Berkeley: Ten Speed Press.

Smith, Bruce D. 1998. *The emergence of agriculture.* New York: Scientific American Library, A Division of HPHLP.

Sutton, D. E. 2001. *Remembrance of repasts: An anthropology of food and memory.* Oxford: Berg.

Wilk, Richard. 2009. "The edge of agency: Routines, habits and volition." In *Time, consumption and everyday life: Practice, materiality and culture*, ed. Elizabeth Shove, Frank Trentmann, and Richard Wilk, 143–56. Oxford: Berg.

The Transnational Dish of the Motherland
The African Roots of Rice and Beans

Michael W. Twitty

New York City 2011

There is no better place in the world to understand the global import of the legacy of rice and beans as a dish of African and Afro-Creole origins than the boroughs of New York City and the surrounding metropolitan area. Termed by Robert Farris Thompson, the "secret African city," it is in New York alone where all of the rice and bean dishes of the Atlantic world converge. From West and Central Africa, Latin America, the Caribbean, and the American South come peoples and nationalities representing all different facets of a dish that tells stories of migration patterns, diverse cultural influences, and places and tastes of memory. In New York, it is not just the communities that prepare these various combinations of rice and legumes (lest we forget Middle Eastern and Indian combinations involving lentils) that enjoy the dish, but the wider sea of New Yorkers, born globalized eaters at the end of a long trail leading back to the Doors of No Return. Rice and beans represent something elemental and complex, supplying food to villages without lights and powering the citizens of an electric, wireless civilization.

"Up South," families, descendants of the great black migration may sit down to Hoppin' John from South Carolina in Harlem; while those who fled the aftermath of Hurricane Katrina might tell stories of antediluvian New Orleans over red beans and rice; which not coincidentally is a signature dish of the Haitian community in Flatbush. Pigeon peas mixed with rice, better known as peas and rice, is central to Jamaican and Grenadian foodways in Crown Heights while *arroz con gandules*, the same dish yellowed with annatto seeds and cooked with *sofrito* is central in Puerto Rican homes in Spanish Harlem and with coconut milk among Dominicans in Washington Heights. Black beans and rice make the dish in the Brazilian community of Astoria (*feijão com arroz*), the Cuban community across the river in Union City (*moros y cristianos*), and among the Venezuelans (*pabellon criollo*) and Nicaraguan and Costa Rican communities (*gallo pinto*) scattered throughout the Latin American enclaves of the city. From the other side of the Americas come the growing communities of

Mexican New Yorkers with their *arroz con frijoles*. Rice and beans/peas and rice is sprinkled across the metropolitan area in Afro-Caribbean communities from Trinidad and Tobago (*pelau*), Barbados and the Bahamas (*peas n'rice*), Guyana ("cookup rice"), and other communities where the pigeon pea, other cowpeas, and red beans are the preferred legume.

What links these various peoples together? What makes their consumption of this common, vital, and diverse preparation meaningful? Rice and beans, born out of traditional subsistence patterns, sustaining millions through both prosperity and blinding poverty, have in the post-postmodern world become a dish immediately tied to memory and ethnicity. Other chapters in this volume will help answer those questions. Here, our aim is to define how rice and beans came to be a dish and to follow it from its origins in West Africa across the Atlantic to the slave quarters of the plantations of the New World and the unknowns of emancipation and its aftermath.

Roots: African Rice and African Beans and the Impact of Trade

Even before the arrival and dispersion of Asian rice (*Oryza sativa*) there were several varieties of rice indigenous to West Africa (Figure 2.1). In the Western Sudan, several wild and weedy varieties grew, including *O. longistaminata*, *O. barthii*, and *O. staphii*. These varieties along with certain varieties of fonio and panic grass, form the category of "hungry rice," or famine grains. The most important domesticated African rice is *O. glaberrima*, a reddish variety key to the development and spread of civilization in the Western Sudan and Senegambia (Catling 1992: 108). This was domesticated more than 3,500 years ago in the Inner Delta region of the river Niger, with a second area of domestication in the Guinean highlands around the Casamance and Gambia rivers. Before the introduction of Asian rice, *O. glaberrima* ruled the rice fields of Africa from the Senegal River in the west to Lake Chad, south along the Senegambian coast through the Rice Coast to western Côte D'Ivoire. Asian rice, dispersed through Arab and European trading networks over a period of several hundred years, eventually dominated because of its higher yields. Both varieties are still cultivated in modern times by speakers of either the West-Atlantic or Mande language groups including the Baga to the Malinke, Mende, Diola, Serer, Fula, and others.

Africa was also the home of several indigenous legumes. Most prominent among these are varieties of cowpea (*Vigna unguiculata*), the Bamana groundnut (*Vigna subterraneana/Voandzeia*), the pigeon pea (*Cajanus cajan*), and lablab or hyacinth bean (*Lablab purpureus*). The cowpea, also known by many synonyms and varietal names (including "field pea" and "black-eyed pea"), is the most important, and is consumed across a wide swath of sub-Saharan Africa. Originally domesticated near Lake Chad, the cowpea diffused west and then south with the Bantu migrations into central and southern Africa. The Bamana (or Bambara)

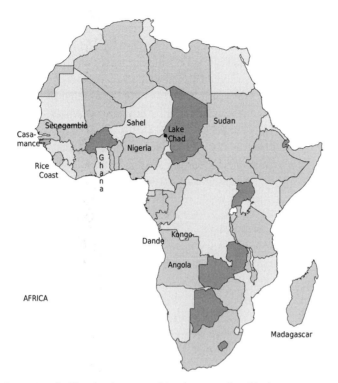

Figure 2.1   Map of Africa showing many of the places mentioned in the text.

groundnut, that grows in the earth like the American peanut, was widespread in western and central Africa while the pigeon pea was more common across eastern and central Africa, most notably the region that would become known in the era of the slave trade as Kongo and Angola, spreading to West Africa during the slave trade by way of the Portuguese.

Rice is as central to sustenance in the African areas of cultivation as bread is in Western and Middle Eastern traditions. Both rice and cowpeas have their symbolic, mythological, spiritual, and proverbial meanings in each specific culture. The successful cultivation and preparation of rice brought individual honor to the grower in the Rice Coast, even as the cowpea stood as a symbol for divine protection, good fortune, and survival in times of hardship in Senegambia. Both foods were significant as offerings to divine forces; placed separately or together on the altars of the ancestors and local and national deities alike. Throughout the rice-growing region, the ceremonial rice spoons, mortars, pestles, hoes, winnowing baskets, and calabashes had sacred meanings that were in turn transferred to the rice plantations and patches of the New World. Rice represented a key cultural niche for West African women who were responsible for most of the work associated with growing, preparing, and cooking it.

Rice and African legumes were commonly paired together in the manner of African entrees, and were used interchangeably in certain recipes. The classic West African pairing of sauce, soup, or stew with starch meant rice was the base over which any of the aforementioned might be ladled or mixed ensuring a hearty meal for hard-working agrarians. Rice could also be made into a one-dish composite meal in the manner of the contemporary dish Joloff rice. Rice was preferred single-grained rather than mushy or glutinous. Overboiled rice or rice flour would often be made into balls to be eaten with stew or the kind of cakes that would be used in ceremonies among the Malinke, and later named among their Gullah descendants in the South Carolina and Georgia Lowcountry as *saraka*. Rice might also be made into fritters as were cowpeas (*akkara*), a tradition that was mirrored in colonial and antebellum New Orleans as hot *cala* fritters made from rice or field peas, and in Brazil with the preparation of *acaraje*. Cowpeas and other legumes were joined in the slave-trade era by American varieties of beans brought in by the Portuguese following the settlement of the Americas, known in Kongo as *lukanza lua Brasil*. Chickpeas, also introduced by the Portuguese, were grown in Angola, notably in the same region (the Dande) known for rice. Throughout West and Central Africa cowpeas were often companion planted with cereals such as sorghum or millet and later maize, so the beans grew up the stalk. It was traditional to serve the cowpeas boiled and seasoned, with the porridge made from the cooked grains.

Returning to modern New York City for a moment, there is an area in Harlem known as Little Senegal where the grandfather dish of all rice and beans preparations is well known. In the small food markets where one can obtain Senegalese and Gambian spices, dried fish, bouillon cubes, leaves, and medicinal herbs, one sees heavy bags of rice and cowpeas in different colors—blue, black, white- and black-eyed, speckled, red—all under the label *niebe*, a West-Atlantic language family (Wolof, Serer, Fula) name for the cowpea. Rice and cowpeas cooked together, as far as we know, a 3,500-year-old or more dish, is known to the Wolof and Serer as *thiebou niebe* (pronounced chebu-neeyebay), a meatless version of other thiebou (rice-based) stews. The connection is immediately spotted by Senegalese master-chef Pierre Thiam who states that *thiebou niebe* "became hoppin' john in the New World" (2008: 16).

In the Diola region of Senegal, called the Casamance, the connection is even clearer in the dish known as *sinan kussak*. Interestingly enough, Thiam suggests using Diola "red rice" (*O. glaberrima*) for the dish, a clue to its antiquity and provenance (2008: 17). Ghana has her *waakye*, a snack dish or spicy rice and beans. In Hausa, a common trade language and lingua franca, *waka* refers to beans while beans are called *adua* in Twi, the predominate language family of central and southern Ghana, hinting that the dish may have spread into that region from the rice-eating cultures of the savanna agricultural belt. The Ga people, a non-Akan group from coastal Ghana, also consume a version called *yoo ke omo*—black-eyed peas and rice mixed together. Later we will see why the Gold Coast littoral became a tertiary center of rice cultivation in the seventeenth and eighteenth centuries.

Rice paired with beans may well have been brought southward into the lower Guinea Coast by Muslim traders from the Hausa, Fulani, and related nations living in the Western Sudan, along with Joloff rice, another transnational rice dish loosely associated with the Wolof of Senegal and their neighbors. The Fulani, the Hausa, and their cousin ethnic groups, involved in the movement of cattle herds or trade, are likely candidates for a pattern of culinary diffusion from Senegambia to the east and south.

The Portuguese were crucial to the spread of rice and beans across tropical Africa. Their quest to economically exploit West and Central Africa even as they claimed to spread Christianity was always followed by the spread of Portuguese culture and language, but the Portuguese had a curious relationship with Atlantic Creoles (African cultures and societies formed on the coastal littoral based on a fusion of African and European cultural elements), ensuring another cross-pollination. West and Central Africans from various parts of the 3,500-mile coastline would come to know each other through the Portuguese as cloth, cheap trinkets, cooking pots, and other goods traveled up and down the coast and later back and forth across the Atlantic with the slave trade. African sailors, traders, and settlers piggybacked on Portuguese trading missions. Goods from one part of the coast were sold to the others, and with them came food, food words, and foodways. As the passage from Brazil to Angola and Nigeria became a two-way street through repatriation, and as cultures from other parts of the enslaved Americas began to voyage back and forth across the Atlantic as returning creolized freedmen, foods traveled back to the motherland and were emplaced as staples of the tropical diet.

The Portuguese colonized Africa from the Cape Verde islands, to the rice heartlands of Guinea-Bissau and to Kongo-Angola and Mozambique. Each one of these centers was bustling with food production, not only with the memory foods of Portugal, almonds, kale, coleworts, chickpeas, herbs, but also with rice and legumes to provision ships. All of those cultural influences were swapped and exchanged creating certain common elements of a Luso-African culture and cuisine that would parallel its language, a growing patois based on Portuguese known as "Krio." This "Creole" identity marked rice and beans dishes born of cultural mixtures and influences as a food intended to travel great distances, serve the needs of multiple ethnicities, and bond previously disparate peoples into a racialized ethnic polity born in the hold of slave ships and on Portuguese trading vessels. Rice cultivation increased in Kongo-Angola with the Portuguese and Luso-Brazilian influence, where it was paired with chickpeas, kidney beans, cowpeas, the newly arrived peanut (known as *nguba* or later "goober peas"), and especially the pigeon pea, which would come to be known in the Americas as the Congo pea. It is possible that there were rice and bean dishes already in Kongo-Angola, but rice cultivation was fairly limited there, largely confined to the lower parts of the Zaire River and the Dande region of Angola (Heywood 2007: 216).

The Middle Passage, Resistance, and the Influence of Ethnicity

The link between slavery, ethnicity, and agricultural production has become a way for scholars to explore the institution of enslavement and its cultural groundings. Several works in English, mostly focusing on North America, have centered on the connection between West and Central African knowledge systems, ethnic preferences among slave traders and planters, the economic impact of this engagement, and its cultural consequences. No link has been more fruitful for this discussion than the movement of rice and rice-growing systems from Africa to the Americas, with particular attention going to the Lowcountry region between the southeastern coast of North Carolina through South Carolina and Georgia to northeastern Florida; with some investigation of the lower Mississippi Valley with an emphasis on the rice plantations of colonial Louisiana. Peter H. Wood's *Black Majority* (1974), Daniel C. Littlefield's *Rice and Slaves* (1981), Gwendolyn Midlo Hall's *Africans in Colonial Louisiana* (1995), Judith Carney's *Black Rice* (2001) and *In the Shadow of Slavery* (2009), and Edda L. Fields-Black's *Deep Roots* (2008) all give considerable attention to the matter of ethnic origins and rice cultivation in the New World.

The ethnic groups most associated with rice cultivation in the Americas came from the same regions that gave rise to combinations of rice and beans/peas; specifically Senegambia, the Rice Coast (modern-day Sierra Leone and Liberia), and the adjacent regions of the Western Sudan—the broad savanna belt of West Africa. Predominately West-Atlantic and Mande speakers, the peoples of Senegambia were the common thread tying together the rice-growing regions of British and French mainland North America, Veracruz in Mexico, the Arbonite region of Haiti, and Maranhao, Amapa, and Para in northeastern Brazil. The Senegambians, although ethnically diverse, were connected through religion, trade, war, and intermarriage, producing what Phillip D. Curtin called "a region of homogeneous culture and a common style of history" (Hall 1995: 29). Early in the European encroachment into West Africa for enslaved individuals, the Senegambians were some of the trade's first victims. As early as the 1450s through the settlement of the Cape Verde islands, and during the initial importation of enslaved blacks in 1502 to Spanish America, the Senegambians were a convenient and sustainable source of enslaved workers. Senegambians were brought in chains to the relatively nearby Iberian Peninsula and Cape Verde where some of the first sugar plantations were created, and in Cape Verde, the Senegambians introduced the cultivation of rice (Carney 2001: 75).

The Senegambians were not merely expert rice growers, but were also renowned for cultivating cotton, tobacco, and indigo. They were familiar with the cultivation of other grains and quickly embraced maize. This would prove instrumental in the establishing of cash crop plantations throughout the West Indies, North America, Spanish America, and Brazil. Ethnicities like the Wolof, Serer, Lebu, Bassari, Baga, Diola, Malinke/Mandingo, Fulbe, Serahuli/Soninke, and Bamana peoples were a collectivity of ethnic groups, who developed relationships across physical and cultural spaces often based on the barter and trade of food items. Some like the Fulbe/ Fula were the pastoralists of the region, others like the Lebu were fishermen, some grew wet rice, some grew dry rice, many were members of castes of craftsmen specializing in blacksmithing, leatherwork, carpentry, and weaving. While Islam was a major religious presence in the region alongside the traditional religions, before the jihadist campaigns of the eighteenth and nineteenth centuries, it was only symbolically adopted, and even then it was a faith intimately tied with creating solidarity with others involved in trade.

Senegambians, skilled in growing multiple cash crops, fishing, pastoralism, hunting, and diverse in their crafts and trades, thus earned the dubious honor of being ideal enslaved persons. In 1627, Alonso de Sandoval wrote of the qualities of enslaved Senegambians:

> The blacks of the rivers and ports of Guinea ... we refr to, because of their excellence, as of law (having a written religion with ethical-legal traditions). They are much more faithful than all the others, of great reason and capacity, more handsome and attractive in appearance; strong, healthy and capable of hard work, and for these reason it is well known that all of them more valuable and esteemed than any of the other nations. (Hall 2005: 80)

According to Gwendolyn Midlo Hall, the trade in Senegambians was further fomented by the "geographic proximity ... favorable winds and currents, and shorter voyages allowing for smaller ships and crews" (2005: 84). The rice- and cowpea-eating Senegambians composed much of the early African presence in Spanish America, particularly in the Caribbean and those areas facing outward toward the Caribbean Sea. In the mid-seventeenth century fully 88 percent of enslaved Afro-Mexicans were of Senegambian origin (Hall 2005: 84). Although rice in Mexico is attributed to Spanish transporting it from North Africa, a number of the early enslaved Iberian Senegambians were brought there as well as Hispaniola/Santo Domingo and may have had a significant role in the transfer of rice and bean dishes to the region. What was true for Mexico was true in much of early Spanish America; Senegambians were a seed-culture and wherever they came, so did rice cultivation and consumption.

Judith Carney states:

> Publications written on areas of black settlement history along the Pacific lowlands of Ecuador and Columbia, eastern Nicaragua, Jamaica and Cuba mention in passing the presence of rice from an early date. But the historical research that might reveal its

linkage to slavery, as Peter Wood meticulously undertook for South Carolina, has yet to be done. This is regrettable since the establishment of rice in Latin America dates more than one hundred years in advance of its cultivation in North America, making such recovery crucial for understanding the role of slaves and African rice in the agricultural history of the Americas. (2001: 78)

The journey to America via the Middle Passage was provisioned from foods from West Africa. The southwestern coastal region of the Gold Coast, populated by the Ahanta and Nzima peoples, became an oasis of rice production in the seventeenth century owing to the Dutch presence at Axim. The many tons of rice grown there supplied European traders and settlers and provisioned ships headed for the New World, mainly Suriname and Brazil. Along with prepared, polished rice came seed rice ready to be planted on plantations in the New World as a subsistence and cash crop (Carney 2005: 338).

Staples brought across the ocean with captives reflected their dietary preferences— yams, cassava, maize, cowpeas, rice, millet, and peanuts were all transported across the Atlantic both as provisions for the enslaved cargo as well as for seeding fields and gardens to feed the enslaved once the ship reached its destination. John Newton's 1750 voyage included food supplies for 200 enslaved Africans including loads of cowpeas and eight tons of rice (Carney 2009: 67). Rice and peas/beans was the predominant dish of many an unfortunate voyager on the dreaded Middle Passage. There was nothing gourmet about the infamous "slabber sauce" made on slave ships; palm oil or lard, grains or tubers boiled into mush, horsebeans, pigeon peas, cowpeas, doused with salt when available and melegueta or chili pepper. The twice-daily ration was often force-fed to those disgusted with it, or some who sought slow suicide by starvation.

Upon arrival, the earliest enslaved Africans became, as Peter H. Wood has put it, "Black pioneers," carving out plantations, building up the human landscape, cultivating new and indigenous crops. Farms supplying foodstuffs developed alongside sugar, tobacco, rice, cotton, indigo, hemp, and coffee plantations. Maroon settlements in the Guianas and Suriname, the West Indies, and Brazil preserved the legacy of African foodways, growing cowpeas, rice, pigeon peas, tamarind, watermelon, Bamana groundnut, peanuts, okra, ginger, sesame, and other crops in neo-African, transethnic settlements. Indigenous Native American, African, and some European crops grew side by side in plantation provision grounds and maroon subsistence fields and gardens. The interplay between manor house, slave quarters, maroon villages, and urban centers in these British, French, Dutch, Portuguese, and Spanish societies would shape and color the tone of food traditions, with Europeans in the tropical regions quickly ceding their classic food traditions for what would come to be known across the region as "Creole food."

As Africans from diverse societies and regions began to mix on the plantations of the New World, recipes were exchanged, survival stories told; nations would emerge from the holds of ships. While many enslaved Africans would find themselves in ethnic blocs, others would assimilate into regional cultures. For example, in Haiti, rice and cowpeas and other beans were grown in the Arbonite region. The Senegambian and Angolan traditions merged, and rice and bean dishes like Haitian red beans and rice and *riz et pois cole* (made with pigeon peas) emerged as staples, influenced by the Arawak/Taino civilization and French cuisine. The trade among islands and between the islands and the mainland would further enrich the complex variety of rice and bean dishes steadily being born in the slave societies of the Americas.

Rice and Beans in Colonial and Antebellum America

While it is generally assumed that Anglo North America was a "last stop" in an archipelago of slave ship anchorings, the Afro-Caribbean role in shaping African American culture, and by extension, foodways was largely supplementary rather than foundational. Exceptions can be found in Charleston and New Orleans based on the relationship between those colonial capitals and Barbados and Santo Domingo, respectively. In the case of rice and beans these dishes owed more to the direct shipment of Senegambians and others than to Caribbean influences. Charleston and New Orleans, like most other North American ports in the slave trade, brought in most of their enslaved workforce directly from Africa, not from already established populations in the Caribbean. There was a strong relationship between mother colonies in the Caribbean and daughter colonies in mainland North America; however, some of the cultural artifacts were parallel developments rather than dispersed hand-me-downs. Furthermore, it is significant to note that some elements of contemporary Caribbean food culture may owe their presence to the number of creolized African Americans in the West Indies— either as the enslaved chattel of Tories or as freedom seekers, especially in the British Caribbean. In other words, it is more likely that Afro-Carolinian and Afro-Latin rice and bean dishes seeded the rice and beans culture of the Caribbean than Caribbean cultures seeded the rice and bean dishes of North America.

Senegambians were perceived to be prized workers in the flow of the slave trade. Their knowledge, skills, and craftsmanship, especially their ability to grow all of the major cash crops that would make slavery lucrative, made them attractive to white planters. In North America this was as much the case in the late seventeenth through late eighteenth centuries as it was for Spanish America, Brazil, and the French Caribbean during the dawn of slavery in 1502 through the early 1700s. Furthermore, North America was a much shorter voyage than other locales, ensuring more captives would be delivered alive and ready for "seasoning" and sale. In the colonial Chesapeake, planters in Maryland and Virginia "expressed a preference for slaves from Senegambia" (Walsh 1997: 79). This was also true in the Upper Chesapeake including Maryland with Virginia down to the Rappahannock River peninsula, where eighteenth-century slave-trading companies imported workers mostly from Senegambia and Upper Guinea to build up the colony and farm tobacco and corn.

In colonial Louisiana, according to the research of Dr. Gwendolyn Midlo Hall, Sene-gambians composed over 64 percent of the French trade to Louisiana and the lower Mississippi Valley and 59 percent of the voyages from Africa between 1770 and 1803 (2005: 92–93). Not only did the French prefer the Senegambians, but they controlled St. Louis and Goree, the ports where enslaved Africans from across Senegambia as far as the Western Sudan, most notably the Bamana, were sourced for bondage. "The survival of French Louisiana was due not only to African labor but also to African tech-nology. The introduction from Africa of rice seeds and of slaves who knew how to cul-tivate rice assured the only reliable food crop that could be grown in the swamplands in and around New Orleans" (Hall 1995: 131). Hall drives home the point that rice and Africans were inextricably linked, stating, "The captains of the first two ships that brought African slaves to Louisiana in 1719 were instructed to try to purchase three or four barrels of rice for seeding and several blacks who knew how to cultivate rice, which they were to give to the directors of the company upon their arrival in Louisiana. By 1720, rice was growing in great abundance all along the Mississippi River; within a few years rice was exported to the French West Indies" (1995: 122).

South Carolina had shifting ethnic preferences. The eighteenth century saw a diverse array of enslaved Africans enter the colony following the "discovery" of rice's profitability in the 1690s. Enslaved Africans there were already growing *O. glaberrima* for their own use when the colony sought to make it profitable to its fac-tors and the Crown, with the arrival of the much more prolific Asian rice. With the famous "seed from Madagascar," the colony's rice production soared, saw the ex-pansion of settlement past the fall line, and quickly grew a black majority (Carney 2009: 150–53). The colony had early importations from Senegambia and significant populations from Ghana and the grandfather colony of Carolina, Barbados, where both Akan and Senegambians could be found. Rice production was expanding in Upper Guinea, and expanded in reaction to the slave trade in Kongo-Angola and the Gold Coast.

Rice and cowpea growers from Senegambia, along with those from the Wind-ward and Rice coasts, made up 36 percent of the known imports in the 1740s, 62 percent in the 1750s, 58 percent in the 1760s, and again 62 percent in the 1770s. "The Slaves from the River Gambia are preferr'd to all others with us save the Gold Coast," stated famed Charleston slave trader Henry Laurens. John Guerard stated he would "chuse all Men of Gambia or Windward Coast," for purchase (Morgan 1998: 67). Like French Louisiana, Carolina would start as a colony born of other colonies, but this period was followed by the direct importation of Africans and the establishment of plantations. The mainland colonies served as provision suppliers to the West Indies:

In particular, Carolina supplied the British West Indies with three commodities—rice, cattle and cowpeas—traditional mainstays of West African subsistence systems. After first establishing itself as a larder to the English Caribbean, the Carolina colony came into its own by the early eighteenth century as the Atlantic world's chief supplier of rice. (Carney 2009: 107)

In colonial Georgia, with its short period of direct importation from West Africa (slavery was legalized in Georgia much later than in other colonies—1750), Senegambians and their cultural cousins in Sierra Leone and Liberia were numerically dominant (Holloway and Vass 1993: 218). Emphasizing that Senegambians were preferred and that they "seeded" enslaved life in certain locales and exercised their influence does not mean that Senegambians were always (or ever) in the majority of the total North American enslaved population. Maryland would maintain a Senegambian/Upper Guinea majority, while Virginia and South Carolina would see their Senegambian imports eclipsed by southeastern Nigeria and Kongo-Angola, respectively. In Louisiana, a mix of peoples from the Bight of Benin, southeastern Nigeria, and especially Central Africa would challenge the Senegambian majority and cultural base. In each region, however, Senegambians, preferred as house servants, cooks, and gardeners, would influence both the enslaved community early on and the tables of white planters, ensuring the reinforcement and continuation of rice and beans as a "dish of memory."

As early as the mid-seventeenth century, rice appears in the colony of Virginia. The association between rice cultivation and the African presence could not be clearer. In 1648, a letter sent to England from the colony stated "we perceive the ground and Climate is very proper for (rice) as our Negroes affirme, which in their Country is most of their food" (Carney 2009: 150). Virginia and Maryland proved too temperate in the long run for rice cultivation, and yet during the American Revolution a planter along the James River was proud to show Captain William Feltman his prize rice paddies (1853: 12). Rice was grown in Anne Arundel County, Maryland, in the 1730s in the sandy and loamy soils around the city of Annapolis and along the South River. The local Annapolis rice, sold by the quart, was preferred over the best imported (Carolina) rice. It was also grown in the Eastern Shore—from Talbot County to those counties near the Virginia border as late as 1860 (Sarudy 1998: 120). This "home rice" grown for private and local consumption across the Chesapeake and Tidewater into northern North Carolina was never grown or consumed to the extent of rice in the Lowcountry of the Carolinas and Georgia or the Lower Mississippi Valley.

We do not know if a rice and beans dish developed in this regional slave society. We know that black-eyed peas and other cowpeas were cultivated in the early Chesapeake, even appearing in the archaeological record from Rich Neck Plantation near Williamsburg in the 1760s, and perhaps appearing earlier. While some rice was grown and eaten in this region, and black-eyed and other cowpeas were certainly grown and consumed from an early date, the Chesapeake never passed down a recipe for cowpeas and rice, if it ever had one to begin with. The Chesapeake diet was dominated by maize, and corn-based foods such as large and small hominy, cornmeal, corn mush, cornbreads, and fresh kernels were the staple dishes of the region.

If there was a rice and beans dish, it might well have been lost in the largest forced migration in American history—the movement of enslaved African Americans from the Upper South to the Deep South during the late eighteenth through mid-nineteenth centuries. Given the high value of rice and prevalence of field peas, the earlier African-born generations may have enjoyed the dish, even as their descendants may have forgotten, abandoned, or simply not preferred it.

In South Carolina and Louisiana, however, the prevalence of rice over corn formed the basis of the "rice kitchen," the complex of foods coming out of the production of rice. Rice was a staple grain for flour, source for breads and dishes both savory and sweet, and as an accompaniment or main body for one-pot meals and entrees. Sene-gambian cooks, male and female, passed down to their children, often domestics like themselves, the dishes and recipes that showed what Karen Hess (2005) called "the African caress" in the New World kitchen. A number of rice and bean prepara-tions argues for their introduction directly from West Africa rather than from the West Indies. Future research might uncover sources showing that rice and pea dishes might have come into the Caribbean equally from North and South America as Brit-ish loyalists fleeing the South brought their enslaved workers with them to the Carib-bean, and as trade continued between the littoral mainland and the chain of islands. It is highly possible that *thiebou niebe*, the Senegalese dish of black-eyed peas or other cowpeas and rice, could be at the root of South Carolina's Hoppin' John. White families were probably enjoying the dish by the mid-eighteenth century, although no recipe occurs until Sarah Rutledge published her *Carolina Housewife* in 1847:

> Hopping John: One pound of bacon, one pint of red peas, one pint of rice. First put on the peas, and when half boiled, add the bacon. When the peas are well boiled, throw in the rice. ... When the rice has been boiling half an hour, take the pot off the fire and put it on the coals to steam, as in boiling rice alone. ... Season with salt and pepper, and, if liked, a sprig of green mint. In serving up, put the rice and peas first in the dish, and the bacon on top. (Rutledge 1979: 83)

While some contemporary African American cooks assume the black-eyed pea was the legume in Hoppin' John, it was the red black-eyed cowpea, specifically a va-riety grown in and around the Sea Islands. This reflects some of the change and transformation that may have taken place as enslaved Gullah/Geechee (the African American communities of the Carolina-Georgia Lowcountry) families prepared their long-simmering dish with vegetables grown in their own gardens. Perhaps the red color of the Sea Island pea reminded them of familiar food aesthetics passed down by their ancestors. In the words of one planter, "There is no vegetable of which negroes are more fond than of the common field pea.... They are very nutritious, and if cooked perfectly done, and well seasoned with red pepper, are quite healthy" (Joyner [1984] 2009: 96). The observation was repeated by architect Frederick Law Olmsted, stating in his 1856 *Journey in the Seaboard Slave States*, "(t)heir chief sustenance is a porridge of cowpeas, and the greatest luxury with which they are acquainted is a stew of bacon and peas, with red pepper, which they call (H)opping John" (506). Native Americans such as the Creek people (Muskogee) had long adopted cowpeas, watermelon, sweet potatoes, and other crops from runaways and from their own population of enslaved Africans (Ethridge 2003: 149). Hoppin' John was likely brought into Florida with those Gullah/Geechee who escaped slavery and went to live with the Seminole who in turn cultivated rice and cowpeas.

In Louisiana the Senegambians there passed down an almost identical dish *Jambalaya au Congri.* From *The* Picayune *Creole Cook Book*:

COWPEAS. *Pois Congris* These peas are utilized by the Creoles in making that famous dish, "Jambalaya au Congri." (See recipe under heading "Louisiana Rice.") On Fridays the rice and peas, which are always boiled separately, must not be cooked with meat, if this day is kept as a fast day. The peas and rice are simply mixed well together and eaten with butter. ([1901] 1922: 190)

Jambalaya au Congri:

1 Cup of Rice. 1 Pint of Cowpeas. 1 Large Onion. Pound of Salt Meat. 1 Square Inch of Ham.

   Chop the salt meat, after washing, into dice, and mince the ham. Boil the cowpeas and the salt meat and ham together. Add the onion, minced very fine. Boil the rice according to recipe for boiled rice. (See recipe.) Chop the meat well. After the peas and the rice are cooked, pour the rice into the pot of peas, which must not be dry, but very moist. Mix well. Let all simmer for five minutes, and then serve hot. On Fridays and fast days the Creoles boil the peas in water, adding a tablespoonful of butter, but no meat. It is again buttered according to individual taste at table. The jambalaya, however, is much nicer when made with the meat. (163)

In the wake of the Haitian Revolution, another dish, more immediately attributable from the Caribbean, would come to Louisiana. *Riz et pois rouge* would become red beans and rice, as refugees from Haiti poured into the United States from the 1790s through the early 1800s. The Haitians would come to have a definite impact on the diet of whites and blacks, introducing peanut confections to Philadelphia; new varieties of peppers, okras, and tomatoes to the Baltimore produce market; and in New Orleans the hearty dish that sustained enslaved Haitians and then became the Monday "wash day" dish in New Orleans. Made of red beans, seasoned with a carrot, onion, bay leaf, butter, ham or salt meat, and salt and pepper, the dish was a rich addition to the city's cultural life.

Prepared with kidney beans and often with pickled pork, this rice and beans dish with "haricots rouge" became a signature dish of New Orleans life, reflecting the interplay between Africa, the French West Indies, and the Lower Mississippi Valley.

Had it not been for the long-term influence of Senegambians in Haiti's Arbonite region, and in the lower reaches of the Mississippi River valley, however, the dish may not have found as hospitable a home.

The American story of rice and beans does not end there. Cowpea- and black-eyed pea-eating Virginians and Marylanders and rice-and-bean/cowpea-eating Gullah would travel to Liberia and Sierra Leone bringing rice and bean dishes back with them, as would Cubans and Bahians to Nigeria, and Cariocas to Angola. The British attempt to close and thwart the slave trade intended to dispose of all captured West Africans in Sierra Leone, forcing dispossessed communities of peoples across a vast area to bring together food traditions, as they tried to make sense of themselves as West Africans, rather than merely representatives of their ethnic groups. On the other side of the Atlantic, African Americans, West Indians, Afro-Latinos, and Afro-Brazilians were cross-pollinating their own Afro-Creole societies through migration and the search for a better life. Rice and bean dishes in North America have been consistently reinforced through migration northward from the Caribbean and Latin America, from the days of the Haitian Revolution onward. West Indian, Puerto Rican, and Cuban enclaves in Manhattan, Brooklyn, Miami, and Boston from the early 1900s onward ensured the further Americanization of rice and beans as a signature ethnic dish, a semblance of home.

Coda: Rice and Beans, Race and Beats, the Official Dish of African Globalism

Africans came to the Americas predominately as enslaved individuals but also as explorers, traders, sailors, and immigrants—and wherever they went they brought the unifying elements of their unique approach to music, dance, spirituality, craftsmanship, visual arts, language, intellectual speculation, and most saliently, food. To these were added the struggle to understand themselves beyond the boundaries of white supremacy, the fight to secure freedom and democratic representation, achieving economic equality and success and the establishment of nations within nations announcing the presence and power of the people. The same collectivity that gave the world jazz, rock and roll, gospel, house music, disco, salsa, meringue, samba, the blues, and reggae, among other musical genres, would import to the vaults of human cultural ingenuity a parallel menu reflecting variations on similar themes. Okra, peanuts, starchy tropical tubers, leafy greens, hot peppers, water and muskmelons, and rice and cowpeas sit alongside the aforementioned list as a culinary soundtrack whose sound is bent to the tastes of the nations that adopted them.

Rice and beans, the transnational dish of the African diaspora—past as well as present—gives us something to chew on as we contemplate the balancing act that was begun more than 500 years ago as Africans and their descendants began the negotiation between their own worlds and that of the West and Western Hemisphere.

Originating as we have seen from Greater Senegambia and the Western Sudan regions of West Africa, rice and bean dishes, like the musical genres that give swing and savor to modern life, were not a product solely of the African experience. Foodways, like other cultural artifacts, began their transformations long before the creation of enslaved people's quarters or the writing of cookbooks. These forms were distilled over a long period process of cultural negotiation and creolization. Trade and economics, fluid ethnic identities, shifts in religious ideologies, and the complex interplay between the cultures of Europe, Africa, and the Americas—as well as the new constructs of worlds in-between—the African Atlantic and African America(s)—are the ingredients essential to the history of this family of dishes and many others.

References

Carney, J. A. 2001. *Black rice: The African origins of rice cultivation in the Americas.* Cambridge, Mass.: Harvard University Press.

Carney, J. A. 2005, December. "Rice and memory in the age of enslavement: Atlantic passages to Suriname." *Slavery and Abolition* 26 (23): 325–47.

Carney, J. A. 2009. *In the shadow of slavery: Africa's botanical legacy in the Atlantic world.* Berkeley: University of California Press.

Catling, D. 1992. *Rice in deep water.* London: International Rice Research Institute/ Macmillan.

Ethridge, R. 2003. *Creek country: The Creek Indians and their world.* Chapel Hill: University of North Carolina Press.

Feltman, W. 1853. *The journal of Lieut. William Feltman: Of the First Pennsylvania Regiment, 1781–1782.* Philadelphia: Historical Society of Pennsylvania.

Fields-Black, E. L. 2008. *Deep roots: Rice farmers in West Africa and the African diaspora.* Bloomington: Indiana University Press.

Hall, G. M. 1995. *Africans in colonial Louisiana: The development of an Afro-Creole culture in the eighteenth century.* Baton Rouge: Louisiana State University Press.

Hall, G. M. 2005. *Slavery and African ethnicities in the Americas: Restoring the links.* Chapel Hill: University of North Carolina Press.

Hess, K. 2005. "Jefferson's table: Evidence and influences." In *Dining at Monticello: In good taste and abundance*, 65–70. Chapel Hill: Thomas Jefferson Foundation/ University of North Carolina Press.

Heywood, J. K. 2007. *Central Africans, Atlantic Creoles, and the foundation of the Americas, 1585–1660.* New York: Cambridge University Press.

Holloway, J., and W. Vass. 1993. *The African heritage of American English.* Bloomington: Indiana University Press.

Joyner, C. [1984] 2009. *Down by the riverside: A South Carolina slave community.* Urbana: University of Illinois Press.

Littlefield, D. C. 1981. *Rice and slaves: Ethnicity and the slave trade in colonial South Carolina.* Baton Rouge: Louisiana State University Press.

Morgan, P. D. 1998. *Slave counterpoint: Black culture in the eighteenth century Chesapeake and Lowcountry.* Chapel Hill: University of North Carolina Press.

Olmstead, F. L. 1856. *A journey in the seaboard slave states: With remarks on their economy.* New York: Dix and Edwards.

The Picayune *Creole Cook Book.* [1901] 1922. New Orleans: Times-Picayune Publishing Co.

Rutledge, S. R. 1979. *The Carolina housewife: A facsimile of the 1847 ed. with an introduction.* Columbia: University of South Carolina Press.

Sarudy, B. 1998. *Gardens and gardening in the Chesapeake 1700–1805.* Baltimore: Johns Hopkins University Press.

Thiam, P. 2008. *Yolele!: Recipes from the heart of Senegal.* New York: Lake Isle Press.

Walsh, L. S. 1997. *Calabar to Carter's Grove: The history of a Virginia slave community.* Charlottesville: University Press of Virginia.

Wood, P. H. 1974. *Black majority: Negroes in colonial South Carolina from 1670 through the Stono Rebellion.* New York: Knopf.

–3–

The More Things Change, the More They Stay the Same
Rice and Beans in Modern Cuba

Anna Cristina Pertierra

Congrí goes with everything, like with a simple tortilla, with a potato tortilla or a plantain tortilla, with a pork stew or a pork steak, with lamb stew, or with fried fish or fish in sauce ... you could even say with a boiled fish! [*laughing*] Imagine, this is a dish very much used in Cuban cooking; very nutritious, and it goes with everything.

Margarita, Santiago de Cuba

Although Cubans have experienced a tumultuous half-century of political revolution, social transformation, and market reform, the presence of rice and beans as a staple diet has always remained the same. Or has it? During the high-Soviet period of the Cuban Revolution (during the 1970s and 1980s), and then again after the economic upheavals that began the post-Soviet era (from the early 1990s), the relationship of Cubans to their everyday foods was changed dramatically. As the Cuban Revolution produced new trade relationships, new agricultural practices, and new rules about everyday shopping, even basic everyday recipes like rice and beans have been altered over time. Severe economic crisis in the 1990s, caused by the end of Soviet support and the tightening of U.S. trade embargoes, commenced an era known as the "Special Period in Times of Peace," or more informally as the "Special Period." The peak of this crisis, in 1993 and 1994, is commonly agreed to have been the most difficult period in Cubans' living memory, and nationwide food shortages created a whole new food culture among Cuban citizens. Although the extreme food shortages of the 1990s were significantly overcome in the following decade, shopping for, cooking, and eating food in contemporary Cuba is still deeply shaped by the notion of scarcity and unpredictability that define Cuban consumption. Figure 3.1 shows Cuba's place in the Caribbean and its proximity to the United States.

Within such a context, the case of rice and beans shows how politics can not only transform access to food and to cooking technologies, but also provokes tricky

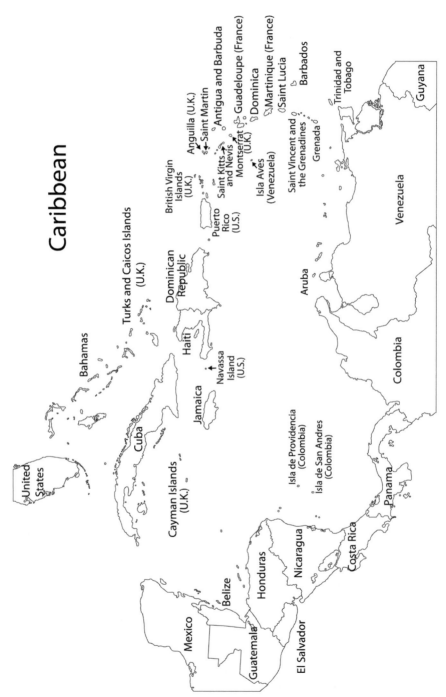

Figure 3.1 Map of the Caribbean showing islands and adjacent mainland discussed in the text.

emotional responses to the practices of cooking and eating good or (as Cubans would describe it) "strong" food. Rice and beans are a daily meal for the average Cuban, and are served in a variety of styles. With fresh memories of the Special Period crisis, and the ongoing consumer shortages that mean that such "special" times have still not entirely ended, the act of preparing daily dishes of rice and beans can be seen by Cubans as a triumph in the context of difficult times, and a physical manifestation of their strength and determination, while also at times marking out the scarcities and shortages that have dominated much of the last two decades in Cuba. Although almost all Cubans would agree that shopping and cooking in everyday life is something of a struggle, such feelings are most often expressed by women who are in charge of feeding their family members and running household domestic economy.

This chapter draws from ethnographic fieldwork in the southeastern city of Santiago de Cuba, conducted over thirteen months in 2003/2004, on the topic of women's domestic consumption practices. But to illustrate how the connection between politics and food is experienced at the level of the individual, the chapter will focus on the stories and recipes of two women, my mother-in-law Margarita and her mother Nena, both accomplished cooks living in Santiago de Cuba. Interviews with Margarita and Nena took place in 2008 and 2009, and neither woman was involved in my earlier field research. Margarita's personal recipe, honed over many years of training with Nena, and provided at the end of this chapter, highlights how the politics and economics of Cuba have been quite materially integrated into this ever-present product of everyday life.

Rice and Beans "Goes with Everything"

Both beans and rice play essential roles in marking a meal as "strong," meaning that it is serious, hearty, nourishing food. Quite simply, a meal is not really a meal in Cuba unless it contains portions of rice and beans, along with some meat or seafood and a serving of starchy vegetables, such as potato, plantain, or cassava; collectively such vegetables are commonly referred to as *viandas*. Vegetables and salads may be served in smaller portions as well; green beans, lettuce, cucumber, avocado, and tomatoes are common accompaniments, but are seen as additions to the true substance of a meal, which is the essential formula of beans + rice + *vianda* + meat. Other styles of food that are a regular part of the Cuban diet, such as sandwiches, spaghetti, pizza, or even corn-based foods such as *tamales*, are more frequently categorized as snacks, and are not considered by most Cubans to be sufficiently sustaining or worthy of description as *una comida fuerte*, a "strong meal." The *congrí* shown in Figure 3.2 is a fine foundation upon which to build a strong meal.

While meat and *viandas* are a necessary presence to make a proper meal, it is the rice and beans that typically form the largest volume of food served on a typical day

Figure 3.2   Margarita's *congrí* from Santiago de Cuba. Photo by the author.

in contemporary Cuba. Meat is highly prized and may be relished in large quantities at special events, but in everyday life whether in home cooking, at workplace
cafeterias, or in state-run restaurants, meat and seafood are too scarce to be served
in large quantities. When necessary, they might be replaced by eggs or by widely
derided manufactured soy proteins, which have since the 1990s become a category
of food worthy of their own cultural analysis in a context of agricultural shortages
and government food distribution. *Viandas*, in contrast, are generally available and
affordable for the average Cuban. Some scholars have suggested that it is *viandas*,
much more than rice and beans, that have a special status in Cuban food culture.
Anthropologist Shannon Lee Dawdy describes cassava and other tubers as being
"worshipped" as a "quasi-divine food" (2002: 57). To lack access to *viandas* would
certainly suggest a state of ridiculous desperation, as signaled by the research of
geographer Marisa Wilson on joking about food shortages in which the punchline to
a cynical joke is "we have no *viandas*!" (2009b).

This does seem quite a contrast to the role of both rice and beans, which are reliable bases upon which the perceived stars of Cuban cuisine, combinations of meat
and *viandas*, are showpieced. Although I have had long conversations with women
who cook for their households in which the details of getting rice and beans cooked
to satisfaction were enthusiastically recounted, in everyday life and by those outside the kitchen, rice and beans are not especially celebrated as the dishes in which

innovation or sensuous delight may be found. Rather, they are a comforting staple, even something to be taken for granted until it suddenly disappears from view.

Perhaps for this reason, celebrations of rice and beans are much more easily found in the nostalgia of the Cuban diaspora; discussed in poems, recreated at community get-togethers, and featuring heavily in the recipes of Cuban American restaurants and food blogs (Charón Cardona 2003; Sánchez 2003; Kandiyoti 2006). Rice and beans are more meaningfully invoked as something specifically Cuban by those who are now away from the island. But it is precisely this taken-for-granted nature of rice and beans for people who still live in Cuba, as the base upon which "strong food" is built, that makes it worthy of analysis. Further, as I will discuss in later sections, the political and economic changes that Cuban residents have experienced since the early 1990s have brought the sometimes-overlooked importance of rice and beans into much sharper relief.

While rice in Cuba is invariably white, the forms of beans used can vary. The most frequently cooked bean—and I believe the most cherished—is the black bean (*frijol negro*) as shown in Figure 3.3, but red beans, chickpeas, and yellow split peas are also common. Beans and rice are often cooked separately, with beans being made into a stew or thick soup that can be served alongside the rice. But there is a special place in most Cubans' hearts for the dishes in which rice and beans are cooked together, which can be known as *moros y cristianos* or as *congrí*. There are varying opinions

Figure 3.3   White rice, black beans, and the base ingredients for making a *sofrito*. Photo by the author.

as to whether these two dishes are one and the same; several sources declare that while *moros y cristianos* is made with black beans, *congrí* is made with red beans (see, for example, Villapol 1981; Sánchez 2003). However, in my own ethnographic fieldwork in the city of Santiago de Cuba, both names are used interchangeably, and vernacular recipes for *congrí* typically use black beans (see also Nuñez González and González Noriega 1991: 148). When I asked about the difference, people frequently suggested that the term *moros y cristianos* is most associated with the western side of the island, in the area surrounding Havana, while *congrí* is the name used for the same dish on the eastern side of Cuba, in which Santiago de Cuba is the largest city. Since it reflects the popular understandings of these terms in my own research experience, for the purposes of this chapter I am referring to *congrí* as a dish made with black beans that is one and the same as *moros y cristianos*, but readers looking for other recipes or scholarly accounts will be likely to find differing opinions on this issue.

The Historical Formation of Rice and Beans as Cuban Cuisine

The name *moros y cristianos*, literally "Moors and Christians," is a racialized metonym that not only alludes to the racial dynamic of blacks and whites living in fairly equal proportions in Cuba, but also points to the legacy of Spanish colonialism by referring to the historical religious divide of (white Spanish) Christians and (black North African) Muslims. To echo a famous analysis of the Cuban stew called *ajiaco* made by the founding father of Cuban anthropology, Fernando Ortíz, rice and beans is a powerful metaphor for both the connections and disconnections that inform Cuban understandings of race (Ortíz 1940). The two main ingredients remain identifiably different in texture and color while mixed together. But in cooking together, the black beans are softened by the rice, while the white rice becomes colored by the bean-tinted water. The interesting background to the term *congrí* is less immediately recognizable, but returning to the work of Fernando Ortíz: "The term *congrí* comes from Haiti, where the coloured beans are known as *congó*, and rice is *riz*, as in French. *Congrí*; drawing from the Haitian Creole meaning 'congos with rice'" (my translation, quoted in Villapol 1981). The prevalence of this term in eastern Cuba would make sense, as it is in this region that many Haitians settled at the beginning of the nineteenth century, including white Franco-Haitians as well as blacks who had lived in differing states of slavery or freedom. Escaping in the wake of the Haitian Revolution, these "French" communities (*franceses*) transformed the cultural life of Santiago de Cuba, establishing, among other things, the coffee industry of the region (Padrón 2005).

In the absence of much other data, we can take Ortíz's etymology as evidence that *congrí* was around at least by the early years of the nineteenth century, the period at which the influence of Haitian culture was most marked in eastern Cuba. However, beans had certainly been present in Cuba since much earlier; some accounts suggest that some kinds of beans were cultivated by the indigenous *Taínos* at the time of Columbus's arrival. While certain kinds of the common *Phaseolus vulgaris*, of which black beans are a variety, may have come to Cuba from Mexico before Spanish conquest, genetic testing indicates that most varieties in use today were probably brought from Mexico and/or Peru through commercial trade routes in the post-Columbian era (Castiñeiras et al. 1991: 5–6). The introduction of rice to Cuba was more clearly a consequence of Spanish colonization (Nuñez González and González Noriega 1999: 146), but again, the origins of rice varieties, and the paths by which they arrived to the Americas, are a matter of debate. In what historians have called the "black rice" thesis, the work of Judith Carney among others suggests that African slaves were responsible for the introduction and cultivation of rice in the southern United States, and Carney lists Cuba as one of a number of Latin American countries in which slaves arriving as part of the plantation economies of the eighteenth and nineteenth centuries were likely to have established rice cultivation (Carney 2001: 196).

The evidence for such a thesis has come under dispute, at least insofar as the influence of African rice-growing techniques, or the value of slaves' rice-growing knowledge in the development of American rice agriculture (Edelson 2010; Eltis, Morgan, and Richardson 2007). Nevertheless, since such debates center upon the constellation of Atlantic plantation economies of which mid-nineteenth-century Cuba was a part, it seems likely that rice production and consumption in Cuba followed roughly the same historical patterns seen in such places as Brazil and the southern United States.

Certainly by the mid-nineteenth century, both rice and beans were recognized as key crops grown in Cuba; in 1854, the North American writer Maturin Murray Ballou reported data from 1830 in which Cuba's annual rice production was valued at $454,230, and the annual production of "beans, peas, onions, etc" at $257,260. While such yields pale in comparison to the more than $8 million worth of sugar produced, it is significant that rice and beans were among the crops included in the report, and that "beans, peas, onions, etc" were calculated separately to the larger category of "vegetables and fruits" (Murray Ballou 1854: 207). Since neither rice nor beans appear in the exports listed by Murray Ballou in a later part of his book, we can conclude that such quantities of both products were cultivated for consumption within Cuba (Murray Ballou 1854: 211).

Despite the African and indigenous origins that have made rice and beans such an excellent metaphor for the mixture of African and indigenous influences in Caribbean societies, at least in the nineteenth century rice and beans seem to have been most frequently eaten by middle- and upper-class Cubans. One reason that *viandas* were more celebrated than rice and beans as the centerpiece of the Cuban diet may be that before the twentieth century, they played a greater nutritional role for poor Cubans, including slaves. Miguel Barnet's oral history of runaway slave Esteban Montejo reports that in the late nineteenth century, small allocated gardening areas provided slaves with important sources of nutrition, growing root vegetables and beans of various sorts. While slaves raised pigs for sale, root vegetables were always kept for personal consumption (Barnet 2003: 59). By this time, rice and beans had appeared in various forms as typical ingredients in the Cuban cuisine that was being increasingly represented as *comida criolla*, the "creole food" of a nationalist middle class that championed the heterogeneous origins of their culture in a local version of the cultural politics of creolization or *mestizaje* that shaped much of nineteenth-century Latin America (Dawdy 2002: 51–55).

Among other cultural forms, cookbooks emerged between the late nineteenth century and the early twentieth century, narrating and celebrating a Cuban cuisine (Folch 2008; Dawdy 2002: 55–56). Cuban intellectuals were directly involved in this deployment of food as part of a nationalist Creole culture, including most famously Fernando Ortíz (1940). For Ortíz, the fusion of ingredients from around the world that make up Cuban cooking has been invoked as the daily expression of the creolization, syncretism, or what Ortíz described as "transculturation" that marks cultures of the Caribbean. As mentioned earlier, Ortíz proposed not rice and beans, but another example of Cuban *comida criolla* as the defining metaphor for Cuban and even Latin American culture: that of the hearty stew called *ajiaco*, combining meat and vegetables to be cooked in what is believed to be an adaptation of indigenous Taíno cooking. Cooked in a cauldron that is literally and figuratively a melting pot, one of the qualities of *ajiaco* that Ortíz saw as representative of Cuban culture was that these distinct ingredients retain their own textures and flavors while mixing together to form this tasty stew (Ortíz 1940; see also discussion in Pérez Firmat 1987).

While nationalist identity ran at an all-time high in the late nineteenth century, through the decades that followed, and indeed for all of the twentieth century, one could argue that both food and politics in Cuba were characterized by alternations between strong nationalist sentiments and a heavy dependency upon foreign imports (see also Dawdy 2002: 54; Pérez 1999: 472). The capacity of the Cuban agricultural sector to provide sufficient food for its population was a fraught political issue, shaped by the dynamics of export economies based in sugar and tobacco, and by political and economic relations with the United States, which were in some ways replicated in subsequent relations with the Soviet Union. Poorer sectors of the Cuban population in the early twentieth century were dependent upon corn and *viandas* as their main sources of carbohydrates, with large amounts of beans but very little rice (Dawdy 2002: 59). But the increasingly affluent middle and upper classes of Cuba had such easy access to imported food items that their diets and lifestyles were largely compatible with those of the North American middle classes.

Imports of consumer goods, including many food items, had long played a central role in the everyday life of affluent Cubans, and by 1959 the rise of processed and packaged food that changed North American life had also come to cities such as Santiago de Cuba, where Philadelphia cream cheese or Quaker oats could be found on the supermarket shelves of local Sears or Woolworths stores (see also Pérez 1999: 72).

With these sizeable differences in access to a variety of foods, and a history of more than a century in which food had been deliberately invoked in nationalist discourse, it is little wonder that the provision of rice and beans, among other staple foods, to even the poorest of urban and rural communities became a significant platform of the Cuban Revolution (Benjamin, Collins, and Scott 1986). While poor Cubans may have been experiencing regular access to idealized Cuban cuisine for the first time, middle-class Cubans experienced a "re-Cubanization" of their diet with the gradual disappearance in the earliest years of the revolution of the many U.S. American food items they had previously taken for granted.

Food and Cooking in the Socialist Era: An Overview

The most famous transformation in twentieth-century Cuba has of course been the revolution of 1959, and the effects of this revolution upon food were profound, if not so much in changing the makeup of Cuban cuisine, then more significantly in determining how much food has been available to the entire population. While it is true that for the first time, rice and beans were a staple diet for all Cubans, this by no means suggests that the Cuban agricultural sector achieved self-sufficiency in the security and provision of food to its population. The increasing integration of socialist Cuba into the Soviet bloc meant that rice, beans, wheat, dairy and poultry products were imported as (despite some unsuccessful early attempts to diversify Cuban farming and exports) the Cuban agricultural sector focused on exporting sugar to the USSR and other socialist countries at highly favorable prices. And not only the foodstuffs like rice and beans were imported; so too were the many technologies required to get them cooked, from the trucks and fuel used to transport food across the country, to the electricity infrastructure powering urban houses, and even the domestic appliances in which rice and beans might be cooked. To this day, imported food items have been a mainstay of Cubans' eating habits across the economic spectrum, and it is necessary to bear this fact in mind, in order to understand the severity of the economic crisis that gripped Cubans, and shook their relationship to everyday foods, by the beginning of the 1990s.

In order to understand how cooking dishes like rice and beans have changed in Cuba from the revolution until today, it is important to outline the basic differences that a socialist economy made to food availability, and to the practices like shopping and cooking that go into the making of a food culture. There is, however, a substantial literature that details the many reforms undertaken in Cuba from the 1960s to the 1990s, which readers looking for more in-depth information may wish to consult (Pérez 2006; Eckstein 2003; Benjamin et al. 1986; Rosendahl 1997). As the Cuban economy became increasing socialist over the first few years of the revolution, most agriculture was nationalized, and food manufacturing plants, marketplaces, and shops were state-run. In urban areas like Santiago de Cuba, for the first time, everybody was able to afford a range of food products, especially the basics of the Cuban diet such as rice and beans. However, whereas previously Cuba had relied on U.S. imports for over 70 percent of essential food items, the withdrawal of U.S. trade relations meant that a wide range of goods that had previously been commonplace for middle-class Cubans disappeared from Cuban shops (Benjamin et al. 1986: 19; Pérez 2006: 55, 61–63, 114). In their place, increasing amounts of food and other consumer items were imported from other countries of the socialist world.

Examples of foods imported from Russia and Eastern Europe that were suddenly affordable for the average Cuban through the 1970s and 1980s included tinned meats, jams and jellies, and pickled vegetables (Benjamin et al. 1986: 40–41). A major shift in food culture during this time, therefore, was the dissolving of significant class divides in diet, resulting in a sense of downward shift for some Cubans, but a significant improvement in quantity and diversity of diet for the urban poor.

Sustenance in Special Times: Food Scarcity in Post-Soviet Cuba

When the Soviet Union collapsed in 1989, this event had largely been unforeseen by the Cuban government, and its previous reliance upon Soviet bloc support across all sectors of the economy left the country adrift. By 1991, the Cuban government announced that the country was in a "Special Period in Times of Peace," in which wartime measures would have to be taken to protect the country from collapse. As the world adjusted to a new post-Soviet era, the economic vacuum left by the demise of the Soviet Union and the COMECON socialist economic alliance was significantly worsened by increases in trade sanctions enacted by the U.S. government that also prevented third-country companies with offices in the United States from engaging in trade with Cuba (Eckstein 2003: 219–27). Despite the severe pressures of the Special Period, Cuba is well known for having adopted a different post-Soviet path to Eastern and Central Europe or indeed to the formerly/formally socialist nations of Asia. While markets were partially opened, the Special Period launched an ongoing coexistence of dual currencies and a mix of a continuing socialist framework within which some sectors of the economy engage in market activities.

While the public health statistics of socialist Cuba have been well documented, the role of food policy in achieving good overall health for Cubans was perhaps less widely known until the crisis of the early 1990s. Food shortages became acute, and within the space of a few years what researchers term a "nutrition transition" shifted a population that had previously been at risk of heart disease and diabetes from excessively fatty food into one that was at risk of malnutrition. Between 1989 and 1993, the per capita availability of caloric energy was reduced by 32 percent and studies showed a decrease in obesity by 53 percent in women and by 61 percent in men compared to a decade earlier (Rodríguez-Ojea et al. 2002: 130). We can conclude that rice, along with *viandas*, took on a crucial nutritional role, as from 1990 to 1993, carbohydrates increased from constituting 64 percent to 79.4 percent of the Cuban diet (Rodríguez-Ojea et al. 2002: 130). In addition to the drastic loss of imports, Cuban agricultural production, heavily reliant upon imported technologies, equipment, and fertilizers, rapidly declined. During this period Cuban milk production fell by half, beef production fell by two-thirds, poultry declined by 80 percent, pigs by 70 percent, and powdered milk production by 90 percent (Pérez 2006: 293).

After the peak of the crisis around 1993, the Cuban government put in place several strategies to regain some of the economic—and nutritional—momentum that it had lost with the withdrawal of Soviet support. First, a Food Program was introduced, supported by international agencies, which included the partial reorganization of agricultural sectors, the encouragement of a return to small-scale independent farming in some rural areas, and the introduction of urban vegetable gardening cooperatives (Altieri et al. 1999; Wilson 2009a: 256–61). Public health programs were geared to address the new health and nutrition problems of Cubans, which started to show results by the mid- to late 1990s (Rodríguez-Ojea et al. 2002: 133). At the same time, parts of the economy were opened to small-scale independent operators; people could get licenses to operate small businesses including the selling of many food products in markets. Remittances from emigrants back to Cuba were legalized, providing to this day an enormous boost to households with friends or family abroad, and the tourist sector was rapidly developed. Cuban shops were also transformed: stores that had previously been restricted to foreign visitors and diplomats were now opened to all Cubans, and became the main source of certain food products that were no longer available through subsidized state outlets—the only problem was that products at these stores were sold in U.S. dollars or its Cuban equivalent, the newly introduced convertible peso, so that one bottle of vegetable oil could cost more than a week's salary. Importantly, food rations at subsidized prices were retained as a central mechanism of socialized food distribution, and have remained to the present; however, the quantity, diversity, and reliability of foods provided through the ration system declined through much of the 1990s, and only provided enough food for between 10 and 15 days on average of a month (Pertierra 2011).

So, what happened to rice and beans through all of this upheaval in post-Soviet Cuba? The short answer is that they became more important than ever before. Imports remained the overwhelming source of both rice and beans—in the early 1990s, only 25 percent of rice in Cuba was locally produced, and wider varieties of beans, including chickpeas and lentils, became increasingly common replacements for black beans in Cuban cooking as they were cheaper to import according to the variable prices of world markets (Castro Ruz 1991). But throughout the crisis of the 1990s, many other foods previously taken for granted disappeared from Cuban shops, kitchens, and tables (including chicken, eggs, milk), and while rice and beans were not literally the only foods regularly consumed, they were among the most reliable, and were recognized by policy makers and consumers alike to be invaluable sources of carbohydrate and protein.

Public and private discourses about the nutritional values of food are extremely visible in Cuba and are in large part a result of the public campaigns led throughout the 1990s to minimize the worst effects of the food security crisis and associated nutrition transition. Television programs, newspaper columns, and political speeches advised the Cuban public about the nutritional qualities of foods, some of which had been previously unfamiliar to the average consumer; Castro's own recognition of this urgent issue is highlighted by the fact that during the five-year period from 1989 and 1994 he gave at least 14 formal speeches that mentioned both rice and beans![1] In one sample speech from 1991, largely devoted to food matters during the Special Period, Castro outlines in the 17th of 118 paragraphs how:

> Three years ago a ton of black beans cost $1,000. Fortunately, the price is lower right now. There is a food that is very rich in protein; lentils. Not too many people eat lentils. There are times when you can buy lentils cheaper than kidney beans. We would prefer to eat kidney beans, but if we can get more, 30 or 40 percent more out of lentils, then we will buy lentils. We have to. There is another food that our people have become accustomed to eating, chick-peas. Chick-peas are 22% protein. A kilogram of chick-peas has more protein than a kilogram of meat. Well, those prices also fluctuate, but it is a nutritious food that generally has a good price. Fortunately, all our students, all of those here who are under 40 years of age, have gotten used to eating chick-peas to such an extent that I know some young people who refuse to eat kidney beans because they want chick-peas. (Castro Ruz 1991)

Within this small excerpt (small in relation to the size of the speech!), we can see how Castro is primarily presenting food in quantifiable terms, measured in prices, weights, and nutritional values. Such a scientific and economic approach to food within Cuban politics and media far outweighs representations of food in more cultural, emotional, or even nationalistic terms. The tendency to discuss food for its nutritional merits is strongly integrated into everyday life, and is second only to the discussion of availability and price in terms of how food might be described in an unprompted conversation (Pertierra 2011).

By the beginning of the new millennium, food security had been sufficiently reestablished that the average Cuban was meeting his or her nutritional needs. But a typical diet today relies more heavily on the traditional *comida criolla* such as rice and beans than ever before. As Shannon Lee Dawdy points out, traditional Cuban cooking has actually prospered as a result of the crisis of the 1990s, because the diversity of imported foods from the ex–Soviet bloc has disappeared, and the prices of imported manufactured foods from Latin America or Asia sold in nonsubsidised stores remain prohibitively expensive (Dawdy 2002: 76). Some of the enduring qualities that made rice and beans useful foods in previous centuries—that is, that both products literally endure through shipping, distributing, and storing for long periods of time without need for refrigeration or extensive packaging—assured their ongoing relevance throughout a period of economic crisis in which foods that are more perishable, less nutritious, or more expensive disappeared from the shop shelves and kitchens of Cuba.

Cooking *Congrí* in Today's Cuba: Everyday Life in Margarita's Kitchen

> As you know, this is a very appetizing dish in Cuban cuisine, and it is always in demand, because it is a dish that is very nutritious; it has frijoles which contain protein, and it includes a cereal—the rice—which is very sustaining. And it combines with all types of meat, such as chicken, fish, pork, lamb.
>
> Margarita

Margarita is a woman in her sixties who has lived most of her life in Santiago de Cuba, who learned to cook at the age of thirteen and prides herself on her excellent skills in the kitchen. Margarita is also my mother-in-law, so over the years I have been able to enjoy the results of the work and love that she puts into her daily cooking. Cuban daughters-in-law would usually join an extended family with their own knowledge of standard Cuban cooking (most Cuban girls take on household chores as teenagers and are expected to know how to cook for their boyfriends and husbands by adulthood). But my foreign origins had given me no training whatsoever in Cuban cuisine, so Margarita has always been very happy and interested to pass on her extensive knowledge to me. Much of her own experience has been gained from cooking alongside her mother, Nena, who in her late eighties has only recently handed over the responsibility of cooking *congrí*, her special forte, to Margarita. While Margarita says that she has been cooking *congrí* pretty much the same way since first taught by Nena, over the years some changes have inevitably taken place, especially with regard to the kitchen equipment (see Figure 3.4) and energy sources that are used in everyday cooking.

Before the revolution, Margarita's (mostly white) family were part of Santiago's (mostly white) middle class, and the 1950s-era houses of their neighborhood already featured tiled kitchens designed to accommodate stovetops, refrigerators, and other modern appliances. However, within this framework, transitions from kerosene to gas-powered stoves, and more recently the introduction of electric rice cookers and electric pressure cookers have clearly made some minor changes to the ways in which *congrí* is prepared. Margarita's recipe for *congrí* calls for the use of an electric pressure cooker to initially soften the beans, but for the main stage in which rice and beans are cooked together, she prefers to use a stovetop pressure cooker instead, in which she feels more comfortable judging the quantities of ingredients and timings.

While Margarita and I discussed the construction of the recipe at the end of this chapter, it became increasingly clear that *congrí* is not the sort of dish for which recipes are generally needed; Margarita cooks almost all of her food-measuring portion

Figure 3.4 Electric pressure cookers are increasingly used to cook rice, soften meat and beans, and to cook stews. Photo by the author.

by sight and judging timings from prior experience. Although she cooks at home every day, Margarita rarely cooks entirely new dishes; she never consults cookbooks but will sometimes trade verbal instructions with other women among her friends and family. While Margarita's cooking knowledge seems informal, that is not to say that she is at all cavalier in her cooking. On the contrary, in drawing from a lifetime of personal practice, Margarita seems to achieve great precision, and knows exactly why each stage of her *congrí* cooking needs to be done just so. For example, in our conversations Margarita has emphasized and explained at considerable length that the proportion of oil, which she measures by sight in the pot, is important:

> because the rice grain is dry and it absorbs a lot ... otherwise when you serve it at the table you will see something pale and without shine, you lose any enthusiasm to eat it if you don't see that slight shininess that is characteristic, that *congrí* should have.

Congrí, therefore, is not the place for innovation in cooking; while there are better or worse executions of the dish, like most *comida criolla*, virtuosity comes in each step being executed carefully, and not from experimenting with significantly new forms. Further, Margarita shares a belief I have frequently heard echoed by women when talking about cooking Cuban food, which is that such typically *criolla* dishes are tastiest when prepared at home:

> I think that my neighbours, for example, would make their *congrí* in the same way that I do. [But] I think that when we compare a *congrí* made in a house with one made in a restaurant, they might leave out steps due to lack of resources. They might leave out the pork fat and use only oil; they don't have the same selection of ingredients which I look for, I really look for them myself. So they're different; for example, you have eaten *congrí* in restaurants; it is really a dry rice dish, it doesn't have the oil, it doesn't look as good … maybe they lack seasoning, they don't use the same seasoning that we do as in that moment they don't have them.

People who have lived or traveled in Cuba in recent decades will recognize that it is no great feat to make food tastier than that served in most restaurants. In referring to restaurants perhaps lacking certain ingredients (in this case, pork fat or seasoning) that she makes a personal effort to attain, Margarita is alluding here to the particular features of the state-run infrastructure that oversees the distribution of most food products in Cuban shops, markets, and restaurants. Especially since the economic crisis of the early 1990s, but also due to fuel shortages, changes to agricultural systems, and problems with both droughts and hurricanes since the early 2000s, state-run restaurants and workplace cafeterias that rely exclusively on government agencies or institutions for the provision of ingredients are usually unable to provide quality versions of even the most staple Cuban foods. In contrast, within individual homes, when people like Margarita have the financial resources and the energy or initiative to actively seek ingredients, they are able to use not only the basic provisions found in state-subsidized outlets, but can also combine products found in a range of other sources, some legal but expensive, some informal but government-tolerated, and others illegal but widely used.[2]

The "Invention" of Cooking: Scarcity in the Post-Soviet Economy

Margarita and other women (for it is almost always women) who are in charge of household provisioning and cooking must be flexible and entrepreneurial in overcoming the vagaries and scarcities of the Cuban food market to make sure they put delicious and varied food on their tables on a daily basis. This capacity to be inventive—not in the cooking, but in the shopping practices that *enable* cooking—is an essential skill of Cuban life that is referred to quite literally as *inventar*, "invention." Being inventive is a necessary quality across all manner of domestic and workplace matters and is especially associated with the Special Period, but women in particular who are of an age to be caring for children and running households will most regularly face the need for invention when trying to resolve unforeseen obstacles in cooking-related areas (Del Real and Pertierra 2008; Pertierra 2011). As anthropologist Mona Rosendahl has argued, cooking and serving "strong food" is a highly valued part of being a woman in Cuba, one upon which identities not only as a caring mother, but also as a loving and capable wife or lover, are hinged (Rosendahl 1997: 36, 49–50). So the very real possibility that many women have encountered since the early 1990s of failing to produce "strong food" can really be understood as cause for deep concern. Even if today most women are regularly able to produce at least one daily meal that would qualify as strong—and my evidence from 2003/2004 suggests that even women on low incomes are largely successful in obtaining and cooking sufficiently nutritious food—the memories and experiences of the previous decade in which even the most dedicated, inventive, and determined cook may not have been able to produce good enough food, or even just enough food, is a trauma that threatens one's purpose in life and, as a consequence, one's identity as a woman.

In response to such a threat, many women are keen to show and share their knowledge and determination in putting in the work that is often necessary to produce a specific meal at a specific time. Even in the following example, in which I will quote extensively from Margarita talking about making *congrí*, it is clear that while by 2009 Cuba was no longer in a state of food crisis, making sure that *congrí* could be made properly for a specific occasion—that of my visit—could still pose several challenges. To understand the following story, it is important to know that the *shopping* is a store at which goods are sold at commercial prices at least as high as those in the United States, and that the prices she quotes are in the second official currency of Cuba, the convertible peso, the value of which is fixed to the U.S. dollar:

> The garlic, onion and pepper you can get in the market, you don't have to pay convertible pesos for them. The rice you receive as part of the basic rations. But look, in the case of the black bean it poses some difficulties, at the moment they are not distributing them in the basic rations. At *this* moment. In months past, they have had them, but at this moment what they are distributing is a red bean. You can make a *congrí* with these, but it won't get that dark colour like when you make it with black beans; instead you will get a sort of pinkish colour, because the bean is sort of reddish pink.
>
> Right now there are no black beans in any market in Santiago; I have done the rounds of all of them and I have not seen one black bean. Either you make it with a coloured bean that they give you in the basic rations, or you can buy the same coloured red beans in the market as well, or else you go to the *shopping* [nonsubsidized store] and you buy one small packet of black beans, which costs 1.05 convertible pesos at some of the shops from the *Panamericana* chain. Because this same little packet, with the same number of grams, if you buy it in the *Cubalse* chain it will cost you 2.00 convertible pesos. That is to say there is a 95 cent difference, and it is the same thing! Because I have walked all over and done the rounds of the shops; since it has been a while since the black bean has not arrived as part of the basic rations, and I wanted to offer it to you here at home—in your

home because this is your house too!—I wanted to make this *congrí* with black beans, so I went around to several of the *shopping* that sell in convertible pesos, and I found that in *Cubalse*, the little 50g packet—with the same brand, and the same producer—cost 2.00 convertible pesos. So I said "Oh, but these seems very expensive here," and I went along to *4ta y Garzón*, which is part of the *Panamericana* chain, and I found the same packet, same brand, same 50 grams, in 1.05 convertible pesos. And that's where I bought it, of course, to save the money.

As we looked over the ingredients for the *congrí* she made that day (see Figure 3.5), Margarita showed very concisely several of the points about cooking in Cuba outlined in this chapter. Even when the main ingredients of a dish are usually part of the rations, some ingredients, in this case black beans, may come or go from the ration-books. At another moment, it could easily have been the case that while black beans were being provided in rations, there happened to be a shortage of onions at the markets. When such scarcities result in going to buy goods at the *shopping*, the unsubsidized store, then the costs of a dish go up astronomically. To put this in perspective, if Margarita had paid 2.00 convertible pesos for her small packet of black beans, this would have equaled around 10 percent of the official *monthly* average salary. As tiring as it may be, doing the rounds of multiple shops to ensure a saving of 95 cents can therefore be a worthwhile undertaking, even in a household like Margarita's that is a regular recipient of remittances. Cooks in households that do not have regular access—through remittances or otherwise—to convertible peso income as part of their domestic budget would simply have made a different type of dish, and never ventured to the *shopping* for basic foodstuffs.

Margarita's moving from the rations to the *shopping*, and her price comparisons across the city, is an example of engaging in *inventar* or invention. It was worth making an extra effort to check different stores, because she wanted to ensure that the *congrí* she made was faithful to her recipe while we were visiting. But even in everyday cooking other examples of the need to *inventar* could equally easily have arisen; for example, with frequent blackouts occurring in Santiago, the beans may have had to be softened using a gas flame rather than their electric pressure cooker, or she may have substituted pink beans for black ones. While such adjustments seem small in themselves, the Special Period years have brought a constant awareness of the likelihood that things will go wrong, and it is this high awareness that carrying out a series of steps like cooking *congrí* will likely be thwarted or challenged along the way that requires women to be inventive in their approach to cooking.

Margarita was interested in explaining these problems as a significant part of her story of making *congrí*. This is consistent with my many conversations with Cuban women about cooking from my first visit to the island in 2002 until this day; any talk of cooking rapidly moves to a discussion of the challenges involved in acquiring the correct ingredients and being able to rely on the appliances and power supply to cook them. Not only are these practices of invention important, but talking about them is

Figure 3.5 Clockwise from top left, lard, vegetable oil, salt, and pork fat. Photo by the author.

also an important part of Cuban women's lives. In successfully navigating what she explicitly presents as a series of slightly challenging problems, Margarita is in effect demonstrating her feminine acumen: her dish of *congrí* is not only an appreciated gesture to me of her valuing my presence, but is also an expression of her ability to overcome minor adversities and fulfill her role as a good mother-in-law and a good woman. Such feelings are not only communicated through the food, but also in the conversations surrounding the food.

Margarita's cooking of rice and beans demonstrates how in some ways the food infrastructure as currently managed by the Cuban government continues to support and enable her endeavors (as when rice and vegetables are easily obtained and cheaply priced), while in other ways the post-Soviet socialist economy is seen on the ground to present puzzling and unpredictable obstacles (as when black beans that have previously been included in rations are only available at wildly varying prices through unsubsidized stores). Within such a context, improvisation and inventiveness are primarily expressed through the acquisition of foods and associated resources in the kitchen and house. In contrast, the food and cooking itself is not a site for creativity so much as for conservative reproduction. Rather than exerting creative energy upon innovations in cooking styles or new food combinations, most Cuban women feel the need to focus, in the midst of such rapid social and political change, on exerting their creative energies to ensure that some features of everyday life—among which food can be the most basic and yet most meaningful—remain relatively familiar.

Clearly, the political economy that determines access to food in Cuba is very different to those found elsewhere in the contemporary Americas. While rice and beans are foods that evoke many sentiments in Cuba—those of heartiness, of familiarity, and above all of normality in a world where normality seems precarious—they do not serve to symbolize Cuban national identity in the way that authors in this volume have identified in Brazil, Costa Rica, and Panama. But the Cuban example also demonstrates a very different situation from that of consumers elsewhere in the postsocialist world. Postsocialist countries in Africa, Europe, and Asia, while divergent in their transition to market economies, have nonetheless generally expanded consumer markets in ways that have massively multiplied the types of foods available for consumers over the past two decades. The rapid transformation of everyday shopping, cooking, and eating caused by the transition from socialist planned economies to different kinds of market economies has been well documented (Humphrey 1995; Yan 2005; Patico and Caldwell 2002). Often, imported foods, especially American or international branded foods and processed convenience foods, shifted within a couple of years from being only accessible by foreigners and elites to becoming a regular part of the middle-class diet (Patico and Caldwell 2002). Anthropologist Melissa Caldwell (2002) has traced the changing role that locally produced food items have played for consumers navigating such transitions in Russia; while imported goods continued to represent superior quality or cosmopolitanism, people were also keen to retain a nationalist pride in Russian food as embodying the collectivist principles upon which socialism was based, and which continued to play an important role in a society that was negotiating its fast insertion into the difficulties and dangers of neoliberal capitalism. In that context, choosing the perceived simplicity and healthiness of locally produced ingredients offers Russians a way to express loyalty to the national collectivist values with which they identified in an era of rapid social change (Caldwell 2002: 313).

In contrast, rice and beans in contemporary Cuba have not been reinterpreted for their nationalist value in the face of increased access to foreign imported foods. Indeed, as described earlier, Cubans have enjoyed a long history of eating imported foods; by 2010 Reuters quoted government sources to report that, despite plans to improve agricultural production, Cuba continued to import the significant majority of its rice and beans (Reuters 2010). But what Cubans and Russians do have in common with regard to their fondness for familiar everyday foods is an understanding of it as the most intimate and emotional connection to traditional values of well-being and strength. As Caldwell and others have shown, political transformations have deep consequences in the everyday experiences of food and eating, both in terms of practical tasks required to cook and eat as before, and in the symbolic or moral significance that certain foods will assume. Particularly in transitions to or from socialist economies, in which the state assumes almost total responsibility for the production and distribution of food, policy developed at the level of government has a deep impact upon consumers' understanding of what constitutes a good life—or at least a good enough life—and the foundation role that food plays in securing such well-being (see also Gronow 2003). Rice and beans in Cuba may not be celebrated as spectacular foods, nor are they invested with the morals or identity of the Cuban nation. But to eat rice and beans is to have, if not the good life, then a good enough life—the power of rice and beans is measured not so much by its presence, as by how difficult it would be to live without.

There remains much scope for further work on the relationships that entangle global politics and food security with gendered identities, household practices, and specific foods such as rice and beans. Judith Carney has elaborated upon the influential work of Sidney Mintz to argue that there is a need for more research that focuses upon the results that the gendered effects of global capitalism have upon food production and consumption, and the taking up of specific foodways (Carney 2008: 128). These issues in a context of global *socialism* have been just as worthy of study, and in at least one corner of the Americas, remain relevant. While unable to discuss here the complex and uneven ways in which women's relationship to paid employment has changed over the course of the Cuban Revolution, this chapter suggests that women's roles as consumers and as household managers are deeply related to the retention of specific foods, including but not limited to, rice and beans. Particularly since the onset of the Special Period, women's identities and practices have become even more closely tied to domestic reproduction than they were in the Soviet years (Pertierra 2008). This has made the ability to cook "strong food" an even more important way to validate and express womanhood than in previous decades. As the base upon which strong food is built, rice and beans have therefore moved somewhat from the background of Cuban cooking to become a more explicit site of domestic labor and inventive production.

As the growing body of food scholarship demonstrates, and as the contributors to this volume have shown, studying food is an excellent way to understand how global politics and economics can shape the most basic practices of everyday life. Whether in the studies of global scale that show how increases of food consumption in one country may rely on exploitative modes of production in another, or in the ethnographies of small-scale communities in which the cultural meaning of specific foods changes over time, or even in the individual case study of a woman like my mother-in-law Margarita, we can appreciate how the most quotidian of activities—such as switching on the pressure cooker to make a good *congrí* for the children and grandchildren—is affected by specific policies such as those of Cuban socialism, as well as by more long-standing forces such as understandings of gender.

Perhaps more than any other country in the Americas, Cuba saw significant and tumultuous change over the twentieth century and into the first decade of the twenty-first century. Throughout such transformation, though, the everyday processes of cooking *congrí* and other standard dishes using rice and beans have changed remarkably little. This in itself is interesting; the many structures and practices that surround the making of a dish like *congrí* have changed, even while the dish itself has largely remained stable—in other words, the more things change, the more they stay the same. In their stability and predictability, rice and beans can also take on some quiet significance. For people who have recently experienced the vulnerability of sudden food scarcity, and for whom the activities that are required to make even standard fare such as *congrí* can still require some inventive and entrepreneurial efforts, there is a certain pleasure and triumph for women like Margarita in being able to provide rice and beans cooked to perfection, to share around the table with loved ones.

Recipe: *Congrí*

Margarita's message

This is a traditional dish, and the recipes pass from generation to generation; from my grandmother it passed to my mother, from my mother to me. I hope that you will be able to prepare this recipe in your house, and that all those reading this recipe decide to cook it. Remember that it was brought to you by Anna Cristina in collaboration with me, Margarita, her mother-in-law, and may you all enjoy this delicious *congrí*! With great pleasure I bring you this recipe.

Ingredients

3 cups of white rice
1 cup of black beans
One strip of bacon (optional)
1 small onion
1 medium chilli pepper
5 to 7 garlic cloves
Olive oil (or pork lard)
Salt

Directions

After soaking the black beans in a large pot of water overnight, put the beans and their water in an electric pressure cooker. Add finely chopped pieces of bacon and cook for 35 minutes or until beans are soft.

While the beans are cooking, finely chop the onion and the chilli pepper. Mash the garlic in a mortar and pestle.

Once beans are cooked, separate the beans from their water using a colander, but saving the water as this will be used for cooking the rice. Measure out the quantity of black bean water required for cooking three cups of rice (Margarita recommends six cups of water for three cups of rice, but reminds us that higher-quality rice grains could require two-thirds or half that amount).

Wash the rice well using regular water and put it aside. Using a large frying pan and a low heat, add 4 or 5 soup-spoons of vegetable oil to the bottom of the pan (Margarita only recommends pork lard as a substitute when bacon has not been used). Add the garlic, onion, and chilli pepper and sauté on a low flame until the ingredients have softened, but have not burned; this combination of ingredients sautéed in oil is the classic Cuban *sofrito*.

Add the washed and drained rice to the frying pan and sauté it in the *sofrito*. Once the rice grains start sticking to the bottom of the pan, transfer them to a stovetop pressure cooker and add the beans. Stir gently for one or two minutes before adding the six cups of black bean water (or adjusted quantity). Add one-third of a soup-spoon of salt, but no more. Place the lid on the pressure cooker and cook for 12 to 13 minutes. Next, turn off the heat but do not open the lid until the pressure subsides; this usually takes about 20 minutes. Using a fork, stir the rice and beans to separate them from the sides and bottom of the pot. Margarita emphasizes that using a fork and not a spoon is important, as this fluffs the rice up and allows some of the vapor to escape. Now your *congrí* is ready to transfer to a large dish and serve.

Notes

1. I carried out a quick survey of Fidel Castro's speeches using the Castro Speech Data Base of the Latin American Network Information Center (LANIC) at the University of Texas, which can be found online at: http://lanic.utexas.edu/la/cb/cuba/castro.html. Searching its database of speeches from 1959 to 1996, results showed 50 speeches in which Castro mentioned both "rice" and "beans," with speeches heavily concentrated toward the earliest years of the revolution (when radical redistribution was taking place and new food goals being set) and from the mid-1980s to the early 1990s (as Cuba started losing USSR imports and subsidies and slid into the Special Period crisis). More broadly, between 1959 and 1996 "food" was mentioned in 173 Castro speeches. While I chose to use the LANIC database for its search facility and the quality of English translation, an even more comprehensive online database of Castro speeches in Spanish and in translation, from 1959 up to 2008, is managed by the Cuban government at http://www.cuba.cu/gobierno/discursos/index.html.

2. Since the 1990s, the development of tourism and the partial opening of the economy to allow small business, including home-based private restaurants, has developed a small sector within which a few Cubans may be able to eat out and enjoy food comparable or superior to a home-cooked meal. But the vast majority

of Cubans cannot afford such places, and the majority of nondomestic cooking takes place in cafeterias for students and workers, which are free or very cheap, but which prize quantity over quality, and are not always able to even achieve the former.

References

Altieri, M. A., N. Companioni, K. Cañizres, C. Murphy, P. Rosset, M. Bourque, and C. I. Nicholls. 1999. "The greening of the 'barrios': Urban agriculture for food security in Cuba." *Agriculture and Human Values* 16: 131–40.

Barnet, M. 2003. "Biography of a runaway slave." In *The Cuba reader: History, culture, politics*, ed. A. Chomsky, B. Carr, and P. M. Smorkaloff, 58–64. Durham, N.C.: Duke University Press.

Benjamin, M., J. Collins, and M. Scott. 1986. *No free lunch: Food and revolution in Cuba today.* New York: Grove Press.

Caldwell, M. L. 2002. "The taste of nationalism: Food politics in postsocialist Moscow." *Ethnos* 67: 295–319.

Carney, J. A. 2001. *Black rice: The African origins of rice cultivation in the Americas.* Cambridge, Mass.: Harvard University Press.

Carney, J. A. 2008. "Reconsidering *Sweetness and power* through a gendered lens." *Food and Foodways* 16: 127–34.

Castiñeiras, L., M. Equivel, L. Lioi, and K. Hammer. 1991. "Origin, diversity and utilization of the Cuban germplasm of common bean (*Phaseolus vulgaris* L.)." *Euphytica* 57: 1–8.

Castro Ruz, F. 1991. "Speech by President Fidel Castro Ruz at the closing session of the Fifth National Agricultural, Livestock, and Forestry Workers Union, SNTAF, Congress held at the Cuban Workers Federation Lazaro Pena Theater in Havana on 22 November." Available at: http://lanic.utexas.edu/project/castro/db/1991/19911123.html. Accessed February 12, 2011.

Charón Cardona, E. 2003. "Yellow cassavas, purple bananas." *Humanities Research* 10: 149–57.

Dawdy, S. L. 2002. "La comida mambisa: Food, farming and Cuban identity, 1839–1999." *New West Indian Guide* 76: 47–80.

Del Real, P., and A. C. Pertierra. 2008. "Inventar: Recent struggles and inventions in housing in two Cuban cities." *Buildings and Landscapes* 15: 78–92.

Eckstein, S. E. 2003. *Back from the future: Cuba under Castro.* New York: Routledge.

Edelson, S. M. 2010. "Beyond black rice: Reconstructing material and cultural contexts for early plantation agriculture." *American Historical Review* 115: 125–35.

Eltis, D., P. Morgan, and D. Richardson. 2007. "Agency and diaspora in Atlantic history: Reassessing the African contribution to rice cultivation in the Americas." *American Historical Review* 112: 1329–58.

Folch, C. 2008. "Fine dining: Race in prerevolution Cuban cookbooks." *Latin American Research Review* 43: 205–23.

Gronow, J. 2003. *Caviar with champagne: Common luxury and the ideals of the good life in Stalin's Russia.* Oxford: Berg.

Humphrey, C. 1995. "Creating a culture of disillusionment: Consumption in Moscow, a chronicle of changing times." In *Worlds apart: Modernity through the prism of the local*, ed. D. Miller, 43–68. London: Routledge.

Kandiyoti, D. 2006. "Consuming nostalgia: Nostalgia and the marketplace in Cristina García and Ana Menéndez." *MELUS* 31: 81–97.

Murray Ballou, M. 1854. *History of Cuba; or, Notes of a traveller in the Tropics.* Boston: Phillips, Sampson and Co. Available at: http://www.gutenberg.org/ebooks/32812. Accessed February 15, 2011.

Nuñez González, N., and E. González Noriega. 1999. "Antecedentes etnohistóricos de la alimentación tradicional en Cuba." *Revista Cubana de Alimentación y Nutrición* 13: 145–50.

Ortíz, F. 1940. "Los factores humanos de la cubanidad." *Revista Bimestre Cubana* 21: 165–69.

Padrón, C. 2005. *Franceses en el suroriente de Cuba.* Havana: Ediciones UNION.

Patico, J., and M. Caldwell. 2002. "Consumers exiting socialism: Ethnographic perspectives on daily life in post-Communist Europe." *Ethnos* 67: 285–94.

Pérez, L. A. Jr. 1999. *On becoming Cuban: Identity, nationality, and culture.* Chapel Hill: University of North Carolina Press.

Pérez, L. A. Jr. 2006. *Cuba: Between reform and revolution.* Oxford: Oxford University Press.

Pérez Firmat, G. 1987. "From ajiaco to tropical soup: Fendando Ortíz and the definition of Cuban culture." *LACC Occasional Papers Series 93. Dialogues (1980–1994).* Florida State University. Available at: http://digitalcommons.fiu.edu/laccopsd/16. Accessed February 1, 2011.

Pertierra, A. C. 2008. "*En casa*: Women and households in post-Soviet Cuba." *Journal of Latin American Studies* 40: 745–69.

Pertierra, A. C. 2011. *Cuba: The struggle for consumption.* Coconut Creek, Fla.: Caribbean Studies Press.

Reuters. 2010. "Cuban efforts to reduce bulk imports on track." January 3. Available at: http://www.reuters.com/article/2010/01/03/cuba-food-idUSN0322348420100103. Accessed January 20, 2012.

Rodríguez-Ojea, A., S. Jiménez, A. Berdasco, and M. Esquivel. 2002. "Nutrition transition in Cuba." *Public Health Nutrition* 5: 129–33.

Rosendahl, M. 1997. *Inside the revolution: Everyday life in socialist Cuba.* Ithaca, N.Y.: Cornell University Press.

Sánchez, J. 2003. "Moro or congrí." *Iowa Review* 33: 158–59.

Villapol, N. 1981. *Cocina al minuto.* Havana: Editorial Orbe. Available at: http://cocina.cuba.cu/cult_cul.php?idsab=4. Accessed February 12, 2011.

Wilson, M. 2009a. "'*La lucha (de provisiones)*': National and local moral economies of food provisioning in Tuta, Cuba." PhD diss. University of Cambridge.

Wilson, M. 2009b. "*No tenemos viandas!* Cultural ideas of scarcity and need." *International Journal of Cuban Studies* 2: 73–80.

Yan, Y. 2005. "Of hamburger and social space: Consuming McDonald's in Beijing." In *The cultural politics of food and eating: A reader*, ed. J. L. Watson and M. L. Caldwell, 80–103. Oxford: Blackwell.

–4–

Jamaica Coat of Arms
Rice and Peas

B. W. Higman

Jamaica had a coat of arms three hundred years before it acquired its own flag and the associated trappings of a modern nation-state. Granted in 1661, soon after the island became an English colony, Jamaica's coat of arms had at its center a shield inscribed with a red cross and five pineapples, the latter thought to symbolize hospitality (Senior 2003: 114). On the crest was a crocodile. To the right and the left of the shield stood a male and a female Indian (Taíno), their feet resting on a banner bearing the motto *Indus Uterque Serviet Uni*, translated to mean "The Indians twain shall serve one Lord." The unique emblems—Taínos, pineapples, and crocodile—were all indigenous.

In 1961, on the eve of Jamaica's independence, Frederic G. Cassidy (1961: 197) observed that "*Rice-and-peas* (that is, beans), a favourite dish, is nicknamed *Jamaica coat-of-arms.*" Precisely how this naming came about remains a mystery, but the association shows that rice and peas had been promoted as a popular representation of identity long before Jamaica installed its official national emblems—bird, flower, tree, and fruit. Not all of these were indigenous: the national fruit, the ackee, had its roots in West Africa. However, this did not prevent its combination with imported salted codfish to create what came to be known informally as Jamaica's "national dish," ackee-and-saltfish (Higman 2008: 2–3). Similarly, the rice of rice-and-peas was not indigenous and often it was imported rather than locally grown. These dishes were "Creole" in the Jamaican sense, meaning the neotropical offspring of intro-duced elements that could not claim indigeneity. Thus, all of these introductions were given new life and made "Jamaican" through the creativity of Creole combina-tion and the particularity of language.

Jamaicans call beans "peas" and beans and rice "rice and peas." The choice of "peas" to describe these legumes is ancient, firmly established by the seventeenth century, and rarely challenged. "Rice and peas" as the preferred name for the seed-combining dish is relatively recent, though firmly in place by the end of the nine-teenth century. Naming it this way put a local stamp on the dish and served to create a difference between Jamaica and those territories that preferred alternative versions such as "peas and rice," "beans and rice," and "rice and beans." Jamaicans also em-phasized that they followed the practice of combining the ingredients in a single pot, at an early stage in the cooking process, in contrast to those—such as their Cuban neighbors—who kept the rice and the peas separate almost until the very end.

Recipe: Rice and Peas

To cook rice and peas in the Jamaican style, the peas are first simmered in coconut milk and, when tender, the rice is added with seasonings and water sufficient to steam or boil the rice until soft but not sticky, leaving the rice grains flavored by the seasoning and the peas evenly distributed.[1]

Ingredients

2 cups rice
1 cup red peas
Milk of 1 dried coconut (grated and juiced) [or 1 can coconut cream]
Salt
Country pepper, scallion, thyme to taste

Directions

1. Boil peas in 3 cups of water until tender.
2. Add coconut milk, salt and seasoning.
3. Boil for 15 minutes, add rice.
4. Stir gently, cover and simmer until water has dried out and rice is soft.

A Cultivated Landscape

The fact that Jamaica should follow a route somewhat different from that taken by both its fellow members of the British Empire and Commonwealth, most of these territories far away in the Eastern Caribbean, and different also from its avid beans-and-rice eating, Spanish-speaking, nearer neighbors is not in itself surprising. Jamaica was notoriously isolated, less open to Caribbean currents and influences than might be expected. It followed a separate path in several significant respects in its social and cultural development. Jamaicans had their own version of callaloo (Higman 2007), for example, and in eating the ackee were regarded with horror by other Caribbean peoples who recognized the fruit's poisonous potential. The notion of an individualistic Jamaican identity had its roots in the island's very geographical location and the character of its settlement history.

Third largest of the islands of the Caribbean, Jamaica possessed from the beginning a potential for uniqueness. This potential was reinforced by its location to the south of the other islands making up the Greater Antilles—Cuba, Hispaniola, and Puerto Rico—and its status as an oceanic island, never having been connected by dry land with the continental Americas or with any other island. Jamaica's rising from the sea set it apart. Not only did the geophysical facts limit the kinds of plants and animals that could find their way to the island, it determined equally that those that did manage to get there were able to develop high degrees of endemism. Thus, whereas the biodiversity of Jamaica was limited, the unique species that flourished on the island often lacked counterparts elsewhere. The maritime isolation of Jamaica also placed it off the beaten track of human migration (Wilson 2007: 100). Whereas its immediate neighbor Cuba was settled by people from Yucatan by about 6000 B.P., the first people to live in Jamaica arrived as late as A.D. 600, long after almost all the other Caribbean islands had been populated and less than a millennium before the fateful landing of Columbus in 1494.

Neither rice nor peas were part of Jamaica's natural mix of plants. Cereals and legumes traveled poorly by wind and water, lacking the capacity to float long distances possessed by fruit such as the coconut. There was no native variety of rice in any region of the Americas and even maize moved slowly to the islands. The food culture developed by the first people to reach Jamaica had its focus in cassava, a tuber carried from the continental mainland. The Taíno people, the builders of complex societies in the islands, had little place in their system for the consumption of seeds. However, although Jamaica lacked the higher versions of the complex societies that emerged elsewhere in the Greater Antilles, the Taíno did create a highly productive and seemingly sustainable horticultural landscape capable of supporting a moderately dense population.

Spanish colonization was immensely destructive. The population of Jamaica was decimated and the carefully articulated food supply system developed by the people ruined. Ironically, when Columbus was marooned on the north coast of Jamaica from June 1503 to March 1504 his crew became dependent on the Taíno to keep them alive. But by the end of the Spanish colonial period, the island was overrun by feral pigs, cattle, and horses, brought to the island from Europe. Meat dominated the diet. Citrus trees spread through the forest. Cassava and other tubers remained important starches. Rice and peas waited their time.

The English conquest of Jamaica in 1655 established a long-lasting imperial status that continued until the island gained independence in 1962. At the time of the conquest, the island had a population of just 3,000 people, slave and free. The English quickly transformed the fertile plains and interior valleys into sugar plantations, and brought in tens of thousands of enslaved Africans to perform the heavy work required in field and factory. The food of the enslaved was partly produced on the plantations, establishing continuity with the Taíno landscape through the cultivation of cassava and other tubers. Introduced plants in this new food system included, from Africa, plantain and banana, yam and taro, and rice. The breadfruit came from the Pacific and a vast range of fruits and spices from Asia. Many of these plants prospered in the fertile fields of Jamaica.

Slaveowners also imported a wide range of foods from abroad, most of it coming from the north Atlantic. Some of these foods were intended solely for the tables of the planters but, in the absence of canning and refrigeration, were not always successfully transported—as, for example, butter and cheese. The wealthy also enjoyed the exotic delicacies of Jamaica, including highly praised endemics such as the black crab, the mountain mullet, and the ringtail pigeon. Enslaved people occasionally consumed these local delicacies but generally lacked the time and opportunity to hunt and fish. Slaveowners imported other more common foods, such as salted fish (dried), pickled fish (packed in brine in barrels), pickled pork and beef, flour, and rice. These were shared, unequally, with enslaved plantation workers. Salted fish was considered superior to pickled fish, which tended to go rotten (Higman 2008: 319). Rice was generally distributed to the enslaved only when alternatives were in short supply or when individuals fell ill (Higman 1984: 270). Peas and beans of all sorts rarely formed part of such distributions.

What was unusual though not strictly unique about Jamaican food culture during slavery was the so-called provision ground system. This was adopted by planters who preferred not to use regular plantation labor to produce food crops or to have responsibility for distributing rations or cooked meals. Rather, these planters allocated areas of land on which the enslaved people had to grow their own food crops, in their own time. Generally the system had at least two elements. In the first, the people grew plants around their houses and kept chickens and hogs in pens. Peas of various species were often included in this house-garden culture. The second part of the provision ground system was made up of more distant plots, where crops that needed less care and supervision might be grown, particularly the tubers and plantains. Maize and rice could be grown in these grounds, where the conditions were right.

After the abolition of slavery in 1838, the plantation system struggled to maintain its position in the economy. New sources of labor were tapped, most important, indentured laborers from India who brought with them new skills and sometimes plants. Many plantations were abandoned and a thriving peasantry quickly emerged. These small farmers typically maintained a crop-mix reminiscent of the provision grounds. Bananas became a major export crop by the end of the nineteenth century, at first as a peasant crop but later produced on a large scale by multinational plantations. Food habits changed in the twentieth century, with a strong shift away from the tubers and carbohydrate fruits of the provision grounds toward increasing reliance on the grains rice, flour, and corn, following patterns and pressures that were global in scale (Boomgaard 2003). Wheat was never grown in the island. Corn and rice were produced in some quantity, but came to be swamped by imports. As rice became increasingly commonplace on Jamaican tables, so too did "rice and peas."

Cultivating Peas

The range of peas grown in Jamaica was quite large, and they were known by an often confusing variety of names. In the next chapter of this volume, Berleant sets out in some detail the broad principles of the botany of Caribbean beans. Here it is necessary only to focus on the three that have been commonly associated with the dish rice and peas in Jamaica. These are *Phaseolus vulgaris* (red pea), *Cajanus cajan* (gungo pea), and *Vigna unguiculata* (black-eyed pea). These three pulses, together with the cereals, provide the greater part of the plant protein consumed by Jamaicans.

The "common bean" (*Phaseolus vulgaris*), known variously in Jamaica as red pea, kidney bean, and cockstone, belongs to a tribe of perhaps fifty-five species, all of them of New World origin. Domestication occurred in Mexico as early as six or seven thousand years before the present. Although the seeds of the common bean are very variable, throughout the Americas, preferences are quite refined, with high values placed on particular characteristics (Norman, Pearson, and Searle 1995).

In the seventeenth century, the English in Jamaica sometimes called these peas "Indian peas," but they were also known as "calavanc, or calavances." William Hughes in *The American Physitian* said they grew on low branched plants, with long pods like kidney beans (1672: 17–18). He thought them "very good food," easily digested and suited to the hot climate of Jamaica, "because the stomack is not very strong, by reason of the external circumambient heat which doth much debilitate and weaken nature." Compared to English peas, said Hughes, calavances caused less trouble with wind and were more nourishing. The colonists in Jamaica, said Hughes, boiled and buttered them when green or dried, and ate them with pork (1672: 18).

Hans Sloane, the English surgeon and naturalist who lived in Jamaica at the end of the seventeenth century, observed the planting of "clay colour'd and red pease," to be harvested when dry in about two months and "boiled as pease in England" (Sloane 1707, 1: lxxv–lxxvi). He said "*Jamaica* red-pease" were "counted very good provision" and believed "clay coloured pease, or six weeks pease" were regarded as "very good provision for Negroes, white servants, or to fatten hogs withal, and very much planted for those uses" (Sloane 1707, 1: 183–84). In the eighteenth century, Henry Barham declared in his *Hortus Americanus* that the "calavances" belonged to the *phaseoli*, the pods containing "a small white pea, resembling the kidney." The peas, he said, were "very good and sweet, green or dry, and easy of digestion; and therefore proper for a hot climate" (1794: 28). Patrick Browne in his *Civil and Natural History of Jamaica*, first published in 1756, called *Phaseolus vulgaris* "calavances, or red pease" (1756: 292), while the planter-historian Edward Long referred to "calavances, or red bean" (1774, 3: 786). By the late twentieth century, the terms *red peas* and *kidney peas* were sometimes used interchangeably, the latter suggesting the beginning of a renaming of the kidney bean. The well-known Jamaican cook and food writer Enid Donaldson (1993: 91) said that "red peas or kidney beans, whether stewed in soup, or cooked with rice and coconut milk, are the most used and best liked of the legumes."

In Jamaica, gungo or gungu pea (*Cajanus cajan*) is known inter alia as pigeon pea, Congo pea, and Angola pea, the last two suggesting an African origin though an ultimate South Asian source is probable (Barham 1794: 19; Lunan 1814, 1: 336–37).

The peas come from pods produced by a large shrub that grows to about ten feet. They can be eaten both green and dried, the latter having the advantage of relatively long storage qualities but requiring long boiling to soften them. When dried the seeds are grey in color but sometimes speckled with pink and red tones.

One of the great attractions of the gungo pea plant is its capacity to survive and produce in dry places without needing close attention. This was particularly important during the period of slavery and for this reason it became common in the provision grounds of the enslaved. It was also valued for being a perennial. As early as 1672, Hughes referred to it as the "seven year pease," meaning that it required planting only every seventh year (1672: 20). Later writers thought two to five bearings more typical but continued to praise the plant's hardiness. Hughes also noticed that on plantations the peas were often planted close to houses and used as fences. He declared them "very good food, and well tasted" but observed that they had to be eaten in moderation because they caused wind (Hughes 1672: 21). This last claim has sometimes been disputed, though it is generally affirmed by Jamaicans and is apparently related to tannin content. Unlike some other peas and beans, the digestibility of gungo is not improved by cooking.

Long claimed that the "pigeon, or Angola pea" was "chiefly cultivated by the Negroes in their gardens and grounds, because it is perennial, and does not require much care." He thought "the seeds, or peas, are a hearty wholesome food, and generally in use, green or dried" (Long 1774, 3: 787). In the last years of slavery, James Macfadyen declared in his *Flora of Jamaica* that the Congo pea was coarser than many other peas but could be found "around every cottage in the island, growing luxuriantly in the parched savannah, and mountain declivity, as well as in the more fertile and seasonable districts" (1837: 297).

By the 1980s the gungo pea was hailed as a "great favourite," esteemed for its flavor and texture, and valued for its ability to grow in almost any conditions. Three varieties were recognized, "the black or brown skinned, the striped skinned which might well be a hybrid, and the green skinned." It was then claimed that "The distinct flavour of gungo combines best with salted meats—salt pork, salt beef, ham, corn beef and corn pork, bacon, sausage" (A.W.D. 1986). Green gungo was available from Christmas to the end of March, thereafter the pea was available only dried. In gungo soup, the peas were fortified by meat (such as salt beef or corned pork, and chopped pig's tail), yam, coco, flour dumplings, coconut milk, and seasonings (Jacobs 1991). In 1987 green gungo soup was declared the "top ranking" peas recipe, because it retained the "full bodied" characteristic flavor of the peas (A.W.D. 1987).[2]

The cowpea (*Vigna unguiculata*), of which the black-eyed pea is a subspecies, is today the most significant legume cropped in West and Central Africa and a major dietary source of protein. In West Africa, where domesticated cowpeas have been part of agriculture for more than three thousand years, the green pods are consumed fresh and the seeds boiled or roasted and ground into flour for breads. The plant grows well in dry and marginal environments where other crops struggle, producing a harvest within just two or three months (D'Andrea et al. 2007). The black-eyed pea is about five mm long, pale with a black spot.

All three of these peas prospered in Jamaica, as products at first of enslaved people's gardens and grounds and later of free small farmers. They supplied bags of peas to local markets, where the produce was decanted by higglers using tin cups to measure out the peas by the gill (quarter-pint). Some of this product also found its way into the stores of merchants and shopkeepers. Growing demand led these merchants to look outside Jamaica for additional and perhaps cheaper sources. Bags of black-eyed peas and barrels of red kidney beans were imported from the United States by the 1880s, if not earlier. Local growers soon began to complain about this competition. For example, in 1940 a "peas planter" claimed that the usual prices before 1914 had been ten shillings per bushel for black-eyed peas, and 16 shillings for red peas. From 1930, however, he said, the government had allowed the importation of cheap Chilean red peas and thus driven down its relative price.[3] Imports of peas and beans per capita peaked in the 1960s and 1970s, challenging local production (Higman 2008: 259). Into the 1980s imported red peas were on the market even when there had been a bumper harvest locally.[4]

Cultivating Rice

Whereas peas prospered in Jamaica, even when challenged by cheap imports, rice ultimately gave up the struggle. By the 1970s almost all of the rice consumed in the island came from overseas. Only in brief periods of Jamaican history did locally grown product play a significant role. During slavery, the sugar planters showed little interest since they could make much larger profits from sugar and coffee, while the slaves lacked time and resources, particularly to carry out milling by hand (Carney 2001: 158). Sloane said "Rice is here planted by some Negros in their own plantations, and thrives well, but because it requires much beating, and a particular art to separate the grain from the husk, 'tis thought too troublesome for its price, and so neglected by most planters." He also argued that rice was neglected because "the use of it may be supplied by other grains, more easily cultivated and made fit for use by less labour" (1707, 1: xix, 103). By the 1700s, Long was advocating that it should only be cultivated where the fields could be flooded. These places he thought "naturally adapted" to rice, "if it should be thought worthwhile to cultivate it, as an additional supply of food for the Negroes" (Long 1774, 3: 768).

The problem was not a lack of knowledge. Indeed African rice (*Oryza glaberrima*) was an important food crop in much of West Africa, including regions from which the enslaved people were taken. African rice was a voyaging food in the Atlantic slave trade. In other parts of the Americas it became a profitable plantation crop through which planters took advantage of the skills of the enslaved. Attempts to grow African hill-rice continued into the 1840s.[5]

Although Asian rice (*Oryza sativa*) was imported from India to Jamaica as early as the 1820s, and its planting did have the occasional advocate (Titford 1811: 58), it was not cultivated in the island until after abolition. Extensive cultivation had to wait on the arrival of indentured laborers, brought to Jamaica to work in the canefields. By the 1890s, however, Indian immigrants had begun growing *Oryza sativa* in low-lying lands not wanted for other crops (Shepherd 1994: 128–30). When rice from Asia became scarce during World War II Jamaicans substituted green bananas and cornmeal but did also experiment with the cultivation of dryland rice crops.[6]

After the war, local rice growing declined and effectively disappeared by the end of the 1980s, when U.S. rice began to dominate the supply. Ironically, Jamaicans became, for the first time, heavily dependent on rice. The roots and tubers lost their significance, because they came to be portrayed as wasteful, time-consuming, and nutritionally deficient. In the 1980s, the poor came to have no choice but to eat rice "with gravy or a vegetable sauce for their main meal." Rice was promoted for its many virtues of convenience and versatility.[7] The result was that rice was installed as Jamaica's most popular starch, increasingly eaten simply as steamed white rice.

Making Rice and Peas

It is striking that the first edition of the comprehensive *Dictionary of Jamaican English*, published in 1967, included "rice-and-peas" only in a last-minute supplement, and defined wrongly as "a dish made with rice, coconut oil, and usu[ally] red peas" (Cassidy and Le Page 1967). (It should be coconut milk, not oil.) The phrase was recalled to be "common" around Kingston by 1915 but the earliest contemporary documented use cited in the dictionary was from 1947. This suggests a late emergence of rice and peas as a current term. Certainly it took quite a time to enter the written record, with citations earlier than 1930 few and far between, but it seems equally likely that it was part of the vernacular by the middle of the nineteenth century or soon after.

The first known reference to rice and peas is found in the *Gleaner*, Jamaica's leading newspaper, in the course of a report on a murder trial in 1872. Burmah, an indentured Indian man working on a sugar plantation, was charged with the murder of Soranee, a woman employed on the same property. The two had become friends on the boat from India, witnesses testified, but quarreled ever since. Burmah claimed that he had not himself killed Soranee but did admit to helping her killers dispose of her body in a pond. In the trial, "rice and peas" was mentioned only tangentially in the evidence, a witness saying Soranee had been given a dish to eat. Burmah was found not guilty.[8]

The next example took twenty more years to appear in the record, in the context of an 1892 inquest into death presumed caused by ackee poisoning. Those who died had eaten for dinner "akee and rice," the rice bought at a shop and the ackee picked from a tree in the yard. The man of the house, whose wife was among the dead, testi-fied that he had survived by eating instead "rice and peas" with beef and bread.[9] The third example came in yet another murder case and this time the dish was directly implicated in the death. In 1898 a woman accused of attempted murder had served "a dish of peas and rice" or "plate of rice and peas" to the intended victim. The meal later proved to contain ground glass and brick. She was found not guilty.[10] These are the only known references from the nineteenth century.

In 1904 a man was accused of beating a woman who later died. In this case a doc-tor performed a postmortem but found insufficient evidence of violence to explain her death. He did, however, tell the court that the woman was "very fat" and had a heart condition. Her stomach contained "a large undigested meal of red peas, rice and water" and the doctor declared that "he would have found sufficient cause of death in the enormous meal of rice and peas which she had taken."[11] Another murder case, in 1919, had the victim's stomach "full of rice and peas."[12] In all of these cases, "rice and peas" was the common term used, "peas and rice" occurring just once.

Although documented references may be scarce, by 1900 "rice and peas" was regarded as an institution, essential at least to every Sunday dinner of the Kingston poor, and described as "a food equal to a diet of meat" (Moore and Johnson 2000: 78). In 1936 Dr. Dahlia Whitbourne, school medical officer, called "rice and peas" one of the "favourite dishes" of Jamaica (1936: 69). Two years later, the newspaper editor H. G. De Lisser, visiting Jigger-Foot Market, got from a vendor for 1½ pence "a fair quantity of rice and peas, some stewed meat, and a little bit of stewed vegetable stuff in a tin plate."[13] A man of the world, De Lisser recognized the existence of "various forms" of the dish throughout the tropical Americas.[14]

As early as World War II, the occasional observer claimed to notice the decline and even imminent fall of rice and peas. Thus in 1941 one writer recalled a time (unspecified) when rice and peas was "the mainstay of Kingston, and the working people did not consider they were well fed unless they had rice and peas. I don't think it is so popular today, nor is pepper-pot and the art of cooking them properly will soon be lost."[15] The dish did not die. Rather, it spread beyond its initial special appearances on Sundays to become a much more common food. Even in the hard times experienced in 1938 school lunches provided to the needy included rice and peas, served several times a week on any day from Monday to Friday.[16] By 1991 it could be said "no longer is rice and peas, reserved for Sunday's dinner" but, in some homes, served seven days a week.[17]

None of these observers specified the variety of pea used, though red peas might seem to be the default. In 1929 the American ethnologist Martha Beckwith described as a popular crop "a small red bean no bigger than a couple of pinheads, used for the familiar 'rice and peas' of the Jamaica Negro" (1929: 18–19). However, this sounds more like the gungo (which Jamaicans sometimes confusingly called "red pea") rather than the true red pea or kidney bean. In 1938, for the first time with clear precision, De Lisser identified the three main types used in Jamaica as red peas, black-eyed peas, and gungo peas.[18] Donaldson in 1993 (41) said that rice and peas was usually made from "red kidney beans" but also green gungo peas, in season, and dried gungo. Those who had no rice sometimes used a substitute known as "corn-and-peas" (Ayre 2002: 89–90).

In spite of the high visibility of rice and peas throughout the twentieth century—whatever the variety of pea used—it remains true that the dish lacked this prominence in earlier times and gained public notice only after 1870. No doubt it existed before this date but it failed to achieve attention in the public record. Certainly the notion that rice and peas existed as a dish—even a "luxury" dish—in Jamaica during slavery remains to be corroborated (Mintz 1974: 227). It may be that the beginnings of the dish can be found in food given enslaved people in the French Atlantic slave trade, as early as the end of the seventeenth century, when cauldrons were boiled on board combining rice and beans from both African and European grounds, along with other ingredients (Mandelblatt 2008: 411–23). However, there is no evidence of this being transposed to Jamaica during slavery.

The origin of rice-and-peas in its Jamaican manifestation seems more likely to emerge in the period following the abolition of slavery in 1838 and may perhaps be related to migrant movement from Jamaica to the Hispanic Caribbean. Small-scale movement of individuals and groups had been common since the seventeenth century, though beans-and-rice was probably not a popular dish in this early period (see Preston-Werner, chapter 10, this volume). Even in the 1850s, when Jamaicans went to work on the Panama railroad, their food supplies depended heavily on root crops and seem not to have included rice (Newton 1984: 121). Substantial migration to Hispanic America did not occur until after 1870, when "rice and peas" had already entered the Jamaican record. Workers on the Panama Canal, after 1900, protested when compelled to consume company-kitchen meals that included beans and (poorly cooked) rice but not necessarily beans-and-rice (Newton 1984: 147).

In the Hispanic lands of the Americas the dish is generally called beans-and-rice or more specifically red beans-and-rice. The practice of coating the rice in oil is Spanish rather than African, with the rice and the beans cooked separately and combined only at the point of serving (McCann 2009: 174). An earlier version was black beans-and-rice but this seems not to have been known in Jamaica. Related dishes are jambalaya and paella, Egyptian rice-and-lentils and the Indian pillau. The fundamental concept could travel without necessarily carrying with it the precise formula and name of a specific dish.

The Jamaican style of preparation was closely matched by Belize, a British enclave in Spanish Central America. There, "rice and beans" was noticed first in 1895 but achieved the status of "national dish" by the end of the twentieth century (Wilk 2006: 101). As the settlement and colony of British Honduras, Belize had a long close association with Jamaica and it may be that the island had a culinary influence rarely repeated in Central America (see Wilk this volume).

In view of this potential relationship, it is not difficult to conceive of an independent creation occurring in Jamaica. The combining of food elements in a single pot or dish must often have resulted from simple necessity. A cook with varied ingredients but just one pot has little creative choice beyond deciding how and when to add each item, or whether to cook separate servings in sequence. Something similar can be argued for the emergence of ackee and saltfish, the so-called national dish of Jamaica (Higman 2008: 156–58). As with rice and peas, there is no record of the dish being cooked either by rich or poor people during slavery. Quite possibly, the ackee and saltfish were at first cooked separately, the first steamed and the second fried, in the kitchens of the well-off. Served in separate dishes, the two elements slid together on the eater's plate, until the steamed ackee eventually came to be added to the frying saltfish just before serving. In addition, ackee and saltfish was originally called saltfish and ackee, the name shifting (by about 1930) as the relative weights of the elements were reversed once the fish became expensive and the ackee abundant. Rice and peas could have evolved in much the same way and indeed the rice and the peas are still sometimes cooked and served separately in other islands of the Caribbean. The inversion from "peas and rice" to "rice and peas" may similarly indicate a shift in the relative weights of the elements. These are speculations, awaiting proof or refutation.

Celebrating Rice and Peas

Very important to nutrition—and central to the story of rice and peas—is the fact that the protein quality of legumes is significantly improved when they are combined with cereals.[19] This occurs because legume seeds and cereals are complementary, as a result of the way in which they balance the two essential amino acids methionine and lysine. Combining peas with rice improves their joint protein yield. Maximum protein efficiency occurs when about 80 percent of the total derives from rice and 20 percent from peas. These advantages were recognized quite early, the Jamaican medical officer Dr. W. E. McCulloch declaring in 1955 that rice and peas met a physiological need, with the rice protein supplementing that of the peas to create "a biologically perfect protein mixture" (Jamaica Agricultural Society 1957: 75). Thus, the combination is not simply a culinary coup but also a nutritional triumph.

Earlier, in 1936, Whitbourne (68) had observed that Jamaicans lived on "starchy foods of vegetable origin," a diet deficient in proteins. She said: "Rice and cornmeal are apparently our cheapest foods and most used, because they swell in cooking and provide large quantities of food at a cheap rate." Rice contained no protein or vitamins, claimed Whitbourne, while cornmeal delivered only low-quality protein, but she recognized as "favourite dishes" rice and peas and stewed peas. By the time of Jamaica's independence in 1962, the most common foods eaten by vendors in the island's markets were ackee and saltfish, and rice and peas, the latter served at every meal other than breakfast.[20]

The first identified use of "Jamaica Coat of Arms" to mean rice and peas came in 1930 when A. Bain Alves reminisced about race meetings in Kingston in 1878, recalling the "hundreds of women and men with their tables and tubs where you could get a dish of rice and peas, better known as Jamaica Coat of Arms, with stewed beef or ackee and saltfish for three pence."[21] Poorer people, called by Alves the "quattie-quattie class," would ask for "a quattie rice and peas with a good lively watchman." (A *quattie* was a penny halfpenny, a quarter of sixpence.) In response, said Alves, "The old mother would dip a long iron spoon into a huge yauba pot of rice and peas and put it into a small pudding pan, she would then take her iron spoon and mould up the rice and peas into a small hill [and] on top of that she would put a piece of salt pork that was called the watchman, or look-out. She would then throw over all this two spoonfuls of flour sauce."[22] In 1938 De Lisser said he was "cut to the quick" when he heard people "scorn the dish known as rice-and-peas, the food by which so many of us swear and which has even been described as Jamaica's Coat of Arms."[23] The claim was repeated regularly over the years. Even thirty years after independence, in 1992, it was said "rice and peas is easily the best liked dish in Jamaica, called the coat of arms."[24]

Jamaicans think of rice and peas as something good to eat, a triumph of taste. By the 1960s, vacation guides even listed the dish among "local dishes worth sampling," followed inter alia by saltfish and ackee, curried goat and rice, and jerked pork (Ullman and Dinhofer 1968: 172). Local enthusiasm rose to new heights in the early 1970s (Scientific Research Council 1972). A guidebook written by Clinton V. Black, the government archivist, listed a veritable cornucopia of delights but told tourists that among the "truly Jamaican dishes" the "best known and best loved" were the two combinations ackee and saltfish and rice and peas (1973: 30). In 1984 tourists were told, "No one should leave Jamaica without tasting our pepper pot soup, ackee and saltfish, rice and peas, run-dung [mackerel and coconut, rundown] and curried goat, to name a few" (Beamish 1984: 1).

However, rice and peas did not feature in every list designed to tempt the tourist, and was less likely to appear when the emphasis was placed on spicy and exotic taste. Nor was rice and peas among the many foods Jamaican expatriates loved to take with them on airplanes when they traveled to friends and family or, as expatriates, made their way home to foreign places. In this case, rice and peas was too readily replicated using ingredients available outside Jamaica, where it was in fact eaten quite commonly by expatriates (Sharma et al. 2002: 441). Among the food items stowed in the grips of Jamaicans traveling to foreign places, rice and peas could not compete with roast breadfruit, fried fish, ackee, hard-dough bread, water crackers, bun, cheese, spices, seasonings, and fruit. Once again, rice and peas was missing from the specialized food festivals that proliferated in Jamaica after 2000, which promoted everything from fish to jerk pork, spice, sugar cane, yam, potato, and breadfruit. The absence of rice and peas from the titles of these events was not remarkable. Ackee and saltfish was missing too, as were most dishes as opposed to ingredients. At the same time, the fish and jerk festivals did feature cooked foods, and these were joined by a curry festival in 2002.[25]

Celebration is not the same thing as popularity or simple frequency of consumption. Rice and peas stands out more strongly as one of the common—as well as highly regarded—foods of Jamaica. In the late 1990s studies showed that the most commonly eaten foods in Jamaica were, in descending order, orange, cabbage, ripe banana, carrot, chicken, rice and peas, calalu, sardine, tinned mackerel, plain rice, yellow yam, corned beef, tomato, green banana, and lettuce. The most common dishes prepared at home were chicken (fried, brown stewed, or curried), followed by rice and peas and plain rice (Samuda et al. 1998: 81–82). In this ranking, there was some association between the popularity of a food and its frequency of consumption, but it was far from perfect. Thus although oranges and ripe bananas, and cabbages and carrots, played a large role, it seems improbable many Jamaicans would have named them as favorite foods in the way they claimed rice and peas.

This pattern was quite different from that of a century before. Around 1900 the common people of rural Jamaica rarely ate rice and peas. Indeed it was not mentioned at all for those who lived in the countryside and for townspeople "rice and pease" was an occasional dish, kept for Sundays. Nor was chicken mentioned. It became popular and common only in the second half of the twentieth century. What poor people ate in 1900 was most often the tubers (yam, taro, cassava, and sweet potatoes)—all of which were commonly called "food"—with plantains, bananas, and breadfruit, helped along by herring and saltfish and the occasional tripe or salt beef (Moore and Johnson 2000: 85–86; Leader 1907: 140). Once again, it is only rice and peas that seems to have continuity of status, and this only in town.

Natural Partners

Rice and peas sometimes forms a meal in itself. More often, a small or large serving of rice and peas formed the foundation for a dish to which the contents of other pots were added. The preferred character of such additions typically matched the suffused flavors and textures of the rice and peas. Something with a sauce or gravy that would seep into the rice and peas was ideal, whereas drier items like fried fish or roast yam worked less well. In this way there was generally a doubled process of combining and suffusing, the first taking place in the preparation of the rice and peas itself and the second consisting of the complementary fusion of seeds and juices on serving. The result was not only an appealing flavor but also an attractive texture and mouthfeel.

One of the first of these natural partners of rice and peas was curried goat. From the 1930s, country cricket matches and fairs were typically followed by suppers of "curried goat and rice and peas" (Pringle 1938: 49). Another common association was with fricasseed chicken, a cooking style popular in Jamaica throughout the twentieth century, though losing ground to fried chicken. The Jamaican version of fricasseed chicken involved frying pieces of the bird seasoned with salt, pepper, garlic, thyme, then stewing it with tomatoes, onions, carrots, potatoes, and perhaps some curry powder, simmered down to a rich gravy. The chicken, with lots of the gravy, was best eaten with rice and peas.[26] This method of cooking came to be better known as "brown stew" and was also applied to fish, though the latter was less likely to be accompanied by rice and peas. Similar methods were used in cooking parts from the "fifth quarter" of the cow, most of which required long, slow cooking and were preferred when enveloped in sauce or gravy. For example, cow foot could be cooked with peas or vegetables to make a glutinous gravy, ideal for serving with rice and peas.

Rice and peas could also be associated in the absence of the dish itself but with similar outcomes. Most important, the highly popular dish known as "stew peas and rice" does not combine the rice and peas until the point of serving. Recipes direct the cook to stew and simmer red peas together with pig's tail, salt beef, onion, ketchup, thyme, black pepper, and small elongated flour dumplings ("spinners"). Fresh beef can be added, if it can be afforded. The rice for the dish is cooked separately. In contrast to rice and peas, stew peas and rice may have begun as three separate elements and has not been reduced to less than two. Everything together in one pot would produce a slushy rice. The point of the combination is to have the gravy of the stew peas melting over and embracing the dry, separate white rice grains. The contents of the two pots are brought together on the plate, the rich gravy of the stew peas allowed only then to mingle with the grains of the rice steamed to a state of dry separateness (Cleary 1970: 46). Stew peas could of course be consumed without the accompaniment of steamed rice, but this was uncommon (Cuff 1989: 19). At the same time, to serve stew peas along with rice and peas was never recommended, though it could occur when alternatives were not easily found. In 1992 stew peas and rice was declared "the best dish made in Jamaica."[27]

Like rice and peas itself, the origins of stew peas and rice are difficult to identify. Known by the 1940s, at least, stew peas and rice did not appear in cookbooks before 1970.[28] It could be that, like ackee and saltfish, stew peas and rice is a Jamaican invention. On the other hand, borrowing from Latin America also appears plausible, just as it does for rice and peas. If so, the ultimate roots of these dishes can be sought in Africa.[29]

Conclusion

Calling rice and peas "Jamaica coat of arms" was essentially an informal way of recognizing the high regard in which the dish was held. Although Jamaicans were often aware that rice-and-peas was not unique to the island and that the dish had close equivalents within the region, this knowledge did not prevent them making claims for its centrality in the island's food system. In various subtle ways they sought to distinguish their own particular style, giving a "Jamaican" twist to something more universal. Assuming the uniqueness of elements of Jamaican culture—and hence their local origin—was something common to other areas of island life, from language to music. Often such claims were well founded. In other cases, notions of priority or exclusivity prospered only in the absence of knowledge of a wider world. But the process operated more broadly as a means of constructing identities in the face of imperialism and globalizing influences, as a variety of proto-nationalism.

At independence in 1962, few changes were made to the Jamaican coat of arms. The appropriateness of the Taínos was occasionally questioned but the emblems remained intact. The one major change made to the coat of arms was the replacement of the motto, to now declare "Out of Many One People." Derived from the Latin *E Pluribus Unum*, it was a sentiment shared with several other societies, including the United States. The motto matches the blending of peoples with Virgil's original metaphor in which the ploughman's grinding of (white) garlic with (green) herbs sees the ingredients losing their individuality and merging into a unified, single hue, something new.

The symbolism of rice and peas is somewhat different, however. Even in the Jamaican version, in which the peas and the rice are combined from an early stage of the cooking, the fundamental elements—the seeds and the legumes—retain their identities. The result—in Jamaican rice and peas—is something closer to "Unity in diversity," the motto of modern South Africa, India, and Indonesia (Barnard 2004: 13). Although there are parallels between these multicultural societies and Jamaica, the mixing of concepts of indigeneity, endemism, and Creole creation is more complete in Jamaica, matching the precocious combining of elements in the island's making of rice and peas.

Notes

1. Parts of this chapter draw on material in Higman 2008.
2. Cf. *Gleaner*, January 28, 1938, 10. The *Gleaner* newspaper began publication in Kingston in 1834 and appeared under a variety of titles, reduced here to *Gleaner.*
3. *Gleaner*, April 15, 1880; *Gleaner*, August 6, 1940, 9.
4. *Gleaner*, June 7, 1985.
5. The role of Africans in New World rice cultivation has been debated, most recently in an AHR Forum in the *American Historical Review* 115 (1) in February 2010. See also Behrendt 2001; Carney 1996, 2001, 2004; Eltis, Morgan, and Richardson 2007; Shepherd 1994: 129.
6. *Gleaner*, November 8, 1890; *Gleaner*, January 23, 1942, 6; *Gleaner*, February 2, 1942, 7.

7. *Home, Living and Food Guide, Gleaner*, March 12, 1992, 23; *Gleaner*, January 5, 1994, 17; *Food Supplement, Gleaner*, May 9, 1985, 28; Grains Jamaica Limited 1990: 2, 8, 17, 20.
8. *Gleaner*, May 7, 1872, 4.
9. *Gleaner*, January 22, 1892, 6.
10. *Gleaner*, January 5, 1898, 7.
11. *Gleaner*, July 25, 1904, 6.
12. *Gleaner*, April 3, 1919, 3.
13. *Gleaner*, January 28, 1938, 10.
14. *Gleaner*, August 27, 1938, 12.
15. *Gleaner*, July 23, 1941, 8.
16. *Gleaner*, November 7, 1938, 27. Cf. Wilk 2006: 121.
17. *Gleaner*, May 1, 1991; *Home, Living and Food Guide, Gleaner*, September 3, 1992, 17.
18. *Gleaner*, August 27, 1938, 12.
19. For the nutritional benefits, see Norman, Pearson, and Searle 1995: 186–87; D'Andrea et al. 2007: 690; White and Thompson 1989: 69; Zephirin et al. 2005: 8.
20. *Food Supplement, Gleaner*, September 24, 1964, 18.
21. *Gleaner*, May 10, 1930, 9.
22. *Gleaner*, May 10, 1930, 9.
23. *Gleaner*, August 27, 1938, 12.
24. *Home, Living and Food Guide, Gleaner*, September 3, 1992, 17. See also Carley 1963: 114; Brandon 1963: 54; Benghiat 1985: 77; Cassidy 1961: 197.
25. *Gleaner*, November 14, 2002, D3.
26. Chapman 1952: 98; Donaldson 1993: 70; *Home, Living and Food Guide, Gleaner*, July 14, 1994, 23.
27. *Home, Living and Food Guide, Gleaner*, September 3, 1992, 17.
28. *Gleaner*, October 7, 1946, 4; *Food Supplement, Gleaner*, August 3, 1989, 29; *Supermarket Supplement, Gleaner*, November 25, 1993, 7; Quinn 1997: 50; Mahabee and Mahabee 1987: 90.
29. Leonard 1970: 127; De Andrade 1978: 78–85; Hawkes 1978: 123–25; McCann 2009: 26.

References

A.W.D. 1986. "No greater favourite—gungo peas." *Daily Gleaner Food Supplement*, March 6, 23.

A.W.D. 1987. "Gungo peas—A Jamaican favourite." *Daily Gleaner Food Supplement*, January 8, 23.

Ayre, Sylvester. 2002. *Bush doctor: Jamaica and the Caribbean's almost forgotten folklore and remedies.* Kingston: LHM.

Barham, Henry. 1794. *Hortus Americanus: Containing an account of the trees, shrubs, and other vegetable productions, of South-America and the West-India Islands, and particularly of the island of Jamaica.* Kingston: Alexander Aikman.

Barnard, Alan. 2004. "Coat of arms and the body politic: Khoisan imagery and South African national identity." *Ethnos* 69 (1): 5–22.

Beamish, Richard. 1984. *Restaurants of Jamaica 1983–1984: Featuring traditional Jamaican recipes.* Montego Bay: The author.

Beckwith, Martha Warren. [1929] 1969. *Black roadways: A study of Jamaican folk life.* New York: Negro Universities Press.

Behrendt, Stephen D. 2001. "Markets, transaction cycles, and profits: Merchant decision making in the British slave trade." *William and Mary Quarterly* 58 (1): 171–204.

Benghiat, Norma. 1985. *Traditional Jamaican cookery.* Harmondsworth, UK: Penguin.

Black, Clinton V. 1973. *Jamaica guide.* London: William Collins and Sangster (Jamaica).

Boomgaard, Peter. 2003. "In the shadow of rice: Roots and tubers in Indonesian history, 1500–1950." *Agricultural History* 77 (4): 582–610.

Brandon, Leila. 1963. *A merry-go-round of recipes from Jamaica.* Kingston: Novelty Trading.

Browne, Patrick. [1756] 1972. *Civil and natural history of Jamaica.* New York: Arno.

Carley, Mary Manning. 1963. *Jamaica: The old and the new.* London: George Allen and Unwin.

Carney, Judith. 1996. "Landscapes and technology transfer: Rice cultivation and African continuities." *Technology and Culture* 37 (1): 5–35.

Carney, Judith. 2001. *Black rice: The African origins of rice cultivation in the Americas.* Cambridge, Mass.: Harvard University Press.

Carney, Judith. 2004. "'With grains in her hair': Rice in colonial Brazil." *Slavery and Abolition* 25 (1): 1–27.

Cassidy, F. G. 1961. *Jamaica talk: Three hundred years of the English language in Jamaica.* London: Macmillan.

Cassidy, F. G., and R. B. Le Page, eds. 1967. *Dictionary of Jamaican English.* Cambridge: Cambridge University Press.

Chapman, Esther, ed. 1952. *Pleasure island: The book of Jamaica.* Kingston: Arawak Press.

Cleary, Teresa E. 1970. *Jamaica Run-dung: Over 100 recipes.* Kingston: Brainbuster.

Cuff, Patricia. 1989. *A taste of the old home place: Select Jamaican recipes.* Mandeville, Jamaica: Pat Cuff.

D'Andrea, A. C., S. Kahlheber, A. L. Logan, and D. J. Watson. 2007. "Early domesticated cowpea (*Vigna unguiculata*) from Central Ghana." *Antiquity* 81 (313): 686–98.

De Andrade, Margarette. 1978. *Brazilian cookery: Traditional and modern.* Rio de Janeiro: A Casa do Livro Eldorado.

Donaldson, Enid. 1993. *The real taste of Jamaica.* Kingston: Ian Randle.

Eltis, David, Philip Morgan, and David Richardson. 2007. "Agency and diaspora in Atlantic history: Reassessing the African contribution to rice cultivation in the Americas." *American Historical Review* 112 (5): 1329–58.

Grains Jamaica Limited. 1990. *Rice cook book.* Montego Bay: Grains Jamaica Limited.

Hawkes, Alex D. 1978. *The flavors of the Caribbean and Latin America: A personal collection of recipes.* New York: Viking Press.

Higman, B. W. 1984. *Slave populations of the British Caribbean, 1807–1834.* Baltimore: Johns Hopkins University Press.

Higman, B. W. 2007. "Jamaican versions of callaloo." *Callaloo* 30 (1): 351–68.

Higman, B. W. 2008. *Jamaican food: History, biology, culture.* Kingston: University of the West Indies Press.

Hughes, William. 1672. *The American physitian; or, A treatise of the roots, plants, trees, shrubs, fruit, herbs, &c. growing in the English plantations in America.* London: William Crook.

Jacobs, Ralph A. H. 1991. "Gungo peas soup." *Gleaner Supermarket Shopping Guide,* January 24, 10D.

Jamaica Agricultural Society. 1957. *The farmer's food manual: A recipe book for the West Indies.* Glasgow: University Press.

Leader, Alfred. 1907. *Through Jamaica with a Kodak.* Bristol: John Wright and Co.

Leonard, Jonathan Norton. 1970. *Latin American cooking.* New York: Time-Life.

Long, Edward. 1774. *The history of Jamaica.* London: T. Lowndes.

Lunan, John. 1814. *Hortus Jamaicensis; or, A botanical description (according to the Linnean System), and an account of the virtues, &c. of its indigenous plants hitherto unknown.* Spanish Town, Jamaica: St Jago de la Vega Gazette.

Macfadyen, James. 1837. *The flora of Jamaica: A description of the plants of that island, arranged according to the natural orders.* London: Longman, Orme, Brown, Green, and Longmans.

Mahabee, Linda A., and Milton L. Mahabee. 1987. *A vegetarian cookbook and better living guide.* Mandeville, Jamaica: College Press.

Mandelblatt, Bertie R. 2008. "'Beans from Rochel and manioc from Prince's Island': West Africa, French Atlantic commodity circuits, and the provisioning of the French Middle Passage." *History of European Ideas* 34 (4): 411–23.

McCann, James C. 2009. *Stirring the pot: A history of African cuisine.* Athens: Ohio University Press.

Mintz, Sidney W. 1974. *Caribbean transformations.* Chicago: Aldine.

Moore, Brian L., and Michele A. Johnson, eds. 2000. "'Squalid Kingston' 1890–1920: How the poor lived, moved and had their being." Mona: Social History Project, University of the West Indies.

Newton, Velma. 1984. *The silver men: West Indian labour migration to Panama, 1850–1914.* Kingston: Institute of Social and Economic Research, University of the West Indies.

Norman, M.J.T., C. J. Pearson, and P.G.E. Searle. 1995. *The ecology of tropical food crops.* Cambridge: Cambridge University Press.

Pringle, Kenneth. 1938. *Waters of the west.* London: George Allen and Unwin.

Quinn, Lucinda Scala. 1997. *Jamaican cooking: 140 roadside and homestyle recipes.* New York: Macmillan.

Samuda, Pauline M., Richard A. Cook, Cristanna M. Cook, and Fitzroy Henry. 1998. "Identifying foods commonly consumed by the Jamaican population: The focus group approach." *International Journal of Food Sciences and Nutrition* 49 (1): 79–86.

Scientific Research Council. 1972. *Peas please.* Kingston: Scientific Research Council.

Senior, Olive. 2003. *Encyclopedia of Jamaican heritage.* Kingston: Twin Guinep.

Sharma, S., J. Cade, J. Landman, and J. K. Cruickshank. 2002. "Assessing the diet of the British African-Caribbean population: Frequency of consumption of foods and food portion sizes." *International Journal of Food Sciences and Nutrition* 53 (5): 439–44.

Shepherd, Verene A. 1994. *Transients to settlers: The experience of Indians in Jamaica 1845–1950.* Leeds: Peepal Tree.

Sloane, Hans. 1707–25. *A voyage to the islands of Madera, Barbados, Nieves, S. Christophers and Jamaica, with the natural history of the last of these islands.* London.

Titford, W. J. 1811. *Sketches towards a Hortus Botanicus Americanus.* London: Sherwood, Neely and Jones.

Ullman, James Ramsey, and Al Dinhofer. 1968. *Caribbean here and now: The complete vacation guide to 52 sunny islands and vacation lands in the Caribbean Sea.* New York: Macmillan.

Whitbourne, Dahlia. 1936. "The ordinary diet in Jamaica with comments thereon." *Jamaica Public Health* 11 (9): 68–74.

White, Alison, and Patricia Y. Thompson. 1989. *The Caribbean food and nutrition book.* London: Macmillan.

Wilk, Richard. 2006. *Home cooking in the global village: Caribbean food from buccaneers to ecotourists.* Oxford: Berg.

Wilson, Samuel M. 2007. *The archaeology of the Caribbean.* Cambridge: Cambridge University Press.

Zephirin, Manuelita, Alison White, Wendy E. Clarke, and Rosie Jackman. 2005. *The joys of healthy cooking in the Caribbean.* Kingston: Ian Randle.

–5–

Beans, Peas, and Rice
in the Eastern Caribbean

Riva Berleant

Introduction

The partnership of grass and pulse in human diets is ancient. In the Old World, wild forms of grasses and pulses were important foods even before they were domesticated. The domestication of wheat, barley, and lentils unfolded in the Middle East and southeastern Turkey between ten thousand and twelve thousand years ago. In Africa, indigenous rice was domesticated and used together with Old World bean species. In the Americas, native maize and beans, along with squash, spread from their sources in Mesoamerica and South America to almost all of the places in the pre-Columbian Americas where they could be grown. In both hemispheres these venerable grain and pulse partnerships are made up of food plants whose wild ancestors were indigenous to the regions where they were domesticated.

The history of the rice and bean combination in the Americas, on the other hand, is distinctive. It is an early dish of globalization. Rice, domesticated separately in Africa and Asia, came together with beans and peas of various species and plural provenance—Africa, the Americas, Asia—in a world of conquest, colonialism, merchant capitalism, proto-industrial agriculture, forced migration, and slavery. This mix of African, Native American, Asian, and European has taken distinctive shapes despite those firm institutional stamps, and has developed in a succession of exploitative plantation and tourist economies.

In the small islands of the Eastern Caribbean, rice and beans dishes are widespread and various. This chapter first defines and broadly describes the Eastern Caribbean and its geographical contrasts. Then it moves to rice and beans: it treats them broadly and brings them home to the islands of the Eastern Caribbean, where their braided strands of cultural and economic significance are both particular to the subregion and similar to the greater area known variously as Plantation America, the South Atlantic system, or the Black Atlantic (Mintz 2010: 46; Wagley 1960). Recipes will not be forgotten.

The Eastern Caribbean Region

The Caribbean islands lie scattered from Cuba, off the coast of the United States, to Aruba, off the coast of Venezuela. Of these, the Greater Antilles, consisting of Cuba, Jamaica, Hispaniola (Haiti and Dominican Republic), and Puerto Rico, trend east to west, mainly above eighteen degrees north latitude. All of the others make up the Lesser Antilles, a chain of islands beginning in the north at the Virgin Islands off the eastern tip of Puerto Rico. The chain arches gently south to Trinidad, and then bends west along the Venezuelan coast. This tiny land area, totaling only about 126,145 square kilometers—about the size of Nicaragua—is scattered along a 2,000-kilometer archipelago and includes an astounding variety of physical features. There are high mountainous islands and low islands; humid climates and dry; islands of volcanic, coral, and fault block origin. The islands and the littorals of the Caribbean are prototypical illustrations of the perplexities of regional boundaries and regional definitions.

One way of organizing the Lesser Antilles around some intragroup similarities and differences is to see three principal sets of islands: an outer longitudinal chain, an inner longitudinal chain, and a chain that parallels the South American coast. Let us exclude this last east–west chain. What we have left is the region known as the Eastern Caribbean. The islands of the outer chain are lower and drier; those of the inner chain more mountainous and moister (Blume 1974: 311–82). The Eastern Caribbean is not quite the same as the historical designation "West Indies," since that category includes Jamaica, one of the Greater Antilles. And, as Jane Austen's well-traveled Mrs. Croft so famously asserted, "We do not call Bermuda or the Bahamas, you know, part of the West Indies" (Austen [1818] 1933: 70).

The higher and moister islands of the inner arc, beginning at the northern tip and moving south, are the U.S. Virgin Islands, the British Virgin Islands, St. Martin, St. Barthélemy, Saba, St. Eustatius, St. Kitts, Nevis, Montserrat, Redonda, Guadeloupe and its satellites, Dominica, Martinique, St. Lucia, St. Vincent, the Grenadines, Grenada, Tobago, and Trinidad. Those of the outer, lower, drier chain are Anguilla, Barbuda, Antigua, and Barbados. Not included in the Eastern Caribbean are the islands of Vieques and Culebra, which are geologically allied with the northern Lesser Antilles, but are historically and culturally part of Puerto Rico (Blume 1974: 311–82).

Despite their variations in topography and humidity, all of the islands are tropical, the northeast trade winds blow across them all, and all have rainy seasons. They also share, as a whole unit, a neotropical complex of plant species, with island variations in plant distribution. Local plant communities range from evergreen tropical rainforest in moister islands to thorn woodland and cactus scrub in drier islands. Almost everywhere precolonial plant communities have yielded to human changes, and especially in the drier areas, have xerophytic complexes spread as a consequence of grazing (Watts 1987: 13–37; Harris 1965: 139–42).

In fact, it is scarcely possible to discuss the physical and biotic features of the Eastern Caribbean without considering human agency, for what we see now are cultural landscapes shaped by human activities. The European use of many of these islands for plantation production overrode local variations in soil, climate, topography, and climax vegetation: wherever sugar could be grown, sugar was grown.

But even while sugar re-created vast areas of the Eastern Caribbean, it did not impose an absolutely uniform stamp. The European presence also bred cultural and linguistic variety. Individual islands and the Creole languages spoken throughout the region retain essential Dutch, French, Spanish, and English components. Further, the very processes of plantation production and its accompanying system of slave labor, widespread and heavy-handed as they were, carried in themselves some sources of human adaptation that interpreted and used the landscape in ways different from and even subversive to the plantation. One of these ways was subsistence production on small plots. The role of beans and peas is inseparable from these small food gardens.

There was from the beginning of plantation production both an antagonism and a symbiosis between large-scale plantation production and small-scale production for subsistence and sale. The plantation was a powerful and encompassing institution, but what some human beings did and how they lived in the cracks between plantations was necessary to plantation survival, even while opposition and sabotage went on between plantation and small plot, highland and lowland, provisions and sugar, slave and a master, local market and export economy. Such dualities dramatize and oversimplify the colonial Caribbean, but do, nevertheless, signal more complex processes and relationships.

In early colonial Montserrat, for example, the planter elites of the seventeenth century adopted strategies to maximize plantation production. They tried to eliminate small plots and yeoman cultivators. They legislated against independent market production by slaves. At the same time they tried to attract white militiamen and indentured servants and to promote the raising of maize, sweet potatoes, and cassava for food (Berleant-Schiller 1989). These incompatible goals must not be dismissed as contradictions, but understood as parts of the same system. The plantation wiped out many island differences, but local history and local adaptations maintained variety within pattern. The low dry island of Barbuda, for example, was a place where no plantations thrived, but the island supplied foods and raw materials to the plantation island of Antigua.

The usual defining characteristics of the Caribbean region—in fact the generalizations that have most often been made to explain it—include plantations, enslavement of Africans, and colonialism. These of course have been found elsewhere in the American tropics and subtropics. But some significant features set the Eastern Caribbean islands apart from other American regions of plantation slavery and a colonial past. One is the recency of political independence. Decolonization is not yet complete: Montserrat by choice is still a British colony. Another is the near-destruction of native peoples early in the history of settlement, by contrast, for example, to

Mesoamerica or Brazil. The mosaic of languages and colonizing states in so small a land area is also remarkable. Throughout most of the American tropics, a single colonial power left its cultural and linguistic mark over a great swath of territory. In the Eastern Caribbean, however, Denmark, the Netherlands, Great Britain, the United States, and France have left their marks.

Insufficiently credited is another important aspect of the region's colonial history: the commercial and strategic centrality of the islands during the eighteenth century. The Eastern Caribbean region was central in the early modern processes of empire, finance, labor control, and commodity production, even though its contemporary economic and political status gives no hint of that significant history.

Finally, the very fact of islandness intensifies the cultural and linguistic variety of the region. The islands themselves are not accounted for, either singly or as a group. Discussions of the unity and diversity within the region are far from conclusive and seem inexhaustible. The range of rice and beans dishes throughout the entire Caribbean exemplifies that regional unity and diversity.

Rice and the Eastern Caribbean

Rice, a grain of Old World origin, has been wholly assimilated into the cuisines of the Americas. Other grains from the Old World, such as wheat or oats, have also been assimilated but the case of rice is distinctive. Rice is not only a fundamental part of the daily diet in the American tropics and subtropics; it also bears a unique symbolic load. But why is rice so significant? Why not maize, the American grain that is native to the American tropics, which enslaved Africans grew on their provision grounds, and that small-plot cultivators still grow? Why not guinea corn or sorghum, which also do well in dry tropics and were food crops that enslaved Africans brought with them to the American plantations? How and why did rice become so significant and widespread? The answer lies in the past and in the present, in culture and economy.

Rice began its global career as a food commodity early in the modern period after 1500. That economic status reinforced the historical and cultural circumstances of its arrival in the Americas, which happened early and more than once. Spanish settlers in Hispaniola brought rice from Spain soon after 1492; enslaved Africans brought it repeatedly beginning soon after; Asian indentured servants entering in the nineteenth century reinforced its production and cultural value. Twentieth-century processes contributed too: population growth and its accompanying internal migration and urbanization made rice into the primary source of energy next to sugar everywhere in Latin America and the Caribbean. Let us expand on these factors of the last five hundred years—cultural, economic, historical, and demographic—that together amplified the significance of rice.

Spanish settlers in Hispaniola were growing "small quantities" of rice by 1512, probably *Oryza sativa* brought from Europe, where it had arrived from Asia

(Watts 1987: 115–16). It was a settler subsistence crop at that time and was not the source of later large-scale rice production in the Americas. Rice production on a large scale began in South Carolina, where it became an important export crop in the first part of the eighteenth century. It is now certain that the origins of rice production in South Carolina were African and its human catalysts were enslaved Africans, as Peter H. Wood (1974), Daniel Littlefield ([1981] 1991), Judith Carney (2001), and Edda L. Fields-Black (2008) have shown. West Africans brought the knowledge, the technology, and the rice itself in a complex that allowed rice to become the one of the first real foods (as sugar is not) to be transformed into a global commodity (Carney 2001: 163).

By the late seventeenth century the trans-Atlantic slave trade had stimulated a large and growing new market for the rice produced in the rice coast area of West Africa. The volume of the slave trade made this market a large one, as slave traders purchased tons of rice on Africa's Rice Coast to provision both captives and crews (Fields-Black 2008: 162–65). Rice could be stored in the damp conditions aboard ship, and later dried out. Nevertheless, these origins do not explain subsequent histories and functions, nor does the economics of rice account for its symbolic value and cultural content. We must look further for complete explanations of the significance of rice.

Rice was a widespread and important crop in West Africa long before the Atlantic slave trade brought it to the Americas. Information that we now have points to the first African domestication in the upper Niger River region around 1,700 years ago. Rice cultivation spread throughout West Africa, so that when Portuguese mariners first reached the West African coast in 1446, they found great fields of rice growing in coastal areas (Stokstad 2007). Africans domesticated *Oryza glaberrima* or red rice from indigenous wild African *Oryza* forebears, and its domestication history is separate from that of Southeast Asian rice. *Oryza sativa*, the Asian species, was domesticated in Asia from Asian wild varieties. These two species, *O. glaberrima* and *O. sativa*, are the only two domesticated rice species that exist, even though very recent experimentation is finding ways to combine the most desired qualities of each (Linares 2002: 3630; Stokstad 2007).

Indigenous West African rice carried cultural and symbolic value in addition to its economic and nutritional value. As Judith Carney has shown, enslaved Africans brought it to the Americas as a rich cultural and technological system of knowledge (2001: 163–74). Its symbolic import persists in Africa still. The Jola people of southern Senegal, for example, "still grow African rice for use in ritual contexts" (Linares 2002: 16360). The culture of rice survived the Atlantic slave trade, and "has long served to assert African cultural identity in the Americas" (Carney 2001: 164). Following the emancipation of enslaved Africans in the nineteenth century, Asians from India, Java, and China were brought into the American plantations as indentured laborers. Their dietary needs and preferences reinforced the presence and use of rice in the Caribbean.

Nevertheless, there is as yet no evidence that slaves in the Eastern Caribbean themselves grew rice in their own provision gardens, even though we know that slaves grew subsistence rice in the United States South and in Jamaica (Carney 2001: 154–58). Rice in the Eastern Caribbean was for the most part an imported food ration.

On the sugar plantations of the Eastern Caribbean, planters tried to find an economic balance between the land they wanted for growing cane and the land they were willing to spare for growing food. Sometimes they allotted provision grounds to slaves in areas unsuited to cane. But when it was cheaper to feed the enslaved workforce on imported rations than to grow its food on land that could be put to profitable cane, they put the land to cane. Profit, not food, was always their first criterion. At times their individual decisions in favor of profits led to colonial laws stipulating amounts of land to be set aside for food production. That was the case in Montserrat, as well as in other Eastern Caribbean islands, in the latter seventeenth century. Local law required Montserratian proprietors to plant an acre of cassava or sweet potatoes for every two working persons on their estates whether slave or indentured servant (Berleant-Schiller 1989: 555). Still, food imports were necessary.

As imported food for slaves, rice fell into the category of "dry provisions." These were storable foods that also included peas, maize, guinea corn, beans, flours, and "meals" (Dirks 1987: 57–58). It was possible to grow maize and rice, but maize depleted the soil and rice processing demanded labor and time. These features added too much to the ultimate cost of maize and rice, and the decision to import rather than grow dry provisions depended only on cost (Dirks 1987: 58). Thus the proportion of rice in the diet of Eastern Caribbean slaves changed from year to year according to the profitability of land and labor devoted solely to sugar.

After emancipation in the nineteenth century, which took place at different dates in different European colonies, contract laborers from India, Java, and China entered the Caribbean. Their lot was not necessarily much better than the lot of chattel slaves had been, but the time of their indenture was limited and they had not the legal status of property. Large numbers of workers from China and India entered Trinidad, Jamaica, and Guiana; Javanese workers entered Surinam, unsurprising since Java and Suriname were both Dutch colonies (Hoefte 1998; Look Lai 1993).

Trinidad was the Eastern Caribbean island that received Asian immigrants in substantial numbers. Workers from the East Indies were a small presence in St. Lucia, Grenada, St. Vincent, and St. Kitts. Chinese labor immigrants were a very small presence in Antigua. Labor from India came to the British islands of St. Lucia, St. Vincent, St. Croix, and St. Kitts, and to the French islands of Guadeloupe and Martinique (Watts 1987: 474, 479–80). Most of these immigrants were accustomed to and valued rice as the dietary staple.

Seeking to understand Eastern Caribbean rice only through its colonial and nineteenth-century history is important, but insufficient. We must not assume that the presence of anything in the past satisfactorily explains its existence in the present.

It does not. Continuity and persistence require as much explanation as does change. Why rice? That is an important question that I will take up in the final section of the chapter, when I consider the meanings and the economics of the rice and beans partnership.

Domesticated Beans and the Eastern Caribbean

The family of Fabaceae or Leguminosae is one of the largest families of the green plants. It includes herbs, shrubs, and trees, but all of the species that we call "beans" fall into a single subfamily, the Faboideae. *Bean* is a much more complicated word than *rice* in the Eastern Caribbean. For one thing, every species has many different local common names. For another, crop lists from the Eastern Caribbean literature rarely use binomials, so that the specific referents of "beans" or "peas" on those lists are unknowable. When binomials are used they are often in error, and further, are likely to have been changed since the time that many of the published crop and food lists appeared (Stevens 2001; Angiosperm Phylogeny Group 2003). What was *Dolichos lablab* forty years ago, for example, is now *Lablab purpureus*, and known variously as bonavist, lablab, and hyacinth bean (Harris 1965: 282). In my own research, I confess, the black-eyed pea, *Vigna unguiculata*, was mislabeled *Pisum sativum* (Berleant-Schiller and Pulsipher 1986). Only more field research can remedy these deficiencies.

Many wild genera of the Faboideae subfamily grow in the Eastern Caribbean, some of which may be gathered for human and especially animal food, but here I consider only domesticated species used for human food. Let us begin with a list of the domesticated beans most commonly used in the Eastern Caribbean. They are of both New World and Old World origin. Some are more commonly eaten than others, some are grown in food gardens, and some are imported or canned or both.

Food Beans of the Eastern Caribbean

Species Native to the Americas

Canavalia ensiformis	Horse bean, jack bean, sword bean, overlook bean, maldjo, grudge pea, watchman
Phaseolus coccineus	Scarlet runner bean
Phaseolus lunatus	Lima bean, butter bean, white bean, broad bean
Phaseolus vulgaris	Common bean, string bean, snap bean, kidney bean, red bean, black bean, salad bean (Trinidad only), frijol (Spanish)

Species Introduced from the Old World

Cajanus cajan	Pigeon pea, green pea, congo pea, gandule
Cicer arietinum	Chickpea, garbanzo
Lablab purpureus	White bean, hyacinth bean, butter bean, banner bean, lablab, bonavist bean (formerly *Dolichos lablab)*
Vicia faba	Horse bean, broad bean, fava bean
Vigna radiate	Mung bean (also named *V. aureus*)
Vigna unguiculata	Cowpea, black-eyed pea, black-eyed bean, gub-gub

These are listed alphabetically, but I will discuss them in order of their importance. This importance may be their place in the diet, their place in the garden, their symbolic value, or all of these. In this hierarchy, the pigeon pea, *Cajanus cajan*, comes first.

The Pigeon Pea

Cajanus cajan, the pigeon pea, is the sole member of its genus, *Cajanus indicus*. It is grown and eaten everywhere in the Eastern Caribbean. In our research on Caribbean subsistence gardens, geographer Lydia Pulsipher and I found pigeon peas grown not only on the islands of our field research, Barbuda and Montserrat, but in every island of the Caribbean for which we found published crop lists (Berleant-Schiller and Pulsipher 1986). Pigeon peas are part of what we called the "Caribbean major core complex": four crops that constitute a basic survival complex throughout the region. The three companion crops in this complex are maize (*Zea mays*), sweet potatoes (*Ipomoea batatas*), and cassava (*Manihot esculenta*). These four crops can be and are grown in every moisture and elevation zone, and occupy major space in Eastern Caribbean gardens.

This major core complex blends crop traditions of three continents. Sweet potatoes and cassava, two root crops of South American origin, grew in pre-Columbian conucos. Maize, part of the maize-beans-squash trio, was domesticated in the Meso-american highlands. The pigeon pea, the grain legume in the suite, was domesticated in India and brought to the Americas by way of Africa.

These four crops are, in turn, part of the larger "core complex" that we discovered and that additionally includes bananas (*Musa paradisaica*), first domesticated in Southeast Asia; beans (*Phaseolus* sp.), domesticated in Mesoamerica and South America; pumpkins and squash (*Cucurbita* sp.), domesticated in Mesoamerica and South America; and yams (*Dioscorea* sp.), domesticated in Asia and Africa. When European animals are added—cattle, sheep, and ubiquitous goats—the food production complex is a robust embodiment of Caribbean cultural creolization. Thus the beans used in the Eastern Caribbean are fully embedded in a suite of crops and a cuisine of multicontinental origin and historical depth.

The pigeon pea, so prominent and widespread in Eastern Caribbean diets and gardens, came with the slave trade in the early colonial period before 1700 and is widely distributed in the Eastern Caribbean (Harris 1965: 92–93; Niddrie 1974: 109). Pigeon peas grow best where there is a marked dry season, as there is in Eastern Caribbean trade wind climates. Their shallow, spreading root system allows them to thrive in dry tropical areas and makes them resistant to recurrent droughts, such as Barbuda experiences. They do not require deep or fertile soil (Smartt 1985: 3–5). That tolerance is an important feature, since Eastern Caribbean soils in many islands have been strained by a history of sugar cane production, or lie thinly on coral substrate, as they do in Barbuda and the other dry islands of the outer chain.

Pigeon peas work especially well in Barbudan swidden cultivation, that system of food production that moves garden plots from place to place, using machete and fire to clear the new plot. Pigeon peas continue to grow after the rest of the garden has moved on. Sweet potatoes also persist, at least for a second year, and together the two plants make an invaluable emergency no-labor food source. They are often found intercropped together (Berleant-Schiller and Pulsipher 1986). Like other Faboideae, pigeon pea plants thrive without added fertilizer. But uniquely among the Faboideae, the pigeon pea plant is a shrub rather than a vine or herb.

The shrub habit of the pigeon pea and its perennial growth probably contributed to its symbolic value as a border plant. It is grown in the kitchen gardens of Eastern Caribbean islands not only as a food-producing shrub, but also as a boundary marker. In Barbados it edges cane fields (Handler 1964: 229). These features and functions have been part of the pigeon pea in the Eastern Caribbean since the seventeenth century. Here is part of what Sir Hans Sloane, founder of the British Museum, wrote in 1707 after his voyage to the Caribbean:

Pigeon-Pease

It is ... frequently planted in ... the Caribes [that is the Lesser Antilles] ... chiefly in Alleys as a Hedge, lasts many Years without decaying, and will thrive on barren Land which has been worn out, where scarce any thing else will prosper. ... The Branches with the ripe Pease and Leaves are not only given to feed Hogs, but Horses and all other Cattle, which they fatten very much. ... One Boil, makes them fit for eating. (2: 31)

In addition to marking boundaries, pigeon peas are said to be a remedy of multiple virtues, used against flu, stroke, sorcery, toothache, fish and other poisoning, and uterine bleeding (Ayensu 1981: 140–41). Like other leguminous foods, it is about 24 percent protein and 63 percent carbohydrate. It can be used for forage as well as human food, as Sloane pointed out, and the stems can be used as fuel (CIAT 2001a; European Association for Grain Legume Research 2010; Smartt 1985: 2–15).

Phaseolus *Beans*

How characteristic of the Caribbean that the two most important pulse genera, *Cajanus* and *Phaseolus*, sine qua nons of daily food and garden, come from opposite hemispheres. Eight thousand years ago, a wild *Phaseolus* grew in the Andean region of South America and in the Middle American highlands. This wild vine, domesticated in those highlands, was the source of a major food genus that is now incorporated into diverse cropping systems in diverse environments all over the world. In the Americas, *Phaseolus* species were a basic part of pre-Columbian diet, eventually spreading from their domestication centers to everywhere in the hemisphere that they could be grown. Nevertheless, a chronological and synthesizing sequence of archaeological sites that will show the stages of domestication in and diffusion from Mesoamerica and the southern Andes is yet to be developed (Gepts and Debouck 1991: 7–12; Kaplan and Kaplan 1988: 125–42).

The common *Phaseolus* beans of the Eastern Caribbean are *P. vulgaris*, the common bean, and *P. lunatus*, the lima bean. Much more restricted is *Phaseolus coccineus*, the scarlet runner bean, which requires slightly higher and moister conditions. It is recorded only from herbarium collections taken from very few islands (Howard 1988: 514–15).

The common bean, *P. vulgaris*, comes in diverse phenotypes bearing a host of local names. The edible seed is known as kidney bean, black bean, navy bean, pinto bean, and pea, among other local names. In its edible green pod stage it is the string or snap or salad bean. The lima bean, *P. lunatus*, on the other hand, comes in only two forms, a large-seeded form and a small-seeded form, sometimes called the sieva bean. Both of these *Phaseolus* species were domesticated many times in the Andean region and in Mesoamerica (Salgado et al. 1995: 25). I will not usually distinguish between these two species because crop lists and garden inventories in the Eastern Caribbean literature do not usually distinguish, even though the common names do not overlap and gardeners themselves presumably know the difference. The keys to my own garden maps of Barbuda and Montserrat, for example, use only the term *Phaseolus* sp.

Oddly, we know less about the introduction of *Phaseolus* and other indigenous American Faboideae into the Caribbean than we do about the introduction of Faboideae from Asia and Africa. The earliest records come from post-Columbian sixteenth-century documents. Carl Sauer hypothesized, on the basis of these documents, that the Mesoamerican maize-beans-squash complex was present in Greater Antillean conucos before Columbus. He hypothesized that the complex "came late, by roundabout route south through Central America, east across Tierra Firme, and thence north into the islands," but that beans were "not an important food" ([1966] 1969: 54–55). Using Oviedo and de Las Casas as sources, William Sturtevant reports that "one or more beans (probably *Phaseolus lunatus* L. and *P. vulgaris* L.)" were minor Taíno cultigens at the time the Spanish entered the Caribbean, especially in Hispaniola (1961: 71). We now know archaeologically that at the time of European entry in 1492, the Indians of Cuba and Hispaniola—controversially if convention-ally called Taínos—grew maize of a type that appears to have originated in lowland South America (Newsom and Wing 2004: 200–201; Reid 2009: 57). With maize we expect beans, and beans of some sort might well have been present in Cuba when Columbus arrived there, probably either *P. lunatus* or *P. vulgaris*, growing around the edges of conucos and not important as cultivated food. More firm archaeological evidence is needed.

In the absence of archaeological evidence, some clues have emerged from analysis of seed protein supplemented by observation of seed phenotypes (Gepts et al. 1988: 73–75, 80). This research, which does not supply dates, suggests that the *Phaseolus vulgaris* cultivars of the Greater Antilles came from both the Mesoamerican and Andean domestication centers, but even that information does not answer questions about common beans in the Eastern Caribbean.

Right now there is no archaeological evidence that shows the presence of pre-Columbian *Phaseolus* species in the Eastern Caribbean (Watters 2009). The maize-beans-squash complex, so fundamental in the pre-Columbian seed cultivation systems of Mesoamerica and North America, did not prevail in the Eastern Carib-bean. The Saladoid peoples brought the conuco system of root-crop cultivation to the region from northeastern Amazonia, probably by way of Venezuela, about 2,500 years ago (Reid 2009: 104; Newsom and Wing 2004: 31–32). How *Phaseolus* beans eventually got into Eastern Caribbean food gardens and diets is still an important research question, but the answer is probably linked to the spread of the plantation system.

Africans, both enslaved and free, were present in the American tropics from 1492, even though they did not arrive in great numbers until after 1510 (Deagan 1988: 222). African subsistence foods arrived with them, as we have seen in the case of rice and pigeon peas. So the first question is, how did indigenous American bean species actually get into the Eastern Caribbean? Second, how did they get into the provision gardens of enslaved Africans? And finally, how did the rice-and-beans partnership of today develop?

Jerome Handler offers an important clue to the first question, with a date. He shows that Indians and Africans overlapped and interacted in seventeenth-century Barbados. These Indians were not locals. They had been brought from the Greater Antilles as slaves and like enslaved Africans made important contributions to Bar-badian economy and culture. In 1627 they introduced to Barbados the native food garden complex (1970: 59). So it may be that by 1627 the *Phaseolus* species on the edges of Greater Antillean gardens had moved with displaced American Indians into the Lesser Antilles, where Africans, already familiar with other forms of beans from Africa, made good use of them. Until further archaeological research demonstrates a pre-Columbian *Phaseolus* presence, we must assume a post-Columbian introduction into the Eastern Caribbean, with further research to disclose the whens and wheres of its diffusion.

Canavalia *Beans*

The second bean genus native to the Americas in pre-Columbian times is *Canavalia*, a genus of about fifty species, not all domesticated and not all native to the New World. The domesticated species widespread in the American tropics is *Canavalia ensiformis*. Its domestication may have begun in South America, even though the earliest archaeological occurrence so far is from Mesoamerica, dated to 5,000 years ago (Smartt 1985: 10). In the Eastern Caribbean literature the name *C. plagiosperma* is sometimes used, but this cultivar is at most a geographical race that is not different in any essential way from the *ensiformis* that arose in South America (Smartt 1985: 9–10). Precisely how it got to the Eastern Caribbean is still obscure, just as it is for *Phaseolus*: it could have been brought by American Indians in pre-Columbian times, or distributed later during European conquest (Sauer and Kaplan 1969: 423). Vaughn and Geissler, at odds with Smartt, suggest that its origin was in Central America and the West Indies, but do not cite any sources (1997: 48).

The variety of common names throughout the Eastern Caribbean attests to its widespread presence. The most common name is jack bean. It is also called sword bean, as is its close relative *C. gladiata*, and horse bean, also a common name for other bean species. Horse bean probably refers to its size and coarseness (Allsopp 1996: 297). Its most intriguing common names are grudge pea in Barbados and Trinidad; overlooker or overlook bean in Barbados and Montserrat; watchman in Montserrat; and maldjo in Grenada and Trinidad (Allsopp 1996: 264, 543). The names overlook bean and watchman refer to its function in food gardens as a border plant that will ensure abundant yields, ward off the evil eye from the garden, and stop theft (Brussell 1997: 66–67). That association with evil eye is explicit in the name maldjo (*mal de ojo*), and less explicit in the name grudge pea, which attributes to the bean plant protection against those carrying a grudge against the gardener (Allsopp 1996: 272).

The unfussy jack bean does equally well in conditions from very dry to very moist. The seeds are edible if boiled well, as they may otherwise be toxic (Albala 2007: 94). The green pods are eaten as a vegetable. Nevertheless, it is not so widely eaten in the Eastern Caribbean as is the pigeon pea, perhaps because the pigeon pea, with its continuous and longer history associated with enslaved Africans, is as easy to grow and fills the same nutritional and culinary niche without the toxic hazard of the seeds. Quite possibly the magical and symbolic attributes of the jack bean rather than its food value account for its widespread presence, and possibly their toxicity, when judiciously deployed, may account for their ritual functions. Jonathan Sauer and Lawrence Kaplan observe that it is known archaeologically only from pre-Columbian sites that also show the presence of *Phaseolus*. Since *Phaseolus* species are preferable as food, the uses of *Canavalia*, they write, are "puzzling" (1969: 423). Perhaps the magical and symbolic values indicated by its common names throughout the Eastern Caribbean are a clue to this "puzzling" pre-Columbian presence.

Certainly, as Frederick J. Simoons describes, the association of beans with magic, death, and ritual is very ancient and nearly universal (1998: Ch. 9). Simoons also shows that the ritual value of a plant is widely thought to be enhanced by pairing it with another of similar species (297–99). *C. ensiformis* is, by the way, an excellent, high-yield crop for the livestock originally brought by Europeans (Smartt 1985: 10).

The remaining bean species are of lesser importance today in the Eastern Caribbean. Mung beans, formerly classified as *Phaseolus* but now assigned to *Vigna*, were brought and used by East Indians in Trinidad for making daal. They are not much used outside of Trinidad. The bonavist or hyacinth bean, *Lablab purpureus* (formerly *Lablab niger* or *Dolichos lablab*), is a vine native to Africa that is now grown everywhere in the world tropics (Smartt 1985: 12–13). It is found on almost all the islands of the Eastern Caribbean, both as a feral weed and a cultivated food plant (Carrington 1998: 48; Howard 1988: 501–2), and its many local names attest to wide distribution: white bean in Montserrat, hyacinth bean in Antigua, and banner bean, butter bean, and lablab elsewhere. *Lablab purpureus* arrived in the Americas from Bon Vista, Cape Verde Islands (Allsopp 1996: 110). It was imported in quantity as a food for slaves. Another bean imported as food for the slave labor force is *Vicia faba*, the broad bean or fava bean, known in Barbuda and elsewhere as horse bean (Dirks 1987: 58; Harris 1965: 284). *Vicia faba* too is of Old World origin and is less important today than it was in the eighteenth and nineteenth centuries.

Black-eyed peas or cowpeas, *Vigna unguiculata*, are a little less forgiving of dry climate than many of the other beans used in the Eastern Caribbean. Thus they are not found in flat, drought-prone Barbuda, and in Montserrat we found them only in the highest, moistest cultivation zone (Berleant-Schiller and Pulsipher 1986: 8). Even so, black-eyed peas (gub-gub in Trinidad) are eaten in the moister parts of the Eastern Caribbean, commonly boiled with rice. They were one of the food plants that enslaved Africans brought from home in the 1600s (Allsopp 1996: 105; Carney 2001: 158). Chickpeas or garbanzos (*Cicer arietinum*) are occasionally used, but I have seen no record of their being grown in Eastern Caribbean gardens, nor are they listed in Richard Howard's *Flora of the Lesser Antilles* (1988). They are used in the Greater Antillean island of Puerto Rico, but have not been much grown since the 1970s and now come from cans, as they do in the Eastern Caribbean (Garcia Colón 2010).

Like rice, beans have a history as provisions for enslaved Africans. David Watts mentions that "some beans and peas" were among the crops in the slaves' provision gardens on seventeenth-century sugar estates in Barbados, but he gives no binomials except to mention that *Lablab niger*, the bonavist bean or pea, now called *Lablab purpureus*, arrived in the Caribbean from Africa before 1647 (1987: 194–95).

Robert Dirks shows that rice and "horsebeans" are recorded as slave rations in Antigua in 1789 (1987: 62), and that rice, peas, and beans functioned as alternatives in slave provisions on the island of Nevis in 1789 (63). Further, "Thousands of hogsheads of horsebeans" were imported to "places like St. Kitts" as cheap slave rations in the early part of the eighteenth century (58). "Horsebeans" are a problem, as that common name is applied to more than one species. *Canavalia ensiformis* is called "horse bean" in Barbados, Jamaica, and Trinidad (Allsopp 1996: 297), but *Vicia faba*, the broad bean or fava bean, is also called "horse bean" in some places. If thousands of hogsheads were being imported as cheap food, my guess is that *V. faba* is meant, as it is a venerable Old World crop of broad distribution and use, domesticated in Asia and introduced into Europe early in agricultural times (Purdue University 1998; Simoons 1998: 193). It does not appear in Howard's *Flora of the Lesser Antilles* (1988), but David R. Harris, citing G. Hughes's *The Natural History of Barbados* (1750), says that these beans were "well established as a crop in Barbados, and no doubt also in the Leewards, by the mid eighteenth century" (1965: 222). The species is on his plant list for the Outer Leewards (Anguilla, Antigua, Barbuda) with the common name "horse bean" (1965: 277, 284).

The presence of beans in the diets and gardens of enslaved Africans is attested, but the kinds of beans remain vague. We can guess from their symbolism at the importance of *Canavalia ensiformis*, the overlooker or grudge pea, and of the pigeon pea, border protector and medicinal plant. And surely the ubiquity of *Phaseolus vulgaris* and *Phaseolus lunatus* documented in cuisine and garden of the twentieth century cannot be recent. But, like rice, significance since the twentieth century needs an explanation other than simply continuity from the past.

Rice and Beans since the Twentieth Century

My research in Barbuda and Montserrat focused on rural life: livelihoods, households, food gardens, fisheries, cattle, land use and land tenure, to name the prominent foci of my interest. The villages where I worked were small, though of course not self-contained or separable from structural relations to the outside world. Their residents had personal and economic ties to migrant communities in England, the United States, and Canada, and other Caribbean islands. The villages were also stratified internally, while occupying the bottom of national and global stratification systems. In Barbuda a customary system of land tenure that gives every Barbudan resident equal rights to plentiful undivided lands is one factor that mitigates internal inequality (Berleant-Schiller 1987). But Barbuda is unwillingly tethered in a single state to nearby Antigua, which, after independence in 1981, has held the power. Montserrat has chosen to remain a British colony, to the dismay of its independence faction. In rural Barbuda, therefore, and in the villages of Montserrat, beans and pigeon peas occupy prominent spots in the garden and on the table.

If the satisfactions of a combination dish of rice and beans cannot be explained fully by continuity from the past, even when there is continuity from the past, what factors since the twentieth century have helped perpetuate it? We need to look both at the meanings and the economics of rice and beans.

There can be no quarrel about beans. Clearly the adaptability of beans and pigeon peas in the garden has been a factor in their persistence, even while subsistence gardening slowly declined in the latter twentieth century. But even if you buy them instead of growing them in your garden, they are cheap and nutritious, even though I do not think that that is the conscious reason most people eat them. Rice, on the other hand, must be imported and purchased. So the question of why it is so widespread and popular is intriguing.

According to the International Center for Tropical Agriculture, only in the twentieth century did rice become the food of first choice throughout Latin America and the Caribbean (CIAT 2001b). In the diets of the entire region today, sugar alone supplies more calories. Rice has supplanted such traditional starch staples as maize, sweet potatoes, yams, cassava, and tania. In the 1920s, the annual consumption of rice in the region was 10 kilograms per person. By the 1990s it had risen threefold, to 30 kilograms.

The features of rice that led Eastern Caribbean sugar planters to import it as food for slaves are still persuasive: Rice is durable, storable, compact, and convenient. But other equally significant factors now lead 40 percent of the people at the bottom of the income pyramid in the Eastern Caribbean and indeed throughout Latin America to eat rice as their foundational food. Urbanization and the great migration of people from the countryside to the cities is a major factor in the rise of rice in the diet and the decline of traditional starches grown on small plots (CIAT 2001b). The declining number of persons growing their own food on subsistence plots is another. Rice has filled the gap.

Barbuda is a good example of these processes, even though it is a rural place. In Barbuda, migration keeps the population stable in relation to the availability of land, and Barbudan customary land tenure allows anyone on the island to keep swidden plots (Berleant-Schiller 1987). Barbuda's emigrant communities are far larger than its home population. Jobs are few, so that the remittances sent by émigrés are an important source of income, as they are in Montserrat and most other Eastern Caribbean islands (Philpott 1973; Richardson 1989). Yet cultivating food gardens is, and for a long time has been, mainly the practice of a minority of middle-aged and elderly people, who apparently take it up once youth is passed. Hardly anyone bothers to parch maize on the traditional yabba, except perhaps as a social snack, and I have never seen anyone in Barbuda processing cassava, though I have seen that done in Montserrat, at least before the volcanic eruptions of the 1990s. Even the cornmeal from which Barbudans make funjee, an important traditional dish usually served alongside peas-rice, as Barbudans name their dish, is purchased. The rice is of course imported.

Though imported, the rice was formerly (at least until the 1980s) bought in bulk. Packaged rice came in when a very small self-serve supermarket sort of store opened in Barbuda, some time around 1976. Until then all purchased food came from small shops where customers were served by proprietors. Flour, rice, cornmeal, legumes, spices, and so forth were all weighed out from bulk containers and wrapped up in paper. The rice had to be washed and strained before use.

The new supermarket was immediately popular and perceived as neat and modern. It brought home the experiences of the many Barbudans who have lived abroad. For many people, buying products such as packaged grains or frozen meats and chicken parts became preferable to buying in bulk, killing your own chickens, and buying cuts from the pigs, cattle, goats, and sheep slaughtered in their owners' yards. These changes in provisioning since the 1970s are deep. They free householders from what they see as old-fashioned and unnecessary practices. It is a choice to be modern and Westernized that goes along with choices to drink scotch rather than rum and to eat tinned sardines rather than local goat. It fits with the declarations of self that some—but by no means all—Barbudans made to me with such statements as, "Oh, you won't find anything unusual here. We're very British (or American)." Nevertheless, peas-rice endures as a favored dish, even when the pigeon peas come from a can and the rice from a box. The dish is not a mere verbal declaration, but an enactment of Barbudan comfort and satisfaction.

The rice and beans dishes of the Eastern Caribbean are various, but do have some properties in common. As I have already shown, one regional characteristic is the prevailing use of pigeon peas, though of course red, black, and white *Phaseolus vulgaris* varieties are also much used. Another is the dailiness of rice and beans or peas. By that I mean not that the dish is necessarily eaten every single day, though it may be, but that it is among the most ordinary and frequent of foods. It is so ordinary that it often receives no special mention. It is daily food, even if it is not touted as national cuisine. A third is that the dish is composed in innumerable ways that depend not just on local traditions of what is desirable, but on what is available. Use a bit of meat or a bell pepper and a fresh tomato if you have them; if not, any one of those or just an onion will do. Add bacon or minced beef or not. In Barbuda, for example, the rice and pigeon peas are often cooked together plainly, but dressed up with saltfish, or with the sauce from the cooking of fish or meat. In Montserrat, rum and a bit of bacon or ham with brown sugar and dry mustard season the dish, and it can be baked rather than boiled. In Anguilla, lime juice, salt beef, and hot pepper sauce season the dish. In Trinidad, coconut milk is part of the mix. Black beans in Barbados can be served over rice rather than cooked with rice, and they are flavored with papaya, onion, hot pepper, bell peppers, onion, and lemon juice. In a St. Vincent "cookup," the rice and peas dish is seasoned with salt beef, tomato, and onions, and is served for supper around 8:00 P.M. (Rubenstein 1987: 170).

If we want to know the meaning of rice and beans dishes in the Eastern Caribbean we must look at how the dish is carried out in daily life. Indeed, its very dailiness is worth noting: The dish is cooked and eaten without fanfare. It is vernacular food, not particularly touted as tourist food or holiday food or Sunday food or national food. The dish that residents think of as characteristic or national in several Eastern Caribbean islands—for example, Barbuda, Antigua, and Barbados—is funjee, made of store-bought cornmeal and okra. It is served with pepper-pot or fish. The first is a thick stew of many and variable ingredients; the second another variable dish using any fresh fish or salt cod. The meaning of peas-rice in Barbuda, in the recipe that ends this chapter, is that it is reliable everyday food in itself, and especially enjoyable when it is served as an accompaniment to fish or meat with funjee. Barbudans think that combination is a complete and satisfying meal. When there is no fish or meat at home, peas-rice and funjee will do.

Here is how to make peas-rice with fish and funjee. According to Mrs. Nancy Bunting of Barbuda, one of my Barbudan teachers whom I watched in her kitchen, it is a Barbudan favorite.

Recipe: Barbudan Peas-Rice with Fish and Funjee

Ingredients

1 cup pigeon peas, cooked
1 cup cornmeal
1 cup raw rice
1 onion, chopped (plus some to sauté with the rice)
2 cloves garlic, chopped
6 pods okra or 6 thick prickly pear leaves
2 cups water, plus 1 cup, 2¼ cups, 3 tbsp., 1½ cups
3 tbsp. tomato paste
½ tsp. thyme
½ tsp. curry powder
1 tsp. salt (plus some to sauté with the rice and for fish)
Black pepper
2 tbsp. butter or margarine (plus some to sauté with the rice and for fish)
2 lbs. fish (or beef, pork, lamb, goat, or chicken)

Directions

1. Cook the pigeon peas until tender. Use 1 cup of cooked pigeon peas to 1 cup of raw rice. Sauté the rice with a little chopped onion in butter, add the pigeon peas, 2 cups of water, and some salt. Bring to boil, reduce to simmer, and cook until rice is done.
2. For the funjee, stir 1 cup of any cornmeal into 1 cup of cold water with 1 teaspoon of salt. Cook 6 pods of okra (or 6 thick prickly pear leaves) and slice diagonally. Stir the cornmeal mixture into 2¼ cups boiling water and cook until thick. Stir in the okra with its water and 2 tbsp. butter. Grease a bowl and pack in the funjee-okra mixture. Run a knife edge around the bowl and then invert the funjee onto a plate. Cut into wedges.
3. For the fish: Blend 3 tablespoons of tomato paste with 3 tablespoons of water. Cut up 2 pounds of any fish into any kind of pieces. Sauté 1 chopped onion and 2 cloves

of chopped garlic in oil. Swirl in the tomato paste–water mixture. Add ½ teaspoon of dried thyme, ½ teaspoon of curry powder, and plentiful black pepper to 1½ cups of water. Swirl the fish pieces into the pan to coat, and add the seasoned water. Cover and simmer until the fish is done. Swirl in salt and more butter.

4. Serve the fish with the peas-rice and funjee, spooning sauce over it all. Beef, pork, goat, lamb, or chicken may be used instead of fish. Adjust cooking time.

References

Albala, K. 2007. *Beans: A history.* New York: Berg.

Allsopp, R. 1996. *Dictionary of Caribbean English usage.* Oxford: Oxford University Press.

Angiosperm Phylogeny Group. 2003. "An update of the Angiosperm Phylogeny Group Classification for the Orders and Families of Flowering Plants: APG II." *Botanical Journal of the Linnean Society* 141: 399–436.

Austen, J. [1818] 1933. *Persuasion.* Vol. 5, *The Oxford illustrated Jane Austen.* Oxford: Oxford University Press.

Ayensu, E. S. 1981. *Medicinal plants of the West Indies.* Algonac, MI: Reference Publications.

Berleant-Schiller, R. 1987. "Ecology and politics in Barbudan land tenure." In *Land and development in the Caribbean*, ed. J. Besson and J. Momsen, 116–31. London: Macmillan Caribbean.

Berleant-Schiller, R. 1989. "Free labor and the economy in seventeenth-century Montserrat." *William and Mary Quarterly* 46: 539–64.

Berleant-Schiller, R., and L. M. Pulsipher. 1986. "Subsistence cultivation in the Caribbean." *Nieuwe West-Indische Gids—New West Indian Guide* 60: 1–40.

Blume, H. 1974. *The Caribbean islands*, trans. J. Maczewski and A. Norton. London: Longman Group. (First published as *Die Westindischen Inseln*, 1968.)

Brussell, D. E. 1997. *Potions, poisons, and panaceas: An ethnobotanical study of Montserrat.* Carbondale: Southern Illinois University Press.

Carney, J. A. 2001. *Black rice: The African origins of rice cultivation in the Americas.* Cambridge, Mass.: Harvard University Press.

Carrington, S. 1998. *Wild plants of the Eastern Caribbean.* London: Macmillan Education.

CIAT: International Center for Tropical Agriculture. 2001a. "Common bean: The nearly perfect food." In *CIAT in Focus.* Available at: www.ciat.cgiar.org/ciatinfocus/beans.htm. Accessed February 16, 2011.

CIAT: International Center for Tropical Agriculture. 2001b. "Rice: Latin America's food grain of choice." In *CIAT in Focus.* Available at: www.ciat.cgiar.org/ciatinfocus/rice.htm. Accessed February 16, 2011.

Deagan, K. 1988. "The archaeology of the Spanish contact period in the Caribbean." *Journal of World History* 2: 187–233.

Dirks, R. 1987. *The black saturnalia: Conflict and its ritual expression on British West Indian slave plantations.* Gainesville: University Press of Florida.

European Association for Grain Legume Research. 2010. "Grain legumes." Available at: http://www.grainlegumes.com/aep. Accessed March 3, 2010.

Fields-Black, E. L. 2008. *Deep roots: Rice farmers in West Africa and the African diaspora.* Bloomington: Indiana University Press.

Garcia Colón, I. 2010. Personal communication, e-mail message, January 13.

Gepts, P., and D. G. Debouck. 1991. "Origin, domestication, and evolution of the common bean, *Phaseolus vulgaris.*" In *Common beans: Research for crop improvement*, ed. O. Voysest and A. Van Schoonhoven, 7–53. Wallingford, U.K., and Tucson, Ariz.: C.A.B. International in association with Centro Internacional de Agricultura Tropical.

Gepts, P., K. Kmiecik, P. Pereira, and F. A. Bliss. 1988. "Dissemination pathways of common beans (*Phaseolus vulgaris*, Fabaceae) deduced from Phaseolin electrophoretic variability, I: The Americas." *Economic Botany* 42: 73–85.

Handler, J. S. 1964. "Land exploitative activities and economic patterns in a Barbados village." PhD diss., Brandeis University.

Handler, J. S. 1970. "Aspects of Amerindian ethnography in 17th century Barbados." *Caribbean Studies* 9: 50–70.

Harris, D. R. 1965. *Plants, animals, and man in the Outer Leeward Islands, West Indies.* Berkeley: University of California Publications in Geography, vol. 18.

Hoefte, R. 1998. *In place of slavery: A social history of British Indian and Javanese laborers in Suriname.* Gainesville: University Press of Florida.

Howard, R. A. 1988. *Flora of the Lesser Antilles: Leeward and Windward Islands.* Vol. 4: *Dicotyledoneae—Part 1.* Jamaica Plain, Mass.: Arnold Arboretum of Harvard University.

Kaplan, L., and L. N. Kaplan. 1988. "*Phaseolus* in archaeology." In *Genetic resources of Phaseolus beans*, ed. P. Gepts, 125–42. Dordrecht: Kluwer.

Linares, O. F. 2002. "African rice (*Oryza glaberrima*): History and future potential." *Proceedings of the National Academy of Sciences* 99: 16360–365.

Littlefield, D. C. [1981] 1991. *Rice and slaves.* Urbana: University of Illinois Press.

Look Lai, W. 1993. *Indentured labor, Caribbean sugar: Chinese and Indian migrants to the British West Indies, 1838–1913.* Baltimore: Johns Hopkins University Press.

Mintz, S. W. 2010. *Three ancient colonies: Caribbean themes and variations.* Cambridge, Mass.: Harvard University Press.

Newsom, L. A., and E. S. Wing. 2004. *On land and sea: Native American uses of biological resources in the West Indies.* Tuscaloosa: University of Alabama Press.

Niddrie, D. L. 1974. "The Caribbean." In *Latin America: Geographical perspectives*, ed. H. Blakemore and C. T. Smith, 73–120. London: Methuen.

Philpott, S. B. 1973. *West Indian migration: The Montserrat case.* New York: Humanities Press.

Purdue University, Horticulture and Landscape Architecture. 1998. *Vicia faba* L. Available at: http://www.hort.purdue.edu/newcrop/duke_energy/Vicia_faba.html. Accessed November 27, 2009.

Reid, B. A. 2009. *Myths and realities of Caribbean history.* Tuscaloosa: University of Alabama Press.

Richardson, B. C. 1989. "Caribbean migrations, 1838–1985." In *The Modern Caribbean*, ed. F. W. Knight and C. A. Palmer, 203–28. Chapel Hill: University of North Carolina Press.

Rubenstein, H. 1987. *Coping with poverty: Adaptive strategies in a Caribbean village.* Boulder, Colo.: Westview Press.

Salgado, A. G., A. Gutiérrez, P. Gepts, and D. G. Debouck. 1995. "Evidence for two gene pools of the lima bean." *Genetic Resources and Crop Evolution* 42: 15–28.

Sauer, C. O. [1966] 1969. *The early Spanish Main.* Berkeley: University of California Press.

Sauer, J., and L. Kaplan. 1969. "Canavalia beans in American prehistory." *American Antiquity* 34: 417–24.

Simoons, F. J. 1998. *Plants of life, plants of death.* Madison: University of Wisconsin Press.

Sloane, H. Sir. 1707. *A voyage to the islands of Madera, Barbados, Nieves, St. Christophers, and Jamaica, with the natural history of the last of these islands.* 2 vols. London.

Smartt, J. 1985. "Evolution of the grain legumes, II. Old and New World pulses of lesser economic importance." *Experimental Agriculture* 21: 1–18.

Stevens, P. F. 2001–. *Angiosperm Phylogeny.* Version 9, June 2008, and updated since. Available at: www.mobot.org/MOBOT/research/APWeb. Accessed February 17, 2011.

Stokstad, E. 2007. "American rice: Out of Africa." *ScienceNOW Daily News*, November 16. Available at: http://news.sciencemag.org/sciencenow/2007/11/16-03.html. Accessed January 20, 2012.

Sturtevant, W. C. 1961. "Taíno agriculture." *Antropologica* 3 (Suppl.): 69–82.

Vaughn, J. G., and C. Geissler. 1997. *The new Oxford book of food plants.* Oxford: Oxford University Press.

Wagley, C. 1960. "Plantation America: A culture sphere." In *Caribbean studies: A symposium*, 2nd ed., ed. V. Rubin, 3–13. Seattle: University of Washington Press.

Watters, D. 2009. Personal communication, e-mail message of November 6, with corroboration by L. Newsom in message of November 9.

Watts, D. 1987. *The West Indies: Patterns of development, culture and environmental change since 1492.* Cambridge: Cambridge University Press.

Wood, P. H. 1974. *Black majority.* New York: Knopf.

–6–

Rice and Beans, Beans and Rice
The Perfect Couple

Livia Barbosa

Introduction

Rice with beans and beans with rice are two classic staple combinations of Brazilian cuisine. Inverting these terms is not just a play on words; rather it reflects preferences and tastes about the proportion of both rice and beans on Brazilian plates and the way in which they should be arranged: one on top of the other, side by side, more of one than of the other, and so on. They are often presented as "the perfect couple," in both the nutritional and the symbolic sense, in popular representations and by official organizations such as EMBRAPA (Brazilian National Agriculture Research System).[1] This couple came together in the early nineteenth century and still flourishes in the twenty-first century on the plates of all social classes and in all regions of Brazil, playing a key structural role in the Brazilian diet (see Figure 6.1). Every week in the year, you can rest assured that rice and beans will be included in people's daily hot meals—lunch or dinner (or both).

The fact that these two items are permanent features of the daily menu of Brazilians deserves some reflection, since changes in eating habits are being blamed for rising rates of cardiovascular diseases and obesity, at the same time that traditional eating practices are allegedly being destroyed by the globalization process. This chapter sets out to contextualize the role of this couple in Brazilian society. The first section traces a history of the introduction and adoption of beans and rice in Brazilian eating practices. Next, I describe rice and beans as symbolic representations that define Brazilian alimentary identity, and how they relate to globalization and the developed world. The third section focuses on the empirical description of production and consumption practices; in the concluding section I reflect on the privileged position that rice and beans continues to occupy in Brazilian eating habits and the reasons why this position is sustained.

Figure 6.1   Map of Brazil showing state names and boundaries.

A History of the Perfect Couple

Beans in Brazil

Although we know that *Phaseolus* beans originated in the Americas, various hypotheses exist concerning their domestication on this continent and expansion to others. The first is a Mesoamerican origin, based on wild types found in Mexico and domesticated types found elsewhere in Mesoamerica dating back to 5000 B.C. The second hypothesis suggests that beans were domesticated in South America about 8000 B.C. (the Guitarrero site in Peru) and then transported to the rest of the Americas. The third proposes that there were three primary centers of genetic diversity, both for wild and cultivated species, located in the Mesoamerican region and in the southern and northern regions of the Andes (EMBRAPA 2006). Beans were introduced to Brazil possibly through three different routes. On the first route, small-type beans left Mexico and arrived in

Figure 6.2   Some of the different kinds of beans eaten in Brazil. Reproduced by permission of Jose Valdo De Oliveira Da Silva Junior and Donizeti Da Silva Pinto.

Brazil through the Caribbean, Colombia, and Venezuela. The second route originates in the Andes (Peru), and the beans were of a larger type, while the last and most recent path brought beans from Europe, carried by the Portuguese colonizers and other immigrants (EMBRAPA 2006; Paula Junior and Venzon 2007).[2] (See Figure 6.2.)

Whatever may be the historical origin of the beans that Brazilians eat today, these leguminous plants played an important role in the process of conquering and establishing the Brazilian territory. It was an essential part of the diet of settlers, often grown by women while the men busied themselves with other crops and cattle. Beans were also part of the diet of the Portuguese colonial *bandeirantes*, or scouts, who conquered the interior of the country. The fact that they were easy to transport on a donkey's back, and the practice of planting them along the routes leading to the gold, silver, and precious-stone mines of Minas Gerais, Goiás, and Mato Grosso (states where mining was intensive throughout the seventeenth and eighteenth centuries), as well as their storability and durability, made beans (along with corn, manioc flour, and dried meat) pillars of the Brazilian diet in the colonial period (Pinto e Silva 2005). These foods were so important to early explorers that in 1707 the colonial government required that the *bandeirantes* and the pioneers plant them along the routes that penetrated the interior of the country. In this way the people that would follow them, settlers or other *bandeirantes*, would find crops along the way to feed themselves (Pinto e Silva 2005).

According to Cascudo (1983) beans and flour were the staple diet of the Brazilians during the first half of the seventeenth century. This menu assembled ingredients, cooking techniques, and table and kitchen utensils from the three main ethnic groups—Indians, whites, and blacks—that formed the basis of the Brazilian society. This similarity in the menus of the rich and poor extended to table manners and utensils. Even the most affluent homes had very little furniture such as sideboards, tables, or buffets. Food was served on Indian mats on the floor, with a bowl of flour at the center; diners holding their clay dishes served themselves with their hands. Utensils such as china, glasses, and pewter platters, and tablecloths from India were stored and used only on special occasions and in the presence of visitors or guests. Similarly, the cattle raised in the yard were seen as a reserve one did not touch, except in the case of emergencies, for visitors or guests (Pinto e Silva 2005).

The colonial menu was mostly dominated by the Iberian habit of eating stews, soups, and other types of food with a great quantity of broth, which the Portuguese ate with flour (manioc or corn) to replace wheat bread, together with local ingredients of indigenous origin. The fundamental importance of beans to Brazilian cuisine can be seen in accounts of colonial chroniclers and European travelers to Brazil. In 1587, for instance, the Portuguese Gabriel Soares de Souza praised the taste of beans, though others criticized their "coarseness."[3] However, these accounts are striking in their consistency. Spanning the country from the Amazon to São Paulo, ranging from the seventeenth to the nineteenth century, one finds the same foods, cooking practices, and eating habits in the colonial period. The triad of beans, flour, and dried meat conceals a vast geographic and social diversity (Pinto e Silva 2005).

As the French voyager Saint-Hilaire[4] noted during his travels through Minas Gerais in 1817, "black beans form an indispensable dish on the tables of the rich, and this legume constitutes almost the only gourmet food of the poor." When the German prince Maximilian de Wied-Neuwied visited Brazil from 1815 to 1817, he observed that in Bahia rich men (farmers and traders) ate like their slaves, both in terms of menus—cooked beans with a broth to wet the flour and soften the sundried meat—and manners, using their fingers to mix the beans with the flour (Wied-Neuwied 1942).[5] Carl Friedrich Gustav Seidler, another traveler of Swiss-German descent, visited Brazil in 1826 and made the following comments:[6]

> Beans, mainly black beans, is the favorite dish of Brazilians. It is present in the most refined tables accompanied by *carne seca* (salt dried meat) and a piece of bacon. ... There is no meal without beans, only beans kill your hunger. It is nutritious and healthy, but only after you have been used to it can it be appreciated by the European taste, since its taste is coarse and unpleasant.

All of Brazil's colonial industries, including the sugar-cane monoculture and later on gold mining and coffee production, depended on intensive slave labor. Because the economy was completely oriented toward exporting, food was locally grown by both slaves and settlers, who shared a common repertoire of crops and dishes. Everyone produced their own food in their own yards, gardens, and orchards; even some slaves had small pieces of land inside their owners' property where they could grow some food of their own (Freyre [1933] 2006).

This geographic and social bond may explain why this staple diet proved resistant to foreign influence following the arrival of the Portuguese royal family in 1808. As pointed out by El-Kareh (2008), after the arrival of the Portuguese royal family the daily diet, table manners, and cuisine of the Brazilians underwent a great transformation as new foods and utensils were adopted. Products from various places arrived in the port of Rio de Janeiro to satisfy the tastes of foreign traders—mainly English— who established themselves in Brazil. Still, these new habits did not supplant local ones, which persisted, were combined with the new ones, and today to a great extent define the Brazilian menu, with its various combinations of diverse cooking traditions and ingredients (El-Kareh 2008; Barbosa 2007). From beans, specifically black beans, originates the famous Brazilian *feijoada* (and its numerous variations), the symbol of Brazil's culinary identity and acknowledged as one of Brazil's national dishes.[7]

Rice in Brazil

The history of rice in Brazil, though almost as long as that of beans, is less connected with the conquest and settlement of the national territory. Rice as a crop was introduced into Brazil in the sixteenth century by African slaves and by the Portuguese (Carney and Marin 1999; Portères 1970; Ribeiro 1962; Littlefield 1991; Brooks 1993). For a long time scholars assumed that this was Asian rice (Portères 1976; National Research Council [NRC] 1996). However, recent historical studies lend credence to the possibility that it was African rice (*Oryza glaberrima*), which had been cultivated for more than three thousand years in the region from Senegal to the Ivory Coast (Portères 1976; NRC 1996: 23). The idea that all rice originated in Asia was perpetuated in botanical classifications until the end of the nineteenth century when Steudel, a botanist from Moravia, identified the African variety, which has a reddish color and softer husk (Lewicki 1974; Wood 1974a). Some of the evidence that the Africans were in great part responsible for the dissemination of rice in America comes from the lack of familiarity among white farmers regarding the planting of rice and the slaves' knowledge about production and milling (Wood 1974b; Littlefield 1991; Carney 1993, 1996a,b).

The Cape Verde islands played an important role in exporting African rice to Brazil. Brooks (1993) records a shipment of goods to the country in 1530, just thirty years after the discovery of Brazil, which included rice seeds. This trip was followed by many others that delivered rice seeds to the state of Bahia (Ribeiro 1962; Duncan 1972). In 1587, Gabriel Soares de Souza, noted in his famous book *Tratado Descritivo do Brasil* the importance of the Cape Verde islands in setting the pattern for agriculture and cattle ranching in Brazil, and attributed the origins of rice planting to seeds brought from these islands. He also traces the food patterns of the African slaves in Brazil back to the islands.

Historical documents from the eighteenth century on frequently make references to a red-skinned type of rice in the Amazon region (Primeiro 1818; Marques 1870; Chermont 1885). This type of rice—nowadays known as African rice—became popular at the end of the eighteenth century when the Portuguese supported the creation of rice plantations in the eastern region of the Amazon. Also using white rice from South Carolina, they built rice mills and used twenty-five thousand slaves brought from the area of what is now Guiné-Bissau. The intention was to develop a new export crop in this region, as well as to decrease Brazil's dependence on the rice supply from the Carolinas, which had been disrupted by the American Revolution. However, in 1772, Portugal made planting red rice illegal, and white farmers could be punished with one year in prison plus a large fine, while slaves and Indians were subject to two years in prison. The reason for this regulation is unclear, but it may have been intended to force growers to produce the white rice that was preferred in Portugal.

Regardless of how rice arrived on Brazilian plates, its cultivation began as early as 1587 in the state of Bahia, and by around 1745 the Asian type had reached the state of Maranhão, where local inhabitants began to be called "rice-eaters." From then on rice is found in 1750 in Pernambuco, and in 1772 in Pará. In 1766 the Portuguese Crown authorized the first hulling machine in Rio de Janeiro. From the northeastern states rice spread to the southern states where most producers are concentrated today. Since the late eighteenth century, Brazil has been a major exporter of rice, declining only in the first half of the twentieth century (EMBRAPA 2009; Fernandes 2000).

Another source confirming the antiquity of rice cultivation in Brazil is the Overseas Historical Archive in Portugal, which offers evidence that the Portuguese royal family was consuming rice from plantations in Maranhão as early as the eighteenth century. Shipments of this cereal were regularly sent to Lisbon. When the royal family moved to Rio de Janeiro in 1808, they started receiving the shipments of rice in that city (Bottini 2008). After growing red rice was prohibited, it was still cultivated mainly by Africans in rural areas and was rarely seen in urban centers. Today it is known as *quilombola rice* (maroon rice, or "red rice"), grown mainly in the state of Paraíba, where it is also known as *arroz da terra* (local rice, or "Venice rice"). Red rice is also grown in Ceará and Rio Grande do Sul and is mainly cultivated by *quilombolas* (small farmers who are descended from escaped slaves from the great plantations of colonial Brazil). It plays an important role in local culinary and ethnic identity[8] and also in the political struggles of Maroon social movements seeking to recover and protect their original territories and to reclaim their role in Brazilian history.[9]

Nevertheless, up to the end of the nineteenth century rice played a significantly smaller role in Brazilian cuisine than beans, though it was still appreciated from both culinary and economic perspectives. Because it could grow in both the rainy and dry seasons, rice drew the interest of *sesmeiros* (small farmers who were granted land concessions from the Portuguese Crown) and settlers. Rice was usually eaten as porridge, a kind of thick gruel that sometimes replaced dried cassava flour mixed with hot water. It also appeared as a dessert in the form of "sweet rice" pudding made with coconut milk, a dish that remains popular today, usually topped with powdered cinnamon, both in restaurants and at home.

Rice began to take a larger role in the diet around 1808, when the Portuguese Court arrived in Brazil. After this date rice ascended to the status of a national food, being present in everyday meals of all Brazilian social and economic groups. The first step in this direction was its being adopted for feeding the soldiers of the Brazilian army after 1808, by direct order of Prince Regent D. João (Cascudo 1983). The reason why this decision was taken is not known. At that point it started being consumed regularly with beans and flour (corn and manioc), thereby establishing the necessary conditions for the appearance of the "perfect couple." Rice gradually began to be the ideal complement for beans, leaving to manioc or corn flour the role of the regulator of the amount of moisture in food. The "perfect couple" of the national imagination was formed.

Rice and Beans: Representations, Metaphors, and National Identity

Besides their historical role in Brazilian cuisine, rice and beans are also important in many other ways. They are invoked when we want to indicate that something is ordinary, repetitive, and unchallenging, similar to the way we use the phrase *sexo de papai e mamãe* ("sex between daddy and mommy"). Rice and beans also appear when we want to show that we miss our homeland. In this case, the diminutive *inho* is used to mark both affection and distance from one's country and loved ones: *Estou morrendo de saudades daquele feijãozinho com arroz lá de casa* ("I sure miss that plate of beans and rice from home"). They are the quintessential comfort food, carrying warm memories, security, and reassurance. For this reason, rice and beans figure in many popular reports about Brazilian athletes in the Olympic Games and the World Cup, when images are shown of loving mothers stirring a pot of *feijoada* to welcome the family hero home.

When Brazilians emigrate or go to study abroad, they often worry about their rice and beans supply. They always try to locate other Brazilians in the new city in order to find out where they can find both, as well as manioc flour. They are always nagging their friends coming from Brazil to bring the precious cargo from home.[10]

From the gastronomic point of view, rice and beans are the essence of what Brazilians see as tasty, homey, everyday food, regardless of social class. A survey on eating habits found that the majority of Brazilians think rice and beans should be present at lunch as well as at dinner. Brazilians not only assume that everyone likes it but also that they eat the mixture daily (Barbosa 2007). Here are some quotes from the Brazilian Food Habits (2006) survey.[11]

> "Ha! My dear, rice is something I can't live without! Fluffy rice, *cozidinho* (nice and cooked) ... and beans too." (POA classes D and E/2006)

> "Rice and beans is not considered 'what is for lunch and dinner.' But it has to be there." (RJ. F. A. 2006)

Rice and beans are found as themes in children's games, like *Um dois, feijão com arroz; três quatro, comendo pato; cinco seis, francês inglês; sete e oito, comendo biscoito; e nove e dez, lavar os pés* ("One, two: beans and rice; three, four: eating duck; five, six: French English; seven and eight: eating biscuit; and nine and ten: wash your feet"). The couple is thought of as an essential food for children. Beginning to eat "broth with rice and beans" means transitioning from infant to toddler. They are also the name of musical bands, clubs for children's parties, and are included in the titles and lyrics of love songs, where they act as structural equivalents of Romeo and Juliet.

From the nutritional perspective they are presented as the perfect couple, both by health professionals and the government agency EMBRAPA, which has a special project that constantly monitors the consumption of the two items: the EMBRAPA Rice and Bean Program.

> It is not without reason that the rice and beans combination is perfect! They are two foods that are extremely important to our health, because they are rich in carbohydrates, proteins, mineral salts, vitamins and fibers. Did you know that a plate of rice and beans has the same amount of proteins found in meat? Did you know that when we do not consume them we can have a number of illnesses? Here in this site you will find information about this and much more, like the history of rice and beans, their nutritive power, illnesses caused by the lack of these foods, and delicious recipes for you and your family. At this site you will learn in a simple and fun way that rice and beans are tasty and very nutritious foods. Rice and beans are Brazil's perfect couple. (EMBRAPA 2009)

The key to this perfect pairing is the complementary relationship that they establish: what one lacks in nutrients is compensated for by the other. What one represents symbolically, its symmetrical inverse is represented by the other. This complementarity is explained didactically, like that of a couple whose qualities and deficiencies are pointed out to confirm the popular saying that "opposites attract."

> Rice and beans, two foods extremely rich in nutrients, can be consumed separately in several ways, but together they become a perfect combination. ... For instance, rice is poor in lysine amino acid, which in turn is abundantly found in beans; methyonine amino acid is lacking in beans, but is abundant in rice, and thus they complement each other, becoming a perfect pair. (Silva 2008)

Why rice and beans: "If we ask Brazilians about the dish they do not go without and eat every day, either at lunch or dinner, a majority will say that it is that perfect combination of rice and beans. Considered staple foods in Tupiniquim (Brazilian) cuisine, besides making a delicious partnership they ensure an enviable arrangement of nutrients. According to physicians and endocrinologists … rice and beans are rich sources of carbohydrates, proteins, mineral salts, vitamins, and fibers. 'What one lacks, the other supplies, and thus they complement each other. Together, they offer an excellent combination of proteins. A dish of rice and beans has almost the same quantity of proteins found in meat. What people do not know is that when they do not consume this pair our bodies are prone to develop a number of diseases,' says the physician. Whereas rice on its own, especially polished rice, can 'trigger sugar and insulin increases in the circulation, beans have the power to counter this effect, thereby keeping glucose stable. The blend is, therefore, welcome for maintaining adequate glycemy levels and decreasing the risk of diabetes.'" (Copacabanarunners 2011)

Or the following:

Rice is white, beans are black, which symbolically leads us to our much-spoken-about racial blend. One is dry, the other is wet, which is exactly the contrast between the rainy Amazon and the dry and arid Northeast. One is cold (rice), the other is warm (beans). ("Arroz" 2011)[12]

Although this "perfect couple" is shared with other Latin American countries, such as Costa Rica, Mexico, and Cuba, Brazilians treat it as if it were their own. People often say, "It is our rice and beans" or "Rice and beans is ours." However, the apparent homogeneity of a single name conceals a great diversity. There are many types of beans and rice, cooking techniques, recipes, and forms of consumption, which are neutralized when people talk about food in a generic way. Distinctions, in any form, appear mainly when one wishes to mark a regional identity in opposition to another. For instance, people say, "Black beans are predominantly eaten in Minas, Porto Alegre, and Rio de Janeiro, but here in São Paulo people usually eat common beans (*mulatinho*)." Or, "We seldom eat black beans here in Recife, it is almost always *mulatinho*, but when it is *feijoada* I make it with black beans." Contrary to the Caribbean region, however, beans are almost never cooked with coconut milk or together with rice in one pot. This usually happens only on special occasions like Easter, as is the case of coconut beans in the northeast, or *Baião de Dois*, a regional dish of the northeast.

The particularization of rice occurs less with regard to regions than with regional cooking techniques. Rice is sautéed in Rio, steamed in Recife, fried in other regions. Individual preferences in the manner of consuming rice are also diverse. Rice can be "loose" or "porridge," and these preferences determine the choice of a favorite brand. But when people refer to rice and beans or beans and rice they always have in mind white rice eaten together with beans in a heavy broth, but cooked separately and having as side dishes meat, of any kind, vegetables, potatoes, and salad (see Figure 6.3).

Figure 6.3 A regular portion of rice and beans. Photo courtesy of the author.

In its relationship with the world, and with foreigners (mainly Europeans and North Americans), Brazilian rice and beans has a paradigmatic position. The dish defines our culinary identity and organizes how we understand and experience food and sociability. Brazilians recognize that the dish is aesthetically not very inviting and it can seem strange to those not familiar with it. Taking foreigners out to eat rice and beans or a *feijoada* can be a challenge. A common strategy is to first warn the newcomer about the "ugliness" of the dish. If rice and beans and also *feijoada* are dishes that can seem aesthetically strange or repulsive to outsiders, as far as taste, abundance, and sociability are concerned they are unbeatable from a Brazilian point of view. When abroad, Brazilians will not hesitate to extend an invitation to eat rice and beans or to attend a *feijoada* as a strategy to meet people: the dish functions as a means of communication. According to the testimony of Brazilian expatriates in several European countries and the United States, an invitation to eat one of these dishes allowed them to "break the ice" with work colleagues (Barbosa 2009). A Brazilian executive from a large multinational in London suffered, along with his family, the exaggerated compassion of an English neighbor who tried to give him clothes because he assumed that wearing jogging clothes around the house was a manifestation of Brazilian poverty. In order to show his neighbor that he was neither poor nor needy, the executive invited him over for a *feijoada*, with all that it entails, including human warmth and companionship. Afterward the executive was certain that everything had changed:

> the man had never seen so much food in a single meal. He ate so much that later I laughed to see him walking along the sidewalk to try and digest it. And moreover, everybody was relaxed and laughing together. I think he had never been in a situation like that, sharing affection with strangers in such a natural way. (Barbosa 2009)

Inviting a foreigner to a *feijoada* is seen by Brazilians as a rite of passage into Brazilian culture. Whether they like it or not ultimately makes little difference since in the context of food Brazilians tend to feel culturally superior, especially to North Americans. Hence we have an interesting inversion. While from the point of view of economic development, Europe and the United States are seen as superior (although this perception is rapidly changing), many daily practices, specifically with regard to food and hygiene, reverse this position. Although we may admire Europeans for their culinary traditions, we consider ourselves to have superior personal-hygiene practices, because of our frequent and intimate relationship with water, baths, clothes, and scent (Barbosa 2004). North Americans are admired in neither of these fields. In these two areas, therefore, the positions of developed and underdeveloped are inverted by a classification based on the logic of taste, both culinary and hygienic.

Though rooted in historical and daily Brazilian traditions, the "perfect couple" has been revitalized and updated to meet contemporary challenges. It can be found both in fashionable bars and in the simple, ubiquitous *botequins* (small bars historically frequented by lower-income people. At present, they are very fashionable and popular places to frequent and have become one of the busiest options in Brazilian nightlife). The traditional beans, for example, are cooked in broth in city bars, and served as a tidbit that prepares us for a night of hearty drinking and can also bring the night to a close by lining the stomach and reducing the risk of a hangover. The same is true of rice, which can appear in contemporary reimaginings in the guise of a little round cake filled with Roquefort or Brie cheese. Rice and beans conquered the world through *botequim* gastronomy, exporting the famous *petiscos* (appetizers) typical of this type of establishment to European, North American, and Asian capitals. Even in diets that reject meat, beans and rice have a unique capacity to persevere. Vegan *feijoada*, made with different kinds of vegetables, is the preferred dish of many who relish the sociability of a communal meal. Conde de Bernadotte street in Rio de Janeiro's Leblon neighborhood is home to a gastronomic cluster predominantly made up of bars that serve the most traditional *botequim* gastronomy characterized by a large quantity of fried foods, carbohydrates, and meats. One can find a natural/vegetarian/vegan restaurant whose signature dish is just such a vegan *feijoada*. This example shows not only the adaptability of rice and beans to various dietary requirements, but also the way in which Brazilian society gets around the restriction on sociability that stricter diets can impose on their followers. Instead of setting themselves up in opposition to other establishments that offer an altogether different gastronomy, they provide another option within the same context.

Rice and Beans: Current Production and Consumption

Just as in the colonial period, rice and beans, along with manioc flour, are three of the staple products in Brazil, and daily dietary habits bear witness to their continuing importance. Brazil is the world's largest producer of common beans (*Phaseolus vulgaris l.*), and 70 percent of this production comes from family farms (National Institute of Geography and Statistics [IBGE] 2006/2007). Although bean production has increased, it is still not sufficient to meet the domestic demand and is complemented by imports. Argentina and Uruguay are the main sources supplying beans to Brazil. Of the total bean supply produced in Brazil, 72.4 percent comes from Paraná, Minas Gerais, Bahia, São Paulo, Goiás, and Santa Catarina, states in the south, southeast, and central region of the country.

Data based on aggregate consumption vary widely and are sometimes contradictory, but what is certain is that consumption has been decreasing throughout the years. According to the National Research on Family Budgets (POF) 2002/2003, Brazilians consumed 24.5 kilograms of rice and 12.4 kilograms of beans a year (all types). The POF 2007/2008 indicates a per-capita consumption of 14.6 kilograms of rice and 9.1 kilograms of beans. However, some researchers dispute these numbers because the POFs consider only those beans consumed at home, omitting those consumed in restaurants, schools, and all other institutions. This difference leads us to conclude that the real numbers are higher not only for urban but also rural dwellers. This argument is very important since Brazil has developed a series of public food policies such as the *Programa Cesta Básica* ("Food Basket Program"), the *Programa de Alimentação do Trabalhador* ("Workers' Food Program"), the *Ticket Refeição e Ticket Alimentação* ("Restaurant and Supermarket Ticket") that include physical portions of rice and beans (the Food Basket Program) or allow for their consumption in restaurants, bars, and industrial canteens (the other programs).

More recent data, drawn from a 2009 telephone survey of 54,367 people conducted by the Ministry of Health in association with the Vigitel Project (which regularly monitors the behavior of chronic noncontagious diseases), also show a drop in the frequency of bean consumption when compared with the Diet Habits Survey of 2006.[13] Whereas in that year 71.9 percent of respondents ate beans five times a week, in 2009 the number consuming them was 65.8 percent.

Bean consumption is inversely proportional to income, according to data from the POF 2002/2003 and 2008/2009 (National Institute of Geography and Statistics [IBGE] 2006/2007) and the 2006 PHA. The lower the income, the higher the consumption of beans. Four variables could account for this trend. First, as income increases, people eat out more often, which allows them more food choices. Probably the amount of rice and beans consumed diminishes. For instance in *Per Kilo* self-service restaurants where you pay for the weight of food you consume, there is a huge choice of salads, quiches, Italian food, and meats. Yet rice and beans continue to be the most consumed food even in this type of restaurant. Second, as income increases, part of the per-capita quantity of beans consumed at home is replaced with other food items, as indicated by increases in chicken consumption, which reached a record of thirty-eight kilograms per capita in 2008 (Brazil is a major world exporter of chicken). Third, the higher-income groups are most concerned both with body image and weight control. Consequently, they are more involved in diets and weight-loss regimes, which limit the consumption of beans and rice to "two spoons of rice and one of beans." Other elements that could explain the reduction in the consumption of beans include urban life and the increasing participation of women in the workforce. Because beans take a long time to cook, consumption could be lower due to lack of time for cooking. Usually young married couples do not cook beans at home. They bring them from their parents' house. However, as soon as they have children, rice and beans begin to be cooked at home!

Rice produced in Brazil results from two different production systems: the irrigated and the *sequeiro* (or highland), with most production and consumption originating from the much higher yield of the former. Most of the rice planted is an Indian subspecies, although today Brazilian farmers also have at their disposal (thanks to genetic research carried out by EMBRAPA, the Instituto Agrônomo de Campinas, the Polo Regional do Vale do Paraíba, and the Agência Paulista de Tecnologia dos Agronegócios) new types of rice besides the traditional white variety. Although the amount produced is still small, it is already possible to find black, Italian, *koshini-kare*, and *moti* produced locally, mainly in São Paulo. *Basmati*, the Indian version of rice, will be arriving on the market in 2012 (Bottini 2008). Rice is grown by a mix of small and medium producers, and large agribusinesses, with the latter controlling the packing industry.

Although Brazil was a rice exporter for a long time, today it imports part of its domestic needs, usually less than 10 percent. The annual production of rice in 2009/2010 was around 11,508 million metric tons, less than the 12,602 million tons of 2008/2009 while consumption was around 12,600 million tons. The biggest rice-producing states are Rio Grande do Sul, Santa Catarina, and Paraná (EMBRAPA 2005). Although Brazil is the largest non-Asian consumer, on a global scale it holds the eighth position. The average annual consumption of rice in Brazil is about 75 kilograms per person including hulls, or 55 kilograms dehulled and polished. In comparison to the largest consumers like Myanmar at 210 kilograms per capita, Vietnam at 200 kilograms per capita, and Bangladesh at 180 kilograms per capita, this may not seem like very much. Nevertheless, when compared to European countries, whose average consumption is less than 10 kilograms per year, this represents a great deal.

More rice than beans is currently consumed in Brazil, a reversal of a tradition dating back to colonial Brazil. The reason is clear: while beans are always combined with rice and *cassava* flour, rarely as a dish by themselves, rice has become the universal accompaniment to most meats and savory dishes, a place occupied by the potato and bread in Europe and many other countries. In addition, rice is often a food of choice by itself, in dishes like risotto, *carreteiro* ("hauler's rice," mixed with salt pork meat), baked rice, rice balls, and rice salads.

The same factors influencing the decrease in bean consumption in the home apply to rice. According to the 2006 PHA survey, the frequency of rice consumption in households at lunch and dinnertime is higher than that of beans. As with beans, frequency of consumption varies with the meal, age, and income. Less rice is eaten at dinner, and the sixty to sixty-five age bracket consumes the least. It is worth noting that lower consumption of rice and beans at dinnertime is directly related to the lesser importance of the evening meal in relation to lunch and breakfast. The vast majority of respondents to the PHA survey agreed that "lunch is the most important meal of the day" when we are talking about sustenance, the feeling of being satisfied, full. The importance of dinner, however, is its sociability. It is the occasion for gathering the family together at the end of the day. In terms of food, however, most respondents feel that dinner must be lighter than lunch (Barbosa 2007: 103; Barbosa 2010). Hence, only 71 percent of the respondents eat rice and 68 percent beans at dinnertime, an amount 10–15 percent less than at lunch.

Final Notes

I have sought to demonstrate that rice and beans are structural parts of the Brazilian social context on several different levels. They have been present ever since the dawn of colonization. They have combined as a perfect couple for 200 and are fundamental ingredients in our staple cuisine. They are produced in Brazil by Brazilian enterprises and function as metaphors for our "racial democracy" (invoking the mixture of blacks and whites) and for the superiority of Brazilian food over that of the developed world. They are central elements in everyday meals and in Brazil's self-definition as a people and nation.

This privileged position is reinforced, from an institutional perspective, by government bodies such as EMBRAPA and its program "Rice and Beans, the Perfect Couple" and by health professionals who see this combination as a nutritionally balanced diet. The combination is structurally embedded in government policies such as the food-stamp program for basic food supply, meal vouchers, cash allowances for meals or food, and workers' food policies. Together these two aspects—the structural presence of rice and beans in our history and in our symbolic representation and food habits, plus the institutional policies created by government and reinforced by professional opinion—help explain why the perfect couple has not lost its importance. And this despite a wide range of contrary tendencies such as the growing diversity of food products in Brazilian supermarkets (around twenty-five thousand items), the increased consumption of meals outside the household (30 percent of Brazilian's food expenditure is spent outside the home), the rising consumption of meat, the growing media exposure to new culinary influences, and the participation of women in the workforce. This persistence is notable in a world where theories about food predict greater individualization (people of the same social group eating differently from each other), homogenization (people eating processed food and losing contact with their traditional diet), and the decomposition of traditional meals (change in the structure and the way food is ingested in a meal).

However, if all these changes have not profoundly altered the place of rice and beans among Brazilians, they have certainly changed the nature of Brazilian discussions about what we eat, health, diet, environment, and sensory food experiences. In the context of these discussions, traditional practices such as the rice and beans couple are reevaluated from new perspectives, and become the object of headlines and constant concern every time new research indicates any decline in their consumption. My view is that the new preoccupation with the health and the wellness of societies in general, and particularly in Brazil, has become another factor that helps to reinforce the position of rice and beans on the Brazilian menu. Coupled with ingrained food habits and independence in relation to basic food supply, rice and beans have demonstrated a constant capacity to reinvent themselves in different contexts, where tradition coexists with innovation and imported influences and in so doing raises important questions about globalization and national food habits.

Notes

1. "Perfect Couple" is the slogan adopted by EMBRAPA (Brazilian National Agriculture Research System), an organization linked to the Ministry of Agriculture, Livestock and Food Supply, in a national campaign meant to encourage the population to consume rice and beans, considered "typically Brazilian foods" by EMBRAPA (2006). In the rest of this chapter, "perfect couple" will be used to refer to the close relationship historically established in Brazil between rice and beans, a relationship recognized by the population in daily speech as well as by formal institutions, as mentioned above.
2. For more on this see Berleant in this volume.
3. Gabriel Soares de Souza was a Portuguese who came to Brazil between 1565 and 1569 and wrote a famous book called *Tratado Descritivo do Brasil.* He established himself in Bahia as a small farmer and later on he became the owner of a sugar-cane mill. He married and stayed in Brazil for seventeen years.
4. Augustin François Cesar Prouvençal de Saint-Hilaire was a French botanist and naturalist who came to Brazil in 1816 with the diplomatic mission of the Duke of Luxembourg, and stayed in the country until 1822.

5. Prince Maximilian was also a botanist and naturalist who wrote a very famous book about Brazil, *Travel to Brazil*. The book was published originally in German in 1820 and later in English and French. The prince traveled from Rio de Janeiro to Bahia making notes on the fauna, the flora, and on Brazilian society of the time.

6. Some of the chroniclers who visited Brazil and made comments about foods are Elizabeth Burton (1893), Thomas Ewbank ([1845] 1976), Saint-Hilaire ([1817] 1941), Henry Koster (1810, cited by Elias 2010), Prince Maximilian de Wied-Neuwied (1816, cited by Elias 2010), Jean–Baptiste Debret (1816–1831, cited by Elias 2010), Spix and Martius (naturalists who arrived in the entourage of the first empress of Brazil, Princess Leopoldina), and German Carl Seidler (1826, cited by Elias 2010).

7. For a detailed history of *feijoada* in Brazil see Carlos Alberto Dória's chapter in this volume (Chapter 7).

8. The culinary importance and the social and political meaning attached to red rice can be measured today by various indicators such as its presence in the Slow Food Movement, by the research carried out by the Federação da Agricultura e Pecuária da Paraíba (Paraíba State Federation of Agriculture and Livestock), and mainly by its being indicated by the state of Paraíba as a Product of Geographical Indication to the National Institute of Industrial Property.

9. Another source of production and consumption of the red rice is the gastronomic boom in Brazil, which has opened new possibilities for gastronomical experiences to social groups outside the reach of certain traditional products. The valorization of the origins of certain foods, due not only to gastronomy but also for political, social, and ethical reasons, is another source of the current interest in red rice in Brazil. More recently the EMBRAPA, the Instituto Agrônomo de Campinas, the Polo Regional do Vale do Paraíba, and the Agência Paulista de Tecnologia dos Agronegócios have developed and made available to consumers new types of rice besides the traditional white one. For the impact of new trends in food in the Brazilian food habits, see Barbosa (2009).

10. In the 1970s I went to study at the University of Chicago and lived there for four years. When I arrived, with a small daughter and without knowing anybody, Brazilian women to whom I was introduced immediately instructed me on where to buy rice, black beans, manioc flour, *guaraná*, and guava sweets. In 2008, my middle daughter, a nephrologist, went to live in North Carolina for a year of medical residency. When she got there, the same thing happened to her.

11. The Brazilian Food Habits survey, henceforth referred as BFH, was conducted in 2006 in ten Brazilian state capitals with more than one million inhabitants. It involved 2,136 questionnaires with more than 200 questions about food habits. The research also involved 50 focus groups with 8 people in each, covering all Brazilian economic classes and people between 17 and 65 years old. It was financed by the Brazilian Food Industries and conducted by Toledo Associados (Toledo and Associates) and the School of Advertising and Marketing (ESPM).

12. The notion of cold and hot mentioned here bears no relation to food temperature. It is related to local systems of food classification in the Amazon, northeast, and central regions of Brazil. Hot foods are those considered offensive to the digestive system, whereas cold ones are offensive to the circulatory system, and should not be ingested by individuals with bronchitis and asthma. Many food taboos are constructed around this distinction (Woortmann 2008).

13. The Diet Habits Survey, henceforth called PHA, was conducted in 2006 in ten Brazilian state capitals with more than one million inhabitants. The research had a qualitative as well as a quantitative part. The former involved 400 people in focus groups distributed among the ten capitals. The quantitative part involved 2,136 respondents and focused on several aspects, ranging from what was eaten at each meal during the week, at weekends, and on special occasions, to table manners, knowledge of other culinary traditions, knowledge of healthiness and food ideologies. The PHA survey was carried out by Toledo Associados (Toledo and Associates) and the School of Advertising and Marketing (ESPM).

References

"Arroz." 2011. *Wikipedia.* Available at: http://pt.wikipedia.org/wiki/Agricultura_no_Brasil#Arroz. Accessed November 30, 2009.

Barbosa, L. 2004. "Cleanness, pollution and disgust in modern industrial society." *Journal of Consumer Culture* 4 (3): 385–405.

Barbosa, L. 2007. "Feijão com Arroz e Arroz com Feijão." *Horizontes Antropológicos* 13 (28): 87–116.

Barbosa, L. 2009. *Cultura e Diferença nas Organizações.* São Paulo: Editora Atlas.

Barbosa, L. 2010. "Food and sociability on the contemporary Brazilian plate." *Etnográfica* 14 (3): 567–86.

Bottini, R. L. 2008. *Arroz—História, Variedades, Receitas.* São Paulo: SENAC São Paulo.

Brooks, G. 1993. *Landlords and strangers: Ecology, society and trade in Western Africa, 1000–1630.* Boulder, Colo.: Westview Press.

Burton, E. 1893. *The life of Captain Sir Richard F. Burton. K.C.M.G., F.R.G.S.* London: Chapman and Hall.

Carney, J. A. 1993. "From hands to tutors: African expertise in the South Carolina economy." *Agricultural History* 67 (3): 1–30.

Carney, J. A. 1996a. "Landscapes of technology transfer: Rice cultivation and African continuities." *Technology and Culture* 37 (1): 5–35.

Carney, J. A. 1996b. "Rice milling, gender and slave labour in colonial South Carolina." *Past and Present* 153: 108–34.

Carney, J. A., and R. A. Marin. 1999. "Aportes dos Escravos na História do Cultivo do Arroz Africano nas Américas." *Estudos Sociedade e Agricultura* 12: 113–33.

Cascudo, L. C. 1983. *História da Alimentação no Brasil*, 2nd ed. Belo Horizonte: Itatiaia; São Paulo: Editora Da Usp.

Chermont, T. 1885. "Memórias sobre a Introdução de Arroz Branco no Estado do Grão Pará." *Revista Trimestral do Instituto Histórico Geográfico e Etnográfico do Brasil*, 770–84.

Copacabanarunners. 2011. "O Porquê do Arroz e Feijão." *Copacadana Runners*. Available at: http://www.copacabanarunners.net/arroz-feijao.html. Accessed November 30, 2009.

Duncan, T. B. 1972. *Atlantic islands: Madeira, the Azores, and the Cape Verdes in seventeenth century commerce and navigation*. Chicago: University of Chicago Press.

Elias, R. 2010. "História Da Feijoada." *Portal São Francisco*. Available at: http://www.portalsaofrancisco.com.br/alfa/história-da-feijoada/historia-da-feijoada.php. Accessed November 30, 2009.

El-Kareh, A. C. 2008. "A Vitória da Feijoada ou a Culinária como Afirmação da Identidade Brasileira (1808–1840)." *IV ENEC—Encontro Nacional de Estudos do Consumo*. Rio de Janeiro, September 24–26.

EMBRAPA. 2005. "Cultivo do Arroz Irrigado no Brasil. Importância Econômica, Agrícola e Alimentar do Arroz." *Sistema de Produção*, 3. Available at: http://sistemasdeproducao.cnptia.embrapa.br/FontesHTML/Arroz/ArrozIrrigadoBrasil/cap18.htm. Accessed November 30, 2010.

EMBRAPA. 2006. "Arroz e Feijão, o Par Perfeito do Brasil." *Embrapa Arroz e Feijão*. Available at: http://www.cnpaf.embrapa.br/parperfeito/index.htm. Accessed November 30, 2009.

EMBRAPA. 2009. "Programação Dia de Campo na TV." *Embrapa*. Available at: http://hotsites.sct.embrapa.br/diacampo/programacao/2009. Accessed November 30, 2009.

Ewbank, T. [1845] 1976. *A Vida No Brasil: ou Diário de uma Visita à Terra do Cacaueiro e das Palmeiras*. Belo Horizonte: Editora Itatiaia; São Paulo: Editora da Universidade de São Paulo.

Fernandes, C. 2000. *Viagem Gastronômica Através do Brasil*. São Paulo: SENAC, Editora Estúdio Sonia Robatto.

Freyre, G. [1933] 2006. *Casa Grande e Senzala*. São Paulo: Global Editora.

Lewicki, T. 1974. *West African food in the Middle Ages*. Cambridge: Cambridge University Press.

Littlefield, D. C. 1991. *Rice and slaves: Ethnicity and the slave trade in colonial South Carolina*. Urbana: University of Illinois Press.

Marques, C. 1870. *Dicionário Histórico e Geográfico da Província do Maranhão*. São Luis: Maranhão.

National Institute of Geography and Statistics (IBGE). 2006/2007. *Agricultural census*. Rio de Janeiro: IBGE.

National Research Council (NRC). 1996. *Lost crops of Africa*. Washington, D.C.: National Academy Press.

Paula Junior, T. J., and M. Venzon. 2007. *1001 Culturas—Manual de Tecnologias Agrícola.* Belo Horizinte: EPAMIG.

Pinto e Silva, P. 2005. *Farinha, Feijão e Carne-Seca: Um Tripé Culinário no Brasil Colonial.* São Paulo: Editora Senac São Paulo.

Portères, R. 1970. "Primary cradles of agriculture in the African continent." In *Papers in African prehistory*, ed. J. D. Fage and R. A. Oliver, 43–58. Cambridge: Cambridge University Press.

Portères, R. 1976. "African cereals: Eleusine, fonio, black fonio, teff, brachiaria, paspalum, pennisetum, and African rice." In *Origins of African plant domestication*, ed. J. Harlan, J. Wet, and A. Stemler, 409–52. The Hague: Mouton.

Primeiro, J. 1818. *Compêndio Histórico-político dos Princípios da Lavoura do Maranhão.* Paris: Fougeron.

Ribeiro, O. 1962. *Aspectos e Problemas da Expansão Portuguesa.* Lisboa: Junta de Investigações do Ultramar.

Saint-Hilaire, A. [1817] 1941. *Viagem pelo Distrito dos Diamantes e Litoral do Brasil.* São Paulo: Nacional.

Silva, R. S. 2008. "Arroz e Feijão, um Par Perfeito." *Cyberdiet*, February. Available at: http://cyberdiet.terra.com.br/arroz-e-feijao-um-par-perfeito-2-1-1-44.html. Accessed November 30, 2009.

Wied-Neuwied, P. M. 1942. *Viagem ao Brasil*, 1st ed. São Paulo: Companhia Editora Nacional.

Wood, P. 1974a. *Black majority.* New York: W. W. Norton.

Wood, P. 1974b. "'It was a Negro taught them': A new look at African labor in early South Carolina." *Journal of Asian and African Studies* 9: 160–79.

Woortmann, K. 2008. "Quente, Frio e Reimoso: Alimentos, Corpo Humano e Pessoas." *Caderno Espaço Feminino* 19 (1): 17–30.

Beyond Rice Neutrality
Beans as *Patria*, *Locus*, and *Domus* in the Brazilian Culinary System

Carlos Alberto Dória

Sorting beans borders on writing.

João Cabral de Melo Neto

The Structure of Rice and Beans

The globalization of the economy and culture demands a new territorial approach to the study of food habits. National-level analyses are now insufficient since local development—the expression of increased competition between production regions—has stimulated the definition and promotion of new subnational microspaces. The increase in globalization has paradoxically led to a continuing elaboration of local identities.

This process is widely visible in Europe where development strategies, stimulated by the Organisation for Economic Co-operation and Development (OECD) from the 1980s onward, led to the introduction of national legislation supporting and protecting local production. These laws have proven to be highly effective, especially in countries like Spain and Portugal, which have adopted approaches similar to the traditional French *terroir* model of producing and marketing farm food products. As a consequence, it is possible today to identify, for instance, a wide range of different qualities of olives, as in Spain, and new grape varieties as in Chile—products that used to be "hidden" under more general denominations. The United Nations Educational, Scientific and Cultural Organization (UNESCO) itself, in its effort to value cultural diversity, has been working to promote different types of country heritages, as shown by the examples of Mexican and French cuisine and other geographical approaches, most important the "Mediterranean diet," although Claude Fischler (1996) has shown this to be a relatively recent invention.

When we turn to Brazil, however, it is often difficult to perceive this dynamic of microspatial development since the logic of agribusiness has imposed itself as the dominant tendency across the country as a whole. From the formation of the modern Brazilian state after the 1930 Revolution until very recently there has never been any real concern with protecting or even recognizing the diversity of the productive system, or with addressing the effects of public policies on anything other than large-scale agribusiness. Although national statistics have included a census of small farming, the internal dynamics of small farms are less well known.

The predominance of large-scale agribusiness over small-scale farming practices has produced a kind of "constructed silence," even though the latter supplies many elements of the Brazilian staple diet. Bean production, still mostly confined to small farms, is also relatively invisible. It is this universe of small family farmers that is targeted by initiatives such as the Slow Food Movement, which work to give greater value to the diversity of beans and their many culinary uses. The present study therefore aims to help improve our understanding of this dynamic, largely hidden by the logic of agribusiness.

Rice and beans are the mainstay of Brazilian meals across all income classes and in all corners of the country. In this sense, they constitute the most typical national dish. Rice and beans, separately and combined, express the Brazilian variant of the Western dietary system, in which there is a single grammar for cooking and combining proteins and carbohydrates, while the actual ingredients of these categories vary widely according to local biodiversity (Dória 2009b).

The role of rice and beans in the country's food habits differs fundamentally from the way rice is used in other dietary systems, such as that of China, according to the interpretative schema proposed by Françoise Sabban (2001). She argues that rice is the base of the Chinese diet; its consumption is seen by the Chinese as providing all the nutrients necessary for living. Consequently, everything accompanying the rice is seen as merely a source of pleasure. Given this duality in values, Sabban argues that the Chinese culinary complex is structured by a clear dividing line between "eating to live" (nutrition) and "eating for pleasure."

This duality is very different in Brazil, where rice is not considered high in either cultural or nutritional value. It is much more neutral in meaning, and is sometimes even deprecated from both the nutritional and the gustative point of view. In fact rice consumption became widespread in the country only relatively recently, following on the arrival of the Portuguese Court (see Barbosa's chapter in this volume). Perhaps the only area where rice was highly valued by the lower-income classes was in "saint cooking," or *cozinha de santo*, a cuisine belonging to Bahia's candomblé religion, derived from the traditions of the Islamized former slaves, especially those living in the state of Salvador where the use of the cereal was especially prominent (Querino 1928: 8). This Afro-Brazilian diet, initially religious in origin, only spread widely after the abolition of slavery (1888), the unification of African cults, and increased police tolerance of *candomblé terreiros* (spaces where religious rites were performed, usually improvised in the backyards of households).

In this Africanized tradition, rice sometimes occupies important roles as the *arroz de assuá* (rice boiled in water without salt), and as the *massa* (cooked rice fried in palm oil or cooked in honey). Rice was also made into a drink, dissolved in water with sugar (Querino 1928: 8).

Beans, on the other hand, have a much deeper history. As registered by several researchers, beans have always been loved by working classes and their role as strategic food was recognized very early in Brazilian history. Beans were the sustenance, a way of promoting human energy. They were often eaten slowly, distributed to a circle of participants, in a ceremonial form. For the people, a meal without beans was simply a way of tricking hunger, not a way of feeding oneself. "Without beans there is no meal, only beans assuage hunger," was the refrain in the early nineteenth century (Cascudo 1983: 498).

Beans have been present in the diet of Brazilians since the beginning of European colonization, brought from Europe and Africa by the colonizers and combined with native varieties—although the indigenous cultures did not value or consume beans to any marked degree. But associated with the movement of territorial expansion, beans accompanied the settling of the *sitiantes*, or smallholders, in the four corners of the country, and were cultivated especially by women in fields planted close to their new dwellings. In this way a link was forged between beans and the people that has remained indissoluble throughout the course of history, even though in recent decades beans have declined in importance in the diet of urbanized people.

This profound historical link between beans and colonization generated the popular idiom of "being without a bean plant," synonymous with being short-sighted, careless, and lazy. Corroborating this perception, colonial travelers were almost unanimous in emphasizing beans' central role in people's diets, associated with manioc flour as a starch and accompanied by a protein, especially salted beef. In the case of *baião-de-dois* (the "couple-dance," a dish originating from Ceará, a region known for cattle), manioc flour and salted beef are absent: instead the dish combines rice, beans, and bacon fat (Cascudo 1972: 111).

With a few rare exceptions, there seem to be few direct associations between a bean variety and its use in a specific recipe. Two famous exceptions are *acarajé*—a deep-fried patty, served with a prawn sauce, always made from black-eyed peas— and *feijoada* (black bean stew). But even *feijoada*, a national dish usually associated with black beans, can appear in regional versions with other bean types, such as the *roxinho* bean in Pernambuco, used in a dish that combines different meats with vegetables such as burr cucumber (*Cucumis anguria*) and pumpkin (Saint Maur 2002: 60).

It is important to note, though, that history shows how beans, flour, and salted beef became the staple diet among Brazil's lower classes much earlier than the urban association of beans and rice (Silva 2005), which only took place in the nineteenth century, initially in Rio de Janeiro. But when this association finally took place, beans effectively assimilated and dissolved rice's "neutrality" and the pairing became a unity related to another complementary element added to the meal, the *mistura* or "mixture."

The combination of the *mistura* with rice and beans forms a domestic "full meal." However, when the *mistura* is eaten outside the household, it takes the form of the "ready meal," *prato feito*, known by its initials "PF" in the snack bars of the big cities, showing how the modern food ration is cast in the mold of tradition. Various kinds of PF are available on the market with the *mistura* varying among establishments or the day of the week. More recently restaurants selling a wider variety of cooked food per kilo (by weight) have taken over much of the market previously cornered by the PF option.

It is also worth noting that, in the food classification system distantly inspired by Galenic medicine, the bean is considered a "hot" food while rice is considered "cold." When planted in a multiple crop system, therefore, "a 'hot' plant like the bean should not be planted next to another 'hot' plant, but only next to a plant perceived as 'cold,' such as manioc" (Woortmann 2008: 19).

This is important for various reasons, especially economic ones. Manioc, the staple food for *caboclos* (mixed ethnic rural people) in various regions, requires enormous amounts of labor, both in planting and in processing the wet root into dry flour. Grown alongside manioc, though, beans allow a source of monetary income, or a good that can be exchanged for another food with neighbors, since production usually exceeds the needs of the nuclear family.[1] As well as enabling the balance between the family production unit and the market, beans also help equilibrate the individual helping to balance the diet with a proper combination of "hot" and "cold" foods. The combination of rice and beans therefore constitutes the Brazilian ideal of nutrition because it ensures balanced meals from every point of view. Moreover, it is also a gustative ideal, since references to this food pairing form an indispensable part of every discourse extolling the virtues of Brazilian cuisine.

Bean Diversity

For the historical reasons cited above, Brazilians have a complex relationship with beans, which is expressed in linguistic patterns. Beans are used universally in our cooking, in simple recipes drawing upon an enormous variety of genera, species, colors, and varieties. Despite this universality, beans are seldom mentioned in culinary discourse. On the contrary, a profound silence blankets their existence, reflected in the paucity of recipes in cookbooks. Probably this silence is due to the way methods of cooking beans were embedded in oral tradition and popular culture. Culinary literature (cookbooks) appeared late in Brazilian history, dating only to the last quarter of the nineteenth century and was restricted to the elites of the empire's capital. By contrast, everybody from the working classes must "know how to make" beans, which is a basic requirement of domestic life.

Consequently, any analysis of the history of beans has to start at the lexical and classificatory level. In fact the word *bean* designates different plant species and endless varieties of the species *Phaseolus vulgaris*, *Vigna unguiculata*, *Cajanus cajan*, *Vicia faba*, and *Phaseolus lunatus* (see Berleant this volume). Some Brazilian sources also list various animal fodder species as "beans," as well as others used as manure in coffee plantations. This means that the plants included in the "bean" class are extremely diverse both from a strictly botanical viewpoint and in terms of their use (Pereira 1929: 349–52).

On the other hand, a single variety of bean may be known by many different names, further complicating a lexical approach. In India the cowpea (called *chowlee* or *gubgub*) has been known for more than three thousand years. In Brazil, cowpeas (*Vigna unguiculata*) may be found as *feijão-bongalon*, *feijão-caupi*, *feijão miúdo*, *feijão de corda*, and so on. It first arrived in the northeast, brought from Africa by the Portuguese. Cowpeas may be eaten in the form of green or runner beans (pods), or as green or dried seeds. Black-eyed peas (a variety of cowpea) are used to make *acarajé*, perhaps derived from the Arabian falafel through the influence of Bahia's Islamized black population. Other Afro-Bahian recipes using this variety are *êcurú*, *humulucú* (beans with olive oil), and *abará*, similar to *acarajé*, but cooked in boiling water enclosed in banana leaves, a technique known as "banho-maria" (from the French).

From the viewpoint of *appearance*, beans present an immense array of sizes and colors, forming a spectrum ranging from white to black, passing through yellow, green, brown, and red, as well as mottled patterns in various colors and sizes. Unfortunately this diversity is obscured by statistics, making it difficult to establish any clear quantitative depiction of the regional usage of different beans.

From the quantitative standpoint, the Instituto Brasileiro de Geografia e Estatística's (IBGE) Family Budget Survey (2002/2003) reports that Brazilian households consume around 12.9 kilograms of beans per year, divided into eight of the main varieties among the hundreds grown in the country. In rural areas consumption rises to 23.5 kilograms per year, of which 10.9 kilograms were acquired by nonmonetary means.

The most popular varieties in the IBGE survey are pinto beans (*feijão rajado*), followed by black beans (*feijão preto*), and black-eyed peas (*feijão fradinho*). The last is the most rural variety. Its consumption in rural areas is three times the national average and nonmonetary acquisition of the bean is 2.3 times higher than the amount purchased. Pinto beans are also primarily consumed in rural areas (twice urban consumption) but in contrast to the black-eyed pea, the pinto bean is usually bought rather than grown or bartered.

The two largest supermarket chains sell between eight and thirteen varieties, with regional differences. However, a visitor to the food wholesale district in the center of São Paulo (named *zona cerealista*), where migrants from the poor northeastern parts of Brazil purchase their food supplies, will come across many varieties not sold anywhere else. The diversity found in the large urban centers therefore suggests that beans migrate with their consumers; more than two dozen varieties that are absent from the supermarket shelves are sold in markets. These rare varieties are only found in migrant kitchens and restaurants, part of a chain that links consumers, traders, transporters, and producers, within a kind of culinary ghetto, similar to the urban infrastructure supporting the foreign cuisines of the Jewish, Japanese, and Hungarian communities.

Other beans, unidentified by name in the official statistics, represent around 10 percent of the total consumption. However food preservationist initiatives, led by the Slow Food Movement, have brought to light an immense wealth of other rare varieties, produced and consumed especially in rural communities across the entire country, including cowpeas (*Vigna ungiculata*) with more than 300 varieties identified by the state-owned *Empresa Brasileira de Pesquisa Agropecuária* (Brazilian Company of Agriculture, EMBRAPA) in just one semiarid microregion of southern Piauí state.

When we analyze bean consumption in relation to income, the total amount consumed is slightly higher among the lower-income classes, and the varieties are distributed unequally across socioeconomic sectors. The pinto bean, black-eyed pea, and black bean are more heavily consumed among the poorer sections of the population, while wealthier strata tend to consume more *jalo* beans and very few black-eyed peas (3 percent of total beans, compared to 24 percent among lower-income groups). While black beans and pinto beans cut across the income levels, cowpeas and *jalo* beans differentiate rich and poor. But why this variety in beans? What do the different bean dishes tell us about Brazil?

The *mistura*—the dish that complements rice and beans—always reflects local circumstances, including everything from game meat to salted or fresh beef, pork, chicken, fish, eggs, or cooked vegetables and greens. On the other hand, the strength of the rice-beans association is corroborated by the almost complete absence of recipes that use beans but dispense with rice. Generally speaking, beans, even in simple recipes, are combined with two distinct sets of ingredients: (1) vegetable seasonings (onion, garlic, and bay leaf), and (2) pieces of pork and/or bacon rind. Dishes using pork give rise to the name *feijão gordo*, "fat beans," meaning "nutritious," while those without the addition of animal protein are called *feijão magro*, "lean beans." The advantage of fat bean dishes compared to lean beans is that they form a complete meal in themselves when eaten with rice. Lean beans, though, require *mistura* as well as rice. The most elaborate fat bean dishes are called *feijoada*. Figure 7.1 shows how fat and lean bean dishes are progressively elaborated, including the additions that can be made to them, following culinary practices typically found throughout Brazil. The arrows indicate the additions to fat beans and the subtractions that create lean beans.

Conceptually, a dish becomes fat with the simple addition of bacon rind, which is cooked with the beans. When augmented with other pork-derived ingredients the dish is called a *feijoada*, especially when these additions are made to a black bean stew. Lean beans, irrespective of the variety chosen, are dishes made basically with vegetables, sometimes with the addition of annatto (the most popular seasoning in Brazil, made from the red oil extracted from seeds of the achiote, *Bixa orellana*).

↓	**"Fattening" the Bean: The Path to *Feijoada***	**The Path to Lean Beans**	↑
↓	1. Fresh bacon rind	1. Sautéed in garlic, onion and bay leaves	↑
↓	2. Smoked bacon	2. Parsley and spring onion	↑
↓	3. Salted pork tail and ear	3. Annatto colouring	↑
↓	4. Pork sausages, smoked and unsmoked	4. Chopped spring onion or chopped coriander leaves	↑
↓	5. Salted beef		↑
↓	6. *FEIJOADA*		↑
↓	7. Accompaniments: collard greens, rice, orange slices, etc.		↑

Figure 7.1 Table showing the relationship between "lean" and "fat" beans in the general canon of Brazilian cuisine.

Lean beans are garnished with chopped spring onions or coriander following regional and family preferences: in the southeast, a simple mixture of sautéed onions, garlic, and bay leaf is added, while in the northeast coriander is used. A very simple and common seasoning for lean beans involves pounding together salt, parsley, garlic, and onion. This pesto is made in large batches and then stored for use in small amounts to season the beans cooked on a daily basis.

Feijoada *as a Metaphor*

It is worth analyzing the *feijoada* dish more closely, seeing the prominence given to this bean stew in the academic literature. As Paula Pinto e Silva points out:

> the recipes based on bacon fat and beans, whether black, brown or red, were described exhaustively by travellers, who often confused the name used to designate the dish: called feijoada by some [...] or simply "cooked" (cozido), "turned" (virado) or "fat" (gordo) beans by others. With or without their thick broth, the beans moistened the food and helped create a new taste. (Silva 2007: 14)

Feijoada can be considered the quintessence of "fat beans" enriched to the point of becoming a *prato único*, an "all-in-one dish." However, it cannot be understood without the ritual surrounding it—including the appropriate days of the week for its consumption—and its historical capacity to evoke nationalism. This set of factors transforms this version of "fat beans" into a *feijoada*, eaten on Saturdays or Wednesdays accompanied by collard greens and orange slices, as well as rice and, of course, a *caipirinha* made from limes and sugarcane rum. As one essayist wrote, "the feijoada may appear to us as a totality, as a self-identical unity; however, it may also appear to us as the casual uniting of disparate things" (Pompeu 1986: 18). This calendar of consumption was fixed by the old Rio boarding houses, which offered the dish as a speciality on these days of the week.

The close association between black beans and meat, which together form the *feijoada*, originated in Rio de Janeiro where black beans were popular, rather than on the sugar plantations as the staple food for slaves, as much food folklore insists. In Rio de Janeiro at the end of the eighteenth century, according to the testimony of travelers like Debret, the diet of urban slaves was centered on black beans, manioc flour, oranges, and bananas. The black population, especially the *negros de ganho* (urban blacks slaves who traded for their owners and kept a part of the income for themselves), used part of their income to buy salted beef or bacon fat to add to their beans (Cascudo 1983: 225). The folklorist Câmara Cascudo failed to unearth any reference to *feijoada* as a meal prior to the nineteenth century. But it was the modernists who used the *feijoada* as a sign of Brazilianness beginning in the 1920s. Brazilian modernism was an artistic-cultural movement inspired by futurism and other European aesthetic tendencies that managed, finally, after a long process spanning more than seventy years, to build a consensus around a national identity. Before this, the presence of a large slave population in Brazilian society had hindered the development of any unified notion of the nation or the state.

An endless series of discussions unfolded from the mid-nineteenth century onward, looking for an answer to the question of the place of black people within the Brazilian nation: would they be assimilated through a process of "whitening" the population, or would Brazil become a *mulata* nation, composed of a new type of human strongly shaped by the black presence? Racialist and racist theories in the second half of the nineteenth century informed this discussion, invariably depicting the black population as a factor contributing to the backwardness and degeneration of the Brazilian people.

It was from the modernists onward that a new racial ideology took hold, inverting the negative impression of the nation that had predominated earlier. The *mestiça* (mixed) nation began to be seen as a positive and original aspect of Brazil, thanks especially to works like the classic *Casa Grande e Senzala* (1933), by Gilberto Freyre. His ingenious argument, matched with a captivating style, was a true revolution in the way in which the formation of the Brazilian people was understood. The miscegenation of whites, blacks, and Indians under the control of large rural property owners legitimized the conviction that we Brazilians were all *mestiços* by definition.

Freyre's ideas had already been circulating in Brazilian culture since Modern Art Week of 1922, headed by Oswald and Mário de Andrade. Anthropophagy, cultural "swallowing," was a metaphor found throughout intellectual circles of the period. In the words of poet Jorge de Lima, it involved undertaking a huge enterprise of discovery, abandoning the callow way of seeing ourselves, as though we were Europeans or strangers in our own land, and "finding our own expression." For the modernists, the problem of national culture was *expression*.[2] Insofar as discovering our expression expanded into a program of searching, it also extended to the historical terrain of cuisine.

But cuisine was an almost entirely unexplored terrain in high-brow literature. If we turn to earlier research on Brazilian culture, such as the work of Sylvio Romero, we find almost no descriptions of Brazilian cooking. The exceptions are the pioneering book by Manoel Querino on the culinary arts in Bahia (Querino 1928) and the famous *Manifesto Regionalista*, published in 1926, where Freyre sets out the broad contours assumed by Brazilian national cuisine:

> Three culinary regions stand out in today's Brazil: Bahia, the Northeast and Minas Gerais. Bahian cuisine is undoubtedly the most powerfully imperial of the three. But perhaps it is not the most important from the viewpoint of a sociology of Brazil. Other, less important culinary traditions can be added, each with their own colour, to the map which forms of the variations in meals, deserts and side dishes in our country: the far North region with the predominant indigenous influence and the culinary complexes based on turtles [...] and Brazil nuts, which stands out not only in making sweets, but also in the regional soups—everything refreshed with the celebrated açaí [...]; the region formed by the states of Rio de Janeiro and northern São Paulo—cousin to the northeast in many aspects, conditioned by the very same agrarian-patriarchal traditions—and more than one Rio de Janeiro sub-region, by the abundant use of sugar; the southern region, where the cuisine is somewhat rustic, though more abundant than the others in good meat [...]. The rest could be described from the culinary point of view as the outback: areas still characterized by a rural form of cooking [...] and, in the forests of the country's centre, by the use of game and freshwater fish—all frugal and rustically prepared. Where the Portuguese influence appears to be strongest even today is on the coast, from Maranhão to Rio de Janeiro or Santos [...]. The African influence comes to the fore in Bahia. The Amerindian influence is particularly notable in the far North [...]. But as in other arts, the three great cultural influences found at the base of the principal regional Brazilian culinary traditions and their aesthetics are Portuguese, African and Amerindian, with the regional predominance signalled above. (Freyre 1952)

Gilberto Freyre's analytic starting point was the region. The literature in the 1930s adopted much the same approach and the southeastern industrial section of Brazil needed to discuss the part that was to be played in each region in the total composition of the nation. On the other hand, the complex theme of the coexistence of regional differences—or of the regional factions of the dominant classes within the state—required addressing the integrating level of the nation. The "national discourse" in the period of the New State onward (1937–1945) strongly stimulated the construction of "tradition" by seeking to identify and preserve the national heritage. This period saw the emergence of the National Historical Heritage Service, which today, more than seventy years later, works to identify and landmark the nation's intangible heritage, including its culinary traditions.

Feijoada is today more popular among the lower-income classes, occupying a marginal place in the cuisine of Brazil's elites. It is fairly common to find references to this dichotomy in Brazilian literature, including accounts of popular dishes being secretly consumed by the national elite. Hence we can identify a double standard in the affirmation of culinary tradition. From a perspective critical of the Europeanized elite, the nationalist writer Monteiro Lobato used heavy irony to discuss popular food habits that, in his view, provoked shame among the elite as much as did Brazilian art (painting, literature) freed of the European canons. "Chewing on roast suckling pig, stew, feijoada, maize cakes, muqueca and other savoury delights from our land is just as shameful as painting local landscapes, novelizing local tragedies, or poetizing the feelings of the people" (Sachetta 2008: 16).

Perhaps the dish really is identity-shaping, but the key point here is that while *feijoada* can be seen as a metonym for slavery, with its black beans and white rice, it can also symbolically subvert slavery when it is all eaten together. In and around the *feijoada* we find a practical syncretism of Indians, blacks, and whites, suppressing the knowledge that some were decimated, and others enslaved, while some were cruel exploiters (Doria 2009b).

As an allegorical celebration, *feijoada* has always had a special symbolic place in Brazil's food culture. Even so, it is not a *ceremonial* dish par excellence. Many other dishes compete alongside it. We have pizza and the Sunday pasta in São Paulo, barbecue in the south, and various other regional *dishes*, all of which are more popular and common than *feijoada* in their respective locations. Moreover, any statistical survey of Brazilian food habits shows that *feijoada* is not a daily dish—it is most often eaten on Wednesdays and Saturdays in the bars of the large cities. In sum:

> rejected in rural Brazil, where the festive meal is the barbecue, feijoada became consolidated as the national-popular dish through the triumph of industrial capital [...] having been hoisted as a rallying flag for national pride by urban intellectuals, champions of Brazil as a nation. As a result, enshrined as the national-popular dish in the Rio/São Paulo/Minas Gerais triangle, where the intellectual environment shaped by industrialization was concentrated, feijoada had—and still has—to confront other symbolic dishes in other regions of the country, meaning that its elevation to the status of Brazil's national-popular dish has to be considered as an ongoing process rather than an established fact. (Pompeu 1986)

Understanding the long process involved in creating the symbolic complexity of *feijoada* is essential for anyone studying gastronomy in Brazil. I would argue that this dish functions as a screen hiding an "other" Brazilian cuisine, concealing a vast range of uses of varieties of beans other than black, as we shall see below.

The Bean as Culinary Regionalism

Returning to the IBGE survey, when we focus on the nutritional importance of beans in the Brazilian diet, we can note that their contribution to the total calories consumed in the average diet differs in each federal state. While in Paraíba beans account for 11.9 percent of total calories, for 8.8 percent in Piauí, and 10.5 percent in Ceará, in Amazonas this total falls to 4.3 percent, close to the percentage found in the much richer states of the south and São Paulo, where beans constitute 4 percent of total calories. In the city of São Paulo the amount is equal to 1 percent.

In addition, the data show that in Minas Gerais and the states of the northeast, where the contribution of beans to the diet is higher, their acquisition through nonmonetary means, particularly household subsistence production, is also higher. In Minas Gerais, for example, the nonmonetary acquisition of beans reaches 30 percent of the total, 26 percent through own production and 4 percent through "gifts." In another state, Rio Grande do Norte, 24.6 percent of black-eyed beans are acquired through nonmonetary means, with 26 percent of this category corresponding to own production and 9.7 percent to "gifts," meaning within the web of neighborhood reciprocity. A typical example of reciprocity is the custom in the Pernambuco outback of the *cozinhado* (cooking) using the first harvest of beans, which are offered to neighbors and friends who then reciprocate with cookies or candies, and sometimes clothes for their godchildren within the neighborhood (Suassuna 2010: 63).

Amid all these transactions we can identify beans as a universal ingredient in domestic Brazilian cuisine and, at the same time, as an element fomenting its regional singularity, insofar as there is no nationally uniform type of bean popular everywhere. Hence the bean is a food category which, in the abstract, affirms the unity and uniqueness of the national diet (everyone eats beans) but which take material form as a distinct botanical object in each place (each person eats a type of bean specific to her locality). This way, comparing the uses of various beans with the black bean used in the *feijoada* dish, we can detect the contradictory process defining the nation in culinary terms.

A generalizing discourse on beans hinders us from developing a more intelligible breakdown of the national territory into smaller units, as found in the European practice of focusing on the unique qualities of each *terroir*. Many beans have a strictly local use: *feijão mouro* and *feijão cavalo* are almost exclusively used in Rio Grande do Sul. Others form extensive "islands" within the country, such as the black bean, widely eaten in Rio Grande do Sul and in Rio de Janeiro. Other, highly distinctive beans may change status over time: for example, the "little Santarém butter bean," a small local variety of the cowpea typically eaten in salads in Santarém, Amazonia, but now widely used in haute cuisine. Within the universe of beans in Brazil, this bean is the equivalent of the famous *lentille verte du Puy* in France, the first vegetable to receive Appellation d'origine contrôlée certification in 1996.

Domestic Seasoning

But what happens with beans at the household level? Here I wish to relate two personal observations. Years ago the keeper of a small farm I used to visit on weekends introduced me to his new partner. The following week the woman had already gone. I asked what had happened and he explained: "Ah, you've no idea how badly she seasoned her beans! No way it was going to work!!" Recently I heard various criticisms of a newly opened top restaurant in São Paulo, dedicated to Brazilian cuisine. Most of these complaints concerned the quality of the bean seasoning.

So how do we explain that the main attribute of beans has shifted here from the botanical variety to the additional seasoning? These two episodes, distant from each other in both space and time, lead me to venture the hypothesis that beans function as a more or less neutral counterpoint in Brazilian culinary discourse. Beans are a universal substance appropriated in such varying ways that it excuses us, in everyday life, from having to reflect overly about it. In other words, for me only "my beans" exist and they are linked, by the seasoning, to the subjective universe. At this level of values, the culinary discourse surrounding beans concerns another object—the seasoning. Consequently, it involves an adjectival discourse that refers us directly to domestic space.

Each house possesses its own particular seasoning for beans, usually made from a variety of ingredients that also express regional identity. Whatever the variety of beans used, a home's kitchen will be identified above all by its seasoning, thereby harmonizing domestic cooking with regional and national cooking. It is as though, in this space, *need* assumes the form of *pleasure*—to return to the dichotomy identified by Sabban in Chinese cuisine—as a synonym of *familiarity*, the food in its domestic guise. To the purely nutritional, the home adds pleasure.

This is why a public discourse on the gustative qualities of beans makes no sense. As Brazilian culture does not look to establish a fixed way of seasoning them, what really matters in each home emerges only in domestic discourse or in relations with the immediate neighborhood. My hypothesis is that the same happens with beans as can be observed in relation to the identity-shaping dishes of various traditions, such as the Jewish *gefilte fish*: the dish made by "our mother" is always better than the one made by "our mother-in-law" and so on, to the point where there are very few ethnic restaurants that exploit this intimate cuisine. Only the Arab, Japanese, Italian, and French cuisines, for very specific historical reasons, have managed to break past this domestic barrier to reach a wider public.

The Bean as Cultural Marker

Based on the above considerations, we can advance the general hypothesis that beans are the culinary element linking the country (*patria*) to the region or locality (*locus*) and to the family (*domus*) in a system of complementary similarities as shown in

Figure 7.2. The *national* myth of the *feijoada* locates us historically as a mixed or *mestiço* people, maintaining in particular the memory of the black population (whether in the color of the bean, or in the legend that the dish originated in the *senzalas* or slave quarters). The hundreds of regional varieties locate us spatially in singular communities, segregated "beanwise" but bordering many others. Finally the seasoning and skill of cooking the beans tells us about our family and our idiosyncratic preferences. This is what I call the *silent discourse* of the bean, a discourse that conceals the enormous diversity of the *domus* and which, conversely, becomes more uniform as we approach the *patria*. It tells us that the symbolic plasticity of beans provides Brazilians with what we could call a *cultural marker*, which can be taken as analogous to biological markers, as Lévi-Strauss teaches us:

> a culture consists of a multiplicity of characteristics that it has partially in common (albeit at different levels) with neighbouring or distant cultures from which, in terms of other aspects, it is separated in a more or less accentuated way. These characteristics balance out within a system that must be long-lasting. ... To develop certain differences ... the conditions needed are ... identical to those that stimulate biological differentiation between populations: relative isolation for a prolonged period of time, limited cultural or genetic exchanges. In a certain sense, cultural barriers are the same as biological barriers. (Lévi-Strauss 1971: 19)

Not by chance, the generation of bean varieties through the process of artificial selection projects, on the biological plane, the preferences of the communities involved. As shown by a recent study of farmers dedicated to crop improvement practices, bean varieties are more highly valued by farmers when the strains are lighter in color (Reis Sena 2008: 407). Criteria such as productivity—pursued by rural extension officers—were of much less concern to farmers.

Hence the discourse/silence of this marker is itself expressive and can be used to generate a culinary map markedly different from those with which we are accustomed. But taken by themselves, the species or varieties do not tell us everything; only when cooked according to regional and family preferences do they constitute elements of the "invisible cuisine," to use Esther Katz's apt expression (Katz 2009). By this Katz refers to those dimensions of cooking that embody hidden social realities that are not directly evident in the material practices of food transformation.

Level of representation	Link with beans
Patria	*Feijoada* with black beans
Locus	Hundreds of regional varieties of beans
Domus	Family seasoning

Figure 7.2   Table illustrating the way beans function as representations of different levels of identity.

And what is the role of "invisible" cuisine if not to locate those who share a deter-mined position as bearers of an identity that is not commonly shared and, therefore, not placed in doubt? Beans are the clearest expression of the dynamic of Brazil's culinary heritage. They possess an indisputable and undisputed gustative quality, precisely because all those who share them are both building on original uniformity and diversifying to new varieties of colors and shapes. Strictly speaking, a person only changes her preferential variety of bean when changing her group of reference over the course of life. In becoming urbanized, I abandon my local bean in favor of those sold in the supermarkets, but, while the ties to the rural world persist, I still have access to the "real bean" sent by relatives or available from commercial centers catering to immigrants. And indeed this personal path mirrors the trajectory taken by beans: in a history spanning centuries that begins with the artificial selection of local varieties, and ends with their suppression when they lose their previous symbolic function, being replaced through the adoption of new varieties that help to write the new history of the individual. Hence the "cultural biography" (Kopytof 1986) of the bean—at once univocal and diverse—reveals its importance as a symbolic substrate of the diet of the nation, the community, and the family.

In practical terms, no nation can be taken as a homogenous reality at any level of culture, as explained by Charles Tilly (1992). As I have tried to show here, the example of beans casts light on a historical and cultural dynamic in which families and com-munities, at the same time as they form part of a wider economic and social order, work to maintain the particularities that ensure the discontinuity of space and society. Tilly has demonstrated in another context that the nation is in general a unifying myth con-structed at the cost of repressions and suppressions that nonetheless maintain cultural traits over lengthy periods of time, which reappear when the state's control diminishes. If we let go of our prejudices, we can indeed approach the bean as a *multiplex* capable of teaching us much about the hidden diversity of "being Brazilian" at the table.

Notes

1. Information gathered by the author from manioc producers in Carvão, a locality in the municipality of Mazagão (AP), in July 2009.
2. "Strange, pernicious currents of thought divert the Brazilian spirit from the dis-covery of its expression, its rhythms, its truths. ... The first attempts at national expression were therefore all false through exaggeration" (Lima 1980: 380).

References

Cascudo, C. 1972. *Dicionário do folclore brasileiro*. 1. Rio de Janeiro: Instituto Na-cional do Livro.
Cascudo, C. 1983. *História da alimentação no Brasil*. Belo Horizonte: Itatiaia.

Dória, C. A. 2009a. *A culinária materialista*. São Paulo: Senac.

Dória, C. A. 2009b. *A formação da culinária brasileira*. São Paulo: Publifolha.

Fischler, C. 1996. *Pensée magique et alimentation aujourd'hui*. Les Cahiers de L'OCHAT, Paris, 2–27.

Freyre, G. 1952. "O manifesto regionalista de 1926: Vinte e cinco anos depois." In *Manifesto Regionalista de 1926*. Recife: Região.

Instituto Brasileiro de Geografia e Estatística (IBGE). 2002/2003. *Pesquisas de Orçamentos Familiares*. Available at: http://www.ibge.gov.br/home/estatistica/populacao/condicaodevida/pof/2002aquisicao/default.shtm. Accessed April 1, 2011.

Katz, E. 2009. "Alimentação indígena na América Latina: Comida invisível, comida de pobres ou patrimônio culinário?" *Espaço Ameríndio* 3 (1): 25–41.

Kopytoff, I. 1986. "The cultural biography of things: Commoditization as process." In *The social life of things: Commodities in cultural perspective*, ed. A. Appadurai, 64–91. Cambridge: Cambridge University Press.

Lévi-Strauss, C. 1971. *A cor da pele influencia as idéias?* São Paulo: Escola de Comunicação e Artes/USP.

Lima, J. 1980. "Todos cantam sua terra." *Poesia Completa* 2 (2): 380.

Pereira, H. 1929. *Pequena contribuição para um diccionario das plantas úteis do Estado de São Paulo (indígenas e aclimatadas)*. São Paulo: Typographia Brasil de Rothschild & Co.

Pompeu, R. 1986. *A dialética da feijoada*. São Paulo: Vértice.

Querino, M. 1928. *A arte culinária na Bahia*. Salvador: Papelaria Brasil.

Reis Sena, M. 2008. "Envolvimento de agricultores no processo seletivo de novas linhagens de feijoeiro." *Ciência Agrotécnica* 32 (2): 407–12.

Sabban, F. 2001. *Manger et cuisiner en Chine*. Available at: http://www.clio.fr/BIBLIOTHEQUE/Manger_et_cuisiner_en_Chine.asp. Accessed May 15, 2010.

Sachetta, V. 2008. *À mesa com Monteiro Lobato*. São Paulo: Senac.

Saint Maur, Q. G. 2002. *Muito prazer, Brasil. Variações contemporâneas da cozinha regional brasileira*. São Paulo: A & A Comunicação.

Silva, P. P. 2005. *Farinha, feijão e carne seca. Um tripé culinário no Brasil colonial*. São Paulo: Senac.

Silva, P. P. 2007. "Papagaio cozido com arroz: Livros de cozinha e receitas culinárias no Rio de Janeiro do século XIX." PhD diss., USP (Department of Anthropology), São Paulo.

Suassuna, A.R.D. 2010. *Gastronomia Sertaneja, Melhoramentos*. São Paulo: s.n.

Tilly, C. 1992. *Coerción, Capital y Estados Europeus, 990–1990*. Madrid: Alianza Editorial.

Woortmann, K. 2008. "Quente, frio e reimoso: Alimentos, corpo humano e pessoas." *Caderno Espaço Feminino* 19 (1): 17–30.

–8–

Cookup Rice
Guyana's Culinary *Dougla* and the
Performance of Guyanese Identities

Gillian Richards-Greaves

Introduction

Social scientists have extensively examined the ways that food serves as a source of physical nourishment as well as a code for understanding individual human behaviors and social interactions (Douglas 1971; Counihan 1999; Wilk 1999; Mintz and Du Bois 2002). As a cultural performance, the messages encoded in food are especially crucial to the negotiations of identities, as they exemplify the underlying meanings and values of any society (Fischler 1988: 275). Among Guyanese in Guyana, as well as among those who migrated to other regions of the world, "Guyanese food" is both the "substance and substantiation" of Guyaneseness (Harris-Shapiro 2006: 78). On the Guyanese foodscape, cookup rice occupies an essential place among Guyana's cuisines, presenting a gustatory portrait of the diversity and complexity that is Guyana (see Figure 8.1).

"*Dougla* pot," "mix-up," and "put together" are some of the adjectives used by Guyanese to describe cookup rice, a dish made with rice, peas, coconut milk, and diverse ingredients, and served in virtually every social context.[1] Unlike other Guyanese cuisines, which are inherently connected to a specific "race" or ethnic group, and are often manipulated to deepen the racial divide that is characteristic of the Guyanese society, cookup, by virtue of its potential versatility, is a "no-nation" dish that belongs to everyone and no one simultaneously. I argue, therefore, that cookup serves as a crucial site for examining the nuances of performances of Guyanese identities, including the intersections of race, class, migration, and nationhood, as it presents a "rich symbolic alphabet" (Counihan and van Esterik 1997: 2) of Guyanese embedded systems of meaning. I examine the performance of cookup as "a multilayered discourse employing multiple voices and perspectives" (Drewal 1992: 11), and as a "dialogic" (Bakhtin 1981) in which ideas and influences of food performance flow back and forth between cooks and audiences, homeland and diaspora, creating a sort of "feedback loop" (Nauta 1972).

Figure 8.1 Pigeon peas and red beans cookup, with chicken feet, pumpkin and other veggies, prepared by the author's mom, Waveney. Photo by the author.

Historical Demography of Guyana

The Cooperative Republic of Guyana (formerly British Guiana) is located on the northeastern portion of South America, and is the only English-speaking sovereign nation on the continent. Guyanese often refer to Guyana as "the Land of Six Races," as a way of referencing the country's racial and ethnic diversity, which are informed by slavery, colonialism, and industry, among other factors, and include people from England, Ireland, Portugal, India, and the continent of Africa (Knight and Palmer 1989). *Amerindian* is a term used to refer to a diverse body of native Guyanese Indians, including Wai-Wais, Arawaks, and Makushis. Amerindians primarily reside in the hinterlands and account for approximately 9 percent of the country's population. Europeans account for less than 1 percent of Guyana's population, and include descendants from the British "imperial" diaspora and the Portuguese "labor" diaspora, which was historically categorized as nonwhite or subwhite.[2] The African "victim" diaspora was forcibly migrated during the institution of slavery and is the second-largest ethnic group, constituting about 30 percent of the population. Guyana's largest ethnic group is the East Indian (Indian) "labor" diaspora, which accounts for 43 percent of the population. Their ancestors migrated from India under a system of indentured servitude, to fill the labor vacuum that emerged after the abolition of slavery and the subsequent mass migration of Africans from plantations to urban centers. Although the Chinese "trade" diaspora is historically visible in areas of academics, politics, business, and food production, its members constitute only a minute segment of the population (less than 1 percent). *Douglas* account for 17 percent of the population, and is the fastest-growing and most racially ambiguous ethnic group in Guyana, as it comprises mixed-race individuals.

The term *Dougla* originated from the Bhojpuri and Hindi word *doogala*, meaning "two-necks." *Dougla* also has other meanings, including "many," "mix," and "much," and negative connotations, such as "bastard."[3] In Guyana, the term *Dougla* historically referred to the "offspring of an [East] Indian and African sexual union" (Mehta 2004: 543), where the East Indian parent was more than likely of Madrasi heritage, and resided in close proximity to African Guyanese. Madrasis are the darker-skinned East Indians, who, like their African Guyanese counterparts, were generally regarded by other East Indian (Hindu) Guyanese as "undesirable outcasts" (Mehta 2004: 543). Nowadays, however, the term *Dougla* encompasses all biracial or multiracial individuals, in particular those with observable "African" physical features. Thus, Guyanese use labels such as *Cooley-Dougla* (of East Indian and African ancestry), *Putagee-Dougla* (of Portuguese and African ancestry), and *Bouviander* (of Amerindian and African ancestry) to distinguish between various *Douglas*, by highlighting their racial composition, based on physical features, genealogy, and other factors.[4] More important, *Dougla* does not seem to carry the same negative connotations as it did in the past, or among non-Hindu Guyanese.

Depending on the context, Guyanese would lightheartedly or disparagingly refer to *Douglas* as "all-nation" or "no-nation," as a way of indexing their inability or refusal to belong to any specific race, while at the same time, referencing their membership, often arbitrarily, in several racial groups or "nations." However, the ways *Douglas* self-identify are influenced by a range of factors, including the geographic areas in which they were raised, the relatives among whom they live, and the existing political climate in Guyana. The past two decades, for instance, have witnessed the rise in the percentage of "Mixed" and "Other" racial categories on the Guyana census, possibly indexing *Douglas* exercise of agency to affirm racial identities that are independent of the larger, warring African and Indian populations or other races.[5]

This growth in the *Dougla* population in Guyana has far-reaching implications, as various political factions aggressively vie for their vote. When they migrate to the United States and other regions of the world, *Douglas* adopt a range of racial labels, which sometimes change over time, depending on phenotype and other factors. Some identify as "black," others continue to be "other," some self-identify with

Indian or other nonblack ethnic groups, and some even "become" white. Regardless of what race they identify with, or whether they reside in Guyana or abroad, *Douglas* continue to occupy an ambiguous yet crucial space on Guyana's political and social landscape.

Since gaining independence from England in 1966 Guyana has been marred by racial and political discord, which frequently culminated in physical violence, and contributed to the country's economic and social degeneration (Williams 1991). The two principal opposing factions are East Indian Guyanese, who are predominantly Hindus and Muslims, and African Guyanese who primarily practice Christianity, as well as various African-derived religions. Racial and religious divisions are further complicated by political processes, as the largely East Indian Peoples Progressive Party (PPP) and the predominantly African Peoples National Congress (PNC) consistently vie for control of Parliament and the privileges that accompany such political sovereignty (Rabe 2005). As racialized political divisions continue to worsen, they undermine social cohesion and impede economic development in an already impoverished nation, which some commentators also regard as a failed state (Kissoon 2010).[6] To combat what they perceive to be the ultimate demise of their country, and possibly, to achieve political gain, a few politicians and well-intentioned citizens alike work feverishly to promote some semblance of unity as extolled by the country's motto, "One People, One Nation, One Destiny." It is, however, a difficult task, as the country's ethnic diversity is often a double-edged sword of culinary richness as well as societal divisions.

The appearance of unity and diversity is often enacted through cultural performances, which overwhelmingly highlight the contributions of East Indian Guyanese and African Guyanese. For example, when African Guyanese convene annually on August 1 to celebrate Emancipation Day, which commemorates the liberation of their enslaved African ancestors, they invite black performers from other Caribbean and African nations; pour libations to welcome or appease their ancestors; pray in Swahili and other African languages; perform other Africanized religious rites; wear African attire; engage in *Maafa* dances and African-centered musical presentations; and eat fufu, conkee, and other African foods.[7] Conversely, Indian Guyanese celebrate Indian Arrival Day, where they memorialize *their* ancestors' journey to Guyana and their subsequent struggle. They invite delegates from India; wear saris and other Indian attire; perform Indian songs and dances; eat dahl pouri, curry, and other East Indian foods; and, like their African Guyanese counterparts, honor their *own* heroes. There are cultural performances that celebrate the contributions of other Guyanese ethnicities, such as Chinese Arrival, which honors the contributions of Chinese to Guyana's history and development, and *Guyfesta* (Guyana Festival of Arts), which celebrates artistic and other cultural contributions of all of Guyana's races. However, these celebrations pale in scope and divisiveness to those of the Africans and Indian Guyanese. Although the Guyanese community draws on a plethora of cultural performances, Guyanese foods present particularly observable and resilient cultural performances of diversity, division, and unity.

Guyana's Foodscape

The presence and prominence of food is so pervasive in Guyana that a brief survey of the country would reveal a fascinating gastronomic bricolage that also references the country's racial divide. One of the most prominent and visible features of Guyana's food system is the "market square" (open market), often located toward the central and busiest areas of most towns. Crammed with countless stalls selling locally grown produce, homemade snacks, and imported prepackaged food items, the market square is the primary shopping center for fresh fruits and vegetables, and even apparel. The constant clamor of vendors announcing the nature and cost of their merchandise often overshadows the voices of customers negotiating with sellers the lowest possible price for their items of purchase. In addition to market squares, Western-style supermarkets are food centers that primarily sell dried, canned, and packaged groceries, and in particularly large quantities. More prevalent in Guyana, though less impressive than supermarkets, are the countless "snackettes" (small shops that sell homemade cuisines, and imported prepackaged snacks, and beverages) that populate local neighborhoods and serve as a convenient food source for patrons. The local street-side vendors with their large plastic containers with bowls or parcels of channa (a delicacy made of fried chickpeas), plantain chips (thinly sliced, salted, and fried plantains), and homemade meals are not to be overlooked as they provide nutrition and dialogue for regular customers or impromptu snacks for hungry and curious passersby.

Restaurants constitute another facet of Guyana's foodscape that many Guyanese regard as invaluable to the cultural climate, as they allow for the enjoyment of home-style cooking outside of the home. Guyanese who have lived or traveled abroad, for example, often declare that chow mein (a type of noodle), fried rice, and other "Guyanese Chinese" far exceed those they had eaten abroad, both in presentation and taste. Also Guyanese traveling to other countries often carry boxes of frozen Chinese food, as well as other kinds of Guyanese cuisines as part of their luggage.

Although markets, restaurants, snackettes, and street vendors are crucial components of Guyana's culinary network, the home serves as the principal wellspring and determinant of that complex system. Some Guyanese acquire culinary training in home economics courses in high schools, and from the Carnegie School of Home Economics, but most of them principally learn the art of cooking and "bargaining" for the necessary groceries from the women in the home and community. However, whether Guyanese cuisines are produced in homes or schools, by vendors or housewives, acts of cooking and eating in Guyanese society are ultimately underscored by cultural baggage of race, class, and gender, and serve as symbols of those various identities.

Through food Guyanese carve out the spaces that demarcate husband, wife, mother, children, friend, foe, Guyanese, "foreigner," and more. Mothers prepare their daughters for marriage, and specifically how to be "good" wives and mothers, by teaching them how to cook multiple and varied Guyanese cuisines. A young woman who gets married before first learning how to cook adequately can bring "shame" to her mother, who is principally charged with the nurturing and overall "home-training" of her children. Women also assert their own virtue, as well as subservience to men, by engaging in explicit and covert competitions of food preparation and presentations with other women. For women, cooking is a performance, which is executed to solicit praise for the cook, and to elevate her reputation above other women's (Wilson 1973). Conversely, men's virility, physical strength, reputation, and statuses in society are gauged by the quantity and quality of foods they consume (Kahn 1986: 1).

More often than not, men are ultimate judges of food performances, and their favorable "rulings" on a woman's cooking could earn her financial support, elevated status in the community, and marriage proposals. Food preparation and consumption therefore constitute culinary performances whose success and failure are determined by the participants who consume and evaluate the food. The feedback loop that is created by successful performances of food preparation and subsequent praise facilitates the perpetuation of those performances. It is therefore not surprising that food preparation and presentation, or the lack thereof, serve as crucial justifications for men's abandonment or abuse of women, and the community's deafening silence toward such behaviors (Murcott 1983; Devault 1997: 180). Interestingly, food also serves as a source of power, as women are principally responsible for "food acquisition, preparation, provisioning, and cleanup" (Counihan 2004: 1). Additionally, food is the weapon of choice for many women, who retaliate against physical and emotional abuse by poisoning their offenders' food, or putting obeah in their meals to harm or control them (Behar 1989: 180). Because of this negative power ascribed to food, Guyanese are often apprehensive of eating food prepared by people with whom they are feuding (Meigs 1997: 103).

The importance of food for Guyanese is also exemplified in the ways they personify cuisines and food items to convey specific messages about the speaker, the audience, or the food itself. Some of the more frequently expressed personifications of food include "chow mein is a man that dis sour fast" (chow mein spoils quickly) and "Curry is man that dis sour on you easy, easy and you don't even know" (curry can spoil and yet go unnoticed by the person eating it). There is no consensus on why certain foods are often regarded as masculine, but Guyanese generally grasp the overarching messages that chow mein spoils quickly, and thus should not be exposed or unrefrigerated for any length of time; additionally, one should refrigerate curried dishes or, at least, avoid eating ones that are left exposed. These statements also serve as cautionary measures to prevent possible food poisoning.

Guyanese also add human characteristics to various foods when addressing more risqué subjects. Vegetables, such as plantains, are often used to reference the male genitalia, while broth, soup, and metegee serve as wellsprings for conversations about coitus. The plantain's presumed likeness to the penis, coupled with Guyanese's shared belief that "ground provisions" (plantain, cassava "yuka," and other types of tubers) produce physical strength and virility in men, allow for soup and metegee, which are both prepared with ground provisions, to be effortlessly manipulated in conversations that reference sexual intercourse. In addition to gendered labels and sexual implications, Guyanese often ascribe human and animal characteristics, such as "running," "walking," "strong," and "tiger," to their foods.

Mary Weismantel states, "It is because they are ordinarily immersed in everyday practice in a material way that foods, abstracted as symbols from this material process, can condense in themselves a wealth of ideological meanings" (1988: 7–8). In the Guyanese community, food has the unique ability to symbolize racial diversity and division, as most Guyanese cuisines are inherently linked to specific race. Guyanese foods can generally be traced back to the original homelands from which Guyanese migrated, and, in spite of changes in manners of preparation that have occurred, the overarching constituencies of these foods have survived with some degree of constancy. Thus, Guyanese regard roti and curry as Indian foods, while fufu and metegee (plantain, various types of tubers, and meats, boiled in coconut milk) are African in origin. Pepper-pot, Guyana's national dish, is an Amerindian construct, chow mein is an invented Chinese dish, and so forth.[8] Cookup rice is one of the few cuisines that, like *Douglas*, occupy a relatively ambiguous racial space in the Guyanese community.

Although Guyanese frequently claim race-blindness with regard to "Guyanese food," the average Guyanese is an informed consumer who understands the seemingly inherent linkages between race and food. From early childhood Guyanese are socialized in the practices of racializing food, and this race-based culinary education is continued through higher education, as recipes, images, and the extensive addressing of food preparation and consumption undergird textbook discussions on the contributions of the different races. Guyanese agree that different races produce unique cuisines, but folk sayings, such as "Plantain and duff mek Blackman tuff" (Plantain and dumplings makes the African race physically strong), seem to highlight the underlying assumption that food also produces race. While Guyanese may attend the same schools and places of worship, work at the same jobs, and even enjoy the same cuisines, when they sit down to dine, they can also identify the distinct races represented on their plate.

The perceptions, importance, and place of food within the Guyanese community remain firmly entrenched in their psyche and daily routines long after they relocate to other regions of the world. Although "Guyanese food," regarded as an entity, occupies a central place in the Guyanese community in Guyana and abroad, certain cuisines, such as cookup rice, are regarded as unique, and occupying a crucial place in the said community, as they somehow capture the essence of Guyaneseness. But, how did this rice and peas dish assume such prominence on Guyana's foodscape?

Background of Cookup Rice

Rice has been actively cultivated in Guyana since the late 1800s. During its early stages, rice was produced by hand, but later, oxen were used in cultivation in order to increase production. After World War II, rice production experienced mechanization, as rice farmers in the villages along the coast began using tractors and combines in farming (Richardson 1974: 239). East Indian farmers were, and still are, the principal rice growers, who also implemented newer forms of irrigation and rice farming, which aided in the expansion of rice production in Guyana (Smith 1980: 61–66). This is one of the principal reasons that Guyanese often credit East Indians with the domestication of rice, and with the staple's presence in Guyana, and prominence in Guyanese diet. Recent scholarship has, however, demonstrated that rice was cultivated and consumed in West Africa long before the advent of the Atlantic slave trade, and was more than likely brought to the New World by enslaved Africans (McGowan et al. 2009: 8).

In his research on the origins of rice in South Carolina, Daniel Littlefield (1981) argued that certain ethnic groups in West Africa were targeted during the slave trade specifically for their expertise in rice cultivation (see Twitty this volume). As many of the African ethnicities in California were also brought to Guyana and other parts of the Caribbean, it is arguable that they brought with them the expertise of rice production (Carney 2001: 1), which was later expanded upon by East Indians during indentured servitude. How did the plethora of peas enter Guyanese diet?

Beans and peas originated in diverse regions of the world (Albala 2007), and some types, such as lentils, are well documented in the Bible, as well as other ancient texts. According to Albala (2007), lentils originated in the Fertile Crescent (9–24), lupines in Europe and the Andes (26–35), fava beans in Europe (33–74), and black-eyed peas in Africa (120), which were brought to Guyana by colonizers, slaves, indentured laborers, and other agents during the eighteenth and nineteenth centuries. Often associated with poverty, peas became a crucial part of the diet of slaves, as well as indentured servants, as it provided a "cheap and economically efficient way to meet nutritional requirements" (Albala 2007: 2). Although Guyanese consume an abundance of peas, different races tend to utilize certain types of peas more than others, and particularly in culturally specific contexts. East Indians, for instance, use lentils to prepare dahl (a type of soup), dahl pouri (a type of flatbread "roti" made with ground yellow split peas), while African Guyanese overwhelmingly use black-eyed peas to prepare cookup rice during African-centered events. Although Guyanese might highlight racial differences through the peas they use, Guyanese of all races utilize peas specifically to prepare cookup rice, a dish with an ambiguous history.

In order to better understand the history and place of cookup rice in the Guyanese community, I drew on my varied experiences with the Guyanese community and with the dish, which was informed by birth, migration to the United States, three years of dissertation research, and more than thirty informal interviews, which I conducted via telephone and the Internet. I was born in Linden, Guyana, and resided there for the first seventeen years of my life. It was there that I acquired the skills necessary to prepare a wide array of Guyanese cuisines, and to participate in the obsessive, often arbitrary, judgments of food aesthetics. After migrating to the United States in 1989, I discovered that the issues surrounding identity, food preparation, and consumption are further complicated when Guyanese migrate to other regions of the world and find themselves in a milieu of diverse Caribbean foodscapes (Jackson and Cothran 2003).

I resided in Brooklyn, New York, for almost sixteen years, in areas with high concentrations of Caribbean nationals (West Indians), including Crown Heights, Brownsville, and Flatbush (Kasinitz 1992). I also spent considerable amounts of time in and around Jamaica, Queens, which also has a visible West Indian population. In New York City I observed that members of the various West Indian nationalities often prepare the same or similar foods, but generally claim to be able to distinguish their cuisines from those of other West Indians based on unique aromas and flavors. It is not uncommon to hear, for example, a Trinidadian national say, "This curry tastes like a Guyanese curry" or similar comments in which food is used to index a particular Caribbean nationality. Although a Trinidadian might have prepared the curry, comments like these are rooted in the assumption that each Caribbean country has its own unique blends of herbs and spices that are decipherable by its nationals, making them able to distinguish their country's curry from that of another Caribbean country. These types of responses are also influenced by an acute awareness of self and "Other," which is produced and heightened by constant comparing and contrasting of similar cuisines in diverse contexts. It was my sustained exposure to the ethnic diversity that is New York City, and particularly, to "Caribbean New York" with its presumed culinary sameness of diverse West Indians, that trained me to observe the meticulous, often humorous, ways that Guyanese identities are constructed, contested, performed, and evaluated through food (Wilk 2006).

Between fall 2005 and fall 2008, I inadvertently initiated a sustained examination of the role of food in the Guyanese community, when I embarked on the first phase of a comparative dissertation research project in New York City, to investigate the role of kweh-kweh ritual among the African Guyanese diaspora. I discovered that although singing and dancing are the most visible performances at any kweh-kweh, food is a plumbline, which determines the success or failure of the ceremony. In Guyana, where I conducted the second phase of my dissertation research (fall 2008 to spring 2010), I observed that the abundance, performance, and relentless scrutiny of food at kweh-kweh is especially heightened. More important, "coconut foods," such as cookup rice, which African Guyanese regard as African in origin, are a staple at every kweh-kweh. At one kweh-kweh I attended in Georgetown, Guyana, there were three different types of cookup—black-eyed, split peas, and channa (chick-peas)—and the trays were replenished throughout the night. As kweh-kweh attendees strolled pass the buffet-style table they took servings of each type of cookup and later offered their unsolicited verdict on the quality of the food. By the time I had the opportunity to peel myself away from my camcorder to get a bite, I already knew that the channa cookup "ain't saying nothing" (was not up to standard), while the split peas cookup was "sweet bad" (extremely delicious). As any inquisitive researcher, I tried and enjoyed them all.

In addition to my upbringing and dissertation research, I gained great insight into the place of cookup among Guyanese by asking specific questions about the dish. I spoke with several of my kweh-kweh research consultants, and posed five questions by telephone and the Internet to friends, acquaintances, and other willing participants in various regions of the world. I received responses from more than thirty individuals who were predominantly Guyanese, and who provided varying degrees of detail regarding their experience with cookup rice. Non-Guyanese consultants had close associations with Guyanese through marriage or social networks, or had eaten cookup on several occasions. Five of the respondents were men, four identified as East Indian, and one as Amerindian. It is important to note that almost all of the individuals that provided feedback, and particularly those who identified as "African" or "black," also claimed membership in other racial groups. The questions were as follows:

1. What do you think about when you hear the word *cookup*?
2. As a Guyanese/non-Guyanese, what specifically would you like me to address about cookup rice?
3. Who eats cookup rice?
4. How is cookup rice meaningful/meaningless to you?
5. What question did I not ask about cookup rice that you think is important?

My observations and analyses of the responses to the questions I posed revealed that Guyanese hold differing perspectives on the history and place of cookup rice in the Guyanese community. African Guyanese regard cookup in a similar manner that African Americans regard "soul food"—as involving unique, often-unhealthy food items and methods of preparation, but encoded with the essence and experiences of blackness (Henderson 2007). They argue that cookup, metegee, and other "coconut foods" are the kinds of hearty, nutritious cuisines that nourished their ancestors, from time immemorial, making them physically strong, "tough," and psychologically resilient. African Guyanese also cite the prevalence of black-eyed peas (Albala 2007: 117–26), gizzards, chicken feet, and other animal organs in African and African diasporic cuisines, as evidence of cookup's African origin (Mintz 1996: 33–49). Other Guyanese nationals are not as eager to racialize cookup, but simply categorize it as "Guyanese food." Indian Guyanese, whose ancestors suffered under indentured servitude, also cite the presence of coconut milk and the pervasiveness of animal "scraps" in cookup rice as evidence that the dish could have originated among any ethnic group during the colonial period. Guyanese unanimously agree, however, that cookup originated in the rural "country" areas among the lowest strata of society (Suranyi 2006: 125). They also argue that their cookup's taste is unique, and better than "other people's" rice and peas. Ultimately, Guyanese seem more enthusiastic about discussing cookup as a "*Dougla* pot," rather than emphasizing individual racial or ethnic differences (Wilk 1999: 251).

Michelle, an African Guyanese woman residing in Linden, a bauxite mining town in Guyana, asserted, "When I hear the word *cookup* I think of my favorite: a huge plate of black-eyed peas cookup with 'the works,' with everything from chicken to pork, salt beef—everything. Now, I don't want mine cold, 'brought-forward.' It's got to be 'hot.' It's always better to enjoy that with family or good friends, when visiting people you love, or after a beautiful trip somewhere." Michelle was responding to the question—"What do you think about when you hear the word *cookup*?"—which I posed to several Guyanese and other Caribbean nationals familiar with the dish. In describing her favorite cookup, Michelle highlights a specific type of peas (black-eyed) with which it is prepared, as well as other key ingredients she regards as important. She also emphasizes that her ideal plate of cookup has "the works" (diverse kinds of meats, greens, and vegetables) but that leftovers "brought-forward" are not appetizing. Michelle did not confine her discussion on cookup to personal choice but later, situated the dish within larger social contexts that included special occasions, family, and nation. Interestingly, neither Michelle nor other Guyanese I spoke with provided me with any definitive answers regarding the origin or historical background of cookup, which they seemed to regard as elusive or irrelevant to cookup's place in Guyanese society.

Ingredients of Cookup Rice

Cookup rice is prepared with several ingredients, which I have categorized as primary, secondary, and tertiary based on their perceived importance to the average cookup. Primary ingredients are those that Guyanese regard as fundamental or indispensable to the average cookup, and include rice, peas, and coconut milk or cream. Interestingly, these ingredients are some of the staples in Guyanese diet, which can also be easily acquired. Guyana produces and exports rice, and also imports different types of rice. In New York City, Guyanese also choose from a variety of rice types in creating their favorite cookup. Some Guyanese, for instance, assert that any good pot of cookup will have "loosey" rice and, therefore, must be prepared with brown rice. Others who prefer "pasty" or "sappy" (moist) cookup may choose to prepare with white rice and to modify cooking time and ingredients to reflect the desired constitution.

Although rice influences the constitution of any cookup, it is the type of peas with which it is prepared that generally serves as the defining factor. Without peas, the dish would be regarded as "shine rice" (coconut rice) instead of cookup rice. Thus, Guyanese generally talk about channa cookup with beef, pigeon peas cookup with pork, or like Michelle, cited earlier, "black-eyed peas cookup with 'the works.'" A Guyanese American woman residing in Atlanta responded to my list of questions with a single word, "channa" (chickpeas). By referencing only the peas she was able to index her favorite cookup, including its unique aroma, flavor, color, and taste. The kind of peas chosen is generally influenced by individual taste, but sometimes health-related issues affect that choice. Some Guyanese, for instance, assert that split peas causes heartburn, while others cite bloating as a side effect of eating black-eyed peas. To avoid allergic reactions or other health-related issues caused by a specific type of peas, some Guyanese avoid eating cookup containing that ingredient late in the evening or dismiss it from their diet altogether. Still, there are those who eat the "offending" cookup and "bear their chafe" (endure the pain).

One of cookup's principal ingredients that cannot be substituted or dismissed is coconut milk or cream. Without coconut milk, cookup would not be cookup but a rice and peas dish that is not indigenous to Guyana. One Guyanese woman living in Brooklyn, New York, stated emphatically: "Regardless of the combinations, it is the coconut milk that gives it the kick." While in Guyana, Guyanese acquire dried coconuts, from which the coconut milk is extracted, free of charge, as many people, particularly in rural areas, have coconut trees in their yards. Shelled dried coconuts, canned coconut milk, and coconut cream can also be purchased at the supermarkets, open markets, or from neighbors. In New York City, Guyanese can also purchase canned coconut milk, frozen coconut cream, and prepackaged grated coconut flakes from the supermarket, or shelled dried coconuts from the "Chinese stores." While some Guyanese prefer the taste of freshly grated coconuts, others opt for the simpler, less time-consuming canned or prepackaged coconut milk, cream, or flakes. Guyanese often contend that good (read, well-trained) Guyanese women choose to grate coconuts to make the cookup "from scratch," as "real" Guyanese food cannot be prepared with prepackaged or canned ingredients.

In addition to coconut milk, peas, and rice, Guyanese prepare cookup with various types of meats and vegetables, which I regard as secondary ingredients. Chicken, pork, beef, fried fish, and diverse meat products are added for taste, flavor, and texture to cookup, but are influenced by financial capabilities, personal preference, religion, and other factors. Some individuals prepare their cookup with a combination of different kinds of meats, while those who are poorer, unemployed, or otherwise financially strapped might be compelled to limit the types or amounts of meat they use or forego that pleasure altogether. Meatless cookup is often referred to as vegetable cookup or "ital" cookup, which references the Rastafarian practice of abstaining from salt and meat. Racquel, a Guyanese Canadian, stated that, "Whenever I am broke and [have] no money to buy meat, that's when it's called vegetarian cookup;

on payday it's beef cookup with fried banga-marys with a salad of cucumbers and tomatoes and lettuce." However, chicken, including the "chicken foot" (chicken's feet or scratchers) and innards, are the most frequently used types of meat as these products are cheaper. Interestingly, Guyanese cite the most delicious cookup as those prepared with peculiar animal parts, such as tripe, cow tongue, and cow ears. Although financial resources and personal choice affect the types of meat people use in their cookup, religious beliefs serve as the overriding influence. Practicing Muslims, for instance, will not use pork, while Hindus would generally avoid beef. Additionally, Seventh Day Adventists avoid pork, shrimp, and other "scavengers of the sea"; some Christian sects reject "un-scaled" fish (fish without scales); and Rastafarians generally avoid all kinds of meats, but particularly red meats. Religious values also stipulate the types of meats that can or cannot be eaten on holy days and special holidays. Thus, Catholics, Anglicans, and other Christians only use fish on Fridays, and avoid meat altogether during the Lenten season.

Unlike meats, vegetables are relatively inexpensive and often prove to be less controversial ingredients in cookup, as any religious group can consume them all year round. In Guyana, vegetables are purchased from local farmers and the open markets, or obtained from an individual's kitchen gardens. Though Guyanese abroad also plant vegetables, they overwhelmingly depend on supermarkets and open markets for fresh and frozen vegetables. Calaloo (eddo leaves), bok choy, and other green, leafy vegetable "greens" are added to cookup to enhance nutritional value, taste, and presentation "color" of the dish. As there are no restrictions on the types of vegetables that can be used in cookup, okra, bora (long bean), and various types of squashes are also frequently added to the dish. Additionally, ground provisions (plantain, and various types of tubers) are often included in cookup to add "body" (mass) to the meal, or to "stretch" it (increase its utility). Guyanese often regard cookup as a well-balanced meal, as all of the major food groups can be included in a single dish. Parents with children who dislike vegetables facilitate a healthy diet by adding vegetables to cookup, which then masks distinctive tastes. For many Guyanese, adding vegetables is more a matter of aesthetics than good health. They often bemoan the appearance of cookup that is "too white" (bland in appearance), even after they acknowledge that the taste is delicious. Only "white" people, Guyanese often argue, prepare food with minimal "seasonings" making it bland in taste and appearance. According to one Guyanese living in Trinidad, a good cookup must also be colorful, displaying "a little bit of green, a little bit of red, a little bit of yellow." The assortment of vegetables and other ingredients in cookup often results in variations that mimic the array of *Douglas* in the larger Guyanese community.

In addition to vegetables, Guyanese often enhance the flavor and presentation of cookup by adding tertiary ingredients, such as pepper or pepper sauce, fried yellow plantains, fried fish, and various types of achar.[9] Some of these ingredients, such as pepper and fried fish, are sometimes cooked together with other ingredients of cookup, but they are more frequently used as "sides" to complement the flavor of the dish. Mango achar (pickled mango) is one ingredient that is frequently cited as crucial to the enjoyment of cookup, as its tangy flavor adds contrast and variation to the dish. Although the addition of tertiary ingredients is generally influenced by personal preference and financial means, Guyanese often regard their presence as being crucial to the complete cookup experience.

The ingredients as well as perceptions of the dish, which are influenced by diverse factors, influence Guyanese's consumption of cookup and the context in which they consume it (Counihan and van Esterik 1997). For many Guyanese, like Yusuf, a Guyanese who resides in Montserrat, cookup is a "strong, well-balanced meal" that transcends race, class, and gender to provide "comfort." Others, however, regard cookup as "po-man" (poor people's) food, which should be only consumed in private settings with family and close friends. As a result, they are apprehensive about serving cookup at weddings and other public events where social status and reputation are generally evaluated and ascribed (Kalčik 1984: 40). In many instances, the association of cookup with lower classes of society stems from the fact that the dish can be relatively inexpensive, making it accessible to the masses, and thus, common. Guyanese who work long or irregular hours, as well as those who live overseas, often reject the notion that cookup is a meal for the miserly, as many of them can afford to purchase an assortment of meats and vegetables necessary to prepare a "rich" cookup. For them, cookup is a meal of convenience that allows them to enjoy Guyanese home cooking even when they are pressed for time (Ray 2004: 49).

Contexts of Consumption

Regardless of their motivations for eating cookup, however, Guyanese frequently assert that "everybody," that is, every "true" Guyanese, should eat cookup and in any context. While some Guyanese eat cookup on a regular basis, others regard it as a dish to be consumed on special occasions. Over the weekends many Guyanese spend considerable amounts of time cleaning their homes, doing laundry, grocery shopping, and other chores they might have ignored during the week. During this period many Guyanese reportedly prepared cookup. Aside from weekends cookup is also a prominent fixture on the menus at life cycle rituals such as christenings, kweh-kweh, weddings, and wakes. During these large gatherings, cookup is often the logical choice of foods because it is filling and can be "stretched" by adding relatively inexpensive ingredients. Michelle asserted that:

> you can go to a party and be served cookup, turn up at a wake and in those moments of sadness you can sit over a plate of cookup and talk of the one you lost. It's served almost everywhere ... I had cookup with [Prime Minister] Sam Hinds and I had some with [Minister of Agriculture] Robert Persaud ... see what I mean? (Michelle, Linden, Guyana)

Although cookup is often present at Guyanese celebrations and holidays, such as birthday parties and Christmas, it is said to be indispensable at Old Year's Night (New Year's Eve) celebrations. In *The Sociology of Food and Eating* Ann Murcott argues that, "what and how people eat or drink may usefully be understood in terms of a system whose coherence is afforded by the social and cultural organisation with which it is associated" (Murcott 1983: 1). For Guyanese, Old Year's Night presents a crucial period of celebration, reflection, and preparation for the New Year. During this period they spend exorbitant amounts of time and money to clean and redecorate their homes, and to prepare large quantities of food, as it is their shared belief that the New Year will unfold in the same manner in which it commenced. Amid the abundance of food are various types of cookup, but the menu is considered incomplete unless it also features black-eyed peas cookup. Guyanese who migrate to other parts of the world continue to celebrate Old Year's Night in a similar manner, even if they now refer to the day as New Year's Eve.

As celebrated as cookup is among Guyanese there are those for whom cookup is their "kinna" (the thing they dislike most; the ultimate source of revulsion). These Guyanese often claim that they developed distaste for cookup during their early childhood years, when, for various reasons, they were compelled to eat it on a regular basis. As a result of their past unpleasant experiences with cookup, they "got 'gainst," meaning, they developed a deep-seated revulsion—much like an allergic reaction—toward the dish (Wilk 2009: 189). Others cite allergies to key ingredients in cookup, such as coconut milk or peas, as their reason for avoiding the dish. Nevertheless, even those who dislike cookup overwhelmingly regard it as "real Guyanese food," whose place is firmly etched in Guyanese history, society, and psyche. This sentiment is especially pervasive among Guyanese expatriates who are often the foremost participants in performances of local Guyanese foods.

Cookup Rice, Migration, and Ethnic Identity Negotiation

Claude Fischler (1988) asserts, "Food is central to our sense of identity. The way any given human group eats helps to assert ... both its oneness and the otherness of whoever eats differently" (275). For the Guyanese diaspora in New York City, the preparation and consumption of Guyanese foods is especially crucial to their negotiations of individual and collective Guyanese identities. "Caribbean" restaurants, which specialize in cuisines from nations such as Jamaica, Trinidad and Tobago, and Barbados, allow Guyanese to sample a plethora of cuisines akin to those they enjoyed in Guyana. However, it is this atmosphere of presumed culinary sameness that effects the blurring of parameters that demarcate "Guyanese food" (Bauböck and Rundell 1998: 8). Being constantly inundated by cultural differences of other ethnic groups, including black Africans, African Americans, and West Indians, Guyanese often express the need to authenticate and intensify Guyanese cultural performances in order to safeguard their "culture" (Royce 1982: 40; Waters 1995; Foner 1998; Jackson and Cothran 2003). As food serves as a ready symbol of Guyanese identity, Guyanese cuisines are readily drawn upon and displayed as symbols of ethnic difference. Although Guyanese restaurants, such as Sybil's Bakery and Restaurant in Brooklyn and Bamboo Garden in Queens offer a variety of Guyanese cuisines, the sustained policing of Guyanese ethnic food boundaries often unfolds in individual homes.

In *The Migrant's Table*, sociologist Krishnendu Ray demonstrates how Bengali American women engage in tedious preparations of rice and *jhol* (fish) as a means of preventing the collapse of their culture that comes from Westernization (2004: 126). To combat the encroachment of their ethnic boundaries, Guyanese turn to the "Chinese stores" (open markets similar to those in Guyana), from which they purchase tropical greens, vegetables, condiments, and countless other rations, to cook like they did "back home" (Ray 2004: 1; Harris-Shapiro 2006: 67). As they prepare their cuisines, Guyanese emphasize the importance of keeping recipes as close as possible to those in Guyana, as a way of guaranteeing authenticity. In *What's Cooking in Guyana* (2004), a prominent cookery book produced by Guyana's Carnegie School of Home Economics, the elderly, and sometimes, other Guyanese ethnics, serve as food databases that Guyanese tap in order to erect and reinforce the boundaries of genuine Guyanese cooking. Guyanese constantly evaluate their cooking to ensure their cookup, for example, continues to taste like "real" cookup, as opposed to cookup's "friend," "distant cousin," or "in-law." Although Guyanese express concerns about preserving their "traditional" foodways, they frequently experiment with the ingredients in their cuisines, demonstrating that "tradition is as much a component of creativity as is innovation" (Prosterman 1984: 127; Wilk 2006: 72). Nevertheless, by actively cooking and consuming their own cuisines Guyanese reaffirm the boundaries of their group's ethnic identity by distinguishing "in-group from out-group" (Brown and Mussell 1984: 5).

In asserting ethnic identity through their foodways, Guyanese in New York City and other regions of the world often reference "Guyanese food" as if it were a single entity, comprising segments of equal importance or relevance. Closer examinations would reveal, however, that there are certain cuisines that occupy critical spaces on the culinary landscape of Guyanese cuisines. Guyanese regard such cuisines as unique to Guyana or customized in Guyana to such an extent that they differ considerably and observably from expressions in other cultures. Cookup rice is one such Guyanese dish that evokes strong reactions among Guyanese, who also regard it as one of the truest expressions of the essence of Guyaneseness. Although there are similar expressions of rice and peas cuisines all over the world, including Jamaican cookup and Trinidadian pelau, Guyanese argue that their cookup, with its distinctive blend of ingredients, encapsulates the cultural baggage of Guyanese history and social interactions. Michelle, cited previously, stated: "I went to Trinidad ate pelow and immediately had a deep desire for my own cookup, and boasted seriously that that was nothing compared to 'our' cookup." Sidney Mintz (2003) states that "food binds time," and for Guyanese like Michelle, the complex of life's histories and experiences, which were constructed through cookup and safeguarded in their memory, are only evoked by the unique aromas and flavors that emanate from cookup.

As each act of eating involves the act of remembering, food often functions as the tie that binds people across the expanse of time, even when they are physically separated by great geographic distances, or by death (Sutton 2001: 9; Kalčik 1984: 48). Cookup remains an active food memory for many Guyanese, enabling them to recall specific relationships, landscapes, and previous experiences. In discussing cookup Guyanese frequently use phrases such as "back in the day," "when we were kids," and "I remember when," as framing devices that reference bygone days and transport them to particular spaces among specific people. Even Guyanese who eat cookup on a regular basis preface their conversations with similar phrases as if to validate their expertise with the cuisine, and by extension, their degree of Guyaneseness. Racquel, a Guyanese woman residing in Canada, stated:

> Whenever I hear the word "cook-up" happy thoughts come to mind. I think of my mom asking my dad to grate get two coconuts and this is when the fun begins. The pieces he can't grate are considered treats for us as kids. We would all sit around in the backyard and wait patiently as he grates another piece. (Racquel, Canada)

Although Racquel later explained that she frequently cooks various types of cookup, these more recent enactments were subsumed by her childhood memories and experiences with cookup when asked, "What do you think about when you hear the word *cookup*?" For many Guyanese like Racquel, cookup facilitates the recollection of memories, as well as the symbolic reconstruction of relationships, both with the living and the dead (Corr 2002: 2).

Conclusion

The recollection of memories facilitated by cookup reestablishes the bonds that Guyanese shared with people they knew, but the act of eating cookup also constitutes a larger imagined Guyanese community, or nation. In *Imagined Communities*, Benedict Anderson (1983) argues that a nation constituted an imagined community, as "members of even the smallest nation will never know most of their fellow-members, meet them, or even hear of them, yet in the mind of each lives the image of their communion" (6). For Guyanese, the "image of their communion" is often constructed through the ritualistic acts of food preparation and consumption, which pervade every aspect of their daily interactions. In Guyana, the concept of nationhood appears to be particularly subsumed by the political and racial fragmentation of the Guyanese community, but amid the constant deluge of racial, religious, and political disputes, there are moments when Guyanese are inadvertently silenced by food, and thus, united. Although Guyanese generally eat the same foods, cookup rice and other racially ambiguous "creolized" foods especially enable them to achieve united silence as they eat nationhood.

Sutton asserts that "there is an imagined community implied in the act of eating food 'from home' while in exile, in the embodied knowledge that others are eating the same food" (2001: 84). For Guyanese expatriates, consuming Guyanese food constitutes performances that are "generic means of tradition making" (Kapchan 1995: 479) and nation building through the erection of boundaries that demarcate Guyanese and "Other." This is not to suggest that the religious, racial, and political discord among Guyanese in Guyana automatically dissipates once they migrate, but to emphasize the fact that their displacement and confrontation with exacerbated cultural differences often compels them to seek comfort in the familiarity of shared Guyanese history and cultural experiences. It is in the context of Guyanese "exile" and fear of loss that a local, "po-man" cuisine like cookup emerges as a key symbol of Guyanese national identity (Wilk 1999: 251).

As Guyanese identity is ascribed and affirmed by cultural insiders and outsiders alike, cookup must be considered reliable and predictable by both groups in order to be acknowledged as a symbol of identity; that is, it must "have meaning for both the people who display it and the people to whom it is displayed" (Royce 1982: 148). Over a period of time cookup is imbued with meaning as Guyanese consistently pair this cuisine with Guyanese-specific life histories and experiences in their presentations and performances of Guyanese nationality. Guyanese engaged in exogamous marriages particularly regard cookup as a performance of nationalism, which, much like the use of "slang" among the Kayabi Indians of Brazil, prevents them from "finishing off" (Oakdale 2004: 78) or becoming culturally extinct. Racquel, cited previously, stated:

> As an adult, I have experimented and mastered making this dish for my non-Guyanese husband and friends. I completely enjoy this process of cooking, as this dish always reminds me of my country. A great conversation opening, on introducing and educating others on my rich Guyanese culture.

For Guyanese at home and abroad, cookup rice has become "a force of national unity" (Adair 1986: 50), whose *Dougla* identity momentarily and symbolically halts the segmentation within the Guyanese community that results from the ra-cial profiling of food. Like the dyes and powders that collectively camouflage the physical appearances of participants in Phagwah celebrations among Indians, sym-bolically rendering them casteless and classless, cookup facilitates the conflation of the diverse segments of the Guyanese community. As Michelle puts it, "the great and not so great can come together in one place and enjoy a simple menu which means a lot to them both" (Michelle, Linden, Guyana). As they engage in various

Figure 8.2 Channa cookup with beef prepared by the author. Photo by the author.

cultural and political masquerades in the name of unity, Guyanese continue to celebrate cookup as one of their truest expressions of nationhood. Like Michelle, many Guyanese do not know where or how cookup originated, but they are adamant that "it has surely created more oneness than Banks Beer" (Michelle, Linden, Guyana). (See Figure 8.2.)

Recipe: Cookup Rice

(Channa cookup)

Ingredients

1 small dried coconut (grated) or 1 can of coconut milk
1 pint of long grain parboiled rice
3 lbs. meat (1 lb. pork, 1 lb. beef, 1 lb. tripe)
1 pint of dried chickpeas
1 small onion (finely chopped)
1 plum tomato (diced)
2 green onions or scallions (finely chopped)
2 cloves of garlic (finely chopped)
Other fresh seasonings: thyme, celery (finely chopped or blended)
2 lemons or half a cup of lemon juice
2 bouillon cubes

2 tbsp. butter or margarine (optional)
2 tbsp. browning or soy sauce (for color)
Other (optional) condiments: all-purpose seasoning, black pepper, cumin, basil, red pepper

Directions

1. Wash peas; soak overnight; boil or pressure with minimal salt until half-cooked or parboiled.
2. Wash pork, beef, tripe using lemon juice; rinse.
3. Season meats with chopped or blended fresh seasonings, all-purpose seasoning, black pepper, red pepper, cumin, basil. Meats can be seasoned and refrigerated overnight.
4. Sauté onion, tomato, garlic, and a portion of fresh seasonings.
5. Add seasoned meats and browning or soy sauce to sautéed condiments; stew together until meats are half-cooked.
6. Combine parboiled peas, stewed (half-cooked) meats, coconut milk, bouillon cubes, butter or margarine. Bring to boil for about 15 minutes, then add condiments and seasonings to taste.
7. Cover pot, lower heat, and let cook for about 30 minutes or until rice is soft.
8. Serve with fried yellow plantains, salad, achar.

Notes

The author wishes to thank the editors of this book, Dr. Richard Wilk and Dr. Livia Barbosa, for the insightful feedback they offered during the writing of this chapter. Special thanks also to my research consultants, colleagues, and friends for their support, and without whom this project would not have come to fruition.

1. In this chapter, I do not make a distinction between *peas* and *beans*, as Guyanese often use the terms interchangeably.
2. For discussion on diasporas see Robin Cohen, *Global Diasporas: An Introduction* (Seattle: University of Washington Press, 1997).
3. See http://en.wikipedia.org/wiki/Dougla (accessed April 20, 2011). Scholars and native speakers of Hindi language and culture further substantiated this etymology of *Dougla*. See also Mehta 2004.
4. The terms *Cooley*, *Putagee*, and *Bouviander* are derogatory labels that Guyanese use to describe people of East Indian, Portuguese, and Amerindian ancestry, respectively. However, Guyanese also use these labels in everyday interactions with each other as terms of endearment, as well as modes of inflicting hurt.
5. Guyana Bureau of Statistics, 2002, chapter 2, http://www.statisticsguyana.gov.gy/census.html#popcenfinal (accessed October 31, 2010).

6. Freddie Kissoon is a columnist for the *Kaieteur News* as well as a member of the faculty in the Department of Social Sciences at the University of Guyana. Many politicians also regard Kissoon as an agitator and anarchist.
7. Fufu is a pasty, starchy meal that is made from plantain, cassava, or other tubers, which are boiled, then pounded. Fufu is often served with a stew. Conkee is meal made with cornmeal, wrapped in banana leaves, and boiled.
8. Pepper-pot is a spicy, dark-brown dish, made with various types of meats, pepper, and other condiments. Cassereep, the key ingredient, is a thick dark sauce that is made from cassava "yuka."
9. A type of Indian pickle.

References

Adair, G. 1986. *Myths and memories.* London: Fontana.

Albala, K. 2007. *Beans: A history.* New York: Berg.

Anderson, B. 1983. *Imagined communities: Reflections on the origin and spread of nationalism*, rev. ed. London: Verso.

Bakhtin, M. 1981. "Discourse in the Novel." In *The dialogic imagination, four essays by M. M. Bakhtin*, ed. Michael Holmquist, trans. Caryl Emerson and Michael Holmquist, 259–422. Austin: University of Texas Press.

Bauböck, R., and J. Rundell, eds. 1998. *Blurred boundaries: Migration, ethnicity, citizenship.* Brookfield, Vt.: Ashgate.

Behar, R. 1989. "Sexual witchcraft, colonialism, and women's powers: Views from the Mexican inquisition." In *Sexuality and marriage in Colonial Latin America*, ed. Asuncíon Lavrin, 178–200. Lincoln: University of Nebraska Press.

Brown, L. K., and K. Mussell. 1984. "Introduction." In *Ethnic and regional foodways in the United States: The performance of group identity*, ed. Linda Keller Brown and Kay Mussell, 3–15. Knoxville: University of Tennessee Press.

Carnegie School of Home Economics. 2004. *What's Cooking in Guyana*, 2nd ed. Oxford: Macmillan.

Carney, J. 2001. *Black rice: The African origins of rice cultivation in the Americas.* Cambridge, Mass.: Harvard University Press.

Cohen, R. 1997. *Global diasporas: An introduction.* Seattle: University of Washington Press.

Corr, R. 2002. "Reciprocity, communion, and sacrifice: Food in Andean ritual and social life." *Food and Foodways* 10 (1–2): 1–26.

Counihan, C. M. 1999. *The anthropology of food and body: Gender, meaning, and power.* New York: Routledge.

Counihan, C. M. 2004. *Around the Tuscan table: Food, family, and gender in twentieth-century Florence.* New York: Routledge.

Counihan, C., and P. van Esterik. 1997. "Introduction." In *Food and culture: A reader*, ed. Carole Counihan and Penny van Esterik, 1–7. New York: Routledge.

Devault, M. 1997. "Conflict and Deference." In *Food and culture: A reader*, ed. Carole Counihan and Penny van Esterik, 180–200. New York: Routledge.

Douglas, M. 1971. "Deciphering a meal." In *Myth, symbol, and culture*, ed. Clifford Geertz, 61–83. New York: W. W. Norton.

Drewal, M. T. 1992. *Yoruba ritual: Performers, play, agency.* Bloomington: Indiana University Press.

Fischler, C. 1988. "Food, self and identity." *Social Science Information* 27 (2): 275–92.

Foner, N. 1998. "West Indian identity in the diaspora: Comparative and historical perspectives." *Latin American Perspectives* 25 (3): 173–88.

Harris-Shapiro, C. 2006. "Bloody shankbones and braided bread: The food voice and the fashioning of American Jewish identities." *Food and Foodways* 14 (2): 67–90.

Henderson, L. 2007. "'Ebony Jr!' and 'soul food': The construction of middle-class African American identity through the use of the traditional Southern foodways." *Food in Multi-Ethnic Literatures* (MELUS) 32 (4): 81–97.

Jackson, J. V., and M. E. Cothran. 2003. "Black versus black: The relationships among African, African American, and African Caribbean persons." *Journal of Black Studies* 33 (5): 576-604.

Kahn, M. 1986. *Always hungry, never greedy: Food and the expression of gender in a Melanesian society.* London: Cambridge University Press.

Kalčik, S. 1984. "Ethnic foodways in America: Symbol and the performance of identity." In *Ethnic and regional foodways in the United States: The performance of group identity*, ed. Linda Keller Brown and Kay Mussell, 37–65. Knoxville: University of Tennessee Press.

Kapchan, D. A. 1995. "Performance." *Journal of American Folklore* 108 (430): 479–508.

Kasinitz, P. 1992. *Caribbean New York: Black immigrants and the politics of race.* Ithaca, N.Y.: Cornell University Press.

Kissoon, F. 2010. "Guyana: Lawlessness, chaos and madness in a failed state." Available at: http://www.kaieteurnewsonline.com/2010/10/08/guyana-lawlessness-chaos-and-madness-in-a-failed-state/. Accessed October 8, 2010.

Knight, F. W., and C. A. Palmer, eds. 1989. *The modern Caribbean.* Chapel Hill: University of North Carolina Press.

Littlefield, D. C. 1981. *Rice and slaves.* Baton Rouge: Louisiana State University Press.

McGowan, W. F., J. G. Rose, and David Granger, eds. 2009. *Themes in African-Guyanese history*, 2nd ed. Hertfordshire, U.K.: Hansib.

Mehta, B. J. 2004. "Kali, Gangamai, and Dougla consciousness in Moses Nagamootoo's 'Hendree's Cure.'" *Callaloo* 27 (2): 542–60.

Meigs, A. 1997. "Food as a cultural construction." In *Food and culture: A reader*, ed. Carole Counihan and Penny van Esterik, 95–106. New York: Routledge.

Mintz, S. 1996. *Tasting food, tasting freedom.* Boston: Beacon Press.

Mintz, S. 2003. Review of *Remembrance of repasts: An anthropology of food and memory*, by David E. Sutton. *American Ethnologist* 30 (3): 474–75.

Mintz, S., and C. M. Du Bois. 2002. "The anthropology of food and eating." *Annual Review of Anthropology* 31: 99–119.

Murcott, A. 1983. "Introduction." In *The sociology of food and eating: Essays on the sociological significance of food*, ed. Anne Murcott, 1–13. Aldershot, U.K.: Gower.

Nauta, D. 1972. *The meaning of information.* The Hague: Mouton.

Oakdale, S. 2004. "The culture-conscious Brazilian Indian: Representing and reworking Indianness in Kayabi political discourse." *American Ethnologist* 31 (1): 60–75.

Prosterman, L. 1984. "Food and celebration: A Kosher caterer as mediator of communal traditions." In *Ethnic and regional foodways in the United States: The performance of group identity*, ed. Linda Keller Brown and Kay Mussell, 127–44. Knoxville: University of Tennessee Press.

Rabe, S. G. 2005. *U.S. intervention in British Guiana: A Cold War story.* Chapel Hill: University of North Carolina Press.

Ray, K. 2004. *The migrant's table: Meals and memories in Bengali-American households.* Philadelphia: Temple University Press.

Richardson, B. C. 1974. "Regularities in Guyanese rice cultivation." *Journal of Developing Areas* 8 (2): 235–56.

Royce, A. P. 1982. *Ethnic identity: Strategies of identity.* Bloomington: Indiana University Press.

Smith, R. T. 1980. *British Guiana.* Westport, Conn.: Greenwood Press.

Suranyi, A. 2006. "Seventeenth-century English travel literature and the signature of foreign foodways." *Food and Foodways* 14 (3/4): 123–50.

Sutton, D. E. 2001. *Remembrance of repasts: An anthropology of food and memory.* Oxford: Berg.

Waters, M. C. 1995. "Ethnic and racial identities of second-generation black immigrants in New York City." *International Migration Review* 28 (4): 795–820.

Weismantel, M. J. 1988. *Food, gender, and poverty in the Ecuadorian Andes.* Philadelphia: University of Pennsylvania Press.

Wilk, R. 1999. "'Real Belizean food': Building identity in the transnational Caribbean." *American Anthropologist*, n.s., 101 (2): 244–55.

Wilk, R. 2006. *Home cooking in the global village: Caribbean food from buccaneers to ecotourists.* Oxford: Berg.

Wilk, R. 2009. "Difference on the menu: Neophilia, neophobia and globalization." In *The globalization of food*, ed. David Inglis and Debra Gimlin, 185–196. Oxford: Berg.

Williams, B. F. 1991. *Stains on my name, war in my veins: Guyana and the politics of cultural struggle.* Durham, N.C.: Duke University Press.

Wilson, P. J. 1973. *Crab antics: A Caribbean case study of the conflict between reputation and respectability.* Prospect Heights, Ill.: Waveland Press.

9

All in One Pot
The Place of Rice and Beans in
Panama's Regional and National Cuisine

Carla Guerrón Montero

Introduction

Shared ideologies of food preference are fundamental for national and subnational identities. Food preference is a socially constructed concept in which both consumers and producers define what is "good to eat" (Smith 2006: 480). As Narayan (in Bell and Valentine 1997: 2) notes:

> Thinking about food has much to reveal about how we understand our personal and collective identities. Seemingly simple acts of eating are flavored with complicated and sometimes contradictory cultural meanings. Thinking about food can help reveal the rich and messy textures of our attempts at self-understanding, as well as our interesting and problematic understandings of our relationship to social Others.

Just as nations are difficult to define, so is the concept of a national diet (cf. Mintz 1997; Wilk 1999; Ashley et al. 2004; Long 2004), and of regional identities producing unique diets and dishes (Johnston 1990; Mintz and Du Bois 2002; Sutton 2010). In this chapter, I discuss the meanings and guiding principles of rice and beans as a generic dish within Panama's national cuisine as well as its role as a specific marker of diverse regional identities.

Specifically, I focus on the role of rice and beans in the ethnic cuisine of Afro-Antilleans in the Archipelago of Bocas del Toro, in the northwestern corner of the country. Finally, I address the role of international tourism in fostering both the maintenance and evolution of this dish for Panama's cuisine, particularly among Afro-Antilleans. This chapter is based on my long-term ethnographic research in the Archipelago of Bocas del Toro from 1996 to 2007, and continuous communication with my collaborators until the present time. In my research, I studied the construction of Afro-Antillean identities through ethnic commodities (particularly cuisine and music) as a result of tourism development in the archipelago.

Historical Background

Panama is considered one of the "crossroads of the world." During colonial times, Panama was a strategic place for the Spanish Empire, as the shortest and quickest route from the Pacific to the Caribbean, a transshipment point for commerce between the Viceroyalty of Peru and Spain. In the nineteenth and twentieth centuries, it became a commercial point of connection in the Americas. In 1821, Panama was incorporated into Gran Colombia after its independence from Spain. Panama became a republic in 1903 when it declared its independence from Colombia. Panama has been the location of large and significant infrastructural projects, including the Panamanian Railroad (1850–1855), the French efforts to build a canal (1880–1889), and the U.S. construction of the Panama Canal (1904–1914). These projects have fostered migration of peoples from various cultures and ethnicities, including peoples of African descent from Barbados, Jamaica, Martinique, and Guadeloupe, as well as workers from England, France, Spain, Germany, India, Austria, and China.

Throughout Panama's history, there have been five major migrations of peoples of African descent into the country, with very different characteristics and from different areas. They provided labor as (1) colonial slaves; as workers (2) for the construction of the Panamanian Railroad; (3) on the banana plantations in the province of Bocas del Toro; (4) the French attempt to construct a canal; and (5) the U.S. construction of the Panama Canal. These migrations have influenced and shaped the creation of the nation in dramatic ways. Afro-Panamanians can be divided into two major groups: blacks who landed in Panama as slaves from the sixteenth century until the early nineteenth century, and blacks who immigrated involuntarily or voluntarily to work on different projects in the nineteenth century. The former are commonly known as Afro-Colonials (or *negros coloniales*) and the latter as West Indians, Afro-Antilleans, *criollos*, or *antillanos*.

Afro-Antilleans have contributed to Panama's nation-building project since the early 1800s. Considered the "ideal" labor force for some of Panama's most important infrastructural ventures because of the presumption of being well-adjusted to the tropical environment of Panama and their knowledge of the English language, thousands of workers from the British West Indies migrated—either temporarily or permanently—to Panama to work on the constructions of the Panamanian Railroad and the French- and U.S.-sponsored Panama Canal. When these projects ended, many Afro-Antilleans remained in Panama working for the Panama Canal Company, in Panama City and Colon, or on Bocas del Toro's thriving banana plantations (Guerrón Montero 2008: 743–48). Due to their distinctive cultural traits—in contrast with Panama's assumed "national" mestizo identity—and the racial climate in the country and the region, Afro-Antilleans became second-class citizens, whose many accomplishments have been acknowledged only in recent years. Their marginalization and isolation was more apparent in the Archipelago of Bocas del Toro.

There is a prevalent notion (among academics as well as in popular discourse) of the presence of racial democracy in Panama, which coexists with a strong nationalist rhetoric that portrays a particular kind of Latino or mestizo racial identity as normative. The myth of racial democracy as it is experienced in Panama notes that—contrary to clearly marked inequalities in other parts of Latin America, where marginalized groups experience inequalities, injustices and racism systematically, consistently, unequivocally—racism is not a problem in Panama because of its long history of miscegenation and democratic relations. Therefore inequalities and racist beliefs are the result of the U.S. presence in Panama, which imposed a Jim Crow system in the Canal Zone (cf. Bryce-Laporte 1998; Guerrón Montero 2006a). Thus, a more democratic stance toward racial relations represents a *nationalist* stance against U.S. intervention. At the same time, the "real" Panama is represented by the racial characteristics and cultural experiences of the central provinces. In a multicultural nation-state, these representations inscribe some groups into unequal power structures and foster racialized patterned behavior.

The history of Panama I have detailed above is essential to understand its current economic system. Once the canal began operations in 1914, Panama became heavily dependent on the revenues it received as annual payments from the Panama Canal Company. This was the beginning of a dollarized economy based primarily on a service sector that now accounts for 80 percent of the country's GDP. These services include the operation of the Panama Canal, banking, the Colon Free Zone, and tourism. In 2007, Panama initiated a sizable Panama Canal expansion project at a cost of $5.3 billion. It is expected that the expansion will be completed by 2014; it will more than double the canal's capacity, and will produce a net increase in revenues as a result of higher transit fees and the capability to transit larger ocean-going vessels.

Since the 1990s, the Panamanian government has aggressively pursued tourism as one of its main industries. Facing a serious loss of income estimated at $300 million annually as the day approached when all of the land and properties in the Canal Zone would be turned over to Panama (which occurred on December 31, 1999), the Panamanian government began to seriously promote tourism as a source of foreign income in the 1990s. As a result of these efforts, the tourism industry has grown considerably, becoming in 2003 the largest income earner for Panama ($805 million), surpassing income from the Panama Canal ($690.3 million) (Instituto Panameño de Turismo [IPAT] 2004: 1, 9).

In the early 1990s, the Panamanian government developed a master plan that divided the country into nine tourism zones (currently the plan includes ten zones) and emphasized ecotourism and heritage tourism. Through the Panamanian Bureau of Tourism (*Instituto Panameño de Turismo* [IPAT]), the government began to focus much attention on its now formally acknowledged cultural diversity, and on attracting tourists to locations that had remained "hidden" and "unspoiled." The Archipelago of Bocas del Toro possessed these two characteristics: healthy, rich, and relatively untouched natural landscapes and a wealth of cultural diversity. Not surprisingly, the archipelago was selected as Zone 2 of the master plan, and received considerable governmental attention.

Panama's One-Pot Narrative

Throughout its history as a nation-state, Panama has accentuated its Spanish roots. Since its formation as an independent republic in 1903, Panama's authorities and public intellectuals have emphasized the importance of preserving specific components of its heritage, those that trace the nation's ancestry directly to Spain, and are thus perceived by Panama's dominant elites as "legitimate culture." The master narrative of nationhood prevalent in Panama has been Hispanic or Latino (Spanish-Indian), and rural in nature. A racially, ethnically, and culturally diverse nation was represented almost exclusively by cultural and social values presumably inherited from the motherland (Mendieta and Husband 1997: 204) and most deeply manifested in the central provinces of Panama. The symbols chosen to represent Panama derived directly from a Spanish or mestizo heritage, to identify the nation as one having roots in Latin America in evident opposition to the U.S. presence but also as a result of internal struggles that influenced definitions of legitimacy. For the most part, this project was gendered, racialized, and class-specific: the future of the country was seen to lie in Hispanic or Latino male middle-class intellectuals. Cultural and social values included romanticized "peasant" traditions exemplified in Panama's folklore, music, and cuisine.

As a result of its geopolitical location, Panama's peoples represent a great diversity of cultures and ethnicities, including eight indigenous groups (Ngöbe, Buglé, Naso, Bokotá, Kuna, Emberá, Wounaan, and Bri-Bri), five different waves of migration of peoples of African descent (from the British, Spanish, and French West Indies in the nineteenth and twentieth centuries), and sizeable numbers of immigrants from China, Greece, Spain, and India, among many others. This ethnic diversity has produced a multiplicity of foodways as well as some dishes that are generally viewed as characteristic of the "national cuisine," such as *sancocho* (a kind of soup), *arroz con pollo* (rice with chicken), and *arroz con frijoles* (rice and beans).

The dish *arroz con frijoles* is a prototypical dish in Panama, emblematic of its "typical" or "national" cuisine. In spite of its ubiquitous existence, information about the origin of the dish and systematic research on its variations and relevance throughout the country are not available. *Arroz con frijoles* is a generic dish consumed with different side dishes that frame it. For instance, in the central provinces of Panama, rice and beans are generally consumed accompanied by chicken, although in the 1950s and 1960s iguana substituted for chicken when available. In coastal communities on the Azuero Peninsula fish or chicken is served with rice and red or kidney beans (*Phaseolus vulgaris*). In the province of Chiriquí, rice and pigeon peas (guandú beans, *Cajanus cajan*) are more common. Among indigenous populations, rice and beans are also consumed. Fish is the preferred side dish for rice and beans among the Kuna. The Ngöbe, the largest indigenous group in Panama, consume kidney beans (known as *muma tayn* or "beans that are red") and rice. Traditionally, the beans were served more often with boiled green bananas but these days with the Ngöbe purchasing large amounts of white rice, rice and beans has become the dish of choice (P. Young, personal communication, August 10, 2010). The preferred side dish for rice and beans is not always available, particularly for the poor in Panama, the central provinces, or among indigenous populations. Thus, although undoubtedly there are preferences for side dishes (chicken in the central provinces, or fish among the Kuna), when resources are not sufficient, the dish itself is consumed alone (see Anderson 2005).

Afro-Antillean populations produce and consume rice and red beans in a manner that aligns with their cuisine, and call the dish "rice and beans" or "rice and peas." I now turn my attention to Afro-Antillean cuisine in the Archipelago of Bocas del Toro, where the majority of Afro-Antilleans live (in addition to Panama City [province of Panama] and Colon [province of Colon]), and on the role of international tourism in transforming some aspects of this cuisine.

Afro-Antillean Cuisine

The Archipelago of Bocas del Toro represents a microcosm of the multicultural groups that inhabit Panama, including Afro-Antilleans, Chinese, indigenous groups (particularly Ngöbe and some Kuna), *Panamanian Latinos* (the term used in Panama to refer to mestizos), and resident expatriates, mostly from Europe and North America. Afro-Antilleans in Bocas del Toro are descendants of black slaves from the British West Indies and more recent waves of migration. Afro-Antilleans arrived in Bocas del Toro during the mid- or late eighteenth century (accounts vary) to work as slaves of English and Scottish families who had settled in the region after leaving the islands of Jamaica, Barbados, Providence, and San Andres (Heckadon Moreno 1980; Waisome, Priestley, and Maloney 1981). In the archipelago, Afro-Antillean populations—generally marginalized and ignored elsewhere in Panama—are the majority and have the upper hand in political and social life. The archipelago itself has experienced a cyclical history of boom and bust. Its most recent boom began in the early 1990s with tourism development. As noted earlier in the chapter, since then, the archipelago has become a popular place for an "eco-vacation" for national and international tourists (Guerrón Montero 2005, 2006b).

Most Afro-Antilleans in the archipelago speak Creole English in addition to Spanish (Guerrón Montero 2002: 116, 140–45). From the nineteenth to the late twentieth century, Afro-Antilleans in the archipelago worked mainly for the United Fruit Company, in agriculture and fishing activities for self-subsistence, and in bureaucratic service jobs. This structure changed considerably with the development of tourism in the archipelago in the mid-1990s. Within this context, Afro-Antillean cuisine has become an essential component of the construction of their identities both as Panamanian and Caribbean. Until the late 1980s, the Afro-Antillean region of Bocas remained relatively cut off from the rest of Panama, but was intricately connected with the pan-Caribbean region, producing both cosmopolitanism and isolation. Cosmopolitanism among Afro-Antilleans is expressed in their discursive and material practices linking them with everything deemed "modern," particularly in regard to technological devices, lifestyle, and their outlook on the world and concrete patterns of mobilization. At the same time, the geographic and social isolation they endured contributed to the development and maintenance of a rich culinary tradition, which I detail below.

Afro-Antillean cuisine has some specific characteristics that link it to Jamaican cuisine in particular and Caribbean cuisine in general, from its preparation methods to its ingredients and consumption etiquette (Clarke 1999; Idone 1992; Preston-Werner this volume). In addition to being spicy, Afro-Antillean food is hearty, thick, and filling. A hearty meat-and-tubers soup is a good example of a nourishing food (cf. Sobo 1997: 258). Soups are considered ideal meals in Bocas del Toro, for they contain all these characteristics. For many people in Bocas, especially those with limited economic resources, a dish of a thick soup with meat and tubers represents a very good lunch, and local restaurants offer these soups for a few dollars. Soups are also served at drinking parties, in order to give enough strength to attendants to endure a long party evening. Among the ingredients that are considered essential to cook à la Bocatorenean, breadfruit, coconut, banana, plantain, and rice are the most important, in addition to what Bocatoreneans consider essential condiments, including garlic, onions, curry, cilantro, ginger, celery, sweet hot pepper, and "bull nose" hot pepper (*ají chombo*). Afro-Antilleans also prize deep-fried food, and use large quantities of vegetal or coconut oil to fry their food. Some of the most common dishes in Bocas del Toro are rice and beans, *rondón* (or "run down," a fish soup with coconut milk and tubers), *michilá* (boiled ripe plantain with coconut milk), *chicheme* (boiled hominy with coconut milk, condensed milk, and spices), *bragadá* (codfish cake, breaded with flour and fried), *ackee* with eggs,[1] *ackee* with codfish, pig's tail, *sauce* or *souse* (cooked pig's feet pickled with cucumber and vinegar), *patí* (a turnover of spicy meat), and *Janny* cake (flour bread made with coconut and baked). Some of the most popular desserts are coconut pies; *plantintat* (plantain tart), a turnover with filling of mature banana; yuca (sweet manioc); uyama, a type of squash; otoe (*Xanthosoma sp.*, a tarolike tuber native to the American tropics) pudding; *cocada*, a kind of cookie with sweet coconut; and Bastimentos or Bocas sweet bun (sweet bread). There are also Bocatorenean versions of national dishes, such as the sancocho. Afro-Antillean sancocho has *ñampí* (small gnarled yam [*Dioscorea sp.*]), pig's tail, and beef in addition to the usual chicken, *ñame* (yam), cilantro, and other spices. Some cooks also add flour dumplings, thus making this particular dish almost unrecognizable by Panamanians from the central provinces (Guerrón Montero

2004). When I asked Maritza, a well-known cook who caters for local parties, about the Afro-Antillean version of sancocho, she noted:

> The real sancocho is made only with chicken and ñame, but here we like to add pig's tail, beef, chicken, tubers, and dumplings. We like our food with many ingredients ("complete") and with color, so we add a bit of color to it, with ketchup, and it takes a lovely reddish color. We like our food complete, but what we cook is not the *real* sancocho. (Interview M. W., May 29, 2000)

The meat, tubers, and dumplings used in Bocatorenean cuisine add thickness and consistency to the sancocho, thus rendering this iconic Panamanian dish (Moore 1938) suited for consumption by Afro-Antilleans. Iván González, a Bocatorenean cook, commented to me while having lunch at his restaurant:

> Personally, I do not like sancocho made only with chicken and ñame, the way people in the central provinces and Chiriquí consume it. Here in Bocas we like that deliciously thick soup, with lots of meat. When non-Bocatoreneans come here, they notice the differences in the ways we make sancocho and point them to us. They tell me how proud they are of their version of sancocho, but they love our version too! It all has to do with the tradition of each region. (Interview I. G., May 10, 2000)

As these examples indicate, Afro-Antillean cuisine is utilized as a distinct marker of identity, specifically as a way to signal important identity differences from Latinos (mestizos), indigenous peoples, and more recently, tourists. My collaborators told me, "Indians don't eat with hot peppers or ginger; they only boil their fish and plantains." "Make sure you choose your *ñampies* well; don't buy the purple *ñampi*; that's Indian *ñampi* and it doesn't taste as good."[2] "*Pania* [Latino] food has no flavor; it's white and bland, without spices" (Guerrón Montero 2004). Bocatoreneans, thus, differentiate between "mountain food," by implication cooked and consumed by indigenous peoples (simple, without any condiments other than salt), Afro-Antillean food (thick, spicy, heavy, and "complete"), and "tourist food" (more complex than mountain food in the use of condiments, but lighter than Afro-Antillean food). And still, in spite of these very clearly demarcated gastronomic boundaries, diets, recipes, and cuisines in the archipelago are in continuous flux (cf. Wilk 1999: 244). In Bocas del Toro, the most potentially transforming phenomenon for cuisine is the recently developed tourism industry.

"We Make Rice and Peas in One Pot"

Rice and beans is one of the most prized dishes in Bocas del Toro, "a living relic," the "natural" dish, as some of my collaborators told me. By "living relic," they mean a traditional food, representative of Afro-Antillean identity for countless generations; they consider it a "natural dish," because the combination of rice with beans and coconut milk is viewed as given, natural, and expected.

In Bocas del Toro, both rice and beans are served separately. That is, the fact that they constitute a dish does not preclude Bocatoreneans from consuming these two products independently, particularly rice. Rice accompanies many Bocatorenean meals; beans are sometimes served with rice but not cooked together as rice and beans, rather as a *menestra* (a kind of vegetable stew). However, when rice and beans are combined and made with coconut milk, they become the quintessential Afro-Antillean dish, only comparable to *rondón* in importance, and a treasured symbol of Afro-Antillean's complex identities as Panamanian, Antillean, and Caribbean. The dish is called "rice and beans" or "rice and peas" interchangeably. Although there is limited knowledge among Panamanians of the workings of Afro-Antillean cooking traditions (until the year 2011, there were only two Afro-Antillean restaurants in Panama City), Afro-Antilleans are aware that their gastronomy is unique within Panama. This fact contributes to a sense of belonging to a space and time beyond Panama that incorporates the circum-Caribbean region.

The terms *beans* and *peas* are used in an interchangeable manner among Afro-Antilleans (Higman 2008; Higman this volume).[3] The common preparation of rice and beans is as follows: rice is simmered in a pot with the milk of a medium-sized coconut, and spices such as garlic, scallions, salt, and black pepper are added. Finally, the beans are added to the pot (Figure 9.1). The dish is made all in one pot, and it does not depend on cooking oil.

In regard to consumption, rice and beans in Bocas del Toro is simultaneously an everyday dish (and certainly not a luxury) *and* a special dish in the sense that it so strongly represents Afro-Antillean culture for Bocatoreneans and other Panamanians that it becomes the dish of choice when cooking a special meal for national and international guests. Within the very elaborate cuisine etiquette of Bocatoreneans (which calls for rice with chicken, potato or noodle salad, or roasted meat for special occasions, festivities, and celebrations), rice and beans are widely accepted alternatives. Partly as a result of domestic and international tourism, it is common in several celebrations to offer rice and beans à la Bocatorenean. Thus, in significant events such as November 16 (the celebration of the founding of the province of Bocas del Toro in 1903), Bocatorenean families prepare rice and beans if they have friends, relatives, or tourists visiting. Conversely, rice and beans are prepared daily at small, inexpensive local restaurants and at home, and it is an accessible and pedestrian meal throughout the calendar year.

As in other parts of the Caribbean, rice and beans are consumed every Sunday (cf. Higman 2008; Wilk this volume). On Sundays, practically every Bocatorenean family enjoys rice and beans with coconut milk, stewed or fried chicken, and potato salad. Other salad options include lettuce salad, tomato salad, and noodle salad. Sometimes, pork or beef replaces the chicken.

Figure 9.1   Adding the beans to the rice. Photo by Carla Guerrón Montero.

> It has been a tradition among our ancestors to prepare rice and beans with potato salad and stewed chicken. The sauce in which we make the chicken mixes with the rice and beans and the potatoes and it is the most delicious food ever found. ... My mouth salivates just thinking about it! I think we learned these combinations from our black ancestors and it has been our typical Sunday food for centuries. (Conversation P. W., April 25, 2011)

Women take very seriously the responsibility of cooking the traditional Sunday meal and feel guilty if they change the menu or do not cook on that date: "It doesn't feel like Sunday if we don't cook and eat that meal." Rice and beans is also available to tourists at some restaurants any day of the week, which allows locals to consume it as well. Another reason for deviating from the norm occurs among families where the main cook works on Sunday, and thus chooses to make the dish on another day of the week.

Higman (2008) notes that in the case of Jamaica, it is highly likely that the dish originated among the poor, possibly in the eighteenth century:

> It is possible to conceive the Jamaican dish rice and peas beginning with [...] two separate servings in a plate or bowl spilling together, the seasoned peas flavoring the rice, and eventually cooked together in a single pot, to enhance the flavors and save on tools and energy. (2008: 259)

Actual references to the dish appear even later, in the late nineteenth century and early twentieth century (2008: 260; Higman this volume). The dish was a staple of Sunday dinner of the Kingston poor until the 1990s; nowadays it is no longer reserved for Sundays (2008: 260). It was considered "a very great food in Jamaica" and "a food equal to a diet of meat." It is likely that the dish was brought by Afro-Antilleans to Panama as early as the nineteenth century, although Higman suggests the possibility that Jamaicans who migrated to the Hispanic Caribbean and back in the later part of the nineteenth century might have brought the dish, or versions of it, with them back to Jamaica.

I have not been able to uncover further information about its origins, or whether there were variations of the dish produced by the three main waves of migration of Afro-Antilleans to the country. During my ethnographic research in Bocas del Toro and my conversations with collaborators, I did not observe any difference in preparation, consumption, or relevance of the dish for Afro-Antilleans who descended from these different waves.

In terms of proper consumption, rice and beans should not be eaten after 6:00 P.M. for it is a "heavy" dish (following a heavy/light classification system). Both coconut milk and beans are considered heavy foods, and in Bocas del Toro, foods that are classified as "heavy" cannot be eaten after 6:00 P.M. for they are difficult to digest. *Rondón* (because it is made with coconut milk) and cabbage salad (because it is made with cabbage) are other examples of "heavy" dishes. Additionally, heavy dishes cannot be combined; thus, rice and beans cannot be eaten with *rondón* or any other heavy dish. In the pretourist past, the grammar for rice and beans was strictly chicken and salad, with fried ripe bananas or *plátano tentación* (fried ripe bananas with condensed milk) as common additions. Currently, rice and beans is consumed with fried fish, fish stew, shrimp with garlic, lobster, and a salad and fried ripe bananas.

Rice and beans punctuate special moments for Bocatoreneans. According to Patricia Whitaker, an outstanding Afro-Antillean cook, the dish symbolizes welcoming and renewing connections with relatives and close friends who have been away for a long period of time and return to Bocas for a visit.

> When my friend and English teacher Carla returns to the island and all her friends get together to welcome her, we make a good dish of rice and beans with lobster and vegetables! Also, when executives from another province of Panama come to Bocas and we want to show our cooking abilities and the best of our cuisine, we welcome them with rice and beans and some kind of meat.

Bocatorenean food habits have been generally considered very similar in spite of social class differences. All of my collaborators emphatically asserted that in Bocas del Toro every Bocatorenean family, from the poorest to the most affluent household, had very comparable diets. Bocatoreneans often reminded visitors that "in Bocas nobody dies of hunger." "Why? Because we have the ocean, you take a boat and go fishing, you pick breadfruit, or banana, or coconut; nobody dies of hunger here" (interview J. S., July 24, 1999). Everyone in Bocas del Toro was willing to share a dish with a hungry relative, friend, or even unknown passerby. Angela, the owner of the oldest restaurant in town, noted that every family in Bocas managed to have ham and fruit cake for Christmas, regardless of economic resources (interview A. G., November 23, 1999). As Orlando, a young man who worked at the airport's cafeteria stated, "Rich and poor people eat *rondón.* Maybe because the poor people don't have as many resources, their meals may have fewer ingredients, but poor people here, even if they are quite poor, they find money and make good food, especially on Sundays" (interview O. H., February 21, 2002). Monica Gaskin, a woman who has cooked in different Bocatorenean restaurants and affluent homes, agrees and notes that the food consumed in Bocas is the same, but that well-off families prepare it somewhat differently.

> If you see the actual food, it's the same thing. If a rich and a poor family eat lobster, it is the same lobster, but the preparation is different. The same thing happens with fish. Imagine that a rich family eats a roasted fish; they would want it to be embellished with potatoes, carrots, and things like that. My fish would be plain. I learned from an Argentinean family that I worked for to make lobster with cream sauce, peas and mushrooms. It was delicious; but for my home, I prefer sauté lobster. (Interview M. G., July 10, 2005)

In Bocas del Toro, until the onset of tourism, rice and beans was not just the dish of the poor. Socioeconomic classes were not sharply marked in the pretourist past, and rice and beans was the dish of all social classes in Bocas. The advent of tourism has produced sharper social class distinctions in regard to consumption patterns. Dishes that were considered commonplace are now delicacies. That is the case of lobster and seafood, which now mark social differences. Overfishing has depleted marine resources considerably and this, combined with inflation (partly due to tourism), has made seafood expensive and a signal of special occasions. Thus, when Patricia noted that my friends would welcome me with rice and beans and lobster, she was generously emphasizing the significance of my visit for them. Visits to restaurants that offer international cuisine and cater to tourists are also markers of social class distinctions. Currently, only Bocatoreneans with considerable economic resources are able to consume seafood on a regular basis, or to eat at those restaurants. In spite of these distinctions, rice and beans remains a dish available and consumed by all social classes as well as tourists.

Conclusions

Panama has developed what most Panamanians would consider a typical, national cuisine based on input over the years from a variety of ethnic groups, but has also retained and refined dishes that are considered emblematic of a region or an ethnic group. In contrast to other Latin American and Caribbean nations (see Wilk this volume), Panama has capitalized on the *visibility* of its culinary diversity. As Anderson (2005) reminds us, food is about eating together, and about solidarity and separation.

> Food marks social class, ethnicity, and so on. Food transactions define families, networks, friendship groups, religions, and virtually every other socially institutionalized group. Naturally, one group can try to use food to separate itself, while another is trying to use food to eliminate that separation. (2005: 125)

Rice and beans for Afro-Antilleans in Bocas del Toro represents many experiences including ways to balance economic inequalities by sharing food preferences and tastes that are economically available to all classes. The importance of denoting an everyday, inexpensive meal such as rice and beans as a delicacy and a marker of identity is that it represents an economic leveling in the context of rapid and dramatic changes in this society, where there are no longer solid balances among social classes, and where social boundaries are now demarcated as a result of changes produced mostly by tourism. Thus, in the context of hurried transformations and growth of inequalities, rice and beans and *rondón*, dishes that are considered representative of Afro-Antillean identity but are not delicacies and can be cooked with few economic resources, override class distinctions and are used to represent the identity of Afro-Antilleans to national and international tourists. It could be argued that, similarly to what occurs in Belize (Wilk 2006), tourism has contributed to essentializing Afro-Antillean cuisine, thus producing minimal alterations in its production and only some alterations in its consumption.

Contrary to the views of Belizeans about the influences of tourism and immigration in the respectability of Belizean cuisine (Wilk 2006: 179), esteem for Afro-Antillean cuisine in the eyes of Afro-Antilleans is not the result of tourism, current governmental support, or immigration, but of the historic role that Afro-Antillean cuisine (along with other cultural traits) has played for identity constructions in Panama. Resistance to modify Afro-Antillean cuisine represents a way to assert group identities within the context of a rigid and clearly delineated national identity, although—as it happens in Belize and other parts of the Caribbean—the "insistence on the local is itself a response to global forces" (Caldwell 2006: 99). The globalizing phenomena of tourism and immigration have become venues for this ethnic group to emphasize (and to reinvent, to a degree) its cultural particularities and specific social reconstruction of memory (cf. Wilk 2002; Mintz and Du Bois 2002).

In Bocas del Toro, obligations to share and to return favors through food were highly valued, and thus, distances between the upper, middle, and lower classes in regard to food produced and consumed were not strong until the onset of tourism in the 1990s. When tourism developed on the islands, overexploitation of resources ensued, "tourist food" became available, international cuisine became a consumption option, and the inequalities of social classes flourished.

Narayan (1995) warns about some of the ways in which colonial relationships are replicated in the contacts between producers and consumers of food in postcolonial societies. This particular situation has not taken hold in Bocas del Toro. In spite of the strong emphasis on cosmopolitanism of Afro-Antilleans (Guerrón Montero 2006b), food is a system of communication where there have not been dramatic changes in the preparation and consumption of meals. That is, some pragmatic changes have occurred in order to cater to the needs of the tourists, but there is no desire for cosmopolitan approaches to Afro-Antillean food itself, no experimentation or intent to produce fusions, thus suggesting an unwavering kind of "local patriotism" (Bell and Valentine 1997). There is an emphasis on maintaining the flavors and the rules of preparation, although as indicated above, there is more flexibility when it comes to consumption. Rice and beans are now paired with lobster, fish, or occasionally red meat in addition to chicken and salad. Any sign of sophistication or cosmopolitanism is evidenced in accepting the variations in food preferences of tourists, and in occasional visits to restaurants that offer international cuisine, but not in transforming the living relics.

Rice and Beans by Patricia Whitaker

My dear friend Patricia Whitaker[4] kindly shared her rice and beans recipe for this chapter. Patricia is a well-known cook in Bocas del Toro. She has worked at restaurants and hotels and catered for locals and tourists for several years. Until recently, she worked as the administrator and cook of a bed and breakfast owned by an expatriate family for almost ten years. Currently, she caters food for local events and prepares her mischievously spicy hot sauce "I Be a Bitch," Patti's Original Hot Stuff for sale (Figure 9.2). Her most eager customers are foreign expatriates who administer or own restaurants and hotels in Bocas del Toro.

Patricia was one of the most enthusiastic supporters of my research projects and what anthropologists would call an outstanding key collaborator. Patricia thoughtfully asked me to tell the readers of this volume that she enjoys cooking for friends and guests, and that rice and beans is one of her favorite dishes to make. "After you read this food history, please come to Bocas and have a try. I would love to cook this dish for you."

Recipe: Rice and Beans

Ingredients

1 pound of kidney beans (black-eyed peas or even lentils are options. However, the original dish is made with kidney beans)
1 large coconut or two small coconuts
3 pounds of white rice
1 teaspoon of sugar (Patricia's secret)

Figure 9.2 "I Be a Bitch," Patti's Original Hot Stuff. Photo by Patricia Whitaker.

3 whole garlic cloves
1 medium onion cut in half
Salt to taste
A small piece of celery or red pepper
Sufficient water to boil the red beans
3 cups of water to extract the milk from the coconuts
1 bull nose pepper (hot pepper)
2 green peppers

Directions

The first step is to make the beans tender (Figure 9.3). This process takes from 45 minutes to an hour. In order to make the beans tender quicker, Patricia adds garlic cloves, onions, celery, and green peppers to the water where the beans are getting tender.

While the beans are getting tender, grate the coconut and use the 3 cups of water to extract the milk from the grated coconut (Figure 9.4). Then, strain the coconut milk. Then, add this to the beans, and add the salt and the sugar. After you have tasted the flavor, you may leave the ingredients to boil. Add 1 cup of water or sufficient water so when the rice is added (the rice should have been rinsed before adding it), once the water has boiled, there is 1 inch of water over the rice. This needs to be done little by little in order to avoid adding too much water.

Once the water has evaporated almost completely, add a complete bull nose pepper in the center of the dish, making sure it does not break. Close the pot with

Figure 9.3   Making the beans tender. Photo by Patricia Whitaker.

Figure 9.4   Grating the coconut. Photo by Patricia Whitaker.

Figure 9.5 Rice and beans ready to eat. Photo by Patricia Whitaker.

a lid, and lower the fire. Make sure you check the rice frequently to avoid burning it. If the beans are not tender enough, add a bit of water of coconut milk and leave it on the stove for a few minutes. Once the dish is done, wait for about 10 minutes before serving it (Figure 9.5). You may add a bit of parsley on top of the dish at serving time.

To make the *one pot*, you add pig's tails to the recipe. To make the pig's tails, you boil water for 5 minutes, add the pig's tails and salt, throw out the salty water, and boil the pig's tails along with the beans until they are tender. Then you follow the steps mentioned above to make rice and beans. You may also add dried shrimp or cod fish, but the original recipe calls for pig's tails. The one pot is generally cooked for celebrations, and it is eaten with fried bananas, and is served for festivities for large groups or for gastronomic festivals. Another variant of this meal is "stew peas," made with pig's tails, beans, and coconut milk. (Interview M. W., May 29, 2000)

Notes

I would like to express my deepest gratitude to professors Richard Wilk and Livia Barbosa for their invitation to participate in this fascinating project and for their comments on earlier drafts of this chapter. My sincere appreciation also goes to professors Eugene Anderson, Carole Counihan, and Philip D. Young, for their comments, suggestions, insights, and unwavering enthusiasm for my research. Research for this article was partially funded by the National Endowment for the Humanities and the Schomburg Center for Research in Black Culture's Scholars-in-Residence Program. I thank the fellows at the center, Colin Palmer, and the staff and administrators of the center for their outstanding support and dedication. Any views, findings, conclusions, or recommendations expressed in this publication do not necessarily represent those of the National Endowment for the Humanities.

1. The *ackee* (*Blighia sapida*) is a tree native to tropical West Africa. It was brought to Bocas del Toro from Jamaica. The *ackee* fruit is a common ingredient in Jamaican and Bocatorenean meals and throughout the Caribbean. Currently, there are very few *ackee* trees in Bocas del Toro because the fruit is poisonous unless it is picked up after it is fully ripe. Many families have cut down their trees for fear of having unwanted cases of poisoning among the local children.

2. The Ngöbe do use ginger and hot pepper on occasion, but certainly not as often and not in the quantities used by Afro-Antilleans (P. Young, personal communication, August 10, 2010).

3. Albala (2007) notes that "it is a linguistic accident that we distinguish peas from other beans" (75) as they have a shared genetic history. Both peas and beans belong to the botanical family *Fabaceae* (alternately *Leguminosae*), which contains many genera, among them, *Pisum*, to which the common green pea (*Pisum sativum*) belongs and *Phaseolus*, to which several varieties of common beans, including the kidney bean (*Phaseolus vulgaris*), belong.

4. Patricia requested that her real name be used in this chapter.

References

Albala, Ken. 2007. *Beans: A history.* Oxford: Berg.

Anderson, Eugene. 2005. *Everyone eats: Understanding food and culture.* New York: New York University Press.

Ashley, Bob, Joane Hollows, Steve Jones, and Ben Taylor. 2004. *Food and cultural studies.* London: Routledge.

Bell, David, and Gill Valentine. 1997. *Consuming geographies: We are what we eat.* London: Routledge.

Bryce-Laporte, Roy S. 1998. "Crisis, contraculture, and religion among West Indians in the Panama Canal Zone." In *Blackness in Latin America and the Caribbean: Social dynamics and cultural transformations.* Vol. 1: *Blacks in the diaspora*, ed. Arlene Torres and Norman E. Whitten, 100–18. Bloomington: Indiana University Press.

Caldwell, Melissa. 2006. "Tasting the worlds of yesterday and today: Culinary tourism and nostalgia foods in post-Soviet Russia." In *Fast food/slow food: The cultural economy of the global food system*, ed. Richard Wilk, 97–112. Lanham, M.D.: Altamira Press.

Clarke, Austin. 1999. *Pig tails 'n breadfruit: A culinary memoir.* New York: New Press.

Guerrón Montero, Carla. 2002. "Esclavitud y Relaciones Interétnicas entre Afropanameños Coloniales y Afro-antillanos en Panamá (Siglo XIX) (Slavery and inter-ethnic relations between colonial blacks and Afro-Antilleans in Panama, 19th century)." *Revista Cultural Lotería* 442 (3): 79–96.

Guerrón Montero, Carla. 2004. "Afro-Antillean cuisine and global tourism." *Food, Culture, and Society* 7 (2): 29–47.

Guerrón Montero, Carla. 2005. "Marine protected areas in Panama: Grassroots activism and advocacy." *Human Organization* 64 (4): 360–72.

Guerrón Montero, Carla. 2006a. "Racial democracy and nationalism in Panama." *Ethnology* 45 (3): 209–28.

Guerrón Montero, Carla. 2006b. "Tourism and Afro-Antillean identity in Panama." *Journal of Tourism and Cultural Change* 4 (2): 65–84.

Guerrón Montero, Carla. 2008. "Afro-Panamanians." In *Encyclopedia of the African diaspora*, ed. Carole Boyce Davis, 743–48. Santa Barbara, Calif.: ABC-CLIO.

Heckadon Moreno, Stanley, ed. 1980. "Nota al Lector." In *Memorias de un Criollo Bocatoreño*, by Carlos Reid, 7–14. Panamá: Litho-Impresora Panamá.

Higman, B. W. 2008. *Jamaican food: History, biology, culture.* Kingston: University of the West Indies Press.

Idone, Christopher, with Helen McEachrene. 1992. *Cooking Caribe.* Plano, Tex.: Panache Press.

Instituto Panameño de Turismo (IPAT). 2004. *Análisis Estadístico sobre el movimiento turístico-período enero a Diciembre 2002–2003.* Panamá: Instituto Panameño de Turismo.

Johnston, Ronald John. 1990. "The challenge for regional geography: Some proposals for research frontiers." In *Regional geography: Current developments and future prospects*, ed. Ronald John Johnston, Joost Hauer, and Gerard Hoekveld, 122–39. London: Routledge.

Long, Lucy M. 2004. *Culinary tourism.* Lexington: University of Kentucky Press.

Mendieta, Adela, and Rogelio Husband. 1997. "Contribución del Afro-Antillano a la identidad nacional." Thesis, Universidad de Panama.

Mintz, Sydney W. 1997. *Tasting food, tasting freedom: Excursions into eating, culture, and the past.* Boston: Beacon Press.

Mintz, Sydney, and Christine Du Bois. 2002. "The anthropology of food and eating." *Annual Review of Anthropology* 31: 99–119.

Moore, Evelyn. 1938. *Sancocho: Stories and sketches of Panama.* Trans. Evelyn Moore. Panama City: Panama American.

Narayan, Uma. 1995. "Eating cultures: Incorporation, identity, and Indian food." *Social Identities* 1 (1): 63–86.

Smith, Monica L. 2006. "The archaeology of food preference*." American Anthropologist* 108 (3): 480–93.

Sobo, Elizabeth J. 1997. "The sweetness of fat: Health, procreation, and sociability in rural Jamaica." In *Food and culture: A reader*, ed. Carole M. Counihan and Penny van Esterik, 256–71. New York: Routledge.

Sutton, David E. 2010. "Food and the senses." *Annual Review of Anthropology* 39: 209–23.

Waisome, Felipe A., George Priestley, and Gerardo Maloney. 1981. "Documento Central del Primer Congreso del Negro Panameño." In *Memorias del Primer Congreso del Negro Panameño*, 62–103. Panamá: Impresora de la Nación.

Wilk, Richard. 1999. "'Real Belizean food': Building local identity in the transnational Caribbean." *American Anthropologist* 101 (2): 244–55.

Wilk, Richard. 2002. "Food and nationalism: The origins of 'Belizean food.'" In *Food nations: Selling taste in consumer societies*, ed. Warren Belasco and Phillip Scranton, 67–89. New York: Routledge.

Wilk, Richard. 2006. *Home cooking in the global village: Caribbean food from buccaneers to ecotourists.* New York: Berg.

10

Defending National Foodways
Laying Claim to Tradition
in Costa Rica

Theresa Preston-Werner

Gallo pinto, the quotidian Costa Rican breakfast dish of rice and beans, appears mundane, both to those who eat it daily and to those who regard it as one among many unmarked elements that constitute the landscape of Costa Rica. The Spanish name *gallo pinto* does not literally translate into fried rice and beans. Costa Ricans offer two translations. First, the name of the colorful mixture of rice and beans alludes to the speckled or painted feathers of a rooster (*gallo*). Second, *gallo pinto* may stem from the phrase *¿Quiere un gallito?* ("Do you want a bite of food?"), which is common among Costa Ricans. Despite its ubiquity, very little has been written about *pinto*. Perhaps it is precisely *pinto*'s everydayness that devalues it in the minds of researchers. Costa Rican authors Guillermo García Murillo and Luis Efrén García Brinceño omit any discussion of *pinto*, although, curiously, they write that it is the most preferred meal, and perhaps should be dubbed the national food of Costa Rica (1976: 10). This chapter makes use of foodways, and *pinto* in particular, as a lens through which to explore questions of national identity.

In recent years, municipal governments and national businesses both in Costa Rica and Nicaragua have sponsored "National Day of *Gallo Pinto*" celebrations, marking the food and encouraging patriotic public discourse.[1] These celebrations and the talk they inspire reveal many Costa Ricans' overt xenophobia against Nicaraguans and underlying racism against Afro–Costa Ricans. In what follows, I explain the dish's complex regional history, both within Costa Rica's borders and across the national border between Costa Rica and Nicaragua. In the same vein as my fellow volume contributors, I address the cultural and social context of rice and beans in Costa Rica. Subsequently I argue that the historical complexity, ambiguity, and current controversy surrounding the meal's origin(s) speak to larger issues of nationalism and xenophobia. I begin by suggesting that the meal may have originated in the early twentieth century on Costa Rica's Atlantic Coast. There, Afro–Costa Ricans, indigenous Costa Ricans, Hispanic Costa Ricans, and Nicaraguan migrant laborers worked together on banana plantations. During the second half of the twentieth century, the Costa Rican government passed laws to promote the development of rice agriculture instead of the alternative maize-based foodways eaten in other parts of Central America. At present, regional variations of *pinto* span Costa Rica. Simultaneous to talk that exhibits pride in local recipes, Costa Ricans speak about a generalized national dish of rice and beans. National identity is, in part, maintained by constructing a discursive border through binary distinctions. Costa Ricans, as documented in my fieldwork, others' academic work, and local media coverage, often distinguish themselves from most other Latin American residents, many of whom they consider to be poorer, less academically and socially educated, and less physically attractive. The daily meal of rice and beans speaks directly to this social conflict.

Competing Festivals: Is *Pinto* Costa Rican or Nicaraguan?

On March 21, 2010, Josefinos (residents of San José, the capital of Costa Rica) were delighted when they awoke to a rare cloudy morning; it meant that they could enjoy the day's festivities without suffering from the glare of the sun. That Sunday, Costa Rica celebrated a National Festival of *Gallo Pinto*, sponsored by San José's municipal government and various private businesses. The event was coordinated to occur during the weeklong Festival Internaciónal de Arte and concurrently with the annual celebration of San José, the saint for whom the city is named (Siles Navarro 2010).

Tents flagged the Central Avenue that runs the length of downtown, boasting commercial promotions of national, brand-name goods. More visible were the booths promoting national infrastructure, such as the health care system and water and electricity institutes, and the large and colorful inflatable children's slides. The avenue was closed to vehicles, and residents swarmed the four-lane-wide pavement, pushing children in strollers, riding bicycles and roller skates, walking their dogs, and walking two, three, and even four abreast, hand-in-hand. A half dozen stages set up along the street offered a variety of entertainment, from children's contests to singers and musicians of contemporary and folk music.

At various locations, residents waited in line patiently, and at times, impatiently, to receive free plates of *gallo pinto* with *natilla* (sour cream) and factory-made corn tortillas, presented by a man or woman dressed in either a white chef's uniform or a bright costume dress that harkened days past. Some locations offered additional foods, such as pickled vegetables, and another famous dish, *olla de carne* (a soup of beef, tubers, and vegetables). Josefinos quenched their thirst with complimentary coffee, and then clamored to receive free hats and T-shirts commemorating the event. Families and couples lined the sidewalks, where they leaned against buildings or sat on the pavement enjoying their food. An emcee spoke into a microphone and said,

"Today the men will come home later than usual, and women are unburdened from housework."

Upon finishing their food, people tossed their plates and silverware into trash cans, amid signs reminding them to respect the environment and to keep their country clean. If someone wanted to take a step farther to aid the environment, he or she could sign a petition advocating against privatization of water rights. No signs advertised the *gallo pinto* event, which more than ninety thousand people attended; nonetheless, residents were clear that this was a chance to eat *pinto* together in public and to be part of a cultural experience. Prior to attending the event, Costa Rican informants remarked that surely only poor people and Nicaraguans would seek out the free food. Recognizing the wide range of attendees and the skew toward Costa Rican participants, one man concluded, "Perhaps Nicaraguans don't want to eat Costa Rican *pinto* after all."

Since 2003 public and private organizations in Costa Rica and Nicaragua have declared their respective nation's invention of *gallo pinto* through national gastronomic events. The rival celebrations began with a Costa Rican event sponsored by the nongovernmental public body, Corporación Arrocera Nacional, and held in a public park in downtown San José. Fourteen days later, Pharaoh's Casino in Managua hosted a similar event in Nicaragua, hoping to trump Costa Rica's attempt to secure the record for world's largest dish of rice and beans.[2] Each year the celebrations have become more popular, boasting larger quantities of *pinto*, more types of food and beverages, and a greater diversity of events, including music and dance performances. Residents of each country fiercely protect their claim on the dish's origin. In an interview in 2007, the Marketing Manger of Pharaoh's remarked, "This idea was to demonstrate to Costa Rica that *gallopinto* is Nicaraguan" (Roa 2007).[3] Xenophobic comments appeared in online news articles that documented *pinto* celebrations in each country. Readers frequently criticized residents in the opposite country for having "stolen" their foodway. Such comments often drew parallels between appropriating foodways and other acts of thievery believed to be perpetrated by the other nation.

Costa Rica's event depends on private funding from a variety of businesses, although it has always been held in public locations in San José. The date has changed repeatedly over the years, but in 2008, when the Ministry of Culture and Costa Rican Tourism Institute became involved, the government declared April 13 to be National *Gallo Pinto* Day. In Nicaragua, Pharaoh's Casino sponsored the preparation and handing out of rice and beans in its Managua location from 2003 to 2007, always holding the event on September 15, the day that Nicaragua and Costa Rica both celebrate independence from Spain. Both national events donate their proceeds to various charities. Over the years, plates have cost on average one dollar, though Costa Rica stopped charging for plates in 2009 when the event was expected to draw more than fifty thousand participants (see Quirós 2003; Goodier 2005; Roa 2007;

Raub 2008; Leff 2009; "Free 'Gallo Pinto' for 30.000 on Sunday" 2008; Ana 2009).

Regional Variations in Costa Rica

Generally speaking, *pinto* in Costa Rica involves the mixing of white rice and black beans, both leftover components from the previous day. The mixture is newly fried with vegetable or palm oil for breakfast, and *olores* (aromatics) are added: yellow onion, garlic, sweet pepper, and cilantro. At the very end, Costa Ricans stir in *Salsa Lizano*, a dark, salty, and sweet sauce that tastes much like Worcestershire sauce. Variations on the recipe vary by region, and residents express both feelings of pride toward their own recipes and dislike of other regional variations. In northern Costa Rica, *pinto* is often toasted to a crisp and called by the full name, *gallo pinto*, which may relate to the region's connection to Nicaragua. In the Central Highlands, where the capital, San José, is located, locals say only *pinto* and include plenty of oil to make the dish wetter. Some families cook with red beans, as did my host family in southern Costa Rica, but most people prefer black beans. Only once did I receive an explanation for specific bean choice other than personal preference or whichever happened to be on sale at the grocery. In this instance a woman suggested that members of the urban, middle-class ate black beans while working-class, rural residents ate red beans. Other informants rejected this idea unanimously.

When I asked southern Costa Ricans to discuss regional versions of *pinto*, they sharply distinguished all regional recipes of *pinto* from the version cooked on the Atlantic Coast, which they described as unpalatable and strange. In Costa Rica's Caribbean province, Limón, residents call *pinto* "rice and beans" in English and cook the rice with coconut milk instead of water. Red beans are added (although black can be used as well), as well as a special *pimienta roja* (locally grown spicy red pepper) that gives the dish a kick. Notably the rice-to-bean ratio greatly favors the rice, differing from other versions in Costa Rica, which contain an even mixture.

I can speak to the regularity with which *pinto* is eaten for breakfast. For more than a decade I awoke to the crackle of rice and beans as they mixed together in the cast-iron frying pan on the electric stove.[4] Most often my host mother, Doña Pilar, or one of her two grown daughters, cooked. Doña Pilar's husband or their grown son only cooked when they awoke to an empty house or missed breakfast. Later, I often prepared the morning coffee or the day's rice. *Pinto* is the staple of the breakfast meal, and it often comes accompanied by fried or scrambled eggs, fried sausage or bologna, fried or plain salty cheese, store-bought corn tortillas, toast or bread with sour cream, fresh pineapple, mango, papaya, or watermelon, avocadoes bathed in salt, and always coffee with plenty of sugar and perhaps milk. Occasionally Doña Pilar made fresh corn tortillas, *arepas* (corn pancakes), or *empanadas* (corn and cheese pastries) to accompany the meal.

Many years passed before I began to question my image of Costa Rican breakfast traditions. Then, one day, a young man who was raised in the Central Valley quietly admitted to me that he did not grow up eating *pinto*. He was one of six siblings in a poor family, and he had rarely received more than a cup of sugared coffee and bread or crackers to start his school day. I tell his story here because it impacted my understanding of "tradition." National traditions exist and grow out of local practices, but they may not be the practices of every citizen. Subsequent conversations with informants led me to see the breakfast of my southern family as the breakfast of a middle-class or wealthy family, particularly because meat was frequently served. I learned that *pinto* is commonplace, but so too is a simpler, cheaper breakfast of coffee and toast. When I traveled north to visit another anthropologist, I experienced breakfasts based around gigantic homemade corn tortillas and *pinto*. I also learned that children in some families insisted on eating cornflakes instead of *pinto*. Yet Costa Rican restaurants promote a uniform image of a typical national breakfast; most serve *pinto*, eggs, bread and sour cream, and coffee. Residents, members of the tourist industry, and government officials uphold *pinto* across the nation as the single most culturally identifiable Costa Rican food, but this place at the head of the symbolic table of Costa Rican foodways does not signify universal accessibility.

Nicaraguan Gallo Pinto

Like Costa Rican foodways, contemporary Nicaraguan foodways stem from an amalgamation of indigenous, European, and African foods and cooking practices (Wheelock Román 2007: 7). Nicaraguans, more so than Costa Ricans, emphasized the numerous and commonplace maize-based foods that dominate their culinary traditions, in addition to the omnipresent *gallopinto*. This explains the presence of homemade tortillas in Guanacaste, which belonged to Nicaragua until its annexation by Costa Rica in 1824. By far the most common difference between Costa Rican *pinto* and Nicaraguan *gallo pinto* noted by informants was their preference for different beans. Costa Ricans like black beans, and Nicaraguans like red beans. "No comemos frijoles negros. Somos racistas," joked a young Nicaraguan woman to me as we sat in her small, rented home in San José, Costa Rica. "We don't eat black beans. We're racists," she had said. The woman's double-edged comment communicates a great deal with its wit. Nicaraguans endlessly find themselves the butt of Costa Rican jokes that serve to compare the two nations, and with this quip, the woman simultaneously recognized the extant xenophobia that Nicaraguans endure and empowered herself and her fellow countrymen to be the jokesters (Masís Fernández and Paniagua Arguedas 2008).

Other differences in food preparation and eating customs distinguish Nicaraguan rice and beans (called the full name *gallo pinto* or *gallopinto*). In Costa Rica *pinto* is a breakfast dish (although rice and beans served separately accompany most lunch and dinner meals or can constitute an entire dinner meal). In contrast, the *gallo pinto* mixture can be found on Nicaraguan plates at every meal. Like Costa Ricans, Nicaraguans use leftover rice and beans to create the mixture. Nicaraguan *gallo pinto*, however, involves frying the rice and beans separately in a little cooking oil, then mixing them together, and adding yellow onions and garlic (no sweet red pepper, cilantro, or *Salsa Lizano*). Nicaraguans complained that Costa Rican *pinto* is too full of *olores* (strong-smelling ingredients), which mask the taste of the rice and beans. They described their version of the dish as the most appetizing, describing the rice and beans of other nations across the Caribbean and Central America as too dry, too pretentious in their ingredients, or too sweet. Nicaraguan comments regarding inter-regional taste echo those made by Costa Ricans regarding intranational distinctions.

Pinto's Ambiguous History in Costa Rica

My interest in the social history of *pinto* was piqued when I first noted the differences between Costa Rican foodways and those of nearby countries. Costa Rica is a crossing-point for three regions. As evidenced by archaeology, history, and culture, populations and their goods have crossed Costa Rica as they journeyed south from Mesoamerica, north from South America, and across the sea from the Caribbean. Initially I saw Costa Ricans' preference for rice and beans as curious in light of their location on the southern end of Mesoamerica, a geocultural region known for maize-based foodways. Yet in Costa Rica's southern province, maize-based foods are not eaten daily. Instead rice and beans dominate.

The history of rice and beans as a meal in Costa Rica is one of global political, economic, and social change. Caribbean immigrants, Central American Hispanics, Europeans, and U.S. Americans came together at the turn of the nineteenth century on Costa Rica's Atlantic Coast, bringing with them varying foodways that would eventually define contemporary Costa Rican cuisine. The cultivation of rice dates to 1789 among the Spanish (Cabezas, Porras, and Espinoza 1996). While the Spanish may have grown the grain, it was cultivated in such small quantities that it would not likely have been a staple component of the diet. Instead, many Costa Rican researchers who specialize in foodways argue that African slavery in the Caribbean was the conduit through which rice and beans as a typical food eventually arrived in Costa Rica in the mid- to late 1800s (Cabezas Bolaños and Espinoza Esquivel 2000: 14–17; Ross de Cerdas 2001, 2003: 59–61).[5]

Emancipated slaves moved in large numbers to Costa Rica's Atlantic Coast when slavery was abolished in the Caribbean during the 1800s. Asian workers flooded the Caribbean labor market driving down wages. As a result, more than two hundred thousand former British West Indians relocated to Central and South America to work on railroad construction projects, the Panama Canal, and banana plantations between 1850 and 1910 (Putnam 2002: 35). In particular, Jamaicans immigrated to the Atlantic coast of Costa Rica following abolition in the 1830s. Under the direction of the Bostonian Minor C. Keith, Jamaicans worked to expand the railroad from the inland capital of San José to the Atlantic coastal city of Limón in the 1870s and harvested bananas for the United Fruit Company in the 1890s (Putnam 2002).

Sources differ about whether or not Afro–Costa Ricans banana growers and harvesters grew their own subsistence crops and which foods were typical. Aviva Chomsky writes that the production of basic crops for sale was highly discouraged by the United Fruit Company, although workers did maintain their own small gardens (1996: 83–86). In contrast, Jeffry Pilcher writes that immigrant Afro–Costa Rican workers frequently cultivated their own small plots of rice for subsistence purposes (2000: 1280–81). Philippe I. Bourgois adds, "[The] majority of the West Indian banana workers at the turn of the century were obliged at the same time to be part-time peasants in order to survive" (1989: 68). He notes that during the construction of the cross-country railroads, Keith "kept his labor force from starving or emigrating by arranging for the Costa Rican government to provide his unemployed workers with land upon which to cultivate subsistence crops (Koch 1975: 80)" (1989: 68–69). Finally, Bourgois explains that, like the railroad workers, banana workers were encouraged to grow their own food because this enabled company owners to suppress wages (1989: 69). In her research of foodways among banana plantation workers in the early twentieth century, Patricia Vega Jiménez writes that the black population raised its own animals and planted root cops because they were encouraged to do by company owners who gave them plots of land to cultivate (2002: 102). She adds that Afro–Costa Ricans, more often than other groups, cooked their food at home instead of eating in company dining halls (102).

Rice and beans as a meal may not have been quotidian from the start. Root crops and teas were the basis of Afro–Costa Rican diets, with rice and beans saved as a special meal eaten only on Sundays and holidays (Vega Jiménez 2002: 103). Quince Duncan offers a similar suggestion: "Rice and beans were not, in the beginning, the quotidian dish. On the contrary, it was the special plate reserved for Sundays and special days. Many varieties of beans were planted in the family gardens, as well as the rest of the basic foods" (2005: 126). Nonetheless, the dish of rice and beans transitioned from a special affairs meal to a common dish by the time Carlos Luis Fallas lived and worked on Limón's banana plantations (Vega Jiménez 2002: 107). The famous Costa Rican author demonstrates *pinto*'s ubiquity in the cultural landscape of the Caribbean coast as early as the 1920s when he writes in the novella, *Mamita Yunai*, "In the morning we said to the Shepardess that she must send us the *gallo pinto* with the kitchen helper from Azuola" (1957: 138).

Beginning in 1910, another population joined the Afro-Caribbean immigrants on Costa Rica's Atlantic Coast: Nicaraguan migrant workers and immigrants (Bourgois 1989: 54). By 1927, Lara Putnam writes that of Limón's residents, 37 percent were Spanish speakers, a quarter of whom had been born abroad, 72 percent in Nicaragua (2002: 65). Initially, Nicaraguans migrated to the province of Limón as strikebreakers for the banana industry, but within a few years word had spread that banana workers received twice the pay as did agricultural workers in Costa Rica's Central Highlands, so an increasing number of Nicaraguan and Costa Rican nationals began to move to Limón (181). As early as the late 1800s, many landless Nicaraguan laborers followed the higher wages to Limón, although they often found themselves performing the least desirable tasks, such as clearing the virgin jungle. Many Nicaraguans migrated annually between Nicaragua and Limón. Putnam writes:

> The intermittent waves of migration from Nicaragua over the course of the twentieth century are today the focus of much hostility within Costa Rica, expressed in nationalist terms. But the autobiographies of *campesinos* [peasants] who ended their days in Limón describe not an ongoing Nicaraguan invasion but rather a unified social geography within which people with relatives on both sides of the border moved back and forth over the course of their working lives. (2002: 70)

Banana production peaked in the first decade of the twentieth century, followed by a downward economic turn during World War I. Putnam writes that fewer Hispanic workers (Costa Rican and Nicaraguan) returned seasonally to plantation work (2002: 64).

In addition to Nicaraguan laborers, Costa Rican nationals from the northern Guanacaste province and lighter-skinned Central Valley nationals began to arrive in the mid-1920s and 1930s (Bourgois 1989: 183). Guanacastecans (residents of Costa Rica's Guanacaste province) have long suffered discrimination within Costa Rica for their differentiating cultural and physical characteristics (a tendency toward darker skin, local speech and accent, and poorer economic means). Many present-day residents of the region are of Nicaraguan descent or are Nicaraguan immigrants, further identifying the region as a borderland between the two nations. Oftentimes Costa Ricans refer to Guanacastecans by the racist term, *nicas regalados*, meaning Nicaraguans that have been handed over to Costa Rica. Bourgois notes, however, that many Guanacastecans are fiercely patriotic to Costa Rica (1989: 185–86). The migration of Nicaraguans and Costa Ricans from the Central Valley between their homelands and the Atlantic Coast is one avenue for the transmission of *pinto* and its adoption outside of Limón. In Nicaragua, *gallopinto* first appeared in association with banana plantations and later became an urban food (Wheelock Román 2007: 236–37).

While Limón's residents were heterogeneous during United Fruit's reign in the first third of the twentieth century, the social hierarchy did not favor Hispanics, either Nicaraguan or Costa Rican, planting the seeds for racial and cultural hostilities that exist to this day. Due to their longtime presence in the region, often for more than one generation, Caribbean immigrants were able to purchase small plots of land and exit the plantation system. If not, they rose in rank to become housing construction workers, considered to be easier labor. This was, in part, due to their ease of communication with English-speaking American owners. Hispanic workers, in contrast, were viewed as poor, young, uneducated, and violent (Putnam 2002: 175–77).

Vega Jiménez (2002) shows that pay rates for workers on the railroad in Limón were differentiated by race, and she correlates the rates with workers' cultural foodways (2002: 104). For example, Hispanic Costa Rican workers received 35 cents daily and ate rice, fat, meat, beans, crackers, salt, sugar, and coffee. Italians received 50 cents and ate spaghetti and meat (104). Vega Jiménez does not offer a comparison of wage and food for Nicaraguan or Afro–Costa Rican workers, nor does she locate rice and beans within the Afro–Costa Rican culture; instead, she assigns the dish to a general category of Central American banana workers. Workers who did not wish to eat in the dining hall could purchase goods, including rice and beans, at the company store for a significantly higher price (2002: 107). In a conversation, Vega Jiménez stressed that she believed *pinto* stems from neither solely Afro-Caribbean nor Hispanic Central American foodways.

While Vega Jiménez seems to suggest segregated cultural foodways among plantation workers, other writers portray more blurred cuisine boundaries. Paula Palmer quotes an informant who says that early in the twentieth century white Costa Ricans who lived in the United Fruit Company's camps took on black customs, including cooking preferences (2005: 134). Palmer cites lists of the foods that were prepared at large, group holidays and plantation events; rice and beans appeared first on the list (2005: 180).

Rice and beans developed into a staple in the diets of Caribbean coast banana workers. Still, maize continued to embody most Costa Ricans' foodways for the first half of the twentieth century. Rice in Costa Rica grew very well, with little care and no irrigation. The primary national rice-growing region, however, was located in the northwest and was hard to access, so Costa Rica still imported large quantities of rice from Asia each year (Edelman 1992: 305). The completion of the Pan-American Highway in the 1940s facilitated interregional transport. In 1949, the Ministry of Agriculture pushed to develop improved rice seeds, resulting in the modernization and mechanization of rice cultivation. At the time, most maize was grown by small sharecroppers who were "largely unable ... to assume the financial burdens and risks required to shift to mechanized modern farming" (1992: 306). A final push to increase the production of rice came in 1965 with the establishment of the Central American Common Market (CACM). This was intended to encourage free trade between Central American countries. Because Costa Rica had higher production costs than the other countries, free trade was not advantageous. Costa Rica's National Production Council opposed the CACM and selected one basic food for domestic development out of the four covered by the treaty—rice, maize, sorghum, or beans. Costa Rican officials elected rice because of its "greatest comparative advantage in terms of technological development, productivity, investment capacity of the producers, and geographic location" (Piszk 1982: 4 in Edelman 1992: 306). Only a few years later, when international oil prices grew and affected transportation costs, the Costa Rican government promoted self-sufficiency instead of trade and created a National Basic Grains Program that concentrated on the development of high-yield rice.

From 1960 to 1980, Costa Rica's per capita supplies of maize decreased (Pacheco 1983: 38). In contrast, rice consumption rose. During this time rice growers were supported by crop-insurance policies issued by Costa Rica's National Insurance Institute, which insured nearly the full operating costs and created a boom (Edelman 1992: 307). By 1980, annual per capita consumption of rice surpassed fifty-two kilograms (Edelman 1992: 420 fn 35). Despite programs of structural adjustment that began in 1984 and that lessened support for national rice production, the grain had become a key component of Costa Rican foodways.

Defining National Foodways through Negation and Erasure

In both interviews and community surveys, Costa Ricans described *pinto* as a "traditional" Costa Rican food, identifying it with the nation as a whole. I have come to question whether the dish began organically and then found its place as a nationally recognized food, or if its status as the signature Costa Rican dish is determined more by its promotion in festivals, tourist fare, and local restaurants.[6] Cultural theorist Jorge Larrain cautions that national identity should consider the interconnected role of (1) the public sphere "as articulated discourses, highly selective and constructed from above by a variety of cultural agents and institutions" and (2) the social base "as a form of personal and group subjectivity which expresses a verity of practices, moves of life and feelings which become representative of a nation's identity and which sometimes are not well presented in public versions of identity" (2000: 34). These two perspectives are symbiotic, or dialectic, in practice. Officially sanctioned symbols, as *pinto* has come to be in Costa Rica, most often derive from local cultural groups. They are promoted at a national level and adopted by the nation at-large, albeit after they have been modified from the original creators' use and meaning (Wade 2000; Gal 1991). Costa Ricans conceptualize rice and beans as a "traditional" food based not only on their individual, personal histories, but also due to overarching influences, such as the national government and media, which bolster the image of *pinto* as *the* national food. For instance, in late 2007, Costa Rica's Tourism Institute sponsored both the National Day of *Gallo Pinto* and an exhibit in the National Museum on Costa Rican cuisine that featured *pinto* as the national dish.

The act of labeling a practice or material object "traditional" embodies it with a romantic, ahistorical quality and can wash away the need to remember clear historical details (Preston-Werner 2009; see also Sharman 2006). In interviews, Costa Ricans and Nicaraguans alike listed rice and beans as one of their most typical foods, explaining that they had eaten the dish since childhood. When I pressed individuals to consider *pinto*'s origins, informants imposed their own imagined history and symbolic meaning. Many suggested *pinto* developed in northern Costa Rica. They justified their claims by linking the dish's place of origin with their own—their own families had migrated south from the north, so the dish must have developed there as well. My origin question befuddled them, forcing residents to consider the legacy of something that seemed so innate. Folklorist Henry Glassie explains, "History and tradition are comparable in dynamic; they exclude more than they include, and so remain open to endless revision. They are functionally congruent in their incorporation of the usable past. But the terms cannot be reduced, on to the other" (1995: 395). Conzuelo Cruz, a political scientist, echoes a similar perspective; regarding national history, "the ring of truth is often no more than the ring of the familiar" (2000: 280).

Historian Jeffrey M. Pilcher further supports the call to question the top-down, bottom-up contradiction of national culture creation. To the discussion, he adds the complicated notion of authenticity: "The construction of a national cuisine inevitably reduced complex regional dialects to a few stereotyped dishes, thereby undermining the search for authenticity" (1998: 156). Pilcher cites Jean-François Revel, who denied the existence of national cuisines and focused instead on the purely local (due to the unique environment of ingredients) and international styles (deemed works of art) (157). For residents in Costa Rica, national and regional symbolic meanings collapse into the single dish. *Pinto* at once signifies local and authentic variations and a generalized national version.

Still, no tourist photo album is complete without visual documentation of the ubiquitous *gallo pinto* served at breakfast in Costa Rica. The photos are often accompanied by eaters' critical descriptions of the meal. Tourists variously question how Costa Ricans tolerate eating the same, bland food every day, as if they have or know no other option. Other tourists romanticize the meal, describing it as hardy, flavorful, and satisfying, and adding that they wished they ate as well at home. In a time of political correctness, judgment of food stands in for blatant assessment of Costa Ricans themselves. Foreigners leave Costa Rica with a firm symbolic linkage between food and place, and by extension, people (Trubek 2005). They do not generally know that not all Costa Ricans eat *pinto* each morning, and Costa Ricans' preference for rice and beans often varies by class status. Costa Ricans who can afford to dine at the restaurants frequented by breakfasting tourists might opt for a different breakfast or eat cornflakes or only toast and eggs in their own homes. Hence, restaurants may be catering to and promoting an image of Costa Rica that is the one expected by foreigners. Certainly restaurants located in high-end hotels that serve *pinto* under the label "Costa Rican typical breakfast" are marketing an image of national unity that suggests an easily commodified and packaged identity.

Defending Foodways from the Other

Since at least the nineteenth century Costa Ricans have created an imagined community that links nationalism with egalitarianism and democracy (Sandoval García 2008). Concurrent to this project, though less overt, is an assumption of whiteness

(Molina Jiménez 2005; Appadurai 1993; Anderson 1983).[7] These conceptions of national identity are projected onto local assumptions about taste, in this case regarding *pinto*, simultaneously reaffirming taste as a nationally unifying construct and obscuring from view those individuals who do not fit into the project.

To strengthen Costa Rican national identity, political leaders have historically emphasized Costa Rica's differences from its northern neighbor (Sandoval García 2008; Cruz 2000). Cruz writes, "By 1835 dread of a Nicaraguan 'infection' was very much in the open. ... [A]t every point they confronted the fact of Nicaraguan neighbors, 'possessed of many good and brilliant qualities' but 'generally indolent, accustomed to internal strife, and inclined to fight with neighboring states'" (Cruz 2000: 301, 303). Such fears were intensified by the 1824 annexation of Nicoya by Costa Rica from Nicaragua and the 1854 Cañas-Jérez Treaty regulating the San Juan River that serves as the geopolitical border between the nations (Sandoval García 2008: 155). Cruz argues, "The rhetorical frames that emerge as dominant at critical junctures in the history of a group or a nation" show how the political economies of Costa Rica and Nicaragua derive from purposefully crafted accounts of national history (2000: 276). Costa Rican historians and political figures emphasized positive aspects of their country's social and economic structures, establishing a precedent upheld by future leaders and academics (Cruz 2000). Put more succinctly: "National tradition itself is a political invention" (Cruz 2000: 279). Hence Costa Rica's history of egalitarianism, Castillo heritage (whiteness), and democracy depends as much on long-standing rhetoric as on actual events (Cruz 2000).

Sandoval García complicates this view of national historiography to argue that Costa Rica's national identity is not entirely uniform and has shifted over time. He writes:

> It [the author's analysis of data] has explored the transition between discourses that refer to the colonial times and representations that identify Costa Rica as a middle-class nation ... there is not a singular hegemonic discourse of national identity, but that there are different versions fighting for legitimacy to represent the national sentiment. (2008: 112)

Nonetheless, as Costa Ricans debate their changing identities, both public and private discourses continue to emphasize Costa Ricans' superiority over Nicaraguans. Rice and beans have come to be understood in the minds of individual Costa Ricans as intimately tied to this legacy of nationalism. *Pinto* exists in consumers' minds as the dish of the citizenry. That informants expressed a dual allegiance to the meal as a symbol of a united country and as a symbol of regional cuisine expresses the tension between Cruz's argument for strategic nation-building and that of Sandoval García for the recognition of moments of variation.

Presently, Costa Ricans bemoan the strain on national resources and state infrastructure they attribute to Nicaraguan immigrants (Sandoval García 2008). Spurred by the Sandinista Revolution in 1979, Nicaraguans fled to Costa Rica, initially fleeing political violence and later poverty (Molina Jiménez 2005: 104–8). Until I began to read the literature in which Costa Rican academics document rates of immigration, I was under the impression that one-quarter of the people residing in Costa Rica were foreign-born, and most of those were Nicaraguans. Despite Costa Ricans' perceptions, only 5.9 percent of the population was Nicaraguan from the 2000 census, and only 7.8 percent during the highest times of coffee harvesting (Sandoval García 2008: xvii). Of the immigrant population, Nicaraguans do constitute the largest percentage: 76.4 percent (Castro Valverde 2008: 26), nearly half of whom are between the ages of twenty and thirty-nine (30), and as many women migrate as do men (26).

Regarding the xenophobic and unjust treatment of Nicaraguan migrants in Costa Rica, Lina Morales, coordinator of the Fondo Centroamericano de Mujeres, boldly said:

> When you arrive in Costa Rica they ask you where you are from because the *ticos* [Costa Ricans] have the image that all Nicaraguans are dark-skinned, small, and dark-haired. ... They can't believe that there is a Nicaraguan that can study and be something. ... Well this ... is xenophobia. (Interview, September 16, 2009)

The term *nica* (similar to the shortened Costa Rican descriptor *tico*) has come to mean not only Nicaraguan, but also anyone who is dirty, dark-skinned, uneducated, brutish, or hostile. So pervasive are these stereotypes that schoolchildren relayed them to researchers in surveys (Sandoval García 2008). Costa Rican jokes about Nicaraguans are circulated daily via cellphone and told both in public and private spaces, among friends and strangers. In response, the Nicaraguan band, CPU, wrote and composed the song, "Nica en Costa Rica" ("Nicaraguan in Costa Rica"), which opens with a parody of Costa Rica's famous song, "The Swiss of the Americas" (accompanied by upbeat, traditional marimba music) and quickly switches into a heavy-metal ballad detailing the misadventures of a Nicaraguan man in San José. The animated music video for "Nica en Costa Rica" ends with a drawn image of rice and beans and the caption, "Costa Rica rice and shit." This final statement drives home the point of the song. Costa Rica is not the egalitarian, tranquil nation with distinguished tastes it purports to be—moreover, its food tastes like shit. As evidenced by the song's lyrics, Nicaraguans recognize their stigmatized and subservient societal position, but they will remain neither silent nor hidden.

Academics document and local media emphasize the contemporary discord between the two nations.[8] Most recently, since October 2010, Costa Ricans and Nicaraguans have been embroiled in the latest of a long history of disagreements over land rights ("Dredging up Votes" 2010). Such geographic disputes embolden residents to disparage the opposing country and its residents. Costa Rican and Nicaraguan newspapers revel in the chance to pit the two countries against one another discursively, fanning the flames of xenophobia. The dispute becomes particularly apparent in the dueling festivals celebrating each nation's claim to *pinto*'s origin. The definite origin(s) of *pinto* in Costa Rica is not as important, perhaps, as is individuals' reactions when confronted with the dish's history. While my informants expressed disbelief that *pinto* could have an Afro–Costa Rican origin, both Costa Ricans and Nicaraguans expressed frustration and rage when I suggested the possibility that *pinto* originated in the other's country. One informant, a young Nicaraguan woman who lives in San José and who is married to a Costa Rican, spoke with her sister and me about Nicaraguan foods, especially *gallo pinto*:

Theresa: Well, do you believe that there is a dish that, well, that you would call a national dish?
Woman 1:   *Baho* is.
Woman 2:   It's that the national plates are *baho*, the *nacatamal*, what we call the *vigoron*, pork with *yucca*, and *gallo pinto* with a cheese-filled ripe plantain.
Woman 1:   Which the *ticos* say is theirs.
Woman 2:   No, no but it doesn't belong to the *ticos*. It's Nicaraguan.

This woman's comments, and those of her sister, echo the claim made by both Nicaraguans and Costa Ricans regarding *pinto*; many insist that the dish belongs to their respective nation and that the recipe was stolen by members of the opposing nation.

On the Internet, where anonymity encourages unrestrained thought, Costa Ricans and Nicaraguans call for patriotism and freely make inflammatory xenophobic statements. The food dispute links to other geopolitical or cultural issues, such as the annexation of Nicoya, border disputes over the San Juan River, or an incident in which two Costa Rican Rottweiler guard dogs killed a Nicaraguan trespasser. One middle-aged Nicaraguan woman explained to me:

Theresa: It seems to me that, that sometimes they don't get along [Nicaraguans and Costa Ricans].
Woman: Huh, huh. No.
Theresa: But I don't understand, well, why.
Woman: Because according to the Costa Ricans, the Nicaraguans went in to take their food from them during the war, but the Costa Ricans are thieves as well. They stole various, various, all of what is next to Nicaragua.
Theresa: Of Guanacaste?
Woman: All Guanacaste. Guanacaste was stolen.

While the majority of the comments I encountered online maliciously characterized citizens of either Costa Rica or Nicaragua, depending on the author's nationality, occasionally I came across writers who suggested that a bridge between the nations could be created. One Costa Rican wrote, "I think that your *gallopinto* is very different from ours, perhaps one day I will invite you to eat a plate of Nicaraguan

Gallopinto" ("El Gallopinto es Nica!!!!!!!" 2008). Another writer, of unknown nationality, offered an alternate perspective: "*Gallopinto* is neither Nicaraguan nor Costa Rican, it is a LATIN AMERICAN food" ("Donde se creó el plato de comida gallo pinto?" 2007). These writers' comments, I hope, show that xenophobia between Costa Ricans and Nicaraguans, while pervasive, is not exhaustive. Moreover, individuals' tastes for *pinto*, while learned, intimate, and emotional, can also be flexible and open to change.

Conclusions

In this chapter I have discussed how the ordinary meal of rice and beans links to broader political, economic, and social issues faced daily by Costa Ricans and Nicaraguans. *Pinto* has developed meanings from the ground up as a quotidian breakfast food with regionally specific recipes and from the top down as a symbol to citizens, tourists, and outsiders of national unity. Its unclear history has been easily co-opted by those in power to promote a singular story that plays to values ingrained in the Costa Rican psyche. Nationally sponsored celebrations of *pinto* highlight this effort to unify the Costa Rican and Nicaraguan populations respectively and to downplay undesirable histories or contemporary cultural cleavages. I have pointed to potential elements of the dish's history, such as its suggested link to Costa Rica's Afro-Caribbean community and banana plantation legacy, which remain unacknowledged in public discourse.

The two sets of geocultural distinctions that I have discussed involve both intraregional differences in Costa Rica's rice and beans recipes and international differences between Costa Rican and Nicaraguan rice and beans. These two sets stem, I have argued, from an intertwined history connected to Nicaraguan and Costa Rican labor on banana plantations at the turn of the twentieth century.

While intraregional and international differences at first appear opposed, they are heavily interrelated. Within Costa Rica, Costa Ricans recognize regionally distinct recipes for *pinto*. Rarely are comments of superiority made about regional variations, with the exception being a generalized distaste for the *rice and beans* cooked on the Atlantic Coast by Afro–Costa Ricans. Interestingly, most Costa Ricans offered in interviews that as individuals they have their own secret practices to make the *pinto* their own, such as smushing beans at a particular moment or crushing the garlic instead of mincing it. At the same time that they recognize regional differences, Costa Ricans acknowledge a more generalized national dish of rice and beans.

The promotion of a national dish concretizes Costa Ricans' widely held view of their country as exceptional in regard to other Central American nations. Similarly, their egalitarian view of regional varieties underscores a praxis of popularism. This view exists in concert with a history of imagining the nation as white, highlighted in Costa Ricans' negative feelings toward both the taste of Afro–Costa Rican *rice and beans* and the dish's potential gastronomic history in the Caribbean.

On a daily basis, *pinto* is banal. It is created and consumed most often in the privacy of one's home. Its quotidian place in society does not invite discussion. Not until San José's municipal government began promoting a National Day of *Gallo Pinto* did the meal move into public space. Each year, residents in the Central Valley attend the event, and those who live throughout the country participate through reading newspapers and watching newscast reports on television. In these moments residents discuss how exceptional their national food truly is. One can imagine the frustration felt by the thousands of Nicaraguan immigrants who live in Costa Rica and who believe the food to be theirs.

Nicaragua responded with its own *gallopinto* festival, attempting to outdo its southern neighbor. Such overt competition between the countries fuels extent xenophobia and serves to galvanize nationalist identity-building through the use of binary oppositions. That Costa Rica's festival gained funding from both state and private industry, offers its food for free to consumers, and has been consistently repeated annually, while Nicaragua's festival seems to have petered out after only a couple of years of private sponsorship and charging for plates of food, evinces the political and economic differences between the two nations.

Ultimately, the promotion of *pinto* as the national food of Costa Rica serves three goals. First, the meal unifies residents to bolster national solidarity. This practice speaks to the second goal, which is the differentiation of Costa Rica from other Central American countries. The National Day of *Gallo Pinto* festival epitomizes this goal through the image of the state's ability to feed all of its citizens. Reinforcing national solidarity and differentiating Costa Rica from other Central American countries impact the third goal, of depicting Costa Rica as an idyllic nation to the international community, whose members visit and finance Costa Rica's largest industry—tourism. *Pinto* is commodified for tourists through its appearance on menus in every tourist restaurant and as a souvenir of one's experience through English-language cookbooks, postcards, T-shirts, and posters sold in gift shops.

The recipe below, in fact, comes from one such book, *Sabores Típicos de Costa Rica* (*Traditional Flavors of Costa Rica*, 2008), edited by Jacob A. Eide and Trina N. Tobey, which I purchased as part of my growing collection of Costa Rican cookbooks. The book is a collection of recipes produced by the Association of United Ladies of Agua Buena, an innovative women's group from the southern region of the country that formed to generate employment for families.

Recipe: Costa Rican *Gallo Pinto*

Ingredients

½ whole plus 1 tbsp. diced onion
3 garlic cloves
½ whole plus 4 tbsp. diced red bell pepper

3 tbsp. oil
2 cups rice
3½ tsp. salt
1 lb. beans
2 stalks of cilantro
½ tsp. oregano
1 tbsp. *Salsa Lizano* (or similar Worcestershire sauce)

To prepare the rice at any time

1. Sauté 1 tbsp. diced onion, 1 clove diced garlic, and 1 tbsp. diced red bell pepper in 1 tbsp. oil.
2. Wash 2 cups rice. Add to the onion, bell pepper, and garlic. Sauté for 2 minutes.
3. Add 3 cups water and ½ tsp. salt. Place the cover on the pot.
4. Bring to a boil and reduce heat to low. Cook until the water is absorbed.

To prepare the beans

1. Wash 1 lb. beans. Place them in a pot with 2 quarts of water. Leave the beans to soak overnight.
2. Remove the water and add 2 new quarts of water, 2 cloves of minced garlic, 3 tbsp. diced red bell pepper, 1 stalk of cilantro, and ½ tsp. oregano.
3. Bring to a boil and then reduce heat and simmer for 3 hours until soft.
4. Add 3 tsp. salt.

To prepare the pinto in the morning

1. Sauté ½ diced onion in 2 tbsp. oil for 2 minutes.
2. After the onion is tender, stir in the rice and sauté for 3 minutes.
3. Next, add the beans and cook for 2 minutes.
4. Stir in ½ diced red bell pepper and cook for 1 minute.
5. Then, add 1 stalk of cilantro and cook for 1 minute more.
6. Finally stir in 1 tbsp. *Salsa Lizano* (optional) and cook for 2 minutes.
7. Eat with scrambled eggs, tortillas, and sour cream.

Notes

1. As a primarily Costa Rica–based field researcher, I focused this chapter primarily on Costa Ricans and Nicaraguans living in Costa Rica. Fieldwork specific to this chapter took place in June–August 2002 and August 2006 in southern Costa Rica, and in September 2009 in Nicaragua and Costa Rica, and March and April 2010 in Costa Rica during Nicaragua's and Costa Rica's respective Día del *Gallo Pinto* festivals.

2. In 2009 I visited Pharaoh's Casino to attend the celebration, but when I arrived in Managua, employees explained that the event had never been planned, and I was turned away without an explanation.
3. All translations from Spanish are my own.
4. I have conducted fieldwork in Costa Rica since 1998 and often stay in the home of one family.
5. In a prior publication (2009), I documented highland Costa Ricans' denial of *gallo pinto*'s possible origin among Afro–Costa Ricans living on the Caribbean coast.
6. *Pinto* recipes are common in the Costa Rican English- and Spanish-language cookbooks sold in souvenir and bookshops. For examples, see Coto 2007; Watts 2007; De Musmanni and de Weiler 2001. Acuña's book of Costa Rican jokes may gain readers who reach for its food-focused title *Gallo Pinto* (1990). Juana R. de Aragón's *La cocina costarricense* (2003 [1903]) is considered the earliest published cookbook. It does not contain a *pinto* recipe, suggesting that its publication may have preceded the dish's rise to popularity. Instead, Doña Juana names black beans as the national dish.
7. This vision excludes Afro–Costa Ricans from "deep, horizontal comradeship" and obscures them from public view and cultural memory (Anderson 1983: 7). In his recent article, "Re/Making La Negrita: Culture as an Aesthetic System in Costa Rica" (2006), Russell Leigh Sharman documents this historical praxis through the example of Costa Rica's patroness, a black Madonna called *La Negrita*. While the apparition was witnessed by a part-black girl and the icon once belonged to the Afro–Costa Rican community in the Central Valley, the dominant white segment of society appropriated the symbol to stand for nationalism and class concerns (2006). The social history of *pinto* may not be dissimilar to that of *La Negrita*.
8. For more information on media coverage of Nicaraguan immigrants in Costa Rica and Costa Rican public discourse regarding Nicaraguans, see Campos Zamora and Tristán Jiménez (2009).

References

Acuña, Pio Luis. 1990. *Gallo pinto: (Humorismo Costarricense)*, 2nd ed. Tibás, Costa Rica: Litografía e Imprenta LIL, S.A.

Ana. 2009. "Día del Gallo Pinto." *Diario de una becaria en San José*, May 10. Available at: http://unabecariaensanjose.blogspot.com/2009/05/dia-del-gallo-pinto.html. Accessed August 2, 2009.

Anderson, Benedict. 1983. *Imagined communities: Reflections on the origins and spread of nationalism.* New York: Verso.

Appadurai, Arjun. 1993. "The heart of whiteness." *Callaloo* 16 (4): 796–807.

Bourgois, Philippe I. 1989. *Ethnicity at work: Divided labor on a Central American banana plantation.* Baltimore: Johns Hopkins University Press.

Cabezas, Esteban, Jorge Mario Porras, and Ana M. Espinoza. 1996. "Origen y evolución del género *Oryza* y la introducción y diseminación del arroz cultivado en Costa Rica." *III Congreso Centroamericano de Historia.* San José, Costa Rica.

Cabezas Bolaños, Esteban, and Ana M. Espinoza Esquivel. 2000. "El Arroz en América: Su introducción y primeras siembras." In *Revista de Historia de América*, No. 126: 7–18. México: Instituto Panamericano de Geografía e Historia.

Campos Zamora, Anyelick, and Larissa Tristán Jiménez. 2009. *Nicaragüenses en las noticias: Textos, contextos y audiencias.* San José, Costa Rica: Editorial de la Universidad de Costa Rica.

Castro Valverde, Carlos. 2008. "Dimensión cuantativa de la inmigración nicaragüense en Costa Rica: Del mito a la realidad." In *El Mito Roto: Inmigración y emigración en Costa Rica*, ed. Carlos Sandoval García, 25–50. San José, Costa Rica: Editorial de la Universidad de Costa Rica.

Chomsky, Aviva. 1996. *West Indian workers and the United Fruit Company in Costa Rica 1870–1940.* Baton Rouge: Louisiana State University Press.

Coto, Tatiana. 2007. *Las Mejores Recetas: Costa Rica.* Leon, Spain: Ediciones Jadane, S.A.

Cruz, Consuelo. 2000. "Identity and persuasion: How nations remember their pasts and make their presents." *World Politics* 52: 275–312.

De Aragón, Juana R. [1903] 2003. *La cocina costarricense.* Colección Retorno. San José, Costa Rica: Editorial de la Universidad de Costa Rica.

De Musmanni, Carmen, and Lupita de Weiler. 2001. *Costa Rican typical foods.* Cartago, Costa Rica: Impresos Rapidos.

"Donde se creó el plato de comida gallo pinto?" 2007. *Yahoo! Respuestas*. June 28. Available at: http://es.answers.yahoo.com/question/index?qid=20070628091619 AAqGltS. Accessed August 17, 2009.

"Dredging up votes: Daniel Ortega and the swamps of opportunism." 2010. *The Economist*, The Americas, November 11. Available at: http://www.economist.com. Accessed April 21, 2011.

Duncan, Quince. 2005. "Part III: El negro antillano: Inmigración y presencia." In *El negro en Costa Rica*, 11th ed., ed. Quince Duncan and Carlos Meléndez, 113–75. San José, Costa Rica: Editorial de la Universidad de Costa Rica.

Edelman, Marc. 1992. *The logic of the latifundio.* Stanford, Calif.: Stanford University Press.

Eide, Jacob A., and Trina N. Tobey, eds. 2008. *Sabores Típicos de Costa Rica (Traditional Flavors of Costa Rica).* Asociación Damas Unidas. San Miguel de Agua Buena de Coto Brus. Puntarenas, Costa Rica. Instantpublisher.com.

"El Gallopinto es Nica!!!!!!!" 2008. *Akari Ladon*, December 20. Available at: http://foro.akariladon.com/viewtopic.php?f=101&t=9644. Accessed August 2, 2009.

Fallas, Carlos Luis. 1957. *Mamita Yunai.* San José, Costa Rica: Editorial Costa Rica.

"Free 'Gallo Pinto' for 30.000 on Sunday." 2008. *Inside Costa Rica*, April 10. Available at: http://insidecostarica.com/dailynews/2008/april/10/nac02.htm. Accessed August 2, 2009.

Gal, Susan. 1991. "Bartók's funeral: Representations of Europe in Hungarian political rhetoric." *American Ethnologist* 18 (3): 440–58.

García Murillo, Guillermo, and Luis Efrén García Brinceño. 1976. "Introducción a un estudio sobre las comidas y bebidas de Guanacaste." In *Cuaderno de Guanacaste, Serie Lengua, Literatura, y Folklore.* No. 2. San José, Costa Rica.

Glassie, Henry. 1995. "Tradition." *Journal of American Folklore* 108 (430): 395–412.

Goodier, Robert. 2005. "Costa Rica strikes back in regional gallo pinto war." *Tico Times*, January 1. Available at: http://www.ticotimes.net/dailyarchive/2005_01/daily_-1_11_05.htm#story2. Accessed January 20, 2010.

Koch, Charles. 1975. "Ethnicity and livelihoods: A social geography of Costa Rica's Atlantic Coast." PhD diss., Department of Anthropology, University of Kansas.

Larrain, Jorge. 2000. *Identity and modernity in Latin America.* Malden, Mass.: Blackwell.

Leff, Alex. 2009. "The rice and beans war." *Global Post.* March 23. Available at: http://www.globalpost.com/dispatch/costa-rica/090317/the-rice-and-beans-war. Accessed August 2, 2009.

Masís Fernández, Karen, and Laura Paniagua Arguedas. 2008. "Chistes sobre nicaragüenses en Costa Rica: Barreras simbólicas, mecanismos de control social, constructores de identidades." In *El Mito Roto: Inmigración y emigración en Costa Rica*, ed. Carlos Sandoval García, 339–56. San José, Costa Rica: Editorial de la Universidad de Costa Rica.

Molina Jiménez, Iván. 2005. *Costarricense por dicha: Identidad nacional y cambio cultural en Costa Rica durante los siglos XIX y XX.* San José, Costa Rica: Editorial de la Universidad de Costa Rica.

Pacheco, Jorge A. Reyes. 1983. "A simulated foodgrain security reserve program for maize and rice in Central America and Panama from 1960 to 1980." Master's thesis, Kansas State University.

Palmer, Paula. 2005. *What happen: A folk-history of Costa Rica's Talamanca Coast.* Miami: Distribuidores Zona Tropical, S.A.

Pilcher, Jeffrey M. 1998. *¡Qué vivan los tamales!: Food and the making of Mexican identity.* Albuquerque: University of New Mexico Press.

Pilcher, Jeffrey M. 2000. "The Caribbean from 1492 to the present." In *Cambridge world history of food*, vol. 2, ed. Kenneth F. Kiple and Kriemhild Coneé Orbelas, 1278–86. New York: Cambridge University Press.

Piszk, Ileana. 1982. "La Procucción de arroz en Costa Rica: Políticas estatales y fuerzas sociales." *Avances de Investigación* 46: I-63.

Preston-Werner, Theresa. 2009. "*Gallo pinto:* Tradition, memory, and identity in Costa Rican foodways." *Journal of American Folklore* 122 (483): 11–27.

Putnam, Lara. 2002. *The company they kept: Migrants and the politics of gender in Caribbean Costa Rica: 1870–1960.* Chapel Hill: University of North Carolina Press.

Quirós, Marcela. 2003. "Todos querían gallo pinto." *Nacion*, September 1. Available at: http:www.nacion.com/ln_ee/2003/septiembre/01/pais0.html. Accessed October 17, 2007.

Raub, Erin. 2008. "National Gallo Pinto Day in Costa Rica this Sunday." April 10. Available at: http://www.costaricapages.com/blog/costa-rica-news/gallo-pinto-day/825. Accessed August 2, 2009.

Roa, Doren. 2007. " 'Gallopinteada' del año." *El Nuevo Diario*, September 12. Available at: http://impreso.elnuevodiario.com.ni/2007/09/12/variedades/58710. Accessed January 20, 2010.

Ross de Cerdas, Marjorie. 2001. *Entre el comal y la olla: Fundamentos de gastronomía costarricense.* San José, Costa Rica: Editorial Universidad Estatal a Distancia.

Ross de Cerdas, Marjorie. 2003. *La magia de la cocina Limonense: Rice and beans y calalú.* San José, Costa Rica: Editorial de la Universidad de Costa Rica.

Sandoval García, Carlos. 2008. *Otros Amenazantes: Los nicaragüenses y la formación de identidades nacionales en Costa Rica.* Serie Instituto Investigaciones Sociales. San José, Costa Rica: Editorial de la Universidad de Costa Rica.

Sharman, Russell Leigh. 2006. "Re/making la negrita: Culture as an aesthetic system in Costa Rica." *American Anthropologist* 108 (4): 842–53.

Siles Navarro, Andrei. 2010. "Miles de ticos se comieron su gallo pinto." *La Prensa Libre*, March 22. Available at: http://www.prensalibre.cr/pl/suceso/21729-miles-de-ticos-se-comieron-su-gallo-pinto.html. Accessed January 20, 2012.

Trubek, Amy B. 2005. "Place matters." In *The taste culture reader: Experiencing food and drink*, ed. Carolyn Korsmeyer, 260–71. New York: Berg.

Vega Jiménez, Patricia. 2002. "Alimentos e identidades (trabajadores de las bananeras costarricenses 1934)." *Ciencias Sociales* 98: 99–110.

Wade, Peter. 2000. *Music, race, and nation: Música tropical in Colombia.* Chicago: University of Chicago Press.

Watts, Teo. 2007. *Every day an adventure, every meal a feast.* San José, Costa Rica: Arena Transamérica, S.A.

Wheelock Román, Jaime. 2007. *La Comida Nicaraguense*, 4th ed. Bogotá, Colombia: Quebecor World.

–11–

Nationalizing the Ordinary Dish
Rice and Beans in Belize

Richard Wilk

Today any visitor to Belize will quickly be introduced to the ever-present national dish, the only food served by many restaurants, the self-proclaimed national symbol—rice and beans.[1] Rather than being a single substance, the typical serving includes a set of different elements, which together make a meal. When you order a serving under the name "rice and beans" you get a good deal more than just those two foods, and in the same way, there is a whole complex history and political economy contained in that single meal.

In Belize rice and beans is ubiquitous and omnipresent. It is served at every public event, sold from thousands of informal stands in marketplaces and on the streets during public festivities. If you are invited to a Belizean church dinner, of any denomination, you can be fairly sure that you will be eating rice and beans that evening, and the same goes for a New Year's party, a child's christening, at horse races, or a softball game. It arrives in large aluminum trays at birthday parties, and individual servings on plastic plates or foam clamshell containers appear from boxes in countless offices and government buildings every day at lunchtime. Shorn of its trimmings and accompaniments, it appears as a side dish, next to the formal slices of turkey and ham at wedding feasts and christenings, Christmas and New Year's gatherings. Barbecues appear along roadsides all over the country on weekends, and it goes without saying that your grilled or jerk chicken will come nestled up to a scoop of rice and beans. (See Figure 11.1.)

At a minimum, the dish always includes white long-grained rice and red kidney beans, with coconut milk, sage and other spices, ideally resulting in a somewhat dry mixture where the individual grains of rice and beans are separate. The beans are cooked separately until soft, and then the rice is added, along with the coconut milk to absorb the bean juice as it cooks. This combination is never to be confused with "beans and rice," which means a separate bowl or helping of stewed beans served with a heap of white rice, usually cooked with coconut milk. It is up to the diner to do the mixing.

But most of the time whether you go to a restaurant, buy a plate at the roadside, or dine at home, a Belizean expects that rice and beans will come with three other

Figure 11.1 Sign in front of a small restaurant in Belmopan, Belize, advertising varieties of rice and beans. Photo by the author.

elements: (1) some kind of stewed meat, (2) a scoop of potato salad, and (3) one or more strips of fried ripe plantain. The default option for stewed meat is chicken. If the host or server does not tell you what the meat will be, you should always assume chicken; anything else, such as pork or beef, will be marked as "rice and beans with stew pork" or in the case of seafood, "with fry fish."

Stewed chicken is typically seasoned overnight with a commercial seasoned salt mixture, lime, garlic, black pepper, and red *recado*, a spice paste of Yucatecan origin that is composed mainly of bright red achiote seed (*Bixa orellana*) and oregano. This *recado* was often homemade in the past, but today it is commercially produced in Belize and imported from Mexico. The scoop of cold potato salad is very similar to the kind commonly found in North America; boiled, peeled potatoes, a tin of cooked "mixed vegetables" (peas, carrots, green beans), lubricated with British "salad crème."

This ensemble is such a standard, so much a part of Belizean life that it is the default meal if no food is specified. As the tourism business has eclipsed agriculture and fisheries as the mainstay of the Belizean economy, guidebooks and travelogues, television personalities and visitors have cemented the place of rice and beans as the ubiquitous and ever-present fact of daily life. One guidebook even claims that everyone in Belize has eaten rice and beans since the time of the ancient Maya (Ritz 1994: 61), which is absurd considering that rice was unknown in the New World until the Spanish invasion, but it does convey the degree to which rice and beans dominates the contemporary food landscape.

Yet, there are cracks in the seamless edifice of rice-and-beans monopoly, not just because some Belizeans now feel like the culinary richness of their country has been lost behind the uniform stereotype. More visible to the longtime visitor or resident, though, is the way rice and beans rests on shaky historical grounds. Though it appears today as a timeless feature of the landscape, older Belizeans remember the days when rice and beans was a Sunday special dish; back when chicken was scarce and more expensive than beef, and the domestic supply of rice and beans was precarious, subject to shortages and quality fluctuations, supplemented often by expensive imports. Turn the clock back a few more decades, and the picture shifts dramatically.

The national staples were instead salted beef, salted pork, salted fish, breads made from imported flour and plantains. The stereotypical national dish of the early twentieth century would be saltfish and plantains, often cooked together with coconut milk in a stew with other root crops like cassava and sweet potatoes. Each ethnic group at the time had its own hermetic food culture, related closely to the ways they made a living and their physical location in the country. Latins and Mayans depended on cornmeal and black beans, Garifuna on fish and cassava, and only East Indians and Chinese ate a rice-based diet, though their rice was rarely if ever cooked with legumes. Rice and beans does not appear in the historical record until 1895, when it was served as part of a New Year's dinner for the inmates of the Belize City poorhouse and asylum. (There may still be earlier references in newspapers or other documents, but I have not been able to find them.)

How did rice and beans achieve hegemony, obscuring and causing a mass forgetting of earlier diets? What are the positives and negatives of adopting a national dish that has such tremendous hegemonic power, and how does rice and beans both shape and limit the directions in which Belizean diet, foodways, and culinary patterns can change and grow in the future? Finally, how is the adoption of a national dish related to the broader process of building a nation, especially an underpopulated and insignificantly tiny nation in a region overshadowed by huge neighbors to the north? In the process of answering these questions, I will have recourse to recent anthropological work on the concept of the "ordinary," the everyday taken-for-granted that seems to be so obvious to people in the particular moment and place, but which is actually a continually moving target. I will also draw on material I have presented in *Home Cooking in the Global Village*, which uses the medium of food as a means to talk about Belize's relationship with the rest of the world (2006, 2002), and a more recent paper published in Belize in a volume celebrating Belize's twenty-fifth birthday (2007).

Nationhood and the National Dish

Nationhood, the culmination of more than fifty years of struggle and uneven progress toward political self-determination, finally arrived in Belize at independence in September 1981. A seat in the United Nations, a national flag, a military force, and a set of unique legal codes and political processes—these are the kinds of things that country after country has taken as the goalposts of identity, of reaching the global stage as a member of the club of nations. But many skeptical observers of independence in the Caribbean and Africa have argued that nationhood is not all it seems at first glance; that it ushers in a new era of dependency and neocolonialism (e.g., Sheller 2003; Barongo 1980; Henke and Reno 2003). The balance of power has not changed, they say, but it has just become less visible.

Even the proponents of neoliberalism at the World Bank would agree that nationhood cannot deliver all the promises of independence, for the simple reason that globalization makes independence impossible in the world today. This is especially true for small countries with few energy resources. National boundaries are, after all, imaginary lines on a real world, a world where immense amounts of material goods, and all kinds of intangibles from television signals to electricity, e-mail and wire transfers, move around with little respect for imaginary lines or border guards (Franke 1987). In this new world, industry goes where it wants, tourists travel freely, but working people face all kinds of hazards, guards, and legal penalties when they try to move across borders to find work, though they continue to do so (Hannerz 1996; Barndt 2002). It is thought, for example, that more Belizeans live in Los Angeles than in Belize City, the largest settlement in the country.

Faced with multinational corporations, huge and powerful neighbors, international laws and organizations of all kinds, smugglers and the Internet, and institutions like the World Bank and the International Monetary Fund, the powers of nations appear diminished and weak. In truth, the ideal of the culturally unified nation, firmly defended behind national borders, was never more than an imaginary beast even during the eighteenth century in Europe where the modern idea of the nation was first invented. The solidity of this idea was never completely established in fluid zones like the Caribbean, where islands changed hands with striking frequency, and the colonial empires still hang on in places like Martinique and Dutch Aruba. Sovereignty in micro-nations sometimes has an almost comical aspect, honored in public and on paper, but frayed in daily practice and in businesses where survival usually requires some shortcuts.

Today legal nationhood is also challenged by multinational flows of culture, migration, and massive movements of dollars, investments, and tourists. In twenty short years several offshore islands in the Belizean Cays have been completely transformed into "Paradise playgrounds," covered with international restaurants, condominiums, and hotels, so that the islands appear more as a slightly down-market extension of the tourist meccas of Cancun, Montego Bay, and Miami than they do as an indigenous growth of something uniquely Belizean (see Sheller 2003; Sutherland 1998). Belize is just so much Caribbean real estate, a stage for an increasingly internationalized set of stereotyped neotropical fantasies, reducing the "national" to a simple form of branding, as each country competes to set up safe little "tourist villages" for the amusement of hundreds of thousands of cruise-ship tourists who stay for less than twelve hours in each destination. Their only experience of anything Belizean may just be a single plate of rice and beans on their way to and from a rainforest waterfall, or a patch of tropical reef.

This kind of cultural globalization is barely perceived as a danger in the United States and other powerful countries that control their own national media, and have long-standing national identities and institutions. But in small, fragile, new countries that are just emerging from colonialism, national identity cannot be taken for granted, and people pay a lot of attention to symbolic performances like beauty pageants where national identity is paraded, performed, and questioned on stage (Wilk 1995). Food arguably has a lot more weight and significance in settings where national identity is weak and ambiguous than it does in places where national identity has been long established and taken for granted (see case studies in Belasco and Scranton 2002).

The emergence of a uniquely national set of foodways is particularly complex and difficult in a small country settled for the exploitation of natural resources, like Belize. Because the population was engaged in forestry and then industrial agriculture, and few of the indigenous people survived, laborers and their food, as well as their food customs and preferences, were imported from elsewhere. African slaves, Royalist Tories fleeing the successful American Revolution, English and Scottish buccaneers, Carib Indian refugees, Mayan peasants, and a host of others all brought their own foods and ideas, but ended up eating a great deal of imported food as well, so there was no "natural" local diet grounded in existing culture and practices. This means that Belize had a polyglot experience more akin to the "melting pot" of North America than the slow mixture of Spanish and indigenous cuisines that characterizes the adjacent Central American countries of Mexico, Guatemala, and Honduras. How do you create a national diet out of such an odd assortment of different, often separate, and poorly integrated ethnic groups and fragments of other nations, divided by racism, a colonial regime that plays on ethnic divisions to maintain its own power, and a brutal local economy that has almost no room for a middle class (see Wilk and Chapin [1990] on Belize's ethnic history)?

The History of Rice and Beans

Rice and beans were imported in small quantities to the Crown Colony of British Honduras in the nineteenth century, and some were undoubtedly grown there, but not in the kind of quantity that would allow them to be staple foods. None of the nineteenth century travelers who visited Belize ever mentions either rice or beans, and certainly not as any kind of particular local or even regional dish. So if rice-and-beans is only a bit more than one hundred years old, what were the previous "national dishes"?

The European baymen who settled along the coast to cut wood in the seventeenth century ate all kinds of things, especially game meat, but one visitor claimed their favorite dish was called "pig and pease," a stew of salt pork with dried green or yellow peas (Dampier 1906: 123). Both were brought from Europe on ships, and they were part of the regular diet of sailors, so it makes sense that baymen would eat it, given that many of them had been sailors or buccaneers at one time in their lives. Dried peas and salt pork were spread all over the world by British sailors, and they became part of many local cuisines. The baymen probably also ate Mayan foods, since some of them lived with Mayan women slaves they had kidnapped from indigenous settlements. We know very little about the Mayan cuisine of the period, but can surmise it was based mainly on corn as a staple, eaten as tortillas or tamales, along with a rich variety of stews and sauces.

Later on in Belize, as in many other parts of the Caribbean, African slaves in the mahogany camps were also fed imported rations of salted meat or fish and white flour. They cooked these foods into a dish called "pork and doughboys," which consisted of boiled salt pork and white flour dumplings, washed down with the cooking broth. Over time, however, many slaves began to grow gardens ("plantations") to supplement their rations, and for produce to sell in town markets. All the evidence shows that their favorite crops were ground foods and plantains, rather than rice, maize, or beans. Nineteenth-century visitors report the local staple was salted fish and plantains. This is probably the ancestor of today's "boil up," still a popular dish of mixed root crops, green bananas, plantains, dumplings, salt pork, and fish. A lot of the fish may have been caught, salted, and dried ("corned") in coastal villages, making this dish the first entirely local cuisine, and if it had remained Belize's staple food, Belize would have been able to feed itself. Instead another kind of cultural globalization led many Belizeans to abandon saltfish and plantains.

While poor and rural people were eating saltfish and plantains, the better-off urban dwellers, including the emerging Creole middle class and the British colonial officials, ate imported European food as much as possible. When they did eat local meat or vegetables, they drowned them in imported sauces and gravies. By the beginning of the twentieth century, huge amounts of packaged and tinned foods supported a substantial population who were living in tropical America, but eating as if they were in London. They even imported tropical fruit and fish in tins, in preference over the fresh articles available in local markets.

This history exposes two of the most damaging legacies of colonialism for both Belizean culture and the Belize economy. Foreign food products were always ranked above local ones. Tinned, processed, sterilized food from England and other parts of the empire were thought to be more healthful, more cultured, more civilized than the products of the local oceans, forests, and fields. Because foreign products were "superior," local production for the market was stunted and disadvantaged. Those people in Belize who had the money to spend on food were the ones who sneered at local products, even when they were cheaper and fresher than imports. Generations of historians have blamed poor Belizeans for being "uninterested in agriculture," when the blame should properly belong to urban consumers who would pay more for a single tin of British spinach than they would for ten pounds of fresh callaloo (e.g., Waddell 1961; Tripartite Report 1966; Rogers 1885). Olive oil in beautiful tins and bottles from Italy was sold in all the large shops in Belize City, while local coconut and cohune oil were exiled to street markets, where they were sold in reused liquor or soda bottles sealed with corncobs.

These entrenched ideas about the superiority of foreign food had dire economic consequences for the colony as a whole. The balance of trade shifted sharply to the negative in the 1880s, and was never positive again after 1919. Since then the value of imports has continued to grow at a faster pace than the value of exports, helping to keep Belize in debt, in amounts well exceeding annual GDP. Even during World Wars I and II, when food and fuel were scarce and expensive in the British Empire, British Honduras food imports continued to grow. The constant growth in the cost of imports allowed governments to depend on import duty as their main source of revenue, instead of levying reasonable land or income taxes. This legacy continues to the present day. In March 2006 the government of Belize reported that import and export duties on international trade were still the largest source of tax revenue (Government of Belize 2006).

Anyone living in Belize knows the effects that import duties have on both businesses and daily life. The high cost of imported fuel works its way through the entire economy, raising the sales price of every item, even those produced within the country. The high cost of fuel makes all kinds of domestic activities and transportation very expensive. Farmers find that the high cost of imported equipment, chemicals, parts, and fuel makes it difficult for them to compete with farmers in neighboring Latin American republics, not to mention rich countries that subsidize their own farmers and food exports.[2] The cost of living is higher in Belize than anywhere else in Central America, comparable to much richer Caribbean countries.

The legacy of colonialism contributes to a perception among many Belizeans that imported goods have higher quality than local ones. This makes it very difficult for those who are thinking about local production of competing goods, even with tax incentives and some tariff protection. It is always much less risky to go into the import-export business than into local production, a lesson many Belizean ambitious businesspeople have learned to their regret. At the same time, as Belizeans become more cosmopolitan consumers, through travel, residence abroad, education, and watching imported cable television, they are constantly developing tastes for new kinds of packaged, processed, frozen, canned, fast, and convenience foods that cannot be produced in Belize at all (Andrae and Beckman 1985).

New Markets and Growing Variety

If we go back to the beginning of the twentieth century and look at the import records, we find that most of the rice and beans eaten in the country were then imported from the United States. Rural Creole villages grew corn, rice, and beans and raised livestock for their own consumption, but little of this trickled into urban markets (Ashcraft 1973). The Spanish- and Maya-speaking people of Belize grew and ate their own beans as part of a traditional diet, but these were mostly black beans, which few people in the city wanted to eat.

Facing a financial crisis brought on by the Great Depression, the colonial government began to actively promote local farming in 1932, when it opened an Agricultural Board (later the Marketing Board), which paid farmers fixed prices for corn, rice, and red kidney (RK) beans. Eventually it built two rice mills and drying facilities, and farmers gradually began to increase their production of these crops. The British even financed a mechanized rice plantation, but as Belizeans began to eat more rice and beans, production could not keep up, and special licenses were issued to merchants to import rice and beans to make up the difference (Dumont 1963).

It is clear that the combination of rice and beans acquired high social status during this late colonial period, and even if many urban people only ate it once or twice a week, it was usually reserved for Sunday dinner, an honored event that brought families together for a large meal after church. Furthermore, rice and beans was not clearly identified with any single ethnic group as an emblem of ethnic identity, so it was easily adopted by everyone. This combination of "neutrality" and relative status (at least compared with indigenous foods like root crops, corn, or plantains), as well as the air of modernity surrounding two products that were subsidized, cleaned, and processed by mechanized government facilities, combined to make rice and beans acceptable to a broad public. The government considered them civilized, cheap, and nutritious foods that were amenable to "improvement" through agricultural research and extension, and official policy to promote their production and marketing was accepted with little comment or objection.

After Belize achieved independence, the government continued to encourage local production of rice and beans, and a number of foreign aid programs and projects over the years have tried to increase production and efficiency. On the other hand, no research or subsidies were extended to local crops or common food crops like black beans. In the early 1980s, by spending large amounts money for development and research, Belize finally reached its goal of self-sufficiency in rice and beans, and got very close to providing all its own fresh beef, pork, chicken, and fish.

By 2009, the country was even exporting substantial amounts of RK beans and rice. Did this finally mean that Belize was reducing its food imports and becoming economically more independent?

Just one walk through the supermarkets in Belize City will show why the answer is "no." Rice and beans are popular, but they are no longer *staple* foods in the sense that the majority of people eat them as their major source of calories every day. Instead, urban consumers are turning increasingly to processed and prepared "convenience" foods, like consumers in most developing countries around the world. They are eating more baked goods made from wheat flour (which must be imported), and as their tastes broaden, a lot more cheeses, beverages, prepared and preserved meats, and varieties of fish like tuna and salmon that are not local. More women have entered the formal job market and they must continue working to help support children, so they no longer have time to prepare dishes like rice and beans or tamales, which must be cooked well in advance of serving. Living in a nuclear family instead of an extended one means that there is no relative staying home to cook and care for children, and people are increasingly using day care services or other formal child care arrangements. The prices of many local ingredients like root crops have also gone way up, partially because of the high costs of transportation and labor. With more rushed family schedules, convenience foods, snacks, and restaurant meals are becoming more common all the time, and many of these meals are based on imported ingredients. Even in rural areas, flour tortillas, ramen noodles, and canned meat are everyday fare for the families of workers in banana plantations, shrimp farms, and tourist hotels, because so many people have given up farming.

There are a number of positive recent developments, particularly in the supply of high-quality fresh vegetables and fruits to urban markets. The flood of immigrants who came to Belize as political and economic refugees from Guatemala, Honduras, and El Salvador in the 1980s and 1990s brought a wider variety of crops, which they have enthusiastically brought to flourishing urban marketplaces, and some make cheeses and prepared snack foods as well. Chinese and Taiwanese immigrants who initially lived only in cities have moved into rural areas, where they are growing new fruits and vegetables, like pitahaya and guava, which have been rapidly accepted by Belizean consumers. The steadily increasing number of small Chinese grocery stores has diversified the choices of food available to Belizean consumers in some areas (as well as the ubiquitous Chinese fried-chicken stands), and the government is still willing to offer protection from imports to fledgling local food production and processing (Wilk 2009).

Still, farmers and food processors can never keep up with the avalanche of new food products from the United States.[3] When local businesses are able to produce items like bacon and ham to international standards, they are buried by hundreds of new varieties of imported meat products, everything from turkey bacon to cheese-stuffed hot dogs. For every new vegetable that Belizean farmers painstakingly learn to grow and bring to market, supermarkets can import ten new kinds of cheap American or Mexican vegetables, some frozen in microwave bags with herbed butter sauce.

I have even heard of vegetables being exported from Mexico and Guatemala to the United States, where they are bought in wholesale markets, loaded into refrigerated containers, and then shipped to Belize!

Yet, at the same time, Belizean food and food products have never been more popular, and they are becoming widely celebrated by chefs and diners. Every year the National Agricultural Show attracts more visitors to see new local products, and Belizean food takes center stage in the annual "Taste of Belize" festival (celebrated for the ninth time in 2010). Towns and villages around the country are celebrating local lobster, cacao, cashew, sugar, and citrus at local fiestas, hoping to attract tourists and visitors. How can we reconcile the contradiction between rising food imports and the growing pride in national cuisine?

Ethnic and National Food

The British colonial policy divided the different ethnic groups of the country from one another, encouraged them to stay in their own communities, and emphasized their differences. There was a good deal of mixing in Belize City, where the term *Creole* came to include people of very diverse cultural backgrounds with some African ancestors, though sometimes it was also applied to local people who were considered "white." Rice and beans, the Kriol language, and much of what is now thought of as "Belizean" culture emerged from this mixed urban Creole community. But right up to the 1950s when the British began to grant some local self-government and today's political parties were formed, most of the rural people of the country lived in relatively uniform ethnic communities, eating their own traditional foods and diets.

When I first started working in the predominantly Hispanic communities of northern Belize in the early 1970s, very few people in the villages ever cooked rice and beans at home. Their diet was still based on tortillas and other corn products in a cuisine that could be traced to their Maya and mestizo ancestors in adjacent Mexican Quintana Roo and Yucatan. Rice and beans was still considered Creole food or city food, not a food for every Belizean. In 1978 when I started working in Kekchi communities in Toledo, most indigenous people had never eaten rice and beans together, even though they grew both crops to sell to the marketing board. Many Mopan Maya and Kekchi people doubted that rice and beans could be a nourishing food capable of sustaining hard-working people.

On a superficial level, it might seem that independence made few changes in the ethnic mosaic of Belizean culture and cuisine. There has even been a revival of some ethnic cuisines, as they emerge from kitchens into the public eye of the restaurant trade. So today one can sit down to a Garifuna meal of *hudut* (pounded plantains, in a stew of fish and coconut milk) in Hopkins Village, a Mopan Maya dinner of fish steamed in *obel* (bullhoof) leaves in Maya Centre, and an East Indian feast of chicken *tacari* (turmeric curry) in Punta Gorda. At the same time, however, something that can really be called Belizean cuisine has emerged, and is eaten readily by all ethnic groups in the country.

In 1990 I conducted a survey of the tastes and preferences of hundreds of Belizeans of all backgrounds in urban, suburban, and rural areas (Babcock and Wilk 1998). More than one thousand high school students responded to another questionnaire, which asked them, among other things, to name their favorite foods. Across every ethnic group, rich and poor, young and old, the overwhelming favorite food was rice and beans with stewed chicken and potato salad. More than three-quarters of Belizeans of all backgrounds would rather eat this dish than anything else. Interviews I conducted in 2004 confirmed that Belizeans of all ethnic and cultural backgrounds are much more positive toward local food than before, a trend that can be seen in the constantly growing number of restaurants that proudly serve Belizean food (see Figure 11.2), and a growing number of cookbooks, the festivals mentioned above, and the popularity of local cooking shows on television.

The time since independence, then, has been a period when Belizean food, like other aspects of Belizean culture, has shaken off some of the colonial legacy of low status. As others have found in many parts of the world, travel, migration, tourism,

Figure 11.2 A typical Belizean "cool spot" by the side of the road in the Stann Creek Valley, Belize. This is the kind of place where rice and beans can always be expected as the "default option." Photo by the author.

and other kinds of cultural globalization have not wiped out local culture. Instead, exposure to all these global influences has made many people more aware of what they have at home, and encouraged them to recognize that it is something precious worth preserving, protecting, and developing. Presenting that culture to foreign visitors has become an increasingly important business too, as tourism continues to grow, and at least some tourists are asking for a distinctive Belizean experience. There are stirrings of what might be called culinary tourism, as visitors are attracted to Toledo District by the Cacao Festival, where they meet the Maya and Kekchi people who grow, and now process, cacao, and among students and ecotourists staying in village households and lodges who want to eat exotic local foods, and learn how they are made (see Long 2003).

So in many ways rice and beans, as part of Belizean national culture, has never been more widely valued, more loved as part of Belizean life and a symbol of cultural independence. But this value has not been translated into economic independence. While in the colonial past Belize was both culturally and economically dependent and dominated by foreigners, today cultural independence has grown, while economic dependence has, if anything, become deeper and more complete (cf. Appadurai 1990). Even if the rice and beans themselves are grown in Belize, they are raised with imported tools, fertilizer, pesticides, and fuel, cooked on an imported stove with imported propane and spices, and served on imported plates with potato salad made with imported salad crème and mixed vegetables, and often imported potatoes when the local supply is not sufficient.

Conclusions: The Ordinary

The emergence of rice and beans as a staple dish has had mixed economic effects; in the introduction to this chapter I suggested that there are also some complex cultural and social issues hidden behind the overwhelming dominance of the dish. Guidebooks, tourists, visitors, and even some scholars have tended to dismiss the complexity and breadth of Belizean cuisine and foodways, because for many, nothing is visible and accessible beyond rice and beans (or its less visible partner called "beans and rice," where a bowl of stewed beans is served alongside a plate of white rice, much the way the dish is served in New Orleans, see Beriss this volume). I have heard chefs disparage all indigenous Belizean food using the label *rice and beans* as a condescending term for the monotony that tourists face when they go out to try something "local," which is also familiar enough to be safe. This does an injustice to the richness and diversity of the many different indigenous cuisines and foodways of the country, which draw on hundreds of unique natural ingredients, blending them skillfully with many complex techniques and modes of preparation. Given the startling ethnic diversity of the country and its impressive ecological mosaic of habitats, what is remarkable is the *invisibility* of culinary diversity. With all these many different people, and the incredible variety of produce available in hundreds of gardens and fields, why is it so hard to find anything *beyond* rice and beans in the average Belizean restaurant?

It is tempting to settle on a kind of "which came first—chicken or egg" explanation. Nobody thinks there is anything there, so they don't ask for it, and in the absence of demand, people running restaurants don't try to serve anything else. I regularly get this answer when I ask restaurant owners or resort managers why they don't serve something besides rice and beans (or beans and rice). They say something like, "Oh, once I tried, but nobody ordered it, so I dropped it." Or, "Nobody knew what it was." When they do bulk out their menus, it always seems to be with some safe foreign dish that tourists or well-traveled Belizeans will recognize, such as hamburgers, pizza, nacho chips, or burritos. They will even serve up stir-fry and spicy Thai curries with noodles rather than add something local. Somehow, adding another kind of Belizean dish like *tacari* or *sere* (fish stewed with coconut milk) seems "risky" or dangerous. Why? It turns out that the anthropology and sociology of consumer culture has a very plausible answer.

One of the keys to every system of taste and consumption, first identified by the famous German sociologist Georg Simmel (1902), is a tension between what could be called "fitting in" and "standing out." Most people, according to this theory, and Miller and Woodward's recent amplification (2007), face the world of everyday choices about what to consume with considerable anxiety. We want to be individuals, but we don't want to stand out and be conspicuous. For most of us that means settling on items like blue jeans and simple black dresses, which allow us to feel comfortable and blend in, at the same time that they give us some latitude for expressing who we really are; "a sense of security, of relief from the burden of mistaken choice and anxious self-composition" (Miller and Woodward 2007: 343). The brilliance of blue jeans, like the savor of rice and beans, is that they can be both anonymous and intensely personal at the same time. We can share in the common experience of something that is completely acceptable in public, and also the many individual memories and experiences that are vividly called forth by the taste and smell of food, the sensual experience of flavors and the satisfaction of a full belly.

Beyond their personal nature, blue jeans are also popular because they can be produced with almost infinite subtle variations in colors, fabric, shape, size, and fit. This allows a kind of public coding of subgroup difference, so a person can seek distinction by wearing particularly expensive, fancy, or specially cut jeans, while at the same time she will pass seamlessly through groups of people who are not aware of the significance of her garments. In other words, there are all kinds of subtle differences coded in blue jeans that can be read at varying depths by people with the right knowledge and skills. And over time, a pair of blue jeans mold themselves to the individual body, acquiring even more individuality.

Similarly, most Belizeans have very clear ideas about the exact way they like their rice and beans, and they can discuss at great length the reasons why they do or do not like particular variations. Over the years there have been a number of newspaper and magazine articles addressing the question of who makes the "best" rice and beans, and a close reading of this literature reveals many gradations of quality, and a surprising lack of agreement on whether the dish should be wet or dry, have more or less beans that should be harder or softer. In fact there is infinite variation, so that to a real aficionado, no two plates of rice and beans are the same—especially when you consider the wide variety of stewed or fried meats that can take the place of the stereotypical stewed chicken.

Versatility and adaptability may be a quality that many extremely popular national dishes have in common. It is not hard to think of a thousand variations on the hamburger, and pizza certainly invites the same kind of combination of a constant form with an ever-changing constellation of toppings. But more than anything else, rice and beans allows for the creation of a daily experience of what Miller and Woodward (2007) call "the ordinary," that familiar sense of comfort that reduces anxiety and allows for inclusion.[4] One could argue that in a multiethnic society, riven by multiple divisions of religion, culture, class, and wealth, rice and beans plays a key role in providing a sense of common shared normality. A Belizean friend asked me not long ago what things I thought all Belizeans really shared—what was it that defined a person as a Belizean. After trying and rejecting a whole series of different traits, customs, and ideas, we were left with two things—the Kriol language and rice and beans.

Notes

1. I wish to acknowledge the help of the many Belizeans, too numerous to list here, who have educated me about their country, as well as feeding me, over much of my lifetime. I also wish to thank the best cooks I know, the late Aurora Mendez from San Pedro Columbia in the Toledo District, and Mrs. Gloria Crawford in Crooked Tree Village, for feeding me the delicious meals that sparked my curiosity about Belizean cuisine. Thanks especially to Joseph Palacio, who has generously shared his wisdom about anthropology, food, and Belize with me since I was a teenager. My research on Belizean food and rice and beans has been financially supported by a Fulbright Fellowship, the Wenner-Gren Foundation, USAID, the Economic and Social Research Council of the United Kingdom, and Indiana University.

2. American farmers and food processors collected about $24 billion a year from the U.S. government in direct subsidies in 2008 according to the U.S. Department of Agriculture (2010).

3. According to Lang and Heasman (2004), about twenty thousand new food and beverage products are introduced into U.S. supermarkets each year.

4. Miller and Woodward (2007) make the important point that anthropologists and other social scientists have too often ignored the common lineaments of

everyday life, finding them "blindingly obvious," when in fact these everyday taken-for-granted parts of life are exceptionally important and deserve detailed comparative study.

References

Andrae, Gunilla, and Born Beckman. 1985. *The wheat trap: Bread and underdevelopment in Nigeria.* London: Zed Books.

Appadurai, Arjun. 1990. "Disjuncture and difference in the global cultural economy." *Theory, Culture and Society* 7: 295–310.

Ashcraft, Norman. 1973. *Colonialism and underdevelopment: Political economic change in British Honduras.* New York: Teachers College Press.

Babcock, Elizabeth, and Richard Wilk. 1998. "International travel and consumer preferences among secondary school students in Belize, Central America." *Caribbean Geography* 8 (1): 32–45.

Barndt, Deborah. 2002. *Tangled routes: Women, work, and globalization on the Tomato Trail.* Boulder, Colo.: Westview Press.

Barongo, Yolamu R. 1980. *Neocolonialism and African politics: A survey of the impact of neocolonialism on African political behavior.* New York: Vantage Press.

Belasco, Warren, and Phillip Scranton, eds. 2002. *Food nations: Selling taste in consumer societies.* New York: Routledge.

Dampier, William. 1906. *Dampier's voyages.* Ed. John Masefield. London: E Grant Richards.

Dumont, Rene. 1963. *A development plan for British Honduras, Part 2: The modernization of agriculture.* UN Commission for Technical Assistance, Department of Economic and Social Affairs.

Franke, Richard. 1987. "The effects of colonialism and neocolonialism on the gastronomic patterns of the Third World." In *Food and evolution*, ed. Marvin Harris and Eric Ross, 455–79. Philadelphia: Temple University Press.

Government of Belize, Ministry of Finance. 2006. "Monthly report on fiscal operations, March." Available at: http://www.belize.gov.bz/monthly_report_march2006.html. Accessed September 12, 2011.

Hannerz, Ulf. 1996. *Transnational connections.* London: Routledge.

Henke, Holger, and Fred Reno. 2003. *Modern political culture in the Caribbean.* Mona, Jamaica: University of West Indies Press.

Lang, Tim, and Michael Heasman. 2004. *Food wars: Public health and the battle for mouths, minds and markets.* Washington, D.C.: Earthscan.

Long, Lucy, ed. 2003. *Culinary tourism.* Lexington: University Press of Kentucky.

Miller, Daniel, and Sophie Woodward. 2007. "Manifesto for a study of denim." *Social Anthropology* 15 (3): 335–51.

Ritz, Stacy. 1994. *The new key to Belize.* Berkeley, Calif.: Ulysses Press.

Rogers, E. 1885. "British Honduras: Its resources and development." *Journal of the Manchester Geographical Society* 1: 197–227.

Sheller, Mimi. 2003. *Consuming the Caribbean.* London: Routledge.

Simmel, Georg. 1902. "Fashion." *International Quarterly* 10: 130–55.

Sutherland, Anne. 1998. *The making of Belize: Globalization in the margins.* Westport, Conn.: Bergen and Garvey.

Tripartite Report. 1966. *Report of the Tripartite Economic Survey of British Honduras, May 1966.* Trinational Survey Team: Canada, United Kingdom, and the United States.

U.S. Department of Agriculture. 2010. "Budget summary and annual performance plan." Available at: http://www.obpa.usda.gov/budsum/FY10budsum.pdf. Accessed January 5, 2012.

Waddell, D.A.G. 1961. *British Honduras: A historical and contemporary survey.* London: Oxford University Press.

Wilk, Richard. 1995. "Learning to be local in Belize: Global systems of common difference." In *Worlds apart: Modernity through the prism of the local*, ed. D. Miller, 110–33. London: Routledge.

Wilk, Richard. 2002. "Food and nationalism: The origins of 'Belizean food.'" In *Food nations: Selling taste in consumer societies*, ed. Warren Belasco and Phillip Scranton, 67–89. New York: Routledge.

Wilk, Richard. 2006. *Home cooking in the global village.* Belize City: Angelus Press; London: Berg.

Wilk, Richard. 2007. "Independence, globalization, rice and beans." In *Taking stock: Belize at 25 years of independence*, ed. Barbara Balboni and Joseph Palacio, 310–22. Benque Viejo, Belize: Cubola Productions.

Wilk, Richard. 2009. "Completely unique but appealing to everyone: Managing difference on the globalized menu of national and ethnic foods." In *The globalization of food*, ed. David Inglis and Debra Gimlin, 185–96. Oxford: Berg.

Wilk, Richard, and Mac Chapin. 1990. "Ethnic minorities in Belize: Mopan, Kekchi and Garifuna." Monograph No. 1. Belize City: Society for the Promotion of Education and Research.

–12–

Rice and Beans, a Staple on Even the Most Respectable Mexican Tables

Mari-Jose Amerlinck

Different kinds of beans, of Mesoamerican origin, and rice, of foreign origin, have achieved the status of a common staple in Mexican cuisines, regardless of social class or wealth, and have been omnipresent in everyday and festive meals in Mexico, at least from the early nineteenth century.[1] However, the combination of rice *with* beans has not reached the status of a national dish as in the other countries discussed in this book. This paradox may be explained by the overall cultural and economic dominance of a more versatile cereal, maize, both as an ingredient and as a finished product, and by the large number and significance of regional cuisines in Mexico. Beans and rice are separately combined with animal protein, maize and vegetables, particularly chilies and tomatoes, along with many other local and foreign ingredients, and they accompany elaborate dishes everywhere in Mexico, but rice in partnership *with* beans is particular to some regional cuisines.

Mexican culinary traditions or cuisines—note the plural used in this chapter—draw their strength from popular, local, and regional roots, which have undergone a process of gentrification through the centuries.[2] Some local dishes have achieved national recognition and become part of a national identity, in search of a wider appreciation at global level. Some historical work on Mexican cuisines has overemphasized two factors: the reliance of indigenous agriculture upon the combination of maize, beans, and squash, and the decisive influence of colonial convents in the formation of the various Mexican cuisines. This chapter endorses the view that the quasi-dogmatic reliance on these factors precludes a better understanding of the richness and variety of these cuisines.

The production, preparation, and consumption of food are related to practically every aspect of social life. Taking for granted the platitude that food is not just for sustenance and feeding, but also for socializing and feeling, this chapter begins with some personal memories that may help to illustrate how beans and rice are incorporated in Mexican culinary identity, both personal and social. It then proceeds with a brief account of how locally domesticated beans and rice, introduced by the Spaniards, have achieved such importance, and continues with a discussion about beans *with* rice. Some recipes are interspersed along the way.

Culinary Memories about Beans and Rice

Proust (1981) was a lucky man: he once found a madeleine that triggered fond, in-grained memories because, when dipped in tea, it tasted exactly like his aunt Léo-nie's. We all long to recover some exact taste or smell, but the people and events of our past are not easily recaptured at will. I have tried every recipe of *cocada* (a coconut dessert) that I can find, but have yet to give my husband the pleasure of his Andalusian grandmother's confection. As a result of these failures, no memories are recaptured, but new tastes, new smells, new memories, and personal culinary traditions develop. And, even if the precise nuance that will trigger our mnemonic emotions remains elusive, other memories are at hand to guide our present, as I will attempt to show (see also Sutton 2001).

Rice and beans in Latin American countries and in the Caribbean have a similar status to that of the butter madeleine in France: an unpretentious, everyday food. It is not for me to say whether or not they can trigger treasured memories like Proust's, or inspire a new literary masterpiece, but I for one vividly remember the first time I was served *moros y cristianos* at my maternal grandmother's home. I was less than ten years old, but the name struck me as something not only exotic and interesting, but also playful and fun. I knew from my religious upbringing at home and school that we were all Christians, but Moors appeared only in fairy-tales, along with flying carpets, or in the stories my father told about El Cid, named like my brother. Also it would be fun to "eat people" in the way alphabet soup and pig-shaped bread were eaten. So, it was disappointing that the meal that had enticed my imagination was only plain everyday black beans with rice. The name was too grand, out of proportion, and not mischievous, yet I liked it because I had come to like beans and rice.

A second surprising discovery in relation to beans originated at my paternal grandmother's home, who brought from her native Guatemala the recipe for *rel-lenitos de plátano* (stuffed plantain), a circle of boiled and mashed plantain stuffed with refried black beans, folded in half and fried in oil, then powdered with sugar. The combination of sugar with salty beans, common in Guatemala, is infrequent in Mexico, except for Chiapas, the Mexican province that belonged to Guatemala in colonial times (Figure 12.1).[3] Many traits are still shared between Chiapas and Gua-temala, from features of language, to the colorful ethnic textiles.

In grammar school, we were asked to grow a bean seed in wet cotton, in order to help us learn the plant's name and habits. It germinated really quickly, but smelled terrible. I preferred to play *lotería* (lotto), where each player was given beans of a different color, to mark a card as the names of objects depicted in it were called.[4] When we traveled to Yucatán, the land of my maternal grandfather, which was like a separate country at the time, I discovered many new foods, such as *frijol con puerco* (beans with pork) as a main course, and *frijol colado* (strained beans), as a side dish, a delicacy my mother extolled.

Figure 12.1   Map of Mexico showing some of the places mentioned in the text.

As to rice, it was the most common second course among the regular four or five courses of the main midday meal, in every respectable house I visited. It was always accompanied by another dish, such as guacamole or avocado slices, a fried egg, fried plantain, cream and cheese, a small tortilla dish (*sopes*, or *garnachas*), and a homemade chili sauce. And again, at my Guatemalan grandmother's home, rice was often prepared for dessert as a croquette of rice pudding under another playful name: *bigotes* (moustaches), which made a mess when, out of sight of adults, we children tried to wear them.

Beans and rice, sweet and savory, were thus part of my childhood nourishment and amusements, as the madeleine was for Proust's literary alter ego. But unlike Proust, I enjoyed having a modest role in their preparation. Many evenings I would go to the kitchen and "help" the servants pick out the pebbles and chaff from the brown or black beans, which were then soaked overnight and boiled the next day, in an earthen pot (the pressure cooker was not only slighted for the inferior flavor it gave to food, but also considered quite dangerous). I never questioned why beans had to be cleaned, and were not packed in bags or boxes, ready to be cooked, like rice.[5]

Arroz a la mexicana (rice Mexican-style) is first soaked in hot water, drained until the water runs clear, dried, then sautéed with a clove of garlic until golden, stirred to prevent sticking or burning, and boiled with chopped vegetables (carrots, peas, or sweet corn), as *rojo* (red) rice with a tomato sauce, *blanco* (white), without tomatoes or verde (green), if cooked with mashed *poblano* chilies or ground coriander leaves.

My reward as an upper-middle-class girl sorting out beans was to become both fascinated and exquisitely terrified by the ghost stories I asked the servants to tell. As an adult anthropologist I continue to be interested in the lives and ways of rural peoples, not as migrant domestic workers in the capital, but in their own villages, in *mi tierra*, as they used to say. Following this connection, I will attempt to describe how my personal memories are representative of the cultural traits that accompany the widespread role of beans and rice in Mexican cuisines, and will discuss some local and regional peculiarities.

The Staple of Even the Most Respectable Mexicans

The title for this chapter was inspired by the cookbook-cum-dictionary titled the *Nuevo cocinero americano en forma de diccionario*, published in 1888, as a revised and enlarged edition of *El cocinero mexicano* from 1831. Both included more indigenous Mexican ingredients and techniques than older recipe collections, although the influence of French over Spanish cuisine was more evident in the later version (Barros 2006: 192). Several recipe manuscripts are also known from the eighteenth century, and their mere existence is proof of identity of distinctive Mexican cuisines in the making, although many also reproduce recipes known from medieval Spain. However, it was not until the nineteenth century that a varied assortment of recipe books, geared to a larger audience, was published both in Mexico City and in other provincial capitals such as Guadalajara, Morelia, Puebla, Toluca, and Zacatecas. Some were authored by women, unlike contemporary Europe where matrilineal oral transmission gave way, according to Barnes (2003: 13), to increasingly patriarchal written accounts.[6]

The two books cited above are essential to understanding present-day Mexican cuisines because, like other nineteenth-century collections of recipes, they show that the ingredients and methods of indigenous Mexican cooking, combined with foreign ingredients, were fully adopted and appreciated by the middle and upper classes, which helped to redefine what was considered national (Barros 2006: 166–67). Recipe books were not bought or used by peasants or servants, who in their native environments had handed down the local cooking traditions that give Mexican cuisines their distinctive flavors. They were important to the literate, wealthier urban housewives, for whom cooking, previously delegated to servants, had become a respectable activity.[7] The time was ripe for appreciation of ancestral traditions, whereby everyday cooking was emerging as gastronomical pleasure, on equal standing to the Spanish and French traditions that had dominated formal entertaining after independence. A transculturation process was thus completed, reaching a climax in the twentieth century, when Mexican cuisines came of age not only as worthy exports, but also as a field of scholarly research and culinary experimentation.

This *Diccionario* noted the general use of rice in all kinds of savory and sweet dishes in Mexico, saying "Easterners, like us, employ this grain for everything" (1989: 38). It recommended selecting a clean, whole, white, new, thick, and hard grain, which should be soaked several times and then dried, and if properly chosen, would swell easily after boiling. On the other hand it claimed that beans cultivated in Europe were an inferior product. In Mexico they had become a staple for the poor but were so tasty and nutritious that they were eaten for breakfast and dinner in the more *decente* (respectable) homes as well. In many homes they were also eaten at lunch, the main daily meal then and now. The book suggested seasoning beans with onion, cloves, cumin, *guajillo* chili, *pulque* (fermented agave sap), and cheese—quite a list of ingredients.

Both my personal memories and scholarship attest to the pervasive role of beans and rice in Mexican cuisines, as part of everyday and festive consumption, regardless of class or wealth. Next I will address the historical process that brought this situation into being, and discuss regional and local traditions.

Mesoamerican Beans

Mesoamerica was characterized by a high degree of regional and local cultural diversity in pre-Hispanic times, at the same time that it shared a widespread cultural complex including religious beliefs, artistic styles, and technology, among other traits (Kirchhoff [1943] 1953). The agricultural core, which resulted from a long process of domestication of wild plants, was an essential component of this shared cultural complex.

Of primary importance was the domestication of maize (*Zea mays*) some 6300 B.P. (Smith 2001, 2005), which by 3450 B.P. supported sedentary village life (Marcus and Flannery 2004). Maize is often found by archaeologists in the same contexts as beans (*Phaseolus vulgaris*), gourds (*Lagenaria siceraria*), and squash (*Cucurbita pepo*), evidence for the evolution of complex agricultural practices that eventually reached a very efficient level, not so much because of technology, but through a profound knowledge of plants and hard physical and intellectual labor by both men and women.

The discovery of the *nixtamalization* process permitted farmers to get a higher amount of usable protein from maize, particularly when augmented with beans.[8] This may account for the higher population densities in Mesoamerica, compared to the Caribbean islands, where maize was not so processed (Coe [1994] 2004).[9]

Ongoing genetic research has shed more light on the domestication of squash, beans, chili (*Capsicum annuum*), and other basic crops in the Mesoamerican diet. A species of squash was probably domesticated even before maize, and traces of *Cucurbita pepo* from 10,000 B.P. have been discovered in Oaxaca (Dirzo, Lindig, and Rosenthal 2001: 612; Smith 2005). Five or six kinds of beans, including *Canavalia sp.* were domesticated in America (Kaplan 1981). The oldest traces of cultivated beans in Mesoamerica are runner beans, *P. coccineus* (Delgado Salinas, Bonet, and Gepts 1988). Wild species of the common bean (*P. vulgaris*) have been found throughout Mesoamerica, and the earliest directly dated in the archaeological record in Mexico comes from only about seven thousand years ago. When the common bean was initially domesticated it was probably added into well-established farming economies based on pepo squash and maize, as well as on other crops yet to be fully documented and directly dated (Smith 2001).

Besides the *P. vulgaris*, of which there are some fifty varieties, there is the *P. acutifolius* or *escomite* (tepary bean) suitable for drier areas, and domesticated in the U.S. Southwest or the West Coast of Mexico; *P. coccineus* or *ayocote* (scarlet runner bean), and the lima bean, *P. lunatus* or *patachete*. Many authors also include the year bean, *P. polyanthus* (*acalete*), as a Mesoamerican domesticate (Kaplan and Kaplan 1996). All of them are found in present-day Mexico, where new varieties are constantly being discovered.[10]

It has been asserted, over and over again, that maize has always been the dominant crop in Mesoamerica at the center of the trinity, trio, or triad of maize, beans, and squash. The beans, it is said, grow up the cornstalk and the squash provides protective ground cover. Maize was indeed an important food in all the stages of its growth, and it often had a central symbolic meaning in indigenous culture. Men were made of maize, which was a gift from the gods. All native languages have many names for the different parts of the plant, and for different patterns of color, shape, and number of rows of seed. Populucas in the state of Veracruz have names for sixteen kinds of mature corncobs (Barros and Buenrostro 2002: 23).

The history of food is certainly intertwined with the history of agriculture, but the emphasis on this Mesoamerican crop triad has reached a point of dogmatism, obscuring the fact that both subsistence agriculture and associated culinary practices were far more complex and multiple. Just because maize, beans, and squash were planted together, cultivated together, and harvested at about the same time is insufficient to explain both the complexity of indigenous agriculture and the variety of Mexican cuisines.

A fourth ingredient, chili, was as basic as the other three in both the early Mesoamerican, and in the later Mexican agriculture and diet. Herbs and tomatoes, both the red (*Lycopersicum esculentum*) and the green husk tomato or *tomatillo* (*Physalis philadelphica*), and many other crops should be added to the list of basic and common crops at the foundation of regional cuisine. Archaeological and documentary research attests to the huge regional, climatic, ecological, cultural, and ethnic diversity of pre-Hispanic cuisine, which cannot be reduced to a common denominator of a simple triad. The indigenous population used not only all sorts of vegetal ingredients (seeds, pods, leaves, flowers, fruits, and roots) but also minerals, and animals including various insects, amphibians, and mollusks. Eyewitnesses were impressed by the variety of products found in native markets and traded among indigenous peoples. It is significant that *The Florentine Codex*, compiled by the Franciscan friar Bernardino de Sahagún in the mid-sixteenth century, listed 724 plants used by the Aztecs. While 266 were medicinal, 229 were culinary, and among them, beans were used both as food and for religious offerings (Estrada Lugo 1990: 232; Torres 1989), showing that the boundary between food, religion, and medicine was complex and permeable. Based on sixteenth-century vocabularies and *The Florentine Codex*, Barros and Buenrostro (2002: 9) find thirty-five distinct culinary techniques, fifty kinds of beans, and more than forty kinds of chilies. Even by modern standards this array of procedures and ingredients would denote a very complex and diverse gastronomy. Mexican cuisines must be understood in the context of cooking techniques and diverse indigenous utensils, including the stone *metate* for grinding, the *molcajete* for crushing and mixing, and clay plates and pots, particularly the flat *comal* griddle to make tortillas.

Beans were not only basic in the daily diet, but were also second only to maize in the tax or tribute paid to Aztec and other rulers. They were presented to hungry Spanish conquistadores everywhere they went. New and unfamiliar plants were actively sought by Europeans for use as herbs, medicines, and foods. However, the Spanish easily recognized the similarity of Mexican beans, both in shape, taste, and cooking methods to European legumes such as the broad beans, chickpeas, and lentils.

Coe ([1994] 2004: 51–52) asserts that plants that resembled European categories, such as maize, peanuts, squash, and beans, were more easily adopted and exported back to Europe. "But when unfamiliar substances are taken up by new users, they enter into pre-existing and psychological contexts and acquire or are given contextual meanings by those who use them" (Mintz 1985: 6). Maize and beans are a case in point, since they did not cross the Atlantic together or at the same time. The former was conceived as a new cereal akin to wheat and treated as such, while New World beans were absorbed into the list of existing legumes.

Diversity and Locality

When trying to understand present-day Mexican culinary culture, we find the same ancient Mesoamerican pattern of local diversity alongside common themes. At present around twenty varieties of improved beans plus the fifty ancestral kinds are cultivated all over the country, and recognized with names in all native languages.[11] In any common self-service market in Guadalajara, where I live, at least six kinds of beans are regularly sold (*bayo*, *flor de mayo*, *flor de junio*, *negro*, *peruano*, *pinto*), and more kinds can be found in municipal markets (including *azufrado*, *canario*; different kinds of black beans, such as *negro poblano*, *negro marrón*, *negro negro*; and varieties of *peruano*, such as *bola*, *higuera*, and *vaquita*). There is also a variety of processed and ready-to-eat products made with black, pinto, and *peruano* beans in both markets.

Peasants grow beans for consumption and sale, but the diversity is declining (Pietri and Pietri 1976: 70). Research undertaken among the Purépechas in the state of Michoacán between 1977 and 1982 found five varieties of *P. vulgaris* (Mapes et al. 1990), while in the late 1940s West (1948: 40) reported twenty varieties in the same area, and Foster (1948) found eleven varieties just in the one village of Tzintzuntzan.

Beans have been eaten as vegetables in the pod from pre-Hispanic times. As mature dry seeds they are generally boiled or stewed, but they are also roasted and then finely ground and prepared into patties or beverages.[12] Boiled beans have always been eaten plain, as *frijoles de la olla* (beans from the pot), with the common addition of the herb *epazote* (*Chenopodium ambrosioides*) and diverse spices as a simple soup or side dish. The broth is considered a good meal for a weak stomach. A heartier concoction results when beans are cooked with softened corn grains (hominy), called *gallina pinta* in Sonora. Beans are combined with meat (like the Yucatecan *frijol con puerco*), fish and seafood, fruits like the plantain, and of course rice. Rice and beans are called *moros y cristianos* in Veracruz and the other Atlantic Coast states, showing a close connection with Cuba and other islands in the Hispanic Caribbean, and are called *morisqueta* in the western states on the Pacific.

When mashed, beans may be combined with corn tortillas to make tacos, *gorditas*, or *enfrijoladas*.[13] Mashed beans are often stuffed inside *tamales* prepared with corn dough, sometimes with meat or fish, and inside a wide variety of large dry or fresh chilies and sweet peppers. Plain *frijoles refritos* (fried mashed beans) is the typical side dish for breakfast eggs and main meal entrées. However, the particular procedure of straining the mashed black beans before frying them, which results into the lacquered gleam of *frijol colado*, seems unique to Yucatán and Campeche, two states that share many culinary traditions. It is also common in Yucatán to combine beans with pasta, like the Italian *pasta e fagioli*.[14]

There are regional fervent preferences for one kind of beans over others on the basis of color, usually rationalized as reducing cooking time and better taste. In central, eastern, and southern Mexico black beans are preferred, but as one moves west and north, the brown and yellow lighter kinds are favored.[15] For instance in Michoacán brown beans are preferred, while in Jalisco the lighter the better, and *peruanos* are preferred as faster cooking than other light-colored beans, though they are expensive. Some people will simply not eat black beans, while in Puebla and Veracruz the opposite prevails and people say *frijoles güeros ni regalados* ("light-colored beans, not even for free"). In Yucatán black beans are preferred, but the yellow lima bean (*P. lunatus*), which remains yellow when cooked, is used in religious rituals, a custom uninterrupted from pre-Hispanic times.

I have not discovered a satisfactory explanation for these preferences. There might be a racist undertone, since black beans are preferred in regions with a stronger indigenous component, while less indigenous regions favor lighter-colored beans. The early Spanish colonizers preferred lighter beans, which were more like familiar European legumes, and this may explain preferences in western and northern Mexico, where many indigenous cultures did not survive. In any case, differences in color have been acknowledged in agronomic research, and those varieties in higher demand have been the subject of breeding to produce seeds that are drought-resistant, last longer on the shelf, take less time to cook, and may be industrially processed.

Artisans and artists have also used the diversity of bean colors, creating figurative images of revered saints and decorating ephemeral constructions for village festivities using different seeds. This craft of combining colored seeds, found, for example, in Ixtenco, Tlaxcala, or Tepoztlán, Morelos, has been extended to the urban market, where decorative trivets and decorative balls are covered with rows of seeds forming flowers and other designs often encased in plastic.[16]

Beans are considered a strategic product for rural development and urban diets, and their price was controlled, as it was for maize, for many years. Since the 1980s the per capita consumption of beans has declined, a trend attributed to increasing urbanization and change in eating habits, yet Mexico maintains a significant place among countries with a high per capita yearly consumption of beans, second only to Brazil (Sánchez Rodríguez et al. 2001: 15).

Rice from Overseas

Less is known about how rice attained a role as a staple food in Mexican cuisines, even if it has never displaced maize as the most important cereal. Rice prospers on level irrigated land, and it was adopted as a cash crop by large landowners, much more than by self-sufficient peasants, thus helping erode indigenous patterns of production, appropriation, and distribution.

Asian rice had long traveled westward with the help of Alexander the Great, among others, before it became widely consumed among the expanding Arabic civilization of the Mediterranean. When they expanded into the Iberian Peninsula from A.D. 711, Arab and Moorish conquerors were accompanied by many significant crops that included vegetables and fruits like eggplant, citrus, plantain, mangoes, and sugarcane; spices like ginger; and cereals including sorghum, hard wheat, and, of course, their *ar-ruz* that became *arroz* in Spanish. Arabs introduced cooking procedures like *escabeche* (marinating or pickling in vinegar), and advanced agricultural techniques for irrigation. The estuaries of the Guadiana and Guadalquivir rivers and the marshes of Albúfera in Valencia were sown with rice. Centuries later, Spaniards introduced rice into southern France and northern Italy, where it was widely cultivated by the fifteenth century.

Seafarers from Columbus onward took rice with them, since it was already established as a staple in Spain, although not as esteemed as wheat. In medieval Spain rice was seasoned with spices and cooked with legumes such as chickpeas, lentils, and white beans, a forerunner to *moros y cristianos.* The circle of Spanish rice around the world was completed when explorers traveled west from America and found this cereal again in the Pacific islands and in other Asian countries. This rice would reach back to New Spain in the seventeenth century with the yearly arrival of ships from the Philippines to Mexican Pacific ports like Acapulco, Manzanillo, Navidad, and San Blas. It was widely circulated by means of mule trains to the surrounding regions in what are now the states of Colima, Guerrero, Jalisco, Michoacán, and Sinaloa. This rice was accompanied by a wave of Asian immigrants, generically called *chinos* (Chinese), whose entry was later forbidden by the Crown in 1608 (Sánchez Díaz 2008: 246 fn 14).

This second arrival of rice from Asia would be of great economic and culinary importance, but it had probably been first introduced into Mexico from the Caribbean islands shortly before the fall of Tenochtitlan, the Aztec capital, in 1521. It was planted in La Española (present-day Santo Domingo–Haiti) at least since 1512, and then taken to Puerto Rico (Sánchez Díaz 2008: 245) and Cuba (Le Riverend 1963: 69), the island that became the catering center for exploring the continent.

Francisco López de Gómara, chaplain and secretary to Hernán Cortés, was impressed by the fact that the introduction of wheat into New Spain was due to Juan Garrido, a black slave who successfully sowed the few grains he had found in a bag of rice (López de Gómara [1552] 1856: 452). He also mentioned how Cortés tried to improve the local economy by importing animals, plants, and seeds from the islands when his wife arrived from Cuba in 1522 (López de Gómara [1552] 1856: 403). While this author explicitly mentions sugarcane and silk, he seems to take rice for granted, a sign that the bag with the acclaimed wheat in it was not the first to reach the continent. In fact rice was probably already planted around the port of Veracruz, founded by Cortés in 1519. Up to the present, the coastal states of Veracruz and Campeche are the largest producers of this cereal in the country.[17]

There are too many gaps in our knowledge to attempt a cultural history of how Mexicans developed such a fondness for rice, making it part of their everyday and festive meals. The introduction of wheat by both the Spanish conquistadors and missionaries and the deleterious effects it produced on indigenous agriculture have been more widely studied. History gives us just a few hints that may explain the reasons for the prevalence of rice, until we have a detailed study of local and regional ecclesiastical tithes, and other documents that would give evidence about the development and expansion of rice production and consumption.

Brillat-Savarin stated in 1825 that "gastronomy examines men and things for the purpose of transporting from one country to another all that deserves to be known" (2004: 29). It could be added that "all that deserves to be known" is also "transported" from one social class to another. Thus, in Mexico, in a centuries-long process, native indigenous cooking practices and food products from abroad moved upward and downward the social ladder, by means of employers and rulers, but also through their slaves, nannies, cooks, and other servants. The mixture eventually led to a cuisine at least partially shared by all classes, each according to their means.

The use of tobacco in the Caribbean moved upward in status from the Indians and blacks to the dominant white Europeans. It is easy to imagine a similar upward movement of the indigenous meal structure built around a core carbohydrate (manioc and other tubers or maize), with a flavor-fringe supplement, of tomato and chili sauces, and spicy vegetables including beans (Mintz 1985: 9). The result would be a meeting of rice and beans in the main course, a process that parallels the acceptance of chili for seasoning spiced curries among the rice-eating population in India.

The influence of Moorish migrants and black slaves, already habituated to rice, must not be overlooked, since it was undoubtedly significant (Crosby 1972). Male clerics and missionaries were crucial players in the process of changing indigenous agricultural production and food habits, by introducing and encouraging Spanish agricultural systems that included the use of animals and iron tools and the cultivation of wheat, citrus, and other fruit trees among other Old World horticultural products (Ciudad Real [1872] 1976). Spanish conquistadors, like Cortés himself, introduced market-oriented crops such as sugarcane, which were often grown with forced labor, in the properties they received from the Crown. Their estates and those of other settlers would eventually be converted into *haciendas*, and this form of plantation dominated the Mexican landscape well into the twentieth century.

Prominent literati and gastronomes like Alfonso Reyes (1889–1959; 1953), Artemio de Valle Arizpe (1884–1961; [1933] 1976), and most important, Salvador Novo (1904–1974; 1957) praised the distinctiveness of Mexican cuisines. Their writing brought to the fore what had previously been considered common everyday meals, and encouraged their study. But these authors often merged legend with fact in their aspiration to reconstruct, in fine, often baroque prose, the origins of iconic culinary dishes, such as *chiles en nogada* (chilies in walnut sauce) and *moles* (thick sauces with a variety of dry chilies and spices) (Valle Arizpe [1933] 1976). A host of later authors has uncritically adopted their ideas about the decisive influence of nuns in creating, even "inventing," Mexican cuisines in colonial times.

Transmission of culinary abilities was supposedly achieved either through the education of young upper-class women in convents, and when nuns created dishes as gifts to ecclesiastical and political officers, for sale to the upper classes and charity to the poor. The role of nonreligious servants in transmitting culinary knowledge, and combining local and foreign ingredients, has been overlooked or mentioned just in passing (de Gortari Krauss and Escamilla Soto 2000: 16, 22). Priests, monks, and nuns had servants and slaves who were excluded from the religious life, while working in convents, ecclesiastical households, and monasteries. The first convent in New Spain was founded in the viceregal capital of Mexico City in 1540, followed gradually by foundations in practically all important cities. Many Spanish nuns were accompanied into the convent by Moorish slaves, both in Mexico and Peru (Domingo 1996: 24). Later on, women of Spanish ancestry, already born in Mexico, entered the convent with their native maids.

Another possible means of the transmission of rice into Mexican cooking may have been therapeutic, since rice was part of the medieval pharmacopeia. The devastating consequences of Old World diseases for the New World population that lacked immunity caused a demographic collapse during the sixteenth century. Disease was even more catastrophic because of the nutritional deprivation caused when the consumption of basic pre-Hispanic foods, like amaranth, was discouraged or directly prohibited on religious grounds. Rice might have been used as medicinal nourishment for the sick at a time when religious hospitals run by indigenous people with the help of Augustinians, Franciscans, and other clerics had an important role (Ciudad Real [1872] 1976, II: 68).

Proof of the growing popularity of rice is its presence in all eighteenth-century recipe books, and two *tortas de arroz* (rice cakes) appear in a book wrongly attributed to the famous poetess nun Sor Juana Inés de la Cruz.[18] One recommends boiling rice with milk, and both use saffron to flavor it, and form the cake with layers of rice and ground meat seasoned with typical European ingredients like nuts, capers, olives, raisins, and hard-boiled eggs, as well as local tomatoes and chilies in one recipe.

There is a third rice recipe in this book, for a dish called *Turco* (Turkish). It also contains ground meat seasoned with spices, but instead of layers of rice it uses layers of maize dough prepared "as for tamales." This large-grained maize was at the time called Turkish or Saracen grain, since it was mistakenly thought to be introduced into Europe from the Middle East and was classified as *Turcicum frumentum* by Leonard Fuchs in 1542. This recipe is an interesting case in culinary evolution and transculturation that helps to explain the easy acceptance of rice in Mexico. A similar preparation called *Arroz turco* with rice is common in Mexican nineteenth- and twentieth-century cuisine. This is a good example of the interchangeability of cereals, maize and rice substituting for each other. This would have made it easy to substitute rice for corn in a host of local corn/bean recipes all over the country.

Rice is prepared in many ways in Mexico. As a second course or side dish, it is popularly called *sopa seca*[19] (dry soup), to differentiate it from the first course, a *sopa aguada* (watery or liquid soup). As a main dish, it is cooked together as a casserole with fish and seafood, like the *arroz a la tumbada* of Veracruz, or with chicken or pork and all kinds of vegetables, including beans and other legumes. As dessert it is found in many puddings, and ground into flour it is combined with maize in tamales or *atole* (porridge). Rice flour and sugar mix with water to make the popular beverage *horchata*.

Aguirre Beltrán ([1952] 1995, I: 349) asserts that the cultivation of rice was introduced into central Michoacán before 1650, while tithe registers prove that it was certainly cultivated there before 1679 (Sánchez Díaz 2008: 247). Rice had become an important commercial crop in this region by 1697 (Barrett 1975) and continued as such well into the eighteenth century (Sánchez Díaz 2008: 247), as witnessed by Villaseñor, who claimed this rice supplied other provinces in New Spain (Aguirre

Beltrán [1952] 1995, I: 349). Given the geographical location of Michoacán close to the Pacific, and the fact that there was a wave of immigrants from Asia, as stated above, this rice could have been of Asiatic origin.[20]

The consumption of and demand for rice increased all over the country, and by the end of the eighteenth century its cultivation spread from haciendas and large holdings to peasants in communal properties, who planted it along with maize and indigo on irrigated lands in the lowlands of Michoacán (Tello n.d.; Aguirre Beltrán [1952] 1995, I: 349). It was sent to markets in provincial cities as far as Durango and Zacatecas to the north and Veracruz to the east.

The cultivation of rice extended to other regions after the revolution and independence struggles in the nineteenth century. It was commercially planted, next to sugarcane, in Jojutla in the lowlands of Morelos south of Mexico City from 1836, where a distinctive variety was developed. Jojutla is a short-grain rice, soft and sticky, that absorbs liquid quickly, and is highly valued in many parts of Mexico.

Rice production in Michoacán reached its climax in the first decades of the twentieth century, on the estates of the Cusi family. Its founder was native to the rice-producing region of Lombardy in Italy, and visited Louisiana plantations (Cusi 1952). After several experiments he eventually developed a system that used running water for irrigation and cattle to weed and manure the fields, and then thin and prune the young rice shoots (Aguirre Beltrán [1952] 1995, I: 349–52; Cusi 1952: 112–14). Their production stalled after agrarian reform dismembered the Cusi properties in the 1930s (Cusi 1952).

Today rice is grown in the Atlantic coastal states of Campeche, Tabasco, Tamaulipas, Veracruz, and also in Chiapas, Colima, Guerrero, Morelos, Michoacán, Nayarit, Oaxaca, and Sinaloa. Long-grain rice is now increasingly popular because it cooks more quickly, and much is imported from North America, presenting a threat to local producers, who cannot compete with cheap imports. Since the North American Free Trade Agreement was signed in 1994, rice and bean production have declined due to cheaper imports. Other imported varieties are found in urban markets, for use in particular recipes and in the food trade, such as the middle-sized and round, absorbent *arborio* and *calasparra* for *risotto* and paella; *basmati* with small, long grains eaten with curries; and the long-grained *jasmine* for Asian dishes.

Beans with Rice in Mexican Cuisines

The particular combination of beans with rice explored in this book is known in Mexico as *moros y cristianos* or *morisqueta;* the latter is claimed by the *Tierra Caliente* region of Michoacán, but is actually found in other coastal states along the Pacific, such as Colima and Guerrero. There is a proverb, *Cómicos y abogados, lo mismo hacen de moros que de cristianos*, which translates to "Comedians and lawyers, can play either as Moors or as Christians" (Pérez Martínez 2002: 108). This could also be applied to the versatility of the actual dish of *moros y cristianos*, whose preparation can take several forms. The Christian rice can be cooked in water, stock, milk, or other liquid to be served alongside a serving of cooked beans, or cooked rice can be added to already-cooked beans in the pot, or rice can be added to the pot of boiling Moor beans to finish their cooking together. In all three cases, tomato sauces, chilies, and many other ingredients may be added. *Moros y cristianos* is related to the Caribbean, associated to Cuba, where it is also called *congrí*, and is particularly popular in the states of Veracruz and Tabasco, on the Gulf Coast, where it is eaten with fried plantain.

The Spanish Academy dictionary relates the etymology of *morisqueta* to the historical Moors, and translates it as a facial grimace or the steam-cooked rice, with no salt, typical from the Philippines. In Mexican culinary practice it is generically steamed rice or rice cooked with an excess of water, and up to the mid-twentieth century it was considered food for the sickbed.[21] In the Michoacán Tierra Caliente, *morisqueta* is boiled rice served with a sauce of tomatoes, onion, garlic, and cubes of cheese. Pork or meat is an optional addition to the sauce, which is finally topped with *frijoles de la olla*, and is often eaten with *tostadas* (dried tortillas) or *totopos* (fried, dry tortillas cut in triangles).

In Colima *morisqueta* is cooked Filipino-style with no salt and served with *frijoles de la olla* and a pork dish called *chilayo*, made with chilies and spices. A peculiar custom is that an aluminum cooking implement has been devised to steam the rice, locally known as a *morisquetera* (Figure 12.2). Its role is similar to the cylindrical

Figure 12.2 Steamed rice *morisqueta* and *morisquetera* used in Colima since the late nineteenth century. Photo by Patricia González.

rice tube used in Asia (see Lampe et al. [1999] 2001: 72) and clearly relates Colima *morisqueta* to its Philippine forebears.

Moros y cristianos is also a most widely practiced ritual dance, performed by men wearing masks and costumes in religious festivities in Mexico and in many other Latin American countries. The origins of this dance, also called *morisma*, have been traced to court pageants in medieval Spain, and Warman states that the first mention of a staged combat of Christians against Moors dates from a royal wedding in Catalonia in 1150 (1972: 17). The dance, along with other representations, was explicitly used by the Spanish conquerors and missionaries to instruct and control the indigenous people. First performed in official festivities, it climbed down the social ladder across the centuries, to become part of the cultural repertoire of native Mexicans, who had been dancing on ritual occasions since pre-Hispanic times. One of its many variations is called *Danza de negros* or *negritos* in Michoacán, Veracruz, and in many other places, where black men, probably slaves from the sugar plantations, stood for the Moors or replaced them (Próspero 2001: 29–36).

Moros y cristianos, beans and rice, are undoubtedly an important part of Mexican identity both as food and as dance. In a two-volume work edited by Florescano (1997) on national heritage, the chapter dedicated to food describes a typical Mexican menu for a semifestive occasion, that begins with tequila as aperitif, and that evidently includes rice as a *sopa seca*, second course, and beans as a side dish (Vargas 1997: 275).

That this "typical" meal is now worthy of being included in national heritage shows how cuisine has only gradually been acknowledged by Mexican intellectuals, a process that started with the narratives of foreign visitors who appreciated, or disliked, Mexican food.[22] Then, at the beginning of the twentieth century, mole with beans and rice was served for the first time in an official meal to commemorate the first centennial of independence in 1910, organized by Leopoldo Batres, the first Mexican archaeologist to study the great ruins of Teotihuacan. After the Mexican Revolution (1910–1920), nationalist intellectuals rediscovered all things Mexican, including cuisine.

Another landmark was the inclusion of *huitlacoche* (a black fungus that grows on ears of maize, long eaten by rural indigenous people) filled crêpes at the banquet for the official visit of President Charles de Gaulle of France in the 1960s. This was created by chef Mayita Parada, who had catered for years for respectable and wealthy families in Mexico City. Subsequently, while men of letters celebrated the wonders of Mexican food, some Mexican dishes gradually left home and started to appear in fancy restaurants and financial clubs, particularly in Mexico City (O'Gorman 1972). Provincial cities were slower to follow this trend, perhaps because they had never lost contact with their own regional cuisines.

In any case, it is significant that many upper-middle-class women undertook the task of researching Mexican cuisines (e.g., Corcuera de Mancera [1978] 1990; Castelló 1987), and rediscovering old family and convent recipes (Castelló Yturbide and Martínez del Río de Redo 2000). Some became professional chefs, entered the catering trade, and had their works beautifully photographed and lavishly published by banks and other firms (see Chapa 1983; Caraza Campos et al. 1999, 2000; Palazuelos, Tausend, and Urquiza 1992; and many others). In other social classes women's roles were also changing, particularly with the need to bring home a second wage.

Today two processes run in parallel when it comes to the development of Mexican cuisine. First, there is a wider appreciation of Mexican gastronomy, evident both in academic and culinary research and in the mushrooming of culinary schools all over the country. A great deal of innovation is building a new diversity of Mexican cuisines in restaurants and various kinds of competitions and contests. The national pride in Mexican cuisine is reflected in its recent recognition by UNESCO as a form of intangible cultural property at a global level.

Second, in the private sphere, there is a neglect of traditional cooking. One of the reasons for this was best explained to me by a male taxi driver: "When women lived on our wages, they cooked more, and used to make ends meet; now they prefer to work for their own wages and buy ready made food." Besides changes in women's roles and more individual work habits, cooking places in smaller homes also conspire against the time, space, and labor demands of Mexican cooking—including the everyday preparation and consumption of beans and rice. But this latter consideration deserves another chapter.

Notes

1. I want to thank Livia Barbosa and Richard Wilk for their comments, particularly Rick who edited the final version when I was ill; Riva Berleant-Schiller for persuading me into accepting his invitation and advising on a previous version of this chapter; Lucila Gómez Sahagún for sharing her knowledge on food and culture, her gift of books and references; Julio César Ramírez, librarian at El Colegio de Michoacán, for help with the bibliography; and Patricia González Sánchez for photos of her family's *morisquetera*. This chapter is dedicated to the memory of Luis del Valle, S. I. who passed away before seeing its completion, because he was the best friend and the greatest beans and rice and Mexican home-cooking lover that I have ever met.

2. When revising this chapter I realized Mexican cooking authority Diana Kennedy called her first book *The Cuisines of Mexico* (1972). Her many books based on firsthand research with local cooks of all social classes all over the country spares her from the following criticisms. The precision of her explanations for authentic Mexican cooking also deserves much praise. Foreign authors tend to speak of cuisines in the plural, whereas nationals prefer the singular (e.g., Barros 2006; Chapa 1983; Palazuelos, Tausend, and Urquiza 1992).

3. However, the combination of plantain and beans, fried in pork lard, is common in the dish known as *mogo mogo* in Veracruz and Tabasco, undoubtedly of Afro-Caribbean origin.

4. This game is traditionally played at urban homes and rural fairs, not with numbers but with figures, which are more recognizable for illiterates. It portrays many plants, fruits, and objects used in Mexican cooking, such as agave, prickly pear, watermelon, and clay and copper cookpots.

5. Discriminating bean eaters in Mexico have a preference for "new beans," from the year's harvest, for their superior flavor, and faster cooking. I have seen domestic workers bring beans from their birthplace back to the city.

6. See the section on old Mexican cookbooks in Kennedy (1998: 486–521) for comments and some tested recipes.

7. The Spanish feminist writer Countess Emilia Pardo Bazán advised housewives in 1913 to let the cook handle onion and garlic, for whom smells were not offensive, since "it would be very cruel for ladies to preserve between a ruby ring and the openwork embroidery of the sleeve of their blouse a treacherous and despicable trace of onions" (1996: 18; my translation).

8. *Nixtamalization*, a word derived from the nahuatl *nextli* (ashes) and *tamalli* (corn dough), is the process of cooking the maize grains with an alkaline solution, such as lime or ashes, to soften them before grinding. This procedure substantially increases the nutritive value of maize.

9. The maize-beans-squash complex was incorporated into Caribbean slave gardens in the seventeenth century according to Berleant (this volume) and Berleant-Schiller and Pulsipher (1986: 7).

10. See Conferencia 1995 for a list of fifty-two related species of beans from *P. acutifolius* to *P. xantotrichus*. A recently discovered variety is the natural crossing of *P. vulgaris* and *P. coccineus*, called *P. coccineus Darwinianus*, *acalete* in Puebla and *frijol gordo* (fat bean) in Veracruz (Hernández X., Ramos, and Martínez [1979] 1991). For more information on new varieties see Delgado Salinas in Perales and Aguirre Rivera (2008).

11. Some languages even have names for different stages or kinds of beans: such as boiled, big, small, rotten, and wild. There are also local names in many places for different kinds that are proof of historical and ethnobotanical knowledge (Aguirre Beltrán [1952] 1995, I: 338; Avendaño Reyes and Flores Gudiño 1999).

12. These roasted beans, now found only among rural populations, have nothing to do with industrially dehydrated bean powder, geared to the urban fast food market, which tastes like old rags.

13. *Gorditas* are thick stuffed tortillas. There is a delicious recipe where *gorditas* are stuffed with mashed beans mixed with ground, dry avocado leaves. *Enfrijoladas* is a casserole of fried tortillas folded in half and covered with thick bean broth, some cream and cheese, common for breakfast or dinner.

14. "In the Caribbean pasta is eaten with beans without an Italian immigrant anywhere in the past" (Berleant-Schiller, personal communication, August 8, 2010).

15. Anthropologist and chef Sylvia Kurczyn says that at the northern frontier of Mesoamerica, greens disappear and give place to browns (personal communication, April 7, 2010); so beans are flavored with brown cumin instead of green *epazote*.

16. There is a long-standing tradition in Mexico of creating images and designs using mosaic, from the pre-Hispanic designs in feathers to the use of glass beads among present Huicholes in Jalisco.

17. In Campeche there is a yearly rice fair. Other fairs take place in the rice-producing states of Morelos (in Jojutla), Querétaro, and Sinaloa. In Mexico City, the Mexican Council of Rice, the umbrella association of private producers, demonstrated one hundred ways of cooking rice at its 2009 fair.

18. The *Libro de Cocina. Convento de San Jerónimo* was first attributed to Sor Juana Inés de la Cruz herself, who died in 1693 (cf. Pérez San Vicente 1995; Lavín and Bénitez Muro 2001), but was later proved to be written on eighteenth-century paper (Juárez López 2005: 53).

19. When a carbohydrate other than rice, such as pasta or a tortilla-based dish, is presented after, or instead of, the soup, it is also called *sopa seca*.

20. Consequently, the cultivation of rice in Mexico differed from its introduction by Africans in South Carolina.

21. Sylvia Kurczyn provides the following recipe: Place in a pot a layer of corn husks, add 4 cups of water; when it boils add 1 cup rice and salt, and cover with more corn husks. When the rice is cooked, serve it hot with *frijoles de la olla*, and finely chopped green chilies. "The perfume given by the corn leaves is unbelievable" (personal communication, June 6, 2010).

22. One such person was Edward B. Tylor, the British anthropologist who not only defined culture, but also disliked tortillas, only much later growing fond of them.

References

Aguirre Beltrán, Gonzalo. [1952] 1995. *Problemas de la población indígena de la cuenca del Tepalcatepec*, 2nd ed. México D. F.: Universidad Veracruzana, INI, Gobierno del estado de Veracruz, FCE.

Avendaño Reyes, Sergio, and José Salvador Flores Gudiño. 1999. "Registro de plantas tóxicas para ganado en el estado de Veracruz, México." *Veterinaria México* 30 (1): 79–94. Available at: http://www.medigraphic.com/pdfs/vetmex/vm-1999/vm991k.pdf. Accessed March 17, 2010.

Barnes, Julian. 2003. *The pedant in the kitchen*. London: Atlantic Books.

Barrett, Ellinore M. 1975. *La cuenca de Tepalcatepec. Vol I: Su colonización y tenencia de la tierra. Vol II: Su desarrollo moderno.* México D. F.: SepSetentas 177 and 178 Secretaría de Educación Pública.

Barros, Cristina. 2006. *Los libros de la cocina mexicana.* México D. F.: Conaculta.

Barros, Cristina, and Marco Buenrostro. 2002. "Cocina prehispánica, continuidad cultural. Recetario." *Arqueología Mexicana* Special Issue 12. México: INAH.

Berleant-Schiller, Riva, and Lydia M. Pulsipher. 1986. "Subsistence cultivation in the Caribbean." *Nieuwe West-Indische Gids—New West Indian Guide* 60 (1–2): 1–41.

Brillat-Savarin, Jean Anthelme. [1825] 2004. *The physiology of taste.* Whitefish, Mont.: Kessinger.

Caraza Campos, Laura B. de, Cecilia Prieto de Martinez Gallardo, Ignacio Urquiza, and Alejandra Prieto de Palacios. 1999. *Mi casa es tu casa: La magia de vivir en México: Ambientes y recetas para el buen vivir.* México D. F.: Planeta-Dupuis.

Caraza Campos, Laura B. de, Lorenza Caraza Campos, Martín J. García-Urtiaga, Lucila Flores de Clavé, and Sebastián Saldívar. 2000. *Gastronomía del Club de Banqueros de México.* México D. F.: Club de Banqueros de México.

Castelló, Teresa. 1987. *Presencia de la comida prehispánica.* México D. F.: Fomento Cultural Banamex.

Castelló Yturbide, Teresa, and María Josefa Martínez del Río de Redo. 2000. *Delicias de antaño: Historia y recetas de los conventos mexicanos.* México D. F.: Grupo Financiero BBVA Bancomer.

Chapa, Martha. 1983. *La cocina mexicana y su arte.* Illustrations and texts by several authors. México D. F.: Editorial Everest Mexicana.

Ciudad Real, Antonio de. [1872] 1976. *Tratado curioso y docto de las grandezas de la Nueva España*, rev. 3rd ed., ed. Josefina García Quintana and Víctor M. Castillo Farreras. México D. F.: UNAM.

Coe, Sophie D. [1994] 2004. *Las primeras cocinas de América (America's First Cuisines).* Trans. Ana Pulido Rull. México D. F.: Fondo de Cultura Económica.

Conferencia Técnica Internacional de la FAO sobre los Recursos Fitogenéticos. 1995. *Conservacion y Utilizacion Sostenible de los Recursos Fitogenéticos en América Central y México. Informe síntesis subregional Anexo 2 del Informe de la reunión subregional sobre los recursos fitogenéticos para América Central, México y el Caribe.* San José, Costa Rica, 21–24 agosto FIAT. Available at: http://www.fao.org/ag/AGP/AGPS/PGRFA/pdf/amerce2s.pdf. Accessed January 11, 2010.

Corcuera de Mancera, Sonia. [1978] 1990. *Entre gula y templanza. Un aspecto de la historia mexicana*, 2nd ed. México D. F.: Fondo de Cultura Económica.

Crosby, Alfred W. 1972. *The Columbian exchange: Biological and cultural consequences of 1492.* Westport, Conn.: Praeger.

Cusi, Enzo. 1952. *Memorias de un colono.* México D. F.: Editorial Jus.

De Gortari Krauss, Yuri, and Edmundo Escamilla Soto. 2000. *Guisos y golosos del barroco.* Vol. 3: *Cocina virreinal Novohispana.* México D. F.: Editorial Clío.

Delgado Salinas, A., A. Bonet, and P. Gepts. 1988. "The wild relative of *phaseolus vulgaris* in Middle America." In *Genetic resources of* phaseolus *beans*, ed. P. Gepts. Dordrecht: Kluwer Academic.

Dirzo Rodolfo, Roberto Lindig, Joshua P. Rosenthal. 2001. "Plantas cultivadas y sus parientes silvestres: Sistemas modelo para estudios de ecología química." In *Relaciones químicas entre organismos: Aspectos básicos y perspectivas de su aplicación*, ed. Ana Luisa Anaya, Francisco Espinosa García, and Rocío Cruz Ortega, 607–32. México D. F.: Plaza y Valdes.

Domingo, Xavier. 1996. "La cocina precolombina en España." In *Conquista y Comida: Consecuencias del encuentro de dos mundos*, ed. Janet Long, 17–29. México D. F.: Instituto de Investigaciones Históricas, UNAM.

Estrada Lugo, Erin I. J. 1990. "Códice Florentino: Su información etnobotánica." In *Agricultura indígena: Pasado y presente*, ed. Teresa Rojas Rabiela, 227–37. México D. F.: Ediciones de la Casa Chata, CIESAS.

Florescano, Enrique, ed. 1997. *El Patrimonio Nacional de México*. México D. F.: FCE.

Foster, George M., assisted by Gabriel Ospina. 1948. *Empire's children: The people of Tzintzuntzan*. Publication No. 6. Washington, D.C.: Smithsonian Institution, Institute of Social Anthropology.

Hernández X., Efraím, A. Ramos, and Miguel Angel Martínez. [1979] 1991. "Etnobotánica." In *Contribuciones al conocimiento del frijol* Phaseolus *en México*, ed. E. Mark Engleman, 113–38. México D. F.: Colegio de Posgraduados de Chapingo.

Juárez López, José Luis. 2005. "La faceta culinaria de Sor Juana. Diario de Campo April," 53–55. Available at: http://www.antropologia.inah.gob.mx/pdf/pdf_diario/abril_05/DC_abril_05.pdf. Accessed March 17, 2010.

Juárez López, José Luis. 2008. *Nacionalismo culinario: La cocina mexicana en el siglo XX*. México D. F.: Consejo Nacional para la Cultura y las Artes (CONACULTA).

Kaplan, Lawrence. 1981. "What is the origin of the common bean?" *Economic Botany* 35: 240–53.

Kaplan, Lawrence, and Lucille N. Kaplan. 1996. "Leguminosas alimenticias de grano: Su origen en el Nuevo Mundo, su adopción en el Viejo." In *Conquista y comida—Consecuencias del encuentro de dos mundos*, ed. Janet Long, 183–98. México D. F.: Instituto de Investigaciones Históricas, UNAM.

Kennedy, Diana. 1972. *The cuisines of Mexico*. New York: Harper and Row.

Kennedy, Diana. 1998. *My Mexico: A culinary odyssey*. New York: Clarkson Potter.

Kirchhoff, Paul. [1943] 1953. "Mesoamerica: Its geographic limits, ethnic composition and cultural characteristics." In *Heritage of conquest*, ed. Sol Tax, 1–14. Glencoe, Ill.: Free Press.

Lampe, Klaus, Eckart Witzigmann, Tony Khoo, Christian Teubner, and Sybil Countess Schönfeldt. [1999] 2001. *El gran libro del arroz*. Trans. from German by Ambrosio Berasán Villanueva. León: Everest.

Lavín, Mónica, and Ana Luisa Bénitez Muro. 2001. *Sor Juana en la Cocina.* Cocina vinneinal Novohispania, vol. 4. México D. F.: Clío.

Le Riverend, Julio. 1963. *Historia económica de Cuba.* La Habana: Escuela de Comercio Exterior MINCEX.

López de Gómara, Francisco. [1552] 1856. "Crónica de la conquista de Nueva España (Conquista de Méjico)." In *Historiadores primitivos de indias*, vol. I: 295–455. Madrid: Biblioteca de Autores Españoles.

Mapes, Cristina, Víctor M. Toledo, Narciso Barrera, and Javier Caballero. 1990. "La agricultura en una región indígena: La cuenca del lago de Pátzcuaro." In *Agricultura indígena: Pasado y presente*, ed. Teresa Rojas Rabiela, 275–341. México D. F.: Ediciones de la Casa Chata, CIESAS.

Marcus, Joyce, and Kent V. Flannery. 2004. "The coevolution of ritual and society: New 14C dates from ancient Mexico." *PNAS* 101 (52): 18257–61. Available at: http://www.pnas.org/content/101/52/18257.full.pdf. Accessed April 12, 2010.

Mintz, Sidney W. 1985. *Sweetness and power: The place of sugar in modern history.* New York: Elizabeth Sifton Books.

Novo, Salvador. 1957. *Historia gastronómica de la Ciudad de México.* México D. F.: Editorial Porrúa.

Nuevo cocinero mexicano en forma de diccionario. [1888] 1989. Facsimile ed. México D. F.: Miguel Ángel Porrúa.

O'Gorman, Edmundo. 1972. *México en la cocina del Club de Industriales.* México D. F.: Club de Industriales.

Palazuelos, Susanna, Marilyn Tausend, and Ignacio Urquiza. 1992. *El libro de la cocina mexicana.* México D. F.: Editorial Patria. (Published in English as *The Mexican beautiful cookbook*).

Pardo Bazán, Condesa de. [1913] 1996. *La cocina española antigua y moderna.* San Sebastián: R&B Ediciones.

Perales, Hugo R., and José Rogelio Aguirre Rivera. 2008. "Biodiversidad humanizada." In *Capital natural de México.* Vol. I: *Conocimiento actual de la biodiversidad*, 565–603. México D. F.: Conabio.

Pérez Martínez, Herón. 2002. *Los refranes del hablar mexicano en el siglo XX.* México D. F.: El Colegio de Michoacán/Conaculta.

Pérez San Vicente, Guadalupe. 1995. *Sor Juana y su libro de cocina. Memoria del coloquio internacional Sor Juana Inés de la Cruz y el pensamiento novohispano.* México D. F.: Instituto Mexiquense de Cultura.

Pietri, Anne Lise, and René Pietri. 1976. *Empleo y migración en la región de Pátzcuaro.* México D. F.: Instituto Nacional Indigenista.

Próspero, Rocío. 2001. *Kurpiticha (Los Cúrpites). Herencia tradicional de San Juan Parangaricútiro, Michoacán.* San Juan Parangaricútiro, Mich.: Ayuntamiento Constitucional.

Proust, Marcel. 1981. *Remembrance of things past.* Vol. 1: *Swann's way: Within a budding grove* 48–51. Trans by C. K. Scott Moncrieff and Terence Kilmartin. New York: Vintage.

Reyes, Alfonso. 1953. *Memorias de cocina y bodega.* México D. F.: Fondo de Cultura Económica.

Sánchez Díaz, Gerardo. 2008. *Los cultivos tropicales en Michoacán. Época colonial y siglo XIX.* Morelia: Universidad Michoacana de San Nicolás de Hidalgo, Fundación Produce AC, el Centro de Investigación y Desarrollo del Estado de Michoacán y Fondo Editorial Morevallado.

Sánchez Rodríguez, Guillermo, José Antonio Manríquez Nuñez, Fernando Antonio Martínez Mendoza, and Luis Angel López Ibarra. 2001. "El frijol en méxico competitividad y oportunidades de desarrollo." *FIRA, Boletín Informativo* 316 (33): 1–75.

Smith, Bruce D. 2001. "Documenting plant domestication: The consilience of biological and archaeological approaches." *PNAS* 98 (4): 1324–26. Available at: http://www.pnas.org/content/98/4/1324.full. Accessed April 12, 2010.

Smith, Bruce D. 2005. "Reassessing Coxcatlán Cave and the early history of domesticated plants in Mesoamerica." *Proceedings of the National Academy of Sciences of the United States of America* 102 (27): 9438–45.

Sutton, D. E. 2001. *Remembrance of repasts: An anthropology of food and memory.* Oxford: Berg.

Tello, Isabel. n.d. "Notas sobre la historia de Parácuaro." Available at: http://www.paramich.org/libros.htm. Accessed March 17, 2010.

Torres, Bárbara W. 1989. "Las plantas útiles en México antiguo según las fuentes del siglo XVI." In *Historia de la agricultura Epoca Prehispánica siglo XVI*, ed. Teresa Rojas Rabiela and William L. Sanders, vol. I: 53–128. México D. F.: Colección Biblioteca del INAH.

Valle Arizpe, Artemio. [1933] 1976. *Virreyes y virreinas de la Nueva España. Tradiciones, leyendas y sucedidos del México virreinal.* México D. F.: Aguilar.

Vargas, Luis Alberto. 1997. "Un banquete de la cocina mexicana." In *El Patrimonio Nacional de México*, ed. Enrique Florescano, vol II: 266–88. México D. F.: FCE.

Warman, Arturo. 1972. *La danza de moros y cristianos.* México D. F.: SEP Setentas 46.

West, Robert C. 1948. *Cultural geography of the modern Tarascan area.* Publication No. 7. Washington, D.C.: Smithsonian Institution, Institute of Social Anthropology.

–13–

Red Beans and Rebuilding
An Iconic Dish, Memory,
and Culture in New Orleans

David Beriss

Red Beans and Rice
Quartée red beans, quartée rice,
Little piece of salt meat to make it taste nice,
Lend me the paper and tell me the time,
When papa passes by he'll pay you the dime.

New Orleans jump rope jingle (Bienvenue and Walker 2008: 205, citing
John Churchill Chase's book *Frenchmen, Desire, Good Children
... and Other Streets of New Orleans* [1949] 2001: 225)

Honey, and I just love me some red beans. This is a red bean city here. That's it. If you don't have no red beans you just out.

Willie Mae Seaton, owner of Willie Mae's Scotch
House, New Orleans (Roahen 2006)

In late 2005, about a month after Hurricane Katrina's floods devastated New Orleans, I found myself wandering the aisles of an upscale grocery store in northern Virginia, thinking about what to make for dinner. We were still unable to return to New Orleans and I wanted to make a dish that would remind everyone of home. Red beans and rice, with some nice smoky sausage, seemed like just the thing to please adults and children alike. It was late afternoon and I did not have the three or four hours I needed to make the dish properly, but I figured that that would not be a problem. In New Orleans, when you need to make red beans at the last minute, you heat up a can or two of Blue Runner Red Beans, make some rice, sauté your sausage, and you have dinner. Blue Runner is a convincing alternative to the slow-cooked dish most people prefer and, in any case, the company is local, based in Gonzales, Louisiana, about halfway between New Orleans and Baton Rouge. Everyone falls back on it from time to time. I searched the store for Blue Runner beans. Or any prepared beans that would do the job. No luck. Nor would I have any luck in other stores over the next few months. Blue Runner, it turns out, is not distributed nationally.

It was then that I began to understand the extent to which red beans and rice, a seemingly mundane weekly dish, is a distinctive local tradition. It does not seem like much, after all. Just beans, pork, some spices, some vegetables, slow-cooked and served with rice. Unlike seafood gumbo, shrimp remoulade, or pecan-crusted drum, red beans and rice is not likely to inspire a tourist to write home or a food critic to praise the city as a culinary destination. It is not on the menu in many of the fancier local restaurants. It is, however, arguably one of the core dishes New Orleanians are likely to identify as a sign of home. Neighborhood restaurants often serve it, especially as a Monday lunch special (see Figure 13.1). It is frequently made as staff lunch or dinner in the upscale places. School cafeterias serve it on Mondays, accompanied by corn bread. Families eat it at home on Mondays too.

In the weeks and months following the hurricane and floods, some of New Orleans's most famous chefs set up outside their shuttered restaurants and prepared large quantities of red beans and rice for first responders, journalists, and the few remaining locals. The national and local media recounted stories about exiled New Orleans residents who sought to recapture a bit of home by making the iconic dish, only to discover that many of the ingredients they commonly used—brands of beans, pickled pork—were not easily available in other states. Pundits concerned about

Figure 13.1 Monday red beans, rice, and sausage at Mandina's Restaurant, New Orleans. Photo by the author.

the city's future speculated about whether or not the neighborhood restaurants that kept red beans on their menus would ever be rebuilt. In planning meetings, political events, and art installations, red beans and rice became a metaphor for home and an index of the city's ability to sustain a distinctive culture. Three years after the disaster, the return of restaurant reviews to the city's daily paper, graded by red beans rather than stars, was widely noted as a sign that New Orleans was definitively on the road to recovery (Anderson 2008; Severson 2008). In their post-Katrina exile, red beans and rice was apparently the dish people missed the most, but it also became a kind of explicit symbol of New Orleans distinctiveness and authenticity (Fitzmorris 2010: 161; Bienvenue and Walker 2008: 205; Roahen 2008: 255).

This chapter explores the reasons why that symbol resonates so strongly in the city. Beyond the deaths and the physical destruction—it is worth recalling that more than one thousand people died and 80 percent of the city flooded, much of it sitting in toxic waters for nearly three weeks—there was a deep concern that the cultural fabric of New Orleans could not recover and debate over whether or not the city was worth reviving. American political leaders openly questioned whether rebuilding made sense. Some of the arguments against New Orleans were framed in pragmatic terms, with critics asserting (erroneously) that the city was mostly below sea level and thus indefensible against floods. Others took a kind of neoliberal approach, suggesting that the city and its population had long lost the ability to compete in the rough-and-tumble world of the free market. The city's residents were perceived to be poor, dependent on welfare, and unproductive. Images and rumors from the disaster zone suggested a city in chaos and insurrection. New Orleans seemed, in its destruction, positively un-American.

As they watched this debate unfold, local journalists, activists, and elected officials tried to respond to the critics. The city, they pointed out, was not the victim of a "natural" disaster, but had been devastated by the failure of federally built and maintained flood control systems. The city's economy, they claimed, was not only competitive in particular areas, like the port, oil services, and tourism, it played an essential role in the U.S. economy. They admitted that the city did suffer from a wide range of social problems, including high levels of poverty, elevated crime rates, and a poorly performing public education system. These were problems, they pointed out, that existed in many American cities.

However, the core arguments made in favor of New Orleans focused on cultural issues and suggested a complex relationship between the city and the rest of the country. The "Creole vernacular holy trinity" of music, architecture, and food described by Nick Spitzer (2006: 310) was invoked to legitimize the city's culture as something distinct from, yet also essential to, American identity. Although steeped in poverty, this was the culture that had given birth to jazz. It was the home of particular forms of African American art and performance, from second line parades to Mardi Gras Indians (Breunlin and Regis 2006). New Orleans was a city where Creole craftsmen still worked to produce architectural masterpieces. A large (and still growing) literature appeared defending the city's culture and arguing about its place in the larger American context (Piazza 2005; Abrahams et al. 2006; Chin Music Press 2006; McNulty 2008; Baum 2009; Rose 2005; among many others). Some leaders insisted that this culture represented a valuable national asset that should not be squandered. Others claimed New Orleans constituted a living cultural critique of America's fast-paced, homogenizing consumerist society. Whichever view one took—and many people took both—the relationship between New Orleans and the United States seemed surprisingly unclear.

In what follows, I examine how food, in general, and red beans and rice, in particular, is used to think through the relationship between New Orleans and (the rest of) the United States. This begins with demands for recognition of the city's distinctive culture and, as I have argued elsewhere, for control over legitimate representations and authorized representatives of that culture (Beriss 2007). Ideas about culture and about who may represent it have long provided an important set of symbolic tools for thinking about a wide variety of issues in New Orleans, including ethnicity and race, class conflicts, and even the spatial organization of the city (Breunlin and Regis 2006; Campanella 2008; Gotham 2007; Hirsch and Logsdon 1992). In New Orleans, as elsewhere, people self-consciously draw on culture and history to claim distinctiveness and as a way of controlling how they relate to groups with competitive claims or to the state (Adams 2006; Armstrong-Fumero 2009; Dávila 2004; Saada-Ophir 2006). Anthropologists have called attention to the way in which groups increasingly use culture as a marketable asset, sometimes going so far as to assert that without self-conscious cultural marketing, some identities may in fact cease to exist (Bunten 2008; Cameron 2008; Castañeda 2005; Comaroff and Comaroff 2009; see also Preston-Werner this volume). This is true in New Orleans as well, where efforts to persuade locals of the distinctiveness of the city and of the need to market it as unique have a long history, drawing on slogans like "New Orleans—America's Most Interesting City" as early as the 1920s (Gotham 2007; Stanonis 2006). In the wake of the 2005 disaster, confronted with an apparently hostile neoliberal policy context that threatened to undermine the city's very existence, claims about culture and about how to promote it became especially urgent (Lipsitz 2006). Determining the nature of the relationship between the United States and New Orleans seemed like a critical matter. Is New Orleans the home of America's "Creole soul" (Abrahams et al. 2006) or is it, as journalist Dan Baum has claimed, "a city-sized act of civil disobedience" (2009: xiii)?

While post-Katrina analyses of the city's cultural relationship with the United States have focused on many different aspects of local culture, few have taken a culinary perspective. This seems odd, given the long-standing role food has played in defining the city (Beriss 2007; Stanonis 2009). Certainly, the relationship between cuisine, place, and cultural identity has been explored by scholars (see Appadurai 1988; Avieli 2005; Bell and Valentine 1997; Caldwell 2002; Penfold 2002; Pilcher 1996; Sutton 2001; Wilk 2006, along with the other chapters in this volume for

examples). Food has been an important part of many instances of cultural commodi-
fication, ranging from beer in postsocialist Georgia (Manning and Uplisashvili 2007)
and wine in Languedoc (Barthel-Bouchier and Clough 2005), to foie gras and lardo
di Colonnata within the European Union (DeSoucey 2010; Leitch 2003). Each of
these cases highlights efforts to use food to define group identity, determine whose
use of the food can be authorized as authentic, and assert control over its representation. Further, in each of these cases, food is used to stand for the relationship between
one group (a city, region, or country) and some larger dominant institution (see also
Caldwell 2004; Roseman 2004; Wilk 2006). In what follows, I show how red beans
and rice, and cuisine more generally, has provided key symbols for working out the
relationship—essential soul or cultural critique—between post-Katrina New Orleans
and the rest of the United States.

Practical Mythology

It is difficult to untangle food from symbolism in New Orleans. Food has long played
an important role in defining the city as a distinct place within the United States. As
early as the mid-nineteenth century, the city had developed a reputation as a place
where residents were unusually fond of food and where visitors could expect to eat
exceptionally well. Anthony Stanonis (2009) has shown how the development of
cookbooks starting at the end of the nineteenth century, efforts to promote the city to
tourists, and the representation of the city's cuisine in popular culture worked to associate New Orleans with a particularly well-developed culinary culture (cf. Tucker
et al. 2009).[1] As I have argued elsewhere (Beriss 2007), food is a key symbol people
in New Orleans deploy in efforts to sort out any number of social fractures, including class and race. One central element that makes food an effective symbol for New
Orleanians is a sense that they all share in a common cuisine. The dishes many home
cooks prepare resemble the food available in restaurants, even fine dining restaurants
with world-class reputations. New Orleans eaters can be expected to be knowledgeable about the food they find in local restaurants, and chefs are well aware that they
are cooking for a public that is likely to know how to make a roux and to have very
distinct ideas about what gumbo ought to look like. This certainly distinguishes New
Orleans from much of the rest of the United States, where restaurants are increasingly unlikely to have any connection to local foodways (Dirks 2011). Since the
1970s, many chefs in American fine dining restaurants have promoted the use of
seasonal and local ingredients, a movement that has since expanded into markets
and home kitchens around the country. New Orleans is no stranger to this movement.
However, when chefs and food activists in New Orleans promote local and seasonal
foods, they most often do so by linking those foods to the city's history and people.
Being a "locavore" in New Orleans requires a knowledge of the city's identity and
history, as well as an understanding of seasons and ingredients. Food provides New

Orleanians with a very powerful set of symbols with which to sort out their differences with each other and with the rest of the country.

Red beans and rice are central to both the practice and mythology of New Orleans cuisine. Red beans are hard to avoid if you live in New Orleans. It is rare to attend a party that does not feature red beans and rice, either warming on the stove or simmering in a crockpot. Similarly, massive quantities of red beans are consumed around Mardi Gras, when attendance at parades makes it difficult to find time for daily cooking. Above all, red beans and rice is a weekly ritual, most often consumed on Mondays. Neighborhood restaurants that run it as a weekly special are most likely to do so on that day of the week, accompanied by sausages, fried veal cutlets, or fried pork chops. It is often the main course in school cafeterias on Mondays, accompanied by corn bread. Home cooks are likely to make it on Mondays as well. The main story invoked to explain this tradition focuses on the idea that Monday was, before the advent of washing machines, washing day. Red beans could be left to simmer for long hours mostly unattended, while the washing was completed. This is the story you will most often hear from locals. It appears in cookbooks with nearly every recipe for red beans and rice, as well as in memoirs, biographies, and even novels (see Leathem and Nossiter 2009; Roahen 2008; Collin and Collin 1987 for examples).

A second part of the story invokes the frequent use of a cracked hambone in the red beans. Said to come from the Sunday ham, the hambone provides flavoring and, as the marrow leaks into the beans, a certain unctuousness. The need to use the Sunday hambone could also explain the Monday red bean tradition. Of course, the two explanations are not mutually exclusive. Local grocery stores set aside hambones to sell to people without a leftover from Sunday. But not everyone participates in the hambone tradition, turning instead to smoked ham hocks, tasso (a seasoned smoked pork shoulder), boiled ham or, especially, "pickle meat," or pickled pork. All of these can be found in the same section of local grocery stores as the hambone, along with the other ingredients commonly used in the dish. All can be used to season the red beans, and some cooks use more than one in their recipe. Food writer John Thorne (1996: 291) condemns those who attempt this as "a case of wanting to be everyone's friend and ending up no one's."

The beans are apparently ordinary red kidney beans. I say "apparently" because virtually everyone in New Orleans uses Camellia brand red beans (see Figure 13.2), which are packaged by L. H. Hayward and Company in Harahan, a suburb of New Orleans. One source claims that Camellia beans carry 90 percent of the regional market for red beans, which seems quite reasonable (Leathem and Nossiter 2009: 138), since it is rare to see any other brand on store shelves. As many exiled New Orleanians discovered and lamented after Katrina, Camellia is not national—it is mostly available in Louisiana and Mississippi—but the beans can be ordered online. Although I did not attempt to use other beans while in exile, I should note that one local red beans evangelist, food writer Pableaux Johnson, has been quoted dismissing the very idea that Camellia beans are distinctive (Roahen 2008: 246).

Worse, when Sara Roahen, another local food writer, called up the company to see what distinguished its beans from others, she was told they are just ordinary kidney beans (Roahen 2008: 246).

Virtually every recipe for red beans and rice begins with the Creole *mirepoix*—it is called the "holy trinity" in New Orleans—of diced onion, celery, and bell peppers. This trinity provides the flavor background for many New Orleans dishes. The trinity is sautéed, sometimes nearly carmelized, in some kind of fat (oil, butter, or bacon fat) before the addition of meat, beans, garlic—the pope of Creole cuisine—and water. Bay leaves, cayenne pepper, salt, black pepper, and thyme are common additional spices. The whole thing is left to cook slowly for hours, until the beans more or less collapse and the entire dish becomes more creamy than soupy. The process is often encouraged by squashing some of the beans along the side of the pot and stirring them back in.

The history of the dish is open to debate. The kidney bean is an original product of the Americas, adopted by Europeans by the seventeenth or eighteenth century and used in any number of dishes that somewhat resemble the dish consumed today in New Orleans (Albala 2007). The combination of beans cooked with pork and

Figure 13.2   Camellia brand red beans dominate the New Orleans market. Photo by the author.

sausage can be found in France and in Spain, two of the countries that have contributed significantly to the population and culture of New Orleans. Rice is clearly of African origin and its cultivation and consumption accompanied the rise of slavery in the Americas (Carney 2001; Twitty this volume). The preparation of rice in Louisiana is thus rooted in African practices. Rice has been a major cash crop in Louisiana since the mid-nineteenth century. There are a number of rice dishes made in Louisiana that are clearly of African origin, including *rice calas*, a kind of rice fritter historically sold in the French market by itinerant African American women, and boiled rice accompanies many of the standard dishes served in New Orleans.

One distinctive characteristic of New Orleans rice and beans is that the two main components are cooked and served separately (even if eaters often mix them together on the plate). Some authors note that this manner of preparing the dish resembles practices in at least one region of Cuba, a region that was heavily populated by Haitians who had fled the revolution there (Leathem and Nossiter 2009: 137). Many of those same Haitians (both slaveowners and slaves) eventually came to New Orleans, contributing to the local cuisine and, perhaps, to the preferred way of preparing beans and rice (cf. Sublette 2008). This link is part of what defines New Orleans as a Creole city, as I discuss in the next section. It is unclear just how long it took for the dish to become established, but a familiar recipe does appear in one of the earliest New Orleans cookbooks, *The* Picayune's *Creole Cook Book*, in 1901 (2002: 209), which also notes that "the Creoles hold that the boys and girls who are raised on beans and rice and beef will be among the strongest and sturdiest of people" (2002: 208). The *New Orleans City Guide*, published in 1938 by the Federal Writers Project of the Works Project Administration, also provides a recipe for red beans and rice, adding that the dish is "one of the most popular of all Creole cuisine" (2009: 171). Red beans and rice are understood to be a Creole dish, central to New Orleans cuisine and much less frequently consumed in the rest of south Louisiana or nearby Mississippi. Chef Paul Prudhomme, a Cajun from Opelousas, Louisiana, west of New Orleans, whose cooking brought a great deal of attention to the city in the mid-1970s, has noted that until he moved to the city, he was unaware that "red beans were a cultural phenomenon" (Leathem and Nossiter 2009: 130).[2]

The fact that the consumption of red beans and rice is a weekly ritual for many in New Orleans gives the dish unusual symbolic power. The mythology surrounding red beans and rice provides ample resources for those who would use it to make claims about the city and its culture. As a local dish, red beans and rice allows New Orleans residents to lay claim to cultural distinctiveness in an apparently homogenizing America. Along with other foods, the dish is often invoked as a sign of the city's historical ties to the Caribbean and Central America and of an ongoing resistance to assimilation into the United States. The putative "slowness" of red beans and rice, requiring hours to prepare, is seen as a sign of the city's resistance to the forces of neoliberalism. In a city sharply divided by class and ethnicity, red beans and rice is represented as a comfort food that crosses those lines. It is something that nearly everyone can enjoy, both at home and in restaurants. From tourist propaganda to local cookbooks and even popular history, the discourse around red beans and rice has become strikingly unified, telling a story about what kind of city New Orleans might be (see Besh 2009; Collin and Collin 1987; Johnson 2005; Thorne 1996; Leathem and Nossiter 2009 for examples of this discourse).

Creole City

Most New Orleanians agree that the city is Creole, but whether or not that means the city is distinct from the rest of the United States or at the center of what defines the country as a whole is unclear. Nick Spitzer, anthropologist, folklorist, radio show host, and enthusiastic if often critical booster of the city, argues that New Orleans's Creole nature makes it both American and the contrary: "The various people called 'Creole' and the notion of cultural creolization—making a new social group and cultural expressions from the co-mingling of earlier discreet traditions, in this case African, European and native American—is critical to arguing New Orleans's distinctiveness in the United States and its connection to Afro-Latin aspects of the Caribbean" (2006: 310). Yet he goes on to argue that the processes that make New Orleans Creole are the same that have created American culture in general. What makes New Orleans "Creole soul" distinct within America, Spitzer claims, is that the city's cultural creativity is based on a "cultural simmering of many tastes" and not on a "unidirectional assimilation" (2006: 310). Spitzer uses "tastes" here to refer to general preferences for music and architecture, but he provides a perfect jumping-off place for food as well.

Discussions of what constitutes New Orleans culture and cuisine usually start with the idea that it is the product of a mixture of techniques, ingredients, and recipes brought together by the diverse populations that make up the city. Native Americans, French and Spanish colonizers, African slaves, Germans, Italians, and Irish immigrants are usually cited as having contributed variously to making the city's architecture, accent, tastes, and foods. The result is described as a gumbo, a mixture in which the different elements form a delicious ensemble while still remaining, at least in some instances, identifiable. Versions of this story can be found in most of the city's cookbooks and tourist guidebooks, along with scholarly versions in the publications of historians and other social scientists (see Besh 2009; Collin and Collin 1987; Johnson 2005; and Lagasse and Bienvenu 1996 for examples of the former; Tucker et al. 2009 for the latter). The idea of waves of immigrants contributing to the greater whole as they assimilate is a common American idea. The claim, however, in New Orleans is that the mixture has created something distinct, both American and different. The society produced in this process is marked by the existence of a large population of free people of color and by a resistance to the sharp racial segregation that characterized much of the rest of the country. The resulting tension between creolization and Americanization is one of the core elements in ideas of what makes New Orleans distinct within the United States (Hirsch and Logsdon 1992). This distinctiveness is what links New Orleans culture self-consciously back to the ancestors of the slaves and immigrants who make up the city today.

Most New Orleanians would also agree that the city has a cuisine of its own. This cuisine is rooted in the immigrant populations that have made up the city and is linked in explicit ways back to its places of origin in Europe, Africa, and elsewhere. This is obviously the case with some dishes, like gumbo, whose very name is related to a Bantu word for okra (itself a key ingredient in many versions of the dish). Yet the city's cuisine is often cited as demonstrating that New Orleans is less an American city than the northernmost city in the Caribbean. The idea that New Orleans's particular form of red beans and rice links it to Cuba and Haiti is well known. The mirliton, a squash popular in New Orleans cuisine, is rare elsewhere in the United States but common throughout the Caribbean and Central America (where it is called chayote, christophene, or chocho, among other things) (Harris 1989; Walker 2009). When people invoke the idea of a Creole city, these sorts of ties to the Caribbean are also what they have in mind.

New Orleans is a Creole city in part because a large segment of the population identifies and is identified as Creole. Definitions of who belongs in that category vary, from white descendants of French and Spanish settlers, to people of mixed African and European heritage (Dominguez 1997). The latter population is perhaps the most likely to be identified as Creole today. Creole soul cuisine—which is like soul or Southern cuisine elsewhere in the U.S. South but, as New Orleanians would note, more likely to include seafood and more assertively seasoned—is most often associated with restaurants owned and operated by Creoles of color, such as Leah Chase, owner of the very famous Dooky Chase restaurant. In 2006, the New York–based food writer Alan Richman pilloried New Orleans restaurants for not being more like New York restaurants. Richman specifically claimed that Creoles were themselves a myth, writing that "I have never met one and suspect they are a faerie folk, like leprechauns," despite having interviewed Mrs. Chase himself. He added that he doubted that Creole cuisine still existed in New Orleans (Richman 2006: 297). As the angry response in the local media made clear, there was little doubt among people in New Orleans that Creoles continue to make up a significant part of the local population. Along with people, any number of local things take on the modifier *Creole*, including, of course, food. For example, *Creole Italian* cuisine is a local twist on the red gravy Italian food common in other parts of the United States and *Creole* tomatoes is the term used to refer to the large flavorful tomatoes that grow in the parishes along the Mississippi near New Orleans.

Most residents of New Orleans do not distinguish the cooking of Creole chefs like Mrs. Chase from other parts of the city's cuisine. In fact, they consider that the city's culinary culture forms a whole. There is a perception of continuity between the creative dishes put out by chefs with national reputations such as John Besh or Emeril Lagasse and the food cooked in homes throughout the city and region. Although the dishes served in high-end restaurants may be more complicated than those made by home cooks, they often draw on the same seasonal and local produce and seafood. New Orleanians feel knowledgeable enough about that food, as many chefs have told me, to comment on what they are served by professionals. This is one reason why local food critic Tom Fitzmorris has been able to sustain a three-hour daily call-in show focused exclusively on food and restaurants on commercial radio for nearly twenty years in New Orleans.

Among the prized possessions many New Orleanians lost in Katrina's floods were their recipe collections. Starting in 2005, the food editor of the *Times-Picayune*, the city's daily newspaper, began using her weekly column, "Exchange Alley," to publish requests for lost recipes and to print recipes submitted in response to those requests. In 2008, in collaboration with Marcelle Bienvenu, another *Times-Picayune* food writer, she published "Cooking up a Storm: Recipes Lost and Found from the *Times-Picayune* of New Orleans." The first recipe submitted for the collection was for red beans and rice (Bienvenu and Walker 2008: 205). Radio personality and food writer Tom Fitzmorris wrote in a recent food-focused autobiography that in his own post-Katrina exile "no dish had been on my mind more than red beans, the traditional New Orleans lunch special. My mother made it every Monday, no matter what, when we were growing up. No dish would say 'I'm home!' more convincingly than that one. I had an actual hunger for it. I have eaten more red beans and rice in the four years since Katrina than I did in the previous thirty combined" (2010: 161). The dish itself was essential. But the dish evoked, for these writers and for many others, the entire Creole cuisine of New Orleans.

Slow City

In September 2007, *Commentary* magazine published an essay declaring New Orleans dead as a major American city. The author, Ben Toledano, a native New Orleanian and son of one of the city's elite families, wrote that "although the funeral was not conducted until Katrina struck, the death took place several decades ago" (2007: 27). The cause of death, as Toledano saw it, was rooted in the city's origins under French and Spanish colonial rule. He argued that for the last few hundred years, the city's elites were devoted to inherited privilege rather than to enterprise. Industry and talent were not rewarded. The "American" elites that joined the city in the post–Civil War era adopted that ethic of inheritance, symbolized by membership in the city's elite Mardi Gras clubs. When black politicians succeeded in taking over the city in the late 1970s, they continued the same tradition, one marked, according to Toledano, by a small social and economic oligarchy, virtually no middle class, and a majority of deeply poor, uneducated people. Katrina's floods, he claimed, had simply made all of this more obvious than ever. People who wanted to succeed, to achieve the American dream—have safe streets, good schools, and honest, efficient civil servants—would have to live elsewhere. They would have to give up "exotic cuisine and all that jazz," but it would be worth it (2007: 32). They would have to choose between being American or being New Orleanian.

The critique was not original, having been made many times in the last century, but perhaps more frequently since Katrina. Ironically, the idea that the city lives according to a different rhythm and with a different style has been an essential part of marketing strategies developed by tourism officials since the 1920s. City leaders, as both Anthony Stanonis (2006) and Kevin Fox Gotham (2007) have pointed out, have long tried to show that New Orleans was both a thoroughly modern metropolis, with an efficient Americanized business ethic and, at the same time, a vacation destination where one might escape the hustle and bustle of modern American life. Representing the city as a place where visitors can experience cultural authenticity—contrasted, for example, with the artificial environments of Disneyland—has required city business leaders and officials to work hard at creating and maintaining a "brand" that distinguishes New Orleans from other destinations (Gotham 2007: 135). After Katrina, efforts to lure visitors back to New Orleans used themes and slogans such as "Still America's Most Romantic, Walkable, Historic City," "Authentic and Real: Like No Other Place," and "Fall in Love with New Orleans All over Again" (cited in Gotham 2007: 140). In fact, the "exotic cuisine and all that jazz" is at the core of the narratives used by tourism officials to promote New Orleans as a distinctive place.[3]

Asserting that life in New Orleans is qualitatively different from life in the rest of the United States is not just a marketing strategy developed for tourists. Some city activists and intellectuals argue for making these lifestyle differences the basis for a critique of modern American life. In his "New Orleans Manifesto" (distributed during Mardi Gras 2003, but republished in a post-Katrina collection), Charles Cannon states that New Orleans should be proud of being a slow city and that "we need to convert the slow pace of our daily routines—our eating, transportation practices, pointless street conversation with strangers—from a perceived weakness into ideology" (2006b: 141). In *Why New Orleans Matters*, an ode to New Orleans published shortly after the flood, author Tom Piazza argued that the city's culture represents a kind of spirituality that the rest of America ought to honor. Contrasted with the "Calvinist religion of judgment and renunciation of New England," New Orleans rituals form a culture that celebrates sensuality through "sound, movement, and communal cuisine" (2005: 35). In another brief post-Katrina book, a group of scholars called the city a "land of dreams" (referring to the lyrics of the "Basin Street Blues"), a "symbol of cultural freedoms" and, referring to the city's different pace, distinctive cuisine, architecture, music, and rituals, a "democratically diverse, creative, and romantically reactionary distillation of the American soul" (Abrahams et al. 2006: 10).

Red beans and rice and the slowness of the city's food more generally play a key role in the assertion of New Orleans as a kind of living cultural critique of America. Long before Katrina, Walker Percy observed that "I attach more than passing significance to the circumstance that a man who stops for a bite in Birmingham, Detroit or Queens, spends as little time eating as possible and comes out feeling poisoned, evil-tempered, and generally ill-disposed toward his fellowman; and that the same man can go around the corner in New Orleans, take his family and spend two hours with his bouillabaisse or crawfish bisque (which took two days to fix)" (1991: 20). Cannon's New Orleans manifesto, cited above, was published in a collective publication entitled *Do You Know What It Means to Miss New Orleans?* (Chin Music Press 2006). The collection includes essays, stories, and poems by current and past residents of the city, all meant to plead the case for the significance of New Orleans culture for the rest of the United States. There is an essay that argues for the centrality of New Orleans foodways (Wolnik 2006). There are also several recipes, including, of course, one for red beans and rice (Cannon 2006a: 118). Writers tend to represent the manner in which New Orleanians approach food as something fundamental to the city's culture and also central to what makes the city different from the rest of the country. Piazza, noting the significance of red beans and rice as a washing-day tradition, adds, in a long passage devoted to the relationship between New Orleans food and culture, that food in New Orleans is "rarely a means to an end ... it is an end in itself, and one in which the participants are emotionally invested ... it is the passionate, grateful, sacramental relationship of a kind of nonsectarian communion" (2005: 22).

Shortly after the 2005 floods, at the annual Southern Foodways Alliance meeting in Oxford, Mississippi, a panel convened to discuss the consequences of the disaster for New Orleans culinary culture. The panelists, which included both local and national food writers and thinkers, were convinced that the high-end restaurants would survive. But they were concerned that neighborhood grocery stores and plate lunch restaurants—the very places where you can get red beans on a Monday, located in the most badly damaged neighborhoods—might never return. New Orleans had long been a city of neighborhoods and of neighborhood grocery stores and restaurants. Although the corner store with its plate lunches was already in sharp decline before the floods, a surprising number have in fact returned in the post-Katrina era. According to Tom Fitzmorris, who has been tracking the number of restaurants in the city for years, there are actually more restaurants in the city today—including neighborhood plate lunch and po'boy restaurants—than there were before August 2005 (Fitzmorris 2010: 213). This is especially surprising in a context in which independent restaurants (the term is used to refer to nonchain restaurants) have declined nationally (Brandau 2010). It is precisely the local independent restaurants that have thrived in post-Katrina New Orleans, serving their slow-cooked New Orleans dishes.

When I make red beans and rice, I need three to four hours, not including the overnight soaking of the beans. There are ways to speed up the process, of course. Some resort to premade brands, others are known to use pressure cookers. But generally, people who want red beans and rice at home make it in the traditional manner. The fact that local grocery stores usually gather the necessary ingredients together near each other for shoppers' convenience shows that there is a significant public engaged in this act of slowness. The cultural critics, who see the making of this slow dish as an act of defiance toward the speeded-up life promoted in the rest of America, and the city's tourism officials, who see this and other dishes as useful symbols for attracting visitors seeking a temporary escape from their daily lives, agree on the importance of slowness as a symbol. Earlier in this chapter I quoted journalist Dan Baum's claim that "in the context of the techno-driven, profit-crazy, hyperefficient self-image of the United States, New Orleans is a city-sized act of civil disobedience" (2009: xiii). Perhaps making red beans in New Orleans is an act of defiance. But it might simply be a way to temporarily escape the pressures of contemporary American life. One of the current (as of early 2011) slogans used by tourism officials suggests as much: "It's New Orleans: You're different here."

Chocolate City

In the weeks and months following Katrina, the city was increasingly framed by an American discourse that focused on race and class. Images in the news and commentary focused on black victims of the floods, turning New Orleans, in the view of many, from majority black to entirely black. Similarly, the city's middle classes vanished from view and representations of New Orleans suggested that the population had been overwhelmingly poverty-stricken. New Orleans was either becoming a poster child for all American urban ills or it had been transformed into a domestic version of Haiti (Masquelier 2006). Not everyone thought it was worth saving such a city, but some who did insisted that it would have to become whiter and more middle class than they presumed it had been. Reacting to this kind of critique, early in 2006, Mayor Ray Nagin gave a Martin Luther King Day speech in which he asserted that New Orleans "should be chocolate," adding "I don't care what people are saying Uptown or wherever they are. This city will be chocolate at the end of the day. This city will be a majority African-American city. It's the way God wants it to be" (Pope 2006).

Contrary to the idea of a Creole city (see above), the mayor's comment seemed like a stark insertion of American racial ideology into the political and cultural life of New Orleans. This was not the first time the city was confronted with this ideology. Since the end of the Civil War, New Orleans has walked a fine line between the binary poles of American racial politics and categories and complex realities of race and class that have developed out of the city's colonial history (Hirsch and Logsdon 1992). As a self-consciously Creole city, in which at least some of the population has been historically defined as existing somewhere outside of (or perhaps between) American racial categorizations, New Orleans has long stood out in the U.S. South—and perhaps in the country as a whole—for defying American racial codes. At the same time, the city was an historic center for the slave trade and was legally segregated like the rest of the South for decades after the Civil War. Thus, even self-defined Creoles were—and remain today—also black, following the American idea that any African ancestry (the "one drop" rule, according to which one drop of African blood is all it takes) makes a person black and subject to Jim Crow discrimination. One of the central tensions in the city's political and social life since at least the Civil War has been between this American racial binary and the more complex Creole calculus of identity and culture. In the wake of the 2005 disaster, the city's presumed black-ness, whether viewed as problematic or positive, seemed to radically simplify that history, fitting postdisaster New Orleans wholly into the American mold.

Historians, anthropologists, and cultural critics have long argued that one of the keys to New Orleans creative culture has been its ability to blur lines of race and ethnicity that are more sharply drawn elsewhere in America. Locals claim that this is especially evident in the city's cuisine. I have heard Tom Fitzmorris (who is white) tell of visiting black restaurants in the Tremé neighborhood and discovering the red beans and rice that most resembled his mother's homemade version (cf. Fitzmor-ris 2010: 27). In fact, it is not at all uncommon for white writers to discover black restaurants in New Orleans and find the food exceptionally good. The most famous of these was Buster Holmes's restaurant in the French Quarter, which closed in the early 1990s. Holmes was specifically known for making excellent red beans and rice. Reviewing it in 1973, Richard Collin noted that "this is a popular place for poor blacks, poor whites, poor artists, poor French Quarter residents, and lovers of good beans" (1973: 145). Describing soul food in general, Collin, who was perhaps the city's first professional food critic, observed that "most New Orleans blacks have grown up on the same food as other Orleanians" (1973: 143).

At the same time, the fact that the food is the same but that restaurants might nev-ertheless still be defined as black (or white) suggests that the history of segregation is still alive in New Orleans and that the lines, although blurrier and more easily crossed than in other American cities, nevertheless exist. New Orleans restaurants are, as I have noted, staffed by many skilled African American cooks, but very few of them have be-come media stars. Before Katrina, Austin Leslie had significant success, first cooking at Chez Helene and later in other restaurants, before dying tragically during the evacu-ation. In the aftermath of the floods, Ken Smith, who eventually left the profession to become a priest, was recognized nationally for his cooking. However, neither of them ever received the recognition that has made someone like Emeril a household name.

If restaurants run by African Americans have received recognition, it often seems as if it is more for contributions to history and community than for the excellence of their food. Dooky Chase, owned and run by Leah Chase, has long been recognized for serving as a social center for the Creole community in New Orleans. Located in the Tremé neighborhood, Chase's restaurant was a central gathering place for families at a time when Jim Crow laws kept people of color out of other restaurants in New Orleans. In addition, Dooky Chase was open to groups organizing during the civil rights movement in the 1950s and 1960s. Leah Chase's commitment to the community is well recognized and, at least locally, the restaurant is also appreciated for its classic Creole soul cuisine. Similarly, Willie Mae Seaton's restaurant, Wil-lie Mae's Scotch House, has long been recognized as an important neighborhood gathering spot in Tremé. Famous for the eclectic customer base and for fried chicken, Seaton won a James Beard award in 2005, but as an "American Classic" rather than as a high-powered chef. She was 89 at the time and nearing the end of her career.

Following Katrina's floods, the return of restaurants all over the city was celebrated. Each restaurant that opened represented a new space where returning residents could seek each other out, hear stories, and exchange information. The reopening of high-end restaurants also signaled the revival of the city's economy. Each one was a business that managed to find workers (who were thus back in the city) and customers. The return of some restaurants, anchored in historic neighborhoods, signaled the revival of those neighborhoods or, at least, the belief that the community would rebuild. The return of many neighborhood restaurants was celebrated and noted in the press, but the rebuilding of Dooky Chase and Willie Mae's struck a deeper chord than most. Both were preceded by months of events that included fundraisers, often hosted by some of the city's most famous restaurateurs, that could help finance the rebuilding. Each was owned by a dynamic elderly lady who seemed to embody an important element of the city's history and culture. People from different ethnic and class backgrounds worked hard—in the case of Willie Mae's, the rebuilding effort was completed mostly by volunteers over the course of eighteen months (York 2006). Like Willie Mae's customer base, the volunteers, led by John Currence, a native New Orleanian and chef/owner of restaurants in Oxford, Mississippi, were both white and black and crossed class and neighborhood lines in order to accomplish the task of rebuilding the restaurant.

In a sharp critique of Toledano's obituary for New Orleans, Charles Cannon argues that Toledano focuses too much attention on the city's elite and thus loses sight of some of the central elements that make New Orleans not only distinct, but distinctly and interestingly alive. In particular, Toledano misses "the great contribution of New Orleans civilization to the world: a culture created largely by and for poor and working people ... street music, street dancing, red beans, po'boys, public celebrations with free entertainment," all of which contribute to a rich social fabric that defies race and class in ways not found elsewhere in the United States (Cannon 2008: 90). This culture is a product of immigrants from many origins and of the descendants of slaves and of free people of color. Everyone eats red beans and rice. As Willie Mae Seaton said in the interview cited at the head of this chapter, "This is a red bean city here. That's it. If you don't have no red beans you just out" (Roahen 2006).

Conclusion: Rethinking America

After Hurricane Katrina and the federal floods nearly ruined the city, New Orleanians learned a few things they may not have seriously considered previously. They discovered that their cuisine really was different. In fact, reproducing it while in evacuation was often an insurmountable problem. This was true even of a dish as elementary as red beans and rice. If this did not lead them to question whether or not their home city was actually part of the United States, the debates about the city that followed the floods certainly demonstrated that other Americans were not convinced. In the wake of the disaster, a combination of neoliberal ideology and racial politics raised the question of whether or not New Orleans really deserved to exist. The city, with its strange culture and distressing problems, seemed to resemble a foreign country.

None of this was new. Rather, the disaster forced people to confront the relationship between New Orleans and America and made some of the terms of that relationship explicit. The notion that New Orleans was a Creole city, with a distinct population mixture and history had long made the city both an example of the processes that define the United States and an example of a Caribbean culture on the banks of the Mississippi. The city's celebrated slowness can be understood as either a failure to embrace the high-speed lifestyle necessary to achieve the American dream or as a critique of that dream itself. Like most American cities, New Orleans has been deeply shaped by the work and imaginations of people of African descent. But New Orleans has been more ready to acknowledge that fact, something that may mark the city as not quite American.

Walker Percy once observed that New Orleans "is a most peculiar concoction of exotic and American ingredients, a gumbo of stray chunks of the South, of Latin and Negro oddments, German and Irish morsels, all swimming in a fairly standard American soup" (1991: 12). Food has long been at the center of the way people think and talk about what makes New Orleans distinct. It is central to determining the manner in which the city relates to the rest of the United States. Red beans and rice is one of the main dishes that people think of when they consider what makes New Orleans different. One of the city's most famous sons, jazz great Louis Armstrong, was so devoted to the dish that he signed his correspondence "red beans and ricely yours." Restaurant critic Gene Bourg established the use of red beans, rather than stars, to indicate the quality of restaurants he reviewed in the *Times-Picayune* in 1985. This is still the metric used by the newspaper's critic today. In fact, the return of those red bean–graded reviews to the paper in 2008, as I noted above, was widely remarked upon nationally (Severson 2008). You can purchase red bean jewelry in fancy local shops and a red bean–themed shirt is one of the signature souvenirs available at the annual New Orleans Jazz and Heritage Festival. You can attend a red bean–themed parade during Mardi Gras (see Figure 13.3). This is indeed a red bean city. Whether or not it is an American city remains open for debate.

Red Beans and Rice

(adapted and inspired by Collin and Collin 1987; Lagasse and Bienvenu 1996; and Besh 2009)
Serves 8–10, assuming you serve some corn bread on the side

1 cup chopped onions
1 cup chopped red bell pepper
1 cup chopped celery

Figure 13.3   Red bean costume, Mardi Gras 2011. Photo by the author.

1 teaspoon salt (or more to taste)
½ teaspoon cayenne
½ teaspoon black pepper
1 teaspoon thyme
3–4 bay leaves
1 lb. boiled ham, cut into cubes, or 2 smoked ham hocks (leave whole)
1 lb. andouille or other smoked sausage
1 lb. dried red beans, soaked overnight and drained
3 tablespoons chopped garlic
8–10 cups water
Enough boiled rice for everyone (see below for recipe)

Heat the oil in a large heavy dutch oven (cast iron is best) over medium high heat.
Sauté onions, bell peppers, celery, salt, cayenne, black pepper, and thyme for
4 or 5 minutes, until softened. Add bay leaves and meat and sauté for another
5 or so minutes. Add beans, garlic, and enough water to cover everything in
the pot (usually about 6 or 7 cups at this point). Turn up the heat and bring

the pot to a boil. Then reduce the heat to medium and let cook, uncovered, for about 2 hours. Stir from time to time and add water if the mixture gets too dry. After 2 hours, use a spoon to smash about half the beans against the side of the pot. Then continue cooking for another 1½ hours, until the mixture reaches a creamy, soft texture, but don't let it get too thick. Add more water if necessary. Remove the bay leaves and serve with rice, corn bread, and maybe a nice salad.

Boiled rice

Serves 8–10.

2 cups rice
3½ cups water
Salt
1 tablespoon butter (optional)

Put all the ingredients in a pot, bring to a boil and let boil for 2 minutes. Reduce heat to simmer and cover. Simmer for 20 minutes. Remove from heat and let sit for 5 or 6 minutes. Serve with red beans.

Notes

I would like to thank Richard Wilk and Livia Barbosa for organizing this collection and for their comments and insights in editing this chapter. An earlier version of this chapter was presented at the joint annual meeting of the Association for the Study of Food and Society, the Agriculture, Food and Human Values Society, and the Society for the Anthropology of Food and Nutrition, June 2–5, 2010, Bloomington, Indiana.

1. There are many representations of New Orleans that include food as a central element. Some of the more well known ones include Frances Parkinson Keyes's novel *Dinner at Antoine's* (1948) and John Kennedy Toole's *A Confederacy of Dunces* (1980), and the short-lived CBS television series *Frank's Place* (HBO's more recent *Tremé* also features a great deal of New Orleans food).

2. As a Cajun, Prudhomme is part of a population that is historically based in the rural areas of southern Louisiana. Cajuns are generally defined as descendants of French Canadians who were deported from the Canadian maritime provinces and who migrated to Louisiana in the eighteenth century. Creoles can be variously defined as white descendants of Europeans or people of mixed European and African heritage (Dominguez 1997), including descendants of migrants from Haiti following the revolution there in the early nineteenth century, and are

generally considered to be an urban population, based in New Orleans. Although both populations are originally francophone, a great deal distinguishes them, including cuisine. That said, migration into the city and the work of chefs like Prudhomme have, since the 1970s, contributed to a certain amount of hybridization between Cajun and Creole cooking.

3. See Bruner 1994 for a useful and comparable discussion of the ways tourism officials and other promoters of culture and history deal with the issue of authenticity.

References

Abrahams, Roger D., with Nick Spitzer, John F. Szwed, and Robert Farris Thompson. 2006. *Blues for New Orleans: Mardi Gras and America's Creole soul.* Philadelphia: University of Pennsylvania Press.

Adams, Kathleen. 2006. *Art as politics: Re-crafting identities, tourism, and power in Tana Toraja, Indonesia.* Honolulu: University of Hawaii Press.

Albala, Ken. 2007. *Beans: A history.* Oxford: Berg.

Anderson, Brett. 2008. "What took me so long." *The Times-Picayune*, July 25, Lagniappe section, 33.

Appadurai, Arjun. 1988. "How to make a national cuisine: Cookbooks in contemporary India." *Comparative Studies in Society and History* 30 (1): 3–24.

Armstrong-Fumero, Fernando. 2009. "A heritage of ambiguity: The historical substrate of vernacular multiculturalism in Yucatán, Mexico." *American Ethnologist* 36 (2): 300–16.

Avieli, Nir. 2005. "Vietnamese New Year rice cakes: Iconic festive dishes and contested national identity." *Ethnology* 44 (2): 167–87.

Barthel-Bouchier, Diane, and Lauretta Clough. 2005. "From Mondavi to Depardieu: The global/local politics of wine." *French Politics, Culture and Society* 23 (2): 71–90.

Baum, Dan. 2009. *Nine lives: Death and life in New Orleans.* New York: Spiegel and Grau.

Bell, David, and Gill Valentine. 1997. *Consuming geographies: We are where we eat.* London: Routledge.

Beriss, David. 2007. "Authentic Creole: Tourism, style and calamity in New Orleans restaurants." In *The restaurants book: Ethnographies of where we eat*, ed. David Beriss and David Sutton, 151–66. Oxford: Berg.

Besh, John. 2009. *My New Orleans: The cookbook.* Kansas City: Andrews McMeel.

Bienvenu, Marcelle, and Judy Walker. 2008. *Cooking up a storm: Recipes lost and found from the* Times-Picayune *of New Orleans.* San Francisco: Chronicle Books.

Brandau, Mark. 2010. "U.S. restaurant count continues to fall." *Nation's Restaurant News*, July 20. Available at: http://nrn.com/article/us-restaurant-count-continues-fall?utm_sour. Accessed July 20, 2010.

Breunlin, Rachel, and Helen A. Regis. 2006. "Putting the Ninth Ward on the map: Race, place, and transformation in Desire, New Orleans." *American Anthropologist* 108 (4): 744–64.

Bruner, Edward M. 1994. "Abraham Lincoln as authentic reproduction: A critique of postmodernism." *American Anthropologist* 96 (2): 397–415.

Bunten, Alexis Celeste. 2008. "Sharing culture or selling out? Developing the commodified persona in the heritage industry." *American Ethnologist* 35 (3): 380–95.

Caldwell, Melissa. 2002. "The taste of nationalism: Food politics in postsocialist Moscow." *Ethnos* 67 (3): 295–319.

Caldwell, Melissa. 2004. "Domesticating the French Fry: McDonald's and consumerism in Moscow." *Journal of Consumer Culture* 4 (1): 5–26.

Cameron, Catherine M. 2008. "The marketing of heritage: From the Western world to the global stage." *City and Society* 20 (2): 160–68.

Campanella, Richard. 2008. *Bienville's dilemma: A historical geography of New Orleans.* Lafayette: Center for Louisiana Studies.

Cannon, C. W. 2006a. "Laura's red beans." In *Do you know what it means to miss New Orleans?*, ed. Chin Music Press, 118–19. Seattle: Chin Music Press.

Cannon, C. W. 2006b. "The New Orleans Manifesto." In *Do you know what it means to miss New Orleans?*, ed. Chin Music Press, 137–43. Seattle: Chin Music Press.

Cannon, Charles W. 2008. "Rumors of my death have been greatly exaggerated." *Louisiana Cultural Vistas* 19 (1, Spring): 88–91.

Carney, Judith A. 2001. *Black rice: The African origins of rice cultivation in the Americas.* Cambridge, Mass.: Harvard University Press.

Castañeda, Quetzil E. 2005. "Between pure and applied research: Experimental ethnography in a transcultural tourist art world." *National Association for the Practice of Anthropology Bulletin* 23 (1): 87–118.

Chase, John Churchill. [1949] 2001. *Frenchmen, desire, good children … and other streets of New Orleans.* Gretna, La.: Pelican.

Chin Music Press, ed. 2006. *Do you know what it means to miss New Orleans?* Seattle: Chin Music Press.

Collin, Richard. 1973. *The New Orleans underground gourmet.* New York: Simon and Schuster.

Collin, Rima, and Richard Collin. 1987. *The New Orleans cookbook.* New York: Alfred A. Knopf.

Comaroff, John L., and Jean Comaroff. 2009. *Ethnicity, inc.* Chicago: University of Chicago Press.

Dávila, Arlene. 2004. *Barrio dreams: Puerto Ricans, Latinos, and the neoliberal city.* Berkeley: University of California Press.

DeSoucey, Michaela. 2010. "Gastronationalism: Food traditions and authenticity politics in the European Union." *American Sociological Review* 75 (3): 432–55.

Dirks, Robert. 2011. *Come and get it! McDonalidization and the disappearance of local food from a central Illinois community.* Bloomington, Ill.: McLean County Historical Society.

Dominguez, Virginia. 1997. *White by definition: Social classification in Creole Louisiana.* New Brunswick, N.J.: Rutgers University Press.

Federal Writers Project. [1938] 2009. *New Orleans city guide.* New Orleans: Garrett County Press.

Fitzmorris, Tom. 2010. *Hungry town: A culinary history of New Orleans, the city where food is almost everything.* New York: Stewart, Tabori and Chang.

Gotham, Kevin Fox. 2007. *Authentic New Orleans: Tourism, culture, and race in the Big Easy.* New York: New York University Press.

Harris, Jessica B. 1989. *Iron pots and wooden spoons: Africa's gifts to New World cooking.* New York: Simon and Schuster.

Hirsch, Arnold R., and Joseph Logsdon, eds. 1992. *Creole New Orleans: Race and Americanization.* Baton Rouge: Louisiana State University Press.

Johnson, Pableaux. 2005. *Eating New Orleans: From French Quarter Creole dining to the perfect po'boy.* Woodstock, Vt.: Countryman Press.

Keyes, Frances Parkinson. 1948. *Dinner at Antoine's.* New York: J. Messner.

Lagasse, Emeril, and Marcelle Bienvenu. 1996. *Louisiana real and rustic.* New York: William Morrow.

Leathem, Karen Trahan, and Sharon Stallworth Nossiter. 2009. "Red beans and rice." In *New Orleans cuisine: Fourteen signature dishes and their histories*, ed. Susan Tucker, 128–39. Jackson: University of Mississippi Press.

Leitch, Alison. 2003. "Slow food and the politics of pork fat: Italian food and European identity." *Ethnos* 68 (4): 437–62.

Lipsitz, George. 2006. "Learning from New Orleans: The social warrant of hostile privatism and competitive consumer citizenship." *Cultural Anthropology* 21 (3): 451–68.

Manning, Paul, and Ann Uplisashvili. 2007. "'Our beer': Ethnographic brands in postsocialist Georgia." *American Anthropologist* 109 (4): 626–41.

Masquelier, Adeline. 2006. "Why Katrina's victims aren't refugees: Musings on a 'dirty' word." *American Anthropologist* 108 (4): 735–43.

McNulty, Ian. 2008. *A season of night: New Orleans life after Katrina.* Jackson: University of Mississippi Press.

Penfold, Steve. 2002. "'Eddie Shack was no Tim Horton': Donuts and the folklore of mass culture in Canada." In *Food nations: Selling taste in consumer societies*, ed. Warren Belasco and Phillip Scranton, 48–66. New York: Routledge.

Percy, Walker. 1991. "New Orleans mon amour." In *Signposts in a strange land*, ed. Patrick Samway, 10–22. New York: Farrar, Straus and Giroux.

Piazza, Tom. 2005. *Why New Orleans matters.* New York: HarperCollins.

The Picayune. [1901] 2002. *The Picayune's Creole cook book.* Mineola, N.Y.: Dover.

Pilcher, Jeffrey. 1996. "Tamales or timbales: Cuisine and the formation of Mexican national identity, 1821–1911." *The Americas* 53 (2): 193–216.

Pope, John. 2006. "Evoking King, Nagin calls N.O. 'chocolate' city; speech addresses fear of losing black culture." *The Times-Picayune*, January 17: 1.

Richman, Alan. 2006. "Yes, we're open." *Gentleman's Quarterly* (November): 294–99, 337–38.

Roahen, Sara. 2006. "Willie Mae Seaton." Oral History Project, Southern Foodways Alliance. Available at: http://southernfoodways.org/documentary/oh/neworleans_ eats/seaton.shtml. Accessed November 6, 2010.

Roahen, Sara. 2008. *Gumbo tales: Finding my place at the New Orleans table.* New York: W. W. Norton.

Rose, Chris. 2005. *1 dead in attic.* New Orleans: Chris Rose Books.

Roseman, Sharon. 2004. "Bioregulation and comida caseira in rural Galicia, Spain." *Identities: Global Studies in Culture and Power* 11: 9–37.

Saada-Ophir, Galit. 2006. "Borderland pop: Arab Jewish musicians and the politics of performance." *Cultural Anthropology* 21 (2): 205–33.

Severson, Kim. 2008. "Robust again, New Orleans's dining scene is up for taste tests." *New York Times*, July 25, A: 1.

Spitzer, Nick. 2006. "Rebuilding the 'land of dreams' with music." In *Rebuilding urban places after disaster: Lessons from Hurricane Katrina*, ed. Eugenie L. Birch and Susan M. Wachter, 305–28. Philadelphia: University of Pennsylvania Press.

Stanonis, Anthony J. 2006. *Creating the Big Easy: New Orleans and the emergence of modern tourism, 1918–1945.* Athens: University of Georgia Press.

Stanonis, Anthony J. 2009. "The triumph of epicure: A global history of New Orleans culinary tourism." *Southern Quarterly* 46 (3): 145–61.

Sublette, Ned. 2008. *The world that made New Orleans: From Spanish silver to Congo Square.* Chicago: Lawrence Hill Books.

Sutton, David E. 2001. *Remembrance of repasts: An anthropology of food and memory.* Oxford: Berg.

Thorne, John, with Matt Lewis Thorne. 1996. *Serious pig: An American cook in search of his roots.* New York: North Point Press.

Toledano, Ben. 2007. "New Orleans—An autopsy." *Commentary* (September): 27– 32.

Toole, John Kennedy. 1980. *A confederacy of dunces.* Baton Rouge: Louisiana State University Press.

Tucker, Susan, with Cynthia LeJeune Nobles, Karen Trahan Leathem, and Sharon Stallworth Nossiter. 2009. "Setting the table in New Orleans." In *New Orleans cuisine: Fourteen signature dishes and their histories*, ed. Susan Tucker, 3–27. Jackson: University of Mississippi Press.

Walker, Judy. 2009. "A fan of the iconic New Orleans vegetable, The Mirliton Man, is planting seeds of recovery." *The Times-Picayune*, August 6, Living section: 1.

Wilk, Richard. 2006. *Home cooking in the global village: Caribbean food from buccaneers to ecotourists.* Oxford: Berg.

Wolnik, Dar. 2006. "Food will save us." In *Do you know what it means to miss New Orleans?*, ed. Chin Music Press, 110–14. Seattle: Chin Music Press.

York, Joe. 2006. *Above the line: Saving Willie Mae's Scotch House.* Documentary. Oxford, Miss.: Southern Foodways Alliance. Available at: http://www.southern foodways.com/documentary/film/willie_mae.html. Accessed November 6, 2010.

−14−

Conclusions

Sidney Mintz

Only a seemingly insatiable interest in the subject of food on the part of so many people could have given rise to a book like this one. It is not the same interest as that of the hungry. For a large fraction of global humanity, hunger is still never far away. The wrenching photos of women and children in the refugee camps of Sudan, who had to leave the camps to scavenge for firewood for their families' evening meal, even though knowing that killers awaited them outside, are mute evidence that hunger can make food as precious as life itself.

Nonetheless, during the last half century, as a growing fraction of humankind became well fed and better nourished, there was reason to believe food was losing some of its appeal as a field of study. That it remains a thought-provoking subject, even among the well-fed, merits explanation, for more reasons now than the need we share with all life to be nourished, simply to stay alive.

For those societies around the world that are now somewhat better able to feed their citizens, it is health anxiety that has become paramount. People worry about obesity and its associated pathologies, diabetes and heart disease, and even about the contrary addictions of the well-fed, anorexia and bulimia. Evolution provides us with the rise of new strains of *Escherichia coli*, increasingly resistant to antibiotics, able to kill those whom they afflict. *Salmonella* bacteria continue to turn up in the eggs and flesh we eat, sickening us with gastroenteritis, and worse.

Among the features of this visible health anxiety is the widening recognition that we humans can *feel* well-fed, and yet be obese and badly nourished all the same. There seems little doubt that one health-linked anxiety is the feeling that today's wondrous new globalism may have other, equally disagreeable surprises in store for us.

Beneath these concerns there remain, of course, those countless millions for whom closeness to famine remains every day. In fact the world probably has enough food for everyone, right now. Yet inability or unwillingness on the part of those who have enough to make sure there is enough for those who have too little is a cruelly stubborn fact, more economic than technological. Awaiting us are crises in getting clean water and air. The effects of global warming on world agriculture are only now beginning to surface, even as world population grows relentlessly, each day by an additional quarter of a million.

Yet beyond these frightening realities, food's power as a source of wonderment is not on the wane. In part this stems from a more informed reading public. Food topics once unlikely to arouse much interest now get our attention, and I think this book's subject—rice and beans—makes the point. To offer yet another perspective, I draw here upon personal recollection. I do so to uncover in my own case the very real, half-hidden "pull" that rice and beans, a seemingly prosaic marriage of ingredients, exerts upon me as it does on so many others. I ask the reader's indulgence for a lengthy autobiographical parenthesis.

Puerto Rico 1948–1949

In 1948, as a graduate student in anthropology, I found myself at the start of my first fieldwork overseas, living in a tiny town on the south coast of Puerto Rico. My stay in the town itself was temporary. As soon as I could, I moved to a rural section (*barrio*), to settle down for fifteen months. Thinking back to it now, I realize better how poorly prepared I was for fieldwork. My lack of preparation was at least partly my own fault. Being the son of a cook father who had spent most of his childhood in the kitchen of a diner, I may have been slightly better prepared than other beginners to learn about the food I would be eating. Even in that regard, though, I had a great deal to learn.

I was in an old sugarcane-growing region. Around the world, tropical plantation zones of this sort are ill famed for what they do to local land use, standards of living, and health. In the municipality I had deliberately chosen, almost 100 percent of the arable land was in sugarcane. Unsurprisingly, rural working-class Puerto Ricans in such a region more than sixty years ago were malnourished, landless, and dirt poor. In their tiny yards they were able to produce little more than a few spices and some woebegone fowl—and rarely, a goat. The fresh food they could buy was meager, and because they could muster only weak and intermittent demand, little fresh food was ever offered for sale to them. People gorged on mangoes in season, but the season was short. Bananas, papayas, coconuts, and genips (*quenepas*) were the other main fruits available. *Quenepas* are nutritious, but they are mostly peel and seed, providing so little nourishment that they were considered (and mainly were) the food of children.

Pineapples were cultivated for export on the island's north coast, but people living at any distance had no access to them. Almost all of them were grown, picked, and packed for shipping abroad. Oranges, limes, and lemons grew helter skelter in the central highlands, mostly as shade cover for stands of coffee. Hardly any were marketed on the island's coasts. Coconuts grow well on the island; people ate them as occasional treats and drank their water. But nowhere on the island were they an important part of diet. Their dried meat was used for desserts. Bananas and occasional papayas, grown in those tiny yards of the sugar regions, were the main locally produced fruits. Though it was uncommon to see more than as many as two papaya trees in the same yard, these fruits were regularly used as food. They both could be eaten green, the papayas as conserves, the bananas cooked.

What was a bad situation for fresh fruit was equally bad for vegetables, except onions, garlic, and scallions. Carrots, cucumbers, cabbages, and rarely, sweet and "hot" peppers (all Genus *Capsicum*) were eaten, but not often enough to count as regular food on the south coast. Few Puerto Ricans eat piquant peppers. Tomatoes were few (though imported tomato paste in small cans was sold locally). Flavoring herbs, of course—fresh coriander (*cilantro, Coriandrum sativum*), culantrillo (*reca'o, Eryngium foetidum*), basil (*basilica*), and sage, for instance, grew in the tiny yards.

People were much accustomed to eating edible tubers such as yams, sweet potatoes, taro, the New World tarolike *yautía*, and even "Irish" potatoes. They also liked cooked green bananas and plantains, all affordable and common. There was fairly regular access to tubers and breadfruit, hawked by farmers who owned trucks and would drive down to the coasts from the highlands. These two sorts of fleshy foods, arboreal and tuberous, were eaten mixed, almost every day. But their decline as everyday foods was in progress when I was living there (though I didn't know it). Nowadays they have become quite uncommon.

Sugarcane regions have their harvest seasons and "dead times." However scarce the sellers of fresh food, they would became scarcer yet, in midsummer—though with the huge exception of the mango trucks—only reappearing as Christmas approached. The sharp decline in income that marked the onset of *tiempo muerto* would show visibly in the faces of sugarcane workers, and in the limbs of their children (Mintz 1956).

And whether harvest or slack time, every kind of animal protein was expensive. Fresh fish could be had occasionally, but Caribbean coastal fisheries were already overtaxed. A soup of fish and boiled cornmeal (*funche*) was a rare and welcome meal. That some persons whom I knew ate *funche* secretly strongly suggested that it was considered a "humble" food associated with poverty. Not only was it a common food of the poor; it was also associated with people of color.[1] Some cornmeal was ground in Puerto Rico from highland maize. Rice, albeit a very old crop on the island, was mostly imported.

In the 1940s, salt cod (*bacalao*) had not yet become a food fad of the rich. But this ancient Caribbean plantation "delicacy"—one once spurned in the Americas by everyone but the enslaved—was already costly for my hosts, as was corned beef. Corned beef came in those odd squareish cans used by the North American companies that were then (and are still) shipping it around the world from Argentina. It had given rise in Puerto Rico to a distinctly local dish, known as *carne bif.*

Almost without exception, fresh meat was not to be had without a trip to a town; it was never affordable for cane cutters, anyway. A couple of pigs for annual holidays, scrawny locally raised chickens once or twice each month, and meat from the blue (land) crab, caught and fattened locally, mostly by children, was pretty much what people had in the way of animal protein.

I ate locally (as they say, these days). But as has been true of plantation regions globally for centuries, much of the food I was given to eat was not local at all—it was imported. During my fifteen months (and excluding rare trips to a city nearby or a distant college campus), my meals were regularly prepared by Doña Pola, the wife of a cane cutter who lived next door. These meals were carried from her kitchen to the shack I shared with her brother, Santos, in a special portable meal carrier, called a *fiambrera*. It is a bailed, tiered set of enameled metal food containers, four nesting receptacles that will keep food warm for a fairly long time.

Except for breakfast, my customary daily meals included *viandas*—boiled, unseasoned pieces of tuber: taro (*malanga—Colocasia esculenta*), yautía (*Xanthosoma sagittifolium*), yams (*Dioscorea spp.*), potatoes (*Solanum tuberosum*), and sweet potatoes (*Ipomoea batatas*), and rarely, Guinea arrowroot (*lerenes, Calathea allouia*). Often some pieces of boiled green banana, plantain, or breadfruit (*Artocarpus altilis*) were added. A second dish might have some animal protein: bits of salt cod with onion and thyme; or rubbery "Vienna" sausages; a slice of a large, mysterious bologna known locally as *mortadella*; a bit of canned corned beef; or, on the best days, a piece of cooked fresh fish. But whatever else I got, there was always one container of rice and another of beans. The beans were usually the red beans locally known as *habichuelas* (*Phaseolus spp.*) that we North Americans now call *frijoles*, thanks to our Mexican and Central American neighbors. Now and then there were instead other beans: *garbanzos* (chickpeas—*Cicer arietinum*) or *gandules* (*Cajanus cajan*), for instance. There also were some nutritionally minor yet critical foods, such as the pumpkin (*calabaza—Cucurbita moschata*) and other prized and distinctive flavorings, which I also got to eat. The tastes of many were linked to the *sofrito* or sauce accompanying beans, for rice and beans.

Parenthetically, I must stress that every meal that *I* got was, by local standards, a regal repast. In that barrio in 1948, for the local families of cane workers, to eat any animal protein twice in one day was unthinkable; to eat any animal protein daily was also unthinkable. I was likely to get a bit of animal protein once a day—not every day, but almost. In that single regard I was being fed differently—better than—nearly any adult male in the barrio. I knew only a couple of exceptions: a policeman, two storekeepers, possibly a cane mill mechanic. For the many who could not afford meat—as for those few who could—the season did not matter.

While this description resonates with many contributions by others that precede it in this volume, it has a couple of specific implications for me. Among them is that during my stay in Barrio Jauca, I became fat, and my changed appearance was greeted with approval. I did so even though the fieldwork required a marked rise in my physical activity. My caloric intake increased as its nutritional quality declined. My consumption of animal protein, fresh vegetables, fruits, and dairy products fell. All dairy foods were unavailable, in addition to other foods. My consumption of low-quality but calorie-dense cereals, and of legumes and tubers rose. I adjusted to these changes, but I was aware of them, especially when the opportunity arose to eat fresh vegetables and drink milk elsewhere.

Fullness

I think that my feelings about rice and beans were affected by these other radical changes in diet. But whatever the reasons, from when I first tasted *arroz y habichuelas* until I left Puerto Rico, I was a fully convinced enthusiast. I enter timidly into any discussion of the mystique that surrounds that combination. Readers have probably read enough about that already. But whenever I discussed rice and beans with Puerto Rican friends they referred to the subjective feeling of *fullness*, which they richly described. Rice and beans, as I learned to eat them daily, were conceptually quite different from either as a side dish or a course. They did not appear to correspond either to a *pasta* course in Italian food, for instance, or to any other first course; they might be accompanied by other foods, frequently *viandas*; but they were often the only "main course." Once mixed together—and no two eaters ever seemed to do it exactly the same way—rice and beans were said by most Puerto Ricans I knew at the time to be what provided the eater with fullness. Importantly, too, nearly everyone said that one was never really full *without* rice and beans.

I think the concept of "fullness" is culture-specific—that is, the same concept turns up in other places, but I think what it means is specific to each place. I wonder whether it is experienced by people who are malnourished somehow differently from people who are not. I confess that I have no evidence of this. Similar subjective descriptions of "fullness" and nonfullness are reported from different societies, though the core food in question may differ. Many daily rice eaters in Asia, for example, seem to have that feeling about rice by itself. No amount of other food seems to compensate fully for the absence or meagerness of the core food.[2]

I don't know whether there is any relationship between these feelings of fullness and the actual adequacy of local nutrition in such cases. If there is, then it has not been scientifically established, to my knowledge. I clearly remember feeding a friend from the barrio on the mainland, in New York City. I bought him a steak dinner—something he had never had before. When he complained of hunger a couple of hours later, he had a plate of *arroz y habichuelas*, and he said that it made him full, confirming my expectations. (I was living at the time in East Harlem.)

The phenomenon of culturally specific "fullness" can be observed among people whose principal food is maize, or rice, or sorghum or millet. I suspect that it is most apparent when the people in question usually eat relatively little animal protein, and when the core food that they eat is served with a sauce. The first scientific observer to notice this phenomenon, I believe, was the great British social anthropologist of food (and of a great deal else), Audrey Richards, when she worked among the Bemba, in what was then Northern Rhodesia (Richards 1939).

The Core-Fringe-Legume Pattern (CFLP)

If we try to think analytically of the Puerto Rican *plato* or dish called *arroz y habi-chuelas*, we see it has three distinguishable *parts* (as well as many food *ingredients*): (1) a cereal core, rice; (2) a legume, red beans; and (3) a locally distinctive flavoring. Though other beans are sometimes substituted, a red variety of *Phaseolus vulgaris* is much preferred. The cereal in this dish is always rice. The fringe or flavoring includes *achiote*, tomato, coriander, pumpkin, and much else, some of it reduced in cooking to a thick sauce, together with some of the beans (Ortiz Cuadra 2006). In the present work, we have been given many different examples of combinations of three elements, each such being perceived as distinctive, particular, and *created*— made in each case into what is known by many names, all of which names stand for rice and beans.

At the time when I first put forth the idea of core, legume, and fringe, I was not thinking of rice and beans. At that time my aim was to find a way to begin to compare the basic food patterns of people in old agrarian societies, such as India, China, Eastern and Western Europe, Africa, and elsewhere, in both the Old World and the New. What people ate from place to place was often strikingly different, of course. But in many of them, the everyday plate was composed of, for example, a cooked cereal in the form of a thick soup or porridge; or a large piece of bread; a plate of cooked corn-meal or rice; or perhaps a buckwheat flour pancake (though buckwheat is not really a grass). This would be eaten together with a *legume*, in the form of cooked beans; or a peanut soup; a thick gravy made of chickpeas; or perhaps a heap of lentils. And with those two ingredients would come some *flavoring* (*fringe*), supplied by mushrooms, or garlic, or fermented meat, or toasted cheese, or fresh mint leaves, or chopped cucumbers, or salted or smoked fish, or *practically anything* contrastive in taste.

Three categories, over and over, played in each place by different foods: I was trying to uncover some underlying structure. I set it forth here to suggest that many, if not all, of the societies discussed in this book have such a three-element main plate of this sort.

I have long argued that the core-fringe-legume pattern (CFLP)—in which animal protein can play a part but often does not—is among the basic building blocks of the world's cuisines (Mintz 1984, 1992; Mintz and Schlettwein-Gsell 2001). In such diets, the nutritional and caloric role that is played overwhelmingly by animal protein in modern Western food habits is played instead mostly by legumes. This older pattern is now contracting more and more, in much of the world, to be replaced by more fat and more sugar, sometimes fewer legumes, and less healthy cereals. I believe that the core-fringe-legume pattern does not lend itself readily to scientific study. While it may seem that nothing could be easier than studying exactly how much, and what, a number of people eat during some period—a week, say, or even a forty-eight-hour period—I don't think that is so. Unless you lock the people up only a few other things are harder to study, in my opinion. Even when eating behavior is observed, we are hardly ever told about the relative quantities of different foods eaten, or about the role that class or rank plays in the variety, quality, and quantities of the different foods consumed.

I think that the kind of three-element diets I have in mind may be very old, indeed, changing only when climate, micro-environment, or disaster, human or natural, required it. I do not mean that humans are "naturally" vegetarian or carnivorous. I surely do not think that animal protein was entirely missing from such diets. Barring some religious prohibition of animal food sources, traditional meals of this sort probably included some animal protein, more often than not. But such protein was not likely ever to be the nutritional center of the meal—first of all, I think, because animal protein was usually scarce. In such food systems, the taste and texture of meat must often have been part of the total flavors of the food; but I presume that animal protein would only rarely stand out as a separate, distinguishable offering on the plate.[3] Keep in mind that I write here not of herders or hunters or fisherfolk, or of the wealthy and jaded. I have in mind the mostly rural masses of people in agrarian lands such as India, China, much of Africa, and most of the pre-Columbian New World.

The Rise of Rice

As the reader will have seen, this book is about the seemingly simple twinning of two food ingredients, which, in more than a dozen such pairings—structurally similar but varied in particulars, most of them in the tropical Americas—came to occupy central roles in the food choices of laboring millions of common folk. Everywhere, rice plus a legume, usually with a sauce, began as a humble plebian dish. Over time, and in particular localities, such dishes came to be widely consumed and also greatly cherished. A few became nuanced in the hands of nonprofessional but greatly talented chefs, and lapidated historically as symbols of nationhood. They would turn out nearly everywhere to be markers of social status. In some places, rice and beans is a commoner food than bread.

I think such combinations took shape in many other places, too. I have in mind not these two specific foods, but two foods from the legume and grass (Gramineae) families. Between them the legumes and the grasses have provided a majority of humanity with the bulk of their calories for millennia, and in classically agrarian societies, with the bulk of their protein as well. But there is another, more sobering reference point from which to contemplate rice and beans. It has to do with rice, twenty-odd species in all, but here with but one of the two domesticated species, the preeminent *Oryza sativa.*

Few foods in the modern world have been so attractive to first-time eaters as polished white rice. In the last four decades, more and more people worldwide have become rice-eaters, perhaps most notably in Africa and Latin America. The rise of polished rice has led to important reduction in the consumption of other cereals, such as sorghums and millets in Africa and, I suspect, maize in Latin America. This has led as well as to a declining consumption of tubers, especially noticeable in those same continents. These changes are probably considered part of rising standards (or aspirations) of living, but under some conditions they may be part of declining nutritional adequacy.

The combination of cereal and legume is nutritionally more beneficial than eating the two main ingredients separately. This is true for probably all such combinations. But the benefits of polished rice do not equal those that would be provided by a whole-grain cereal instead. Today, a rising standard of living can imply greater leisure, together with more consumption of fats, sugars, and refined carbohydrates, such as white bread or polished rice. I am not saying that polished rice is a "bad" food. Yet the spread of processed complex carbohydrates, together with other changes, may mean a fall in the consumption of healthier foods. These would include whole-grain cereals, and in Africa and South America, the tubers and arboreal foods (such as breadfruit) that I described earlier. The aggregate consequence of such changes may be a less nutritious daily diet. It is important to make clear—in a book in which so many, including this writer, sing the praises of rice and beans—that there are numerous intersecting factors at work in the composition of diet, and their interaction can sometimes result in a net nutritional loss (Gewertz and Errington 2010; Mintz 2011).

And Finally?

When I was invited to contribute to this volume, I took it as my opportunity to situate what Wilk and Barbosa accurately refer to as a "culture complex"—that is, rice and beans—in a wider setting. It was not my intention to detract from the remarkable success of the "rice and beans" complex. But that success was probably built upon some jostling among rival foods, the gradual loss of interest in earlier favorites, and their replacement by another dish—whether for economic reasons, reasons of taste, or some other reason. The last several decades have been marked by some important nutritional gains, globally. Though there are still famines, they now are occurring to a declining percentage of humanity, and many people are learning to eat and to like new foods. But in the course of these changes, there are other causes for concern. I have tried to suggest that the success of rice worldwide is one aspect of such changes. The losing position of tubers of all kinds, and of certain other foods I have mentioned, such as yams and breadfruit, particularly in Africa and in Latin America, is another. I think this coefficient of rice's success is not nutritionally positive.

Increases in incidence of diabetes, obesity, and kindred pathologies in the developed countries in recent decades is evidence that rising standards of living do not guarantee improved nutrition, even if the general availability of healthful foods has increased. At the same time, what is known about larger changes in consumption suggests that nutrition education may have fallen behind, even as food availability may be rising.

Smil (2002) writes of "the nearly universal trend of drastically declining tuber consumption" that has manifested itself in the last half century. At the same time, he notes that rice was providing more than a third of cereal caloric intake in general and up to 85 percent in those West African countries that were traditional rice producers, such as Gambia, Sierra Leone, and the Ivory Coast. In Sénégal, rice consumption increased by 1,000 percent within 40 years. (That's 10 times over, not a mere 100 percent.) These changes generally appear to have accompanied sharp declines in tuber consumption. With the possible exception of cassava, a New World tuber introduced to Africa long ago and now very popular there, the dietary benefits of tubers such as yams, coco yams (taro), and sweet potatoes are real. To supplant these entirely with polished rice would be nutritionally somewhat risky.

Much the same picture emerges in Latin America, where most of the rice-and-beans complexes discussed in this book are to be found. In Latin America and the Caribbean, Calvert et al. reported in 2006 that rice now supplies more calories to diet than wheat, maize, cassava, or potatoes, and that it was especially important in the diets of the poor. There, too, tuber consumption has fallen sharply.

Such bare information tells us too little. But it seems to me salutary to introduce (partly in response to some of the rhapsodic prose of my fellow authors) a word of caution about the dietary and nutritional consequences of such changes.

It is with this sober note that I conclude. I hope my colleagues will forgive me for being, perhaps, a wet blanket. I believe it prudent to add an ounce of skepticism to the many pints of enthusiasm that rice and beans undoubtedly bring to so many tummies—definitely including this writer's.

Notes

The author wishes to thank Professor Cruz Miguel Ortiz Cuadra, Dr. Claire Cage, and Jacqueline Mintz for their invaluable assistance. Professor Ortiz's comments on Puerto Rican food history were invaluable, and Dr. Cage provided important corrections of the text. Jackie Mintz had to reread and edit the manuscript too many times. Regrettably, all remaining errors are the author's fault.

1. Álvarez Nazario (1961) and Ortiz Cuadra (2006) point to the association of the term *funche* with Africa; Álvarez traces the word to a Kikongo or Kimbundo origin. The trade between Africa and the New World was for centuries so vigorous that it is not surprising that maize and other foods would cross the ocean eastward, only then to return, westward, with new uses.

2. And even so, people seem able to tolerate substitutes, if they are hungry enough and if the *flavors* of the accompanying sauce are faithful. In two remarkable books, Elisabeth Rozin (1973, [1983] 1992) has made much clearer how what she calls "flavor principles" enable us distinguish the tastes of different ethnic cuisines. What I label "fringe" is to some extent a crude version of her flavor

principles. She notes a case in which Vietnamese refugees in the United States were prepared to eat cereal substitutes for rice, as long as the *flavors* of Southeast Asia typified the sauce of the accompanying foods.

3. In his superb study of Sudanese food fermentation, Hamid A. Dirar (1993) makes clear that, while the Sudanese people actually consume only a small quantity of meat, they are among the world's most adept at simulating or preserving the taste of meat in their fermented foods.

References

Álvarez Nazario, Manuel. 1961. *El elemento afronegroïde el español de Puerto Rico.* San Juan: Instituto de Cultura Puertorriqueña.

Calvert, L., L. R. Santint, M. Chatel, and J. Izquierdo. 2006. "Rice production in Latin America at critical crossroads." *International Rice Commission Newsletter* 55: 65–73.

Dirar, Hamid A. 1993. *The indigenous fermented foods of the Sudan.* Wallingford, Oxford, U.K.: Center for Agricultural Bioscience International.

Gewertz, Deborah, and Frederick Errington. 2010. *Cheap meat.* Berkeley: University of California Press.

Mintz, Sidney. 1956. "Cañamelar: The subculture of a rural sugar plantation proletariat." In *The People of Puerto Rico*, ed. Julian H. Steward, Robert A. Manners, Eric R. Wolf, Elena Padilla Seda, Sidney W. Mintz, and Raymond A. Scheele, 314–417. Urbana: University of Illinois.

Mintz, Sidney. 1984. *Sweetness and power.* New York: Viking Penguin.

Mintz, Sidney. 1992. "Die Zusammensetzung der Speise in frühen Agrargesellschaften: Versuch einer Konzeptualisierung." In *Brot, Brei und was dazugehört*, ed. M. Schaffner, 13–28. Zürich: Chronos Verlag.

Mintz, Sidney. 2011. "Imperialism on the cheap." *Anthropology Now* 3 (2): 73–77.

Mintz, Sidney, and Daniela Schlettwein-Gsell. 2001. "Food patterns in agrarian societies: The core-fringe-legume hypothesis." *Gastronomica* I (3): 41–52.

Ortiz Cuadra, Cruz Miguel. 2006. *Puerto Rico en la olla, ¿somos aún lo que comimos?* Aranjuez: Doce Calles.

Richards, Audrey. 1939. *Land, labour and diet in Northern Rhodesia.* London: Oxford.

Rozin, Elisabeth. 1973. *The flavour-principle cookbook.* New York: Hawthorn Books.

Rozin, Elisabeth. [1983] 1992. *Ethnic cuisine.* Lexington, Mass.: S. Greene.

Smil, Vaclav. 2002. *Feeding the world: A challenge for the 21st century.* Cambridge, Mass.: MIT Press.

Index

—